THE TALIBAN COURTS IN AFGHANISTAN

The Taliban Courts in Afghanistan

Waging War by Law

ADAM BACZKO

CNRS Research Associate Professor,
Centre for International Studies (CERI), Sciences Po

Translated by

HENRY W. RANDOLPH

OXFORD
UNIVERSITY PRESS

OXFORD
UNIVERSITY PRESS

Great Clarendon Street, Oxford, OX2 6DP,
United Kingdom

Oxford University Press is a department of the University of Oxford.
It furthers the University's objective of excellence in research, scholarship,
and education by publishing worldwide. Oxford is a registered trade mark of
Oxford University Press in the UK and in certain other countries

First Edition published in 2023

Published in the United States of America by Oxford University Press
198 Madison Avenue, New York, NY 10016, United States of America

British Library Cataloguing in Publication Data

Data available

Library of Congress Control Number: 2023944932

ISBN 978–0–19–889677–7

DOI: 10.1093/oso/9780198896777.001.0001

Printed and bound in the UK by
Clays Ltd, Elcograf S.p.A.

To the many Afghans

striving for a better path,

may the future prove them right

Now, the laws keep up their credit, not for being just, but because they are laws; it is the mystic foundation of their authority; they have no other, and it well answers their purpose. They are often made by fools, still oftener by men who, out of hatred to equality, fail in equity, but always by men, vain and irresolute authors.

Montaigne, *The Essays* (trans. Charles Cotton)

Contents

Foreword

Since its capture of Kabul in August 2021, the Taliban has assumed control over all of Afghanistan. This book, written in the years before the armed movement took over, tells the story of how the Taliban relied on its justice system to impose itself. It explains how the Taliban waged the war through law, that is, through the establishment of courts across much of the country. The armed movement appointed hundreds of judges to whom Afghans living in rural areas turned to settle their disputes. These courts let the armed movement establish itself as the authority in ever-growing swaths of the country and substantiate its claim to embody the state. In tandem with its fighters, the Taliban judges empowered the insurgency as a credible alternative to the government that the US-led coalition had installed in the country in the aftermath of 9/11—and thus ultimately contributed to defeating it.

When I began my investigation in Afghanistan in 2010, this Taliban victory was becoming more and more likely. The movement was advancing throughout the country and installing its own administration, while the military operations of the Western coalition and the practices of the regime led successively by Hamid Karzai and Ashraf Ghani succeeded mostly in antagonizing a growing part of the population. It was clear that the US troop surge ordered by President Barack Obama was only marginally effective in tamping down the insurgency: the reinforcements were deployed to the country's south, where the Taliban were already well established. Meanwhile, the environs of the cities and the North, where the insurgency's presence was more fragile, were neglected by the coalition troops. As it turned out, this strategy would prove even more costly because the surge was supposed to lay the groundwork for the withdrawal of Western troops from Afghanistan. It would therefore leave the regime to confront the insurgency on its own.

Obama's successors in the White House, Donald Trump and then Joe Biden, continued the same trajectory. Donald Trump fatally announced the withdrawal of US troops, and then launched a negotiation process with the Taliban. It was the ultimate tragedy for those of us who had long advocated negotiations with the Islamist movement to see them commence at the worst time and in the worst way. Negotiations in the early years of the international intervention, in 2002 or 2003, would have avoided war, since the Taliban were willing to surrender their weapons in exchange for an amnesty. In the surge years of 2010–11, negotiation with the insurgency might still have yielded compromises, with victory remaining a distant if not distinct prospect. In contrast, all that the process that produced the Doha agreements in February 2020—held without representatives of the Kabul regime—did was to concede a fourteen-month timetable for the withdrawal of American troops. It presaged the collapse of the incumbent regime as only a matter of time.

In the final few months, the lack of resistance from the foundering regime in place since 2001 glaringly pointed up its disintegration and unpopularity. At the same time, the Taliban drive to victory testified to its being a cohesive, ideologically driven armed movement born of the networks of Deobandi religious schools and possessed of a solid political and military apparatus. Its conquest of the country blatantly exposed how far off the mark had been the many analyses churned out over the previous two decades by experts from universities, think tanks, and consulting agencies as they endlessly recirculated clichés about the Taliban. They described the armed movement as an aggregate of local interests and a coalition of tribal segments that could only have produced a fractured movement. As Gilles Dorronsoro has shown, these recurrent errors stemmed from the structuration of transnational field of expertise in which the main incentive was to garner consultancy contracts. It was a highly lucrative business in which influence and access to funding derived not from the accuracy of analyses, but from proximity to the circles of power.[1] Never mind that the facts have repeatedly contradicted the conclusions of these analysts—even today, we still hear the same well-worn clichés about the opposition between 'moderates' and 'radicals' within the Islamic Emirate set up by the victorious Taliban.

The victory of the insurgency affirmed the importance and effectiveness of their judicial system. From early on, the Taliban established themselves in the villages by setting up courts. Their military advance was accompanied—and aided—by a progressive institutionalization of this parallel administration. It was implemented by inserting the courts into a jurisdictional hierarchy, installing a system of rotation of judges to ensure their probity, holding recruitment exams for madrasa graduates, and creating rudimentary but regular procedures. The resulting predictability of the Taliban justice system contrasted in the eyes of rural residents with the legal uncertainty fuelled by the

[1] Gilles Dorronsoro, *Le gouvernement transnational en Afghanistan. Une si prévisible défaite*, Paris, Karthala, 2021.

current regime and the Western coalition. Afghans, including those who were risking their lives to fight *against* the insurgency, viewed the Taliban courts as more accessible, efficient, and impartial than the official tribunals. The popularity of their justice system allowed the Taliban to present verdicts that were largely underpinned by their ideology as merely applying the law, as technical acts for settling disputes.

If law was key in the Taliban victory, the question now presents itself as to its role in their new regime. We still lack the benefit of hindsight, but the first two years of Taliban rule already offer us clues to several dynamics consistent with the societal project carried on by their wartime judicial system (see Chapter 10). Thus, the Taliban, who claim that only the ulama are able to pacify society and represent the public good, have installed a theocratic regime that concentrates all power in the hands of clerics. The Taliban victory established the monopoly of the ulama on defining and embodying the common interest. In doing so, they marginalized two historically competing groups: landowners and other traditional elites on the one hand, and, on the other, Afghan university graduates employed by the former regime, humanitarian organizations, or the various Western agencies present in Afghanistan. As was the case in the 1990s, religious schools have become a prerequisite for access to positions of power.

Moreover, the government set up by the armed movement excludes most if not all representatives of minorities and still combines a discourse denying the ethnic question with practices that clearly favour the Pashtuns. The Taliban relegated the Shia Hazaras to second-class citizenship, putting an end to the social mobility they had experienced since the 1980s. Moreover, the new regime poses as the guarantor of security and property, promoting a conservative vision of society that favours owners and gives short shrift to inequality. The Taliban regime may well secure property rights, one of the foundations of the popularity of the Taliban courts during the war, but these measures will do nothing to alleviate the widespread pauperization of the Afghan population.

Finally, the Taliban established the promised patriarchal order nationwide, restoring discretionary power over the women and children in their families to fathers—and to men more generally. In the weeks following their seizure of power in August 2021, this delegation to men of violence against women erupted in an explosion of liberal urban women being beaten, raped, or killed by neighbours or relatives. The Taliban movement did not directly order or plan this wave of violence, but their political agenda and the impunity they offer to men who perpetrate violence against women have played a key role.

Subsequently, the exclusion of women from university, the refusal to reopen schools to girls, and the numerous restrictions on their movement have barred them from public space and have further increased the arbitrariness of men's behaviour in domestic spaces.

While the courts contributed to the Taliban's victory and provided a window on how they would exercise power, the situation has radically changed now that they control the state. Where the Taliban only had to produce some predictability in their justice system in contrast to the government's cronyism (see Chapter 9), they now have to provide all public services. One of the insurgency's winning strategies consisted of skirting the host of social, economic, and political problems for which they lacked answers. Afghans now look to the Taliban not only to settle a land dispute, or to complain about theft or murder, but also to meet the needs that the insurgency previously had ignored: to feed their families, send their children to school, care for a loved one, or help them find a job. Similarly, they no longer govern only the countryside, where their conservative and patriarchal ideology resonated favourably, but also the cities and the Shia region of Hazarajat, a hotbed of opposition, such as it is, to their return to power.

However, the Taliban are installing their regime in a country bled dry from forty-three years of war and two decades of corrupt, nepotistic government. The largest international intervention in history produced little infrastructure. Much of its resources, some three-quarters, never reached Afghanistan, being captured in Western countries through a cascade of subcontracting arrangements and soaked up by operational costs. And much of what was spent in-country ended up in the pockets of regime potentates (see Chapter 3). On the eve of the Taliban entering Kabul, 75 per cent of the government's budget still came from international aid; many essential services depended on Western co-operation projects and non-governmental organizations. The Taliban cannot count on these resources and their priority has been keeping an anaemic administration running mainly with customs revenues. No figures are available, but while the Taliban recalled a large number of civil servants in September 2021, they subsequently had to lay off many for lack of funds to pay them.

The Taliban are therefore running a state reduced to its bare sovereign functions. This, at a time when the country is being ravaged by a historic famine that was entirely predictable given the record of repeat droughts over the last few years. A staggering 95 per cent of Afghans have fallen below the poverty line, and half the population can no longer feed themselves. Moreover, in the only two areas where Western intervention had led to considerable gains, education and health, the Taliban takeover has led to a precipitous decline. The new regime lacks the means to compensate for the departure of Western organizations, even though schools and clinics are key demands of the Afghan population.

Rebuilding the administration has evidently been the priority for the Taliban. In the wake of their victory, many judges, by virtue of being the movement's most trusted cadres, were redeployed from the bench to assist the new ministers and governors in their duties. The relationship between the old regime's officials and the movement's cadres, however, is fraught. The newly appointed Balkh prosecutor general complained, for instance, of being caught in a vice: on the one hand, he has to work with the lawyers recruited by the previous regime and knowledgeable in the procedures necessary for proper administrative functioning but susceptible to corruption and lack of loyalty, and, on the other hand, with Taliban judges whose loyalty and incorruptibility he has no reason to doubt—yet who lack administrative skills other than the rudimentary ones they acquired running insurgent courts.

The other urgent matter facing the new regime is obtaining international recognition of its authority over the country. As in the 1990s, the Taliban aspire to all the trappings of modern sovereignty, including a seat at the United Nations and embassies. To this end, the movement first tried to present itself as a responsible government that respected international borders, considered human rights, and was eager to work with other countries on issues of terrorism or migration. The repression by the armed movement was thus initially of limited scope compared to the purges that usually follow the victory of one side in a civil war. As a sign of this effort at compromise, the new regime actively collaborated with the United Nations Assistance Mission in Afghanistan.

This strategy of engagement has failed. Traumatized by its defeat, the United States has isolated Afghanistan, blocking the Afghan central bank's deposits with the Fed and imposing sanctions on the regime that block the action of international cooperation agencies and all humanitarian organizations. With no prospect of recognition for their regime in the offing, the Taliban leaders are refocusing on their militant base, made up of young fighters disinclined to compromise. It caused them to tighten their repression throughout 2022, cracking down on feminist activists, multiplying restrictive measures against women, and reinstating the most brutal penalties.

Regardless of this tragic panorama, the Taliban's hold on Afghanistan is assured in the short term because there is no actor on the horizon able to challenge, as of the time of writing, except for an Islamic State confined to carrying out sporadic attacks. However, many of the former regime's supporters have gone into exile, especially the educated elite that underpinned the previous regime. They form a diaspora motivated to mobilize against the theocratic regime from outside. The Taliban victory has, for the time being, dropped the curtain on four decades of armed confrontation between university graduates and religious school graduates for the leadership of Afghan society. However, the civil war is giving way to a no less intractable social struggle. It will pit supporters of the old regime, who see the Taliban as fanatics and barbarians, against partisans of the Islamist movement—the latter accusing the former of being traitors who collaborated with a foreign invasion. As in Franco's Spain or today's Iran under the mullahs, this confrontation is likely to fester and politicize the mass of disputes arising from the war that the country's new masters and their judges will have to dispose of in the years to come.

Adam Baczko
Paris
March 2023

Transcription system

In this book, I opted for a simplified Persian transliteration system so that the non-Persian-speaking reader could easily become familiar with the transcribed terms. I do not distinguish between short and long vowels, nor do I double the consonants or add the diacritics.

Names and titles

The names of people, places, and institutions, as well as technical titles or words, appear as they are commonly found in English-language print media, for instance 'Kandahar' and not 'Qandahar'.

Plural management

To ease the reader's task, for words taken from Persian, Pashto, and Arabic, I use an Anglicized plural, including for irregular plurals, by adding the letter 's' to the singular form. For example, the plural of 'hadith' will be rendered by 'hadiths' and not by '*ahadith*' but, according to usage, that of 'mujahid' by 'mujahideen' and that of 'alim' by 'ulama'.

Moreover, I distinguish '*taliban*', the Persian plural of 'talib', meaning student, from Taliban, a political movement. The distinction is essential: many *taliban* do not belong to the Taliban and numerous Taliban are not *taliban*.

Acknowledgements

This book caps a decade of research during which many people supported me and to whom I owe a debt of gratitude. Because of the war and then the Taliban victory, I will guard in silence the names of most of the Afghans who opened their doors to me and agreed to tell me their stories, but I can express here my particular gratitude to Hyder Akbar, Alain de Bures, Borhan Osman, Amiri Rakhmatullah, and Yama Torabi for their essential role in my investigations in Afghanistan. Among the many people who sheltered me, provided leads, and helped me understand what I was observing or hearing, I wish especially to thank Obaid Ali, Lola Cecchinel, Kate Clark, Lorenzo Deslesgues, Fabrizio Foschini, Antonio Giustozzi, Gran Hewad, Masood Karokhail, Piotr Lukasiewicz, Nassim Majidi, Philippe Marquis, Javed Miri, Guilhem Molinie, Stéphane Nicolas, Hervé Nicolle, Christophe Sivillon, and Habib Khan Totakhil. A host of researchers took the time to discuss my hypotheses and results. I am indebted to Gilles Dorronsoro, who showed me the ropes of fieldwork, for a vision of research as a form of artisanship and of learning as companionable. When many pointed out the impossibilities of my project, Stéphane Audoin-Rouzeau remained resolutely supportive while casting a uniquely sharp eye on my work. During the writing of the manuscript, the team of the ERC 'Social Dynamics of Civil Wars' project, Denia Chebli, Anastasia Fomitchova, Lola Guyot, Tanya Karagyozova, Cléa Pineau, Camille Popineau, Arthur Quesnay, Candice Raymond, Anne-Marine Vanier, and Emmanuelle Veuillet, had my back and were an unfailing fount of enthusiasm and stimulation.

For their close rereadings, their enlightened advice, and their encouragement, I am deeply indebted to Fariba Adelkhah, Amin Allal, Richard Banégas, Rémy Bazenguissa-Ganga, Robin Beaumont, Amélie Blom, Gérard Chaliand, Jean-Pierre Chauveau, Gilles Favarel-Garrigues, Laurent Gayer, Olivier Grojean, Jacobo Grajales, Jean-Vincent Holeindre, Alexandra de Hoop Scheffer, Rainer Maria Kiesow, Éric Léonard, Dominique Linhardt, Victor Louzon, Christian Lund, Alessandro Monsutti, Olivier Nay, Shalini Randeria, Anastasia Shestirinina, Bénédict Tratjnek, and Paul Zawadzki. I would also like to thank Thomas Hirsch of CNRS Éditions for guiding me through a first revision of the manuscript, Henry W. Randolph for the elegant translation of my text into English, my editor Robert Cavooris at Oxford University Press, as well as the three anonymous reviewers who helped me greatly when it came to polishing the final text.

This book grew out of my doctoral dissertation, defended in 2018 at EHESS, for which I was awarded the AFSP Mattei Dogan Foundation Prize, the IHEDN Scientific Prize, and the AEGES Bastien Irondelle Prize. I want to thank the institutions that funded this research, EHESS, IRSEM, the ANR research programme 'Neither War nor Peace', and the Zeit Ebelin and Gerd Bucerius Foundation. I also gratefully benefited from a year at Yale University with Stathis Kalyvas in 2014–15 thanks to a Fulbright Fellowship and an Order, Conflict and Violence Fellowship. My thanks also go to Shalini Randeria for her invitation to spend a semester at the Institute for Human Sciences (IWM) in Vienna. My years of working on the ERC project 'Social Dynamics of Civil Wars', directed by Gilles Dorronsoro, allowed me to deepen the comparative dimension of my research. The CNRS and my research home, Centre for International Studies (CERI)at Sciences Po, furnished the ideal conditions for completing this manuscript.

Finally, my thanks go to my family, Krysia, Olek, and Majka, and my friends, Charles and Florian, for their unflagging support in what turned out to be a long-term adventure if not occasional ordeal. During this challenging time, Adèle Blazquez became my primary reviewer, scholarly sounding board, and unwavering supporter. This book owes much to her.

List of Abbreviations

AFD	Agence française de développement (French Development Agency)
AGF	Afghan Guard Force
AIHRC	Afghan Independent Human Rights Commission
ALP	Afghan Local Police
ANA	Afghan National Army
ANAP	Afghan National Auxiliary Police
AP3	Afghan Public Protection Program
ASG	Afghan Security Guard
AUSAID	Australian Agency for International Development
CBSS	Community-Based Security Solution
CDF	Community Defense Forces
CDI	Community Defense Initiative
CIA	Central Intelligence Agency
CIP	Critical Infrastructure Program
DAI	Development Alternatives Inc.
DFID	Department for International Development
DRA	Democratic Republic of Afghanistan
FARC	Fuerzas Armadas Revolucionarias de Colombia (Revolutionary Armed Forces of Colombia)
FLN	Front de Libération Nationale (National Liberation Front)
GTZ	Deutsche Gesellschaft für technische Zusammenarbeit (German Society for International Cooperation)
HRW	Human Rights Watch
ICG	International Crisis Group
ICRC	International Committee of the Red Cross
IDLO	International Development Law Organization
IED	Improvised Explosive Device, homemade mine
IMF	International Monetary Fund
IRA	Irish Republican Army
ISAF	International Security Assistance Force
ISCI	Interim Security for Critical Infrastructure
ISI	Inter-Services Intelligence
JICA	Japan International Cooperation Agency
JSOC	Joint Special Operations Command
KGB	Komitet Gossoudarstvennoï Bezopasnosti (Committee for State Security)
KHAD	Khadamat-i Atalat-i Dawlati (State Information Services)

LDI	Local Defense Initiative
MSF	Médecins Sans Frontières/Doctors without Borders
NATO	North Atlantic Treaty Organization
NGO	Non-governmental organization
PDPA	People's Democratic Party of Afghanistan
PKK	Partiya Karkeren Kurdistan (Kurdistan Workers Party)
PYD	Partiya Yekitiya Demokrat (Syrian Kurdish Democratic Union Party)
RCD-Goma	Rally for Congolese Democracy-Goma
SIGAR	Special Inspector General for Afghanistan Reconstruction
SNTV	Single Non-Transferable Vote
SPLM/A	Sudanese People Liberation Movement/Army
TLO	Tribal Liaison Office
UNAMA	United Nations Assistance Mission in Afghanistan
UNDP	United Nations Development Program
UNHCR	United Nations High Commissioner for Refugees
UNIFEM	United Nations Development Fund for Women
UNODC	United Nations Office on Drugs and Crime
USAID	US Agency for International Development
USIP	United States Institute for Peace
USSR	Union of Socialist Soviet Republics
VAW	Violence against Woman

Introduction

A sociological approach to law in civil wars

Establishing courts amidst civil war

'Oh no! The Taliban judges are something else. They are fine.'[1] In 2010, during my first fieldwork in Afghanistan, an outspoken opponent of the Taliban movement ended our conversation with this surprising formula. Up to that point he had explained to me how the insurgency was 'terrorizing' the population. A village notable close to President Hamid Karzai, he had been forced by the Taliban to leave his village and take refuge in the city of Kandahar. 'They are not *taliban*. They are *taliban* in name only. They are not educated. *Taliban* means student, while they are not students.'

It was only as we ended our interview that the reason for this seeming contradiction became clear. He told me how a neighbour who was close to the insurgency had tried to take advantage of his forced exile and new rulers' hostility toward him by grabbing his land. The Taliban judge hearing the case, after examining the documents and hearing witnesses for both sides, ruled in the notable's favour.

Seeing my surprise, he reiterated his fierce opposition to the movement, while insisting nevertheless that the Taliban judges are fair and preferable to the government judges. A month earlier, a similar point had been made to me in Kunar by another Taliban opponent: the movement is reactionary, yet when his cattle had been stolen, he filed his complaint with one of their judges.[2] Both of my interlocutors distinguished between their outright rejection of the Taliban movement and their appreciation of the judicial system it had established in the areas under its control. These encounters prompted me to investigate the Taliban courts.

The exercise of justice by an insurgency, far from being unique to Afghanistan, is in fact a salient dimension of contemporary civil wars. In recent

[1] E-74, notable from Maywand district (Kandahar), August 2010.
[2] E-6, inhabitant from Ghaziabad district (Kunar), July 2010.

The Taliban Courts in Afghanistan. Adam Baczko, Oxford University Press. © Adam Baczko 2023.
DOI: 10.1093/oso/9780198896777.003.0001

decades, a host of armed movements have set up courts: the IRA in Northern Ireland, the FMLN in El Salvador, the SPLM/A in Sudan, the Tamil Tigers in Sri Lanka, the FARC in Colombia, the Naxalites in India, the Communist Party of Nepal (Maoist), the Islamic Courts Union in Somalia, the PYD in Syria, the MUJAO in Mali, and the Islamic State in Iraq and Syria.[3] The establishment of *law* by armed movements poses a thorny problem for the institutions that guarantee international humanitarian law, namely the United Nations, the International Committee of the Red Cross (ICRC), and the International Criminal Court (ICC). When they collaborate with the tribunals of an armed group in an effort to rein in the excesses that go unpunished in civil wars, they confer an implicit recognition on them that risks weakening the state basis of international law.[4] Afghanistan was a critical case in this regard. On the one hand, the Taliban movement was ostracized by the international system, particularly for being associated with those responsible for the 9/11 attacks; on the other hand, despite the Western intervention since 2001, the Taliban meted out justice over a significant part of Afghanistan's territory, making the movement a key intermediary for the ICRC, the United Nations, and many NGOs.

This dilemma harks back to the theoretical problem of instituting law, an issue addressed by Augustine in a fictional dialogue between a pirate and the Emperor Alexander:

> 'Justice removed, then, what are kingdoms but great bands of robbers? What are bands of robbers themselves but little kingdoms? The band itself is made up of men; it is governed by the authority of a ruler; it is bound together by a pact of association; and the loot is divided according to an agreed law. If, by the constant addition of desperate men, this scourge grows to such a size that it acquires territory, establishes a seat of government, occupies cities and subjugates peoples, it assumes the name of kingdom more openly. For this name is now manifestly conferred upon it not by the removal of greed, but by the addition of impunity.' It was a pertinent and true answer which was made to

[3] For a comparative perspective on court systems established by recent armed movements, see René Provost, *Rebel Courts: The Administration of Justice by Armed Insurgents*, Oxford, Oxford University Press, 2021.

[4] Jonathan Somer, "Jungle Justice: Passing Sentence on the Equality of Belligerents in Non-International Armed Conflict", *International Review of the Red Cross*, 2007, vol. 89, n° 867, pp. 655–90; Sandesh Sivakumaran, 'Courts of Armed Opposition Groups: Fair Trials or Summary Justice?', *Journal of International Criminal Justice*, 2009, vol. 7, n° 3, pp. 489–513. Recent discussion in Western government circles illustrates certain practical implications of this dilemma: is it legal to let the PYD courts judge their nationals alleged to be members of the Islamic State? Human Rights Watch, *Ensure Fair Trials of Syria ISIS Suspects*, www.hrw.org/news/2018/02/13/ensure-fair-trials-syria-isis-suspects, accessed 13 February 2018.

> Alexander the Great by a pirate whom he had seized. When the king asked him what he meant by infesting the sea, the pirate defiantly replied: 'The same as you do when you infest the whole world; but because I do it with a little ship I am called a robber, and because you do it with a great fleet, you are an emperor.'[5]

In contemporary civil wars, where dispensing justice is at once a juridical activity, a political weapon, and a stake in the war, it raises the following questions: how can an armed movement gain recognition for the decisions of its judges as judicial (and not political) acts, despite their having eminently political effects? How did the Taliban judge—who was a Taliban as much as a judge—get the population to recognize him as such?

Law and civil war: antithetical concepts?

The difficulty in contemplating a Taliban juridical system points to a blind spot in the social sciences. Law and civil war remain commonly regarded as antithetical concepts, with civil wars regularly described as situations where chaos, collapse, and anarchy reign. Since the end of the Cold War, civil wars have persistently been explained as involving rampant criminality, irrationality, and predation, with the recurring figure of the 'warlord' and his global counterpart, the mercenary, playing key parts. These characterizations are sustained by the media, by works of fiction[6] but also in scholarly works.[7] Since the 1990s, many researchers have highlighted the 'new' nature of civil wars in the former Yugoslavia and USSR, in Africa and the Middle East.[8] Unlike the armed conflicts of the Cold War period, contemporary armed movements are supposedly emptied of ideology, more ethnic in their aims, more technologically primitive,

[5] Augustine, *The City of God against the Pagans*, Cambridge, Cambridge University Press, 1998, pp. 147–8.

[6] Specifically American movies have been particularly fond of this depoliticized view of civil wars (*Blackhawk Down*, *Lords of War*, *Blood Diamonds*). It features prominently in recent movies about the American wars in Iraq and Afghanistan, including in how they portray the Afghan and Iraqi armed movements (*Iron Man*, *The Hurt Locker*, *American Sniper*, *Lone Survivor*, *Horse Soldiers*). This bias is equally pronounced in video game franchises like *Call of Duty* and *Medal of Honor*.

[7] William Reno, *Warlord Politics and African States*, Boulder, Lynne Rienner, 1998; Antonio Giustozzi, *Empires of Mud: War and Warlords of Afghanistan*, London, Hurst, 2009.

[8] If the concept of '*new wars*' was forged by Mary Kaldor, the historian Martin Van Creveld was the first to advance the argument in 1991, which numerous journalists, writers, and academics took up and developed. See especially Martin Van Creveld, *Transformation of War*, New York, Free Press, 1991; Mary Kaldor, *New and Old Wars: Organized Violence in a Global Era*, 3rd edn, London, Polity Press, 2012.

and more 'barbaric' in their practices.[9] This discussion has led to another, equally fruitless, debate about the 'real' motives of armed groups in recent civil wars. Economists have thus proposed drawing a distinction between civil wars caused by the *greed* of armed actors for extractable or plunderable resources and those in which combatants, driven by *grievances*, take up arms in response to discrimination based on age, ethnicity, or religion.[10] Even today, this opposition between 'loot-seeking' and 'justice-seeking' armed groups underpins many studies on civil wars.[11] Invariably, such approaches share the same premise: civil wars engender lawlessness and therefore constitute situations of ultimate disorder.[12] This view of civil wars developed in the wake of the literatures on 'failed states' and terrorism. Armed conflicts affecting countries on the periphery of the international system are said to be symptomatic of the 'weak', 'fragile', 'collapsed', 'failing', and even 'ungoverned' nature of such states.[13] These countries, the reasoning goes, therefore pose a threat as potential sanctuaries for terrorist groups hoping to strike Europe and North America.[14]

Conversely, the understanding of legal processes carried out in civil wars is generally stripped of their context: they are described as 'post-conflict' or 'transitional'. This negation of the armed conflict is achieved by transposing the concepts of transitology developed at the end of the Cold War from the relatively peaceful democratizations in Eastern Europe, South Africa, and Latin America to all-out wars in Afghanistan, Iraq, Syria, and Mali. In international organizations, development agencies, and expert circles, this transposition has given rise to an agenda that instrumentalizes law and justice as deterrents for civil wars or for repairing the damage they have caused, processes that would

[9] For a critique by Stathis Kalyvas, see '"New" and "Old" Civil Wars: A Valid Distinction?', *World Politics*, 2001, vol. 54, n° 01, pp. 99–118; Roland Marchal and Christine Messiant, 'Les guerres civiles à l'ère de la globalisation: nouvelles réalités and nouveaux paradigmes', *Critique internationale*, 2003, vol. 18, n° 1, pp. 91–112.

[10] Paul Collier and Anke Hoeffler, 'On Economic Causes of Civil War', *Oxford Economic Papers*, 1998, vol. 50, n° 4, pp. 563–73.

[11] For the distinction, see Paul Collier and Anke Hoeffler, *Justice-Seeking and Loot-Seeking in Civil War*, Washington, World Bank, 1999. For a critique, see Roland Marchal and Christine Messiant, 'De l'avidité des rebelles: l'analyse économique de la guerre civile selon Paul Collier', *Critique internationale*, 2002, vol. 16, n° 3, p. 58; Christopher Cramer, 'Homo Economicus Goes to War: Methodological Individualism, Rational Choice and the Political Economy of War', *World Development*, 2002, vol. 30, n° 11, pp. 1845–64.

[12] Paul Collier et al., *Breaking the Conflict Trap: Civil War and Development Policy*, Washington, World Bank, 2003, p. 41.

[13] Among an extensive literature, see I. William Zartman, *Collapsed States: The Disintegration and Restoration of Legitimate Authority*, Boulder, Lynne Rienner, 1995; Anne Clunan and Harold A. Trinkunas, *Ungoverned Spaces: Alternatives to State Authority in an Era of Softened Sovereignty*, Stanford, Stanford University Press, 2010.

[14] For a genealogy of these concepts, see Sonja Grimm, Nicolas Lemay-Hébert, and Olivier Nay (eds), 'Fragile States: A Political Concept', *Third World Quarterly*, 2014, vol. 35, n° 2, pp. 197–209.

thus take place *before* and *after* the fighting. In cases where the war clearly continues, this framing of legal processes as a matter of rebuilding the rule of law or transitional justice implies ignoring, or even denying, the ongoing armed conflict. Actors and researchers thus establish the premise of the incompatibility of civil war and law.

The idea that civil wars are situations of lawlessness is rooted in the history of the social sciences.[15] It originated with the Renaissance thinkers who forged the main concepts of modern political theory—the state, sovereignty, the law—to contrast with the negative figure of the dissolution of the body politic. Confronted by the internal troubles that ravaged Europe in the fifteenth and sixteenth centuries, these thinkers obsessively searched for cures for what Pascal deemed the 'greatest of evils'.[16] Witnessing the emergence of the modern state—the political form which they conceptualized by observing its genesis—they opposed the protective force of its law to the pervasive violence. Rereading the ancient thinkers (Thucydides, Aristotle, Cicero),[17] they formulated the foundational dichotomy of modern political thought: peace and law versus violence and chaos. If Machiavelli already regarded the exercise of power and the organization of institutions as a response to the internal divisions of the Italian Republics, it was Hobbes, witnessing the civil war in England, who most explicitly develop this *topos* of political theory. In *Leviathan*, he contrasted the state of nature as 'a war of all against all'[18] with a civil state ruled by law. Hobbes thus created the model from which we commonly conceive of civil wars as lawless states in which nothing prevents men from killing one another.[19] Even when Locke, Pufendorf, Rousseau, and Kant refuted the idea of humankind's innate warlike character, they still subscribed to the Hobbesian premise of the

[15] For works stressing the difficulties social scientists have in addressing armed conflicts and civil wars, see Hans Joas, *War and Modernity*, Cambridge, Polity Press, 2003; Stéphane Audoin-Rouzeau, *Combattre: une anthropologie historique de la guerre moderne, XIXe–XXIe siècle*, Paris, Seuil, 2008; Hans Joas and Wolfgang Knöbl, *War in Social Thought: Hobbes to the Present*, Princeton, Princeton University Press, 2012.

[16] Blaise Pascal, *Pensées*, Paris, Flammarion, 2015, pp. 152–3.

[17] The Greek and Latin thinkers do not oppose law and civil war in such a systematic way. For Plato, the civil war is an ordeal, a confrontation with injustice, and therefore a time when the righteous stand out. In Aristotle, political tumult is analysed as causing transformations, good or bad, and therefore has no intrinsic moral quality. Similarly, Cicero excludes civil war from the sphere of just war, describing it as 'the worst of the plagues' but praises it when he leads it against Antony. It is not until the modern era that this opposition becomes systematic. Nicolas Dubos, *Mal extrême: la guerre civile vue par les philosophes des origines à nos jours*, Paris, CNRS Éditions, 2010, pp. v–xix.

[18] Thomas Hobbes, *On the Citizen*, Cambridge, Cambridge University Press, 1998, p. 30.

[19] References to Hobbes surface repeatedly in characterizing warring societies, for example in Afghanistan and the Democratic Republic of the Congo. Shah M. Tarzi, 'Afghanistan in 1992: A Hobbesian State of Nature', *Asian Survey*, 1993, vol. 33, nº 2, pp. 165–74; Chris Hedges, *War Is a Force that Gives Us Meaning*, New York, PublicAffairs, 2002. For other cases, see Stathis Kalyvas, *The Logic of Violence in Civil War*, Cambridge, Cambridge University Press, 2006, pp. 52–86.

inevitable violence that breaks out whenever men must coexist in the absence of law.[20] Civil war was thus understood as a pathological state of the body politic, couched in all sorts of medical metaphors—'heat of a fever' said Francis Bacon[21]—which, however, would reveal in the negative the foundations of a healthy, normal political functioning precisely because it was based on the law.

The social sciences emerged in the nineteenth century by criticizing the fiction of a dichotomy between the state of nature and the sovereign state, replacing it with the gradual specialization and rationalization of social organization. Ferdinand Tönnies, Émile Durkheim, and Max Weber, less marked by the threats of civil war than by the social tensions arising from industrialization and emerging capitalism, underlined the essential part played by rule formalization processes. Unlike theorists of sovereignty, who assumed the absence of rights outside the state, they relied on history and anthropology to conceptualize state formation as a process of monopolizing violent and legal means of administration.[22] They pointed to the more decentralized and less autonomous juridical forms in the European past and in societies described as 'primitive'.[23] However, the evolutionism that underlies their writings led them to identify the law and the state, making law—in its codified form—both an emanation of the modern state and the exit from a liminal state. This identification is particularly prominent in Max Weber's canonical definition of the state:

> A compulsory political organization with continuous operations […] insofar as its administrative staff successfully upholds the claim to the monopoly of legitimate physical force in the implementation of its regulations (die Durchführung der Ordnungen).[24]

The state here holds sway as the institution whose legality and coercion are legitimate, insofar as that legitimacy rests on a monopoly of violence and of the law. Legality legitimizes state authority, but it is the state nature of the authority

[20] This conception is particularly evident with Pufendorf and Rousseau who contradicted Hobbes by picturing mankind as initially dispersed and solitary. It is also found in Kant's idea of the human inclination to resistance and the 'pathological' character of the covenant reached to form society in the fourth proposition of his *Idea for a Universal History with a Cosmopolitan*, Cambridge, Cambridge University Press, 2009.

[21] Francis Bacon, *The Essays*, London, Penguin Books, 1985, p. xxix.

[22] Dominique Linhardt, 'Un monopole sous tension: La double nature de la violence d'État', *Politika*, 2019, hwww.politika.io/fr/article/monopole-tension-deux-visages-violence-detat.

[23] James Whitman, 'At the Origins of Law and the State: Supervision of Violence, Mutilation of Bodies, or Setting of Prices', *Chicago-Kent Law Review*, 1995, vol. 71, pp. 4–84.

[24] I took the liberty of correcting the usual translation of the underlined passage, as 'the enforcement of its order' erases the legal dimension of the Weberian definition. Max Weber, *Economy and Society*, Berkeley, University of California Press, 1978, p. 54.

that determines the legal status of its acts. This circular reasoning effectively evades the problem of legitimizing the law in modern states.[25]

A key difficulty in thinking about law in a context like Afghanistan resides in this association between the law and the state. The conception of civil wars as situations of lawlessness is fundamentally a syllogism: since a civil war results in the usurpation of all or part of the territory from the state and the law is the expression of the state, it would logically follow that the law ceases to apply when a civil war breaks out. If this inference is inherent in political theories of sovereignty, the association between law and state in the social sciences stems rather from the modernist bias of the thinkers of the nineteenth and the first half of the twentieth centuries. Theoretically, the dissociation between law and state is perfectly conceivable in the social sciences, as illustrated by the anthropology of law in non-Western societies. Our task here is therefore to revisit sociological and anthropological approaches to law and the state, so that we can reflect on contemporary societies stricken by civil war.

A relentless struggle between legal systems

Our difficulty in making sense of the courts set up by an armed movement like the Taliban results from civil wars being routinely defined as the collapse or absence of the state and therefore of the law. At its root, this is a misinterpretation of Max Weber's definition of the state: the law would primarily play a legitimizing role and its application would rely on maintaining the monopoly on physical coercion and therefore on the state. Civil wars in that case would be characterized by the loss of this monopoly on coercion—and thus on the law—as a result of violent dissent, making it an essentially 'negative' definition built on a lack or an absence. Empirically, however, the problem with contemporary civil wars is not the collapse or absence of law, but the proliferation of competing legal systems. This plurality is bolstered by the involvement of multiple external actors: international organizations and jurisdictions, foreign armed forces, development agencies, humanitarian organizations, and private companies.

Moreover, this definition makes violence the distinguishing criterion of civil wars. Yet, extremely high levels of violence also characterize situations that do not involve an armed organization trying to overthrow the regime and setting

[25] Weber duly considers the problem of the law's legitimization in the historical formation of states, but he detaches it from his conception of the modern state.

up its own legal system (e.g. in South Africa, Mexico, Nigeria, or Pakistan). Leon Trotsky, reflecting on the Russian Revolution, argued that a distinctive criterion of a civil war was the splitting of the state apparatus into several blocs, which he described, from a class struggle perspective, as a 'dual power', a notion on which Charles Tilly based his definition of revolutionary situations.[26] For that matter, the formation of an alternative juridical system—through the bureaucratic investment and involvement in administering the population that it implies—appears as *the very locus of secession* more than does violence and thus as a far more distinctive criterion of the radical nature of the break with the incumbent regime.

In this regard, there has been a recent body of work considering the establishment of parallel administrations by armed movements as 'rebel governance'.[27] It has prompted legal scholars to focus on 'rebel courts' or 'rebel law' in various past and present civil wars.[28] Regarding Afghanistan, Ashley Jackson relies on this literature to analyse how both civilians and the armed actors bargain in order to promote their interests.[29] However, the 'rebel governance' approach produces comparability between armed groups at the expense of sociological depth, rendering it too reductionist in understanding the emergence of legal systems within civil war contexts. The neopositivist paradigm underlying 'rebel governance' is based on an oversimplified perspective of societies, perpetuating rigid dichotomies (combatants versus civilians, government versus rebels) while disregarding intricate social hierarchies. Moreover, an excessive fixation on quantifiable causal relations drives the pursuit of elusive thresholds or variables that might elucidate the delivery of public services by armed groups or the utilization of these services by the population. These shortcomings are even more critical when dealing with the realm of law, as the focalization on the mere presence or absence of a parallel administration overlooks the most intriguing enigmas such the legitimization of these structures

[26] Leon Trotsky, *History of the Russian Revolution*, Chicago, Haymarket Books, 2008, vol. 1, ch. 11; Charles Tilly, *From Mobilization to Revolution*, New York, McGraw-Hill, 1978.

[27] Zachariah Cherian Mampilly, *Rebel Rulers: Insurgent Governance and Civilian Life During War*, Ithaca, Cornell University Press, 2011; Staniland Paul, 'States, Insurgents, and Wartime Political Orders', *Perspectives on Politics*, 2012, vol. 10, nº 2, pp. 243–64. Ana Arjona, Nelson Kasfir, and Zachariah Mampilly (eds), *Rebel Governance in Civil War*, Cambridge, Cambridge University Press, 2015; Ana Arjona, *Rebelocracy: Social Order in the Colombian Civil War*, Cambridge, Cambridge University Press, 2016.

[28] Frank Ledwidge, *Rebel Law: Insurgents, Courts and Justice in Modern Conflict*, Oxford, Oxford University Press, 2017; Tom Ginsburg, 'Rebel Use of Law and Courts', *Annual Review of Law and Social Science*, 2019, vol. 15, nº 1, pp. 495–507; René Provost, *Rebel Courts: The Administration of Justice by Armed Insurgents*, New York, Oxford University Press, 2021.

[29] Ashley Jackson, *Negotiating Survival: Civilian-Insurgent Relations in Afghanistan*, London, Hurst, 2021.

and their profound social repercussions. Thus, I start from an alternative definition of contemporary civil wars that Gilles Dorronsoro and I developed:

> [W]e define civil war as the coexistence on the same national territory of competing social orders engaged in a violent relationship. By 'social order' we mean an economy of violence, relative values of types of capital, and relations between fields, at varying degrees of institutionalisation. The national territory therefore sees the coexistence of different identity regimes, legal systems, and property rights.[30]

The value of this definition is that it shifts the focus from the loss of sovereignty to the social processes at work in civil wars and thus links these contexts to general sociology.

Social studies that concern themselves with law, in particular anthropology, employ the concept of *legal pluralism* to apprehend a multiplicity of legal systems found in a given national territory. In the decolonization context, anthropologists have highlighted the *coexistence* of conflict resolution bodies operating in parallel in colonial and postcolonial societies.[31] This perspective, which has fuelled many works on law and the state since the 1980s, combines theoretical, practical, and political considerations.[32] First, in contrast to the developmentalist approaches that stress the state's weakness and fragility, if not failure, in the countries of the Global South, researchers inspired by these perspectives have proposed rethinking such configurations as a coproduction of authority and public policy by society.[33] These approaches of a 'politics from the bottom',[34] of the periphery producing the centre,[35] and of a 'negotiated

[30] Adam Baczko and Gilles Dorronsoro, 'For a Sociological Approach to Civil Wars', *Revue française de science politique*, 2017, vol. 67, n° 2, p. 322. In this article, we develop our criticism of neopositivist works on civil wars and the implication of a sociological definition of these contexts.

[31] John Griffiths, 'What is Legal Pluralism?', *The Journal of Legal Pluralism and Unofficial Law*, 1986, vol. 18, n° 24, pp. 1–55; Sally Engle Merry, 'Legal Pluralism', *Law & Society Review*, 1988, vol. 22, n° 5, pp. 869–96; Sally Falk Moore, 'Certainties Undone: Fifty Turbulent Years of Legal Anthropology, 1949–1999', *The Journal of the Royal Anthropological Institute*, 2001, vol. 7, n° 1, pp. 95–116.

[32] For a collection of recent approaches to legal pluralism among a very extensive literature, see Brian Tamanaha, Caroline Sage, and Michael Woolcock (eds), *Legal Pluralism and Development: Scholars and Practitioners in Dialogue*, Cambridge, Cambridge University Press, 2012.

[33] Joel Migdal, *Strong Societies and Weak States: State-Society Relations and State Capabilities in the Third World*, Princeton, Princeton University Press, 1988; Jean-François Bayart, *The State in Africa: The Politics of the Belly*, London, Longman, 1993; Patrick Chabal and Jean-Pascal Daloz, *Africa Works: Disorder as Political Instrument*, Oxford, James Currey, 1999.

[34] Jean-François Bayart, Achille Mbembe, and Comi Toulabor, *Le politique par le bas en Afrique noire*, Paris, Karthala, 2008.

[35] Veena Das and Deborah Poole (eds), *Anthropology in the Margins of the State*, Oxford, Oxford University Press, 2004.

statehood'[36] share a preference for the microsociological scale, as well as an interest in the everyday modes of accommodation, challenge, and bricolage that constitute an authority.[37] Secondly, the concept of legal pluralism has opened up a research agenda that consists of inventorying and describing the many normative or juridical authorities obscured by official law in order to study their entanglement.[38] Later, this concept prompted research on the mobilization of the tools of and around the law in order to promote economic or political interests.[39] For instance, Egor Lazarev shows how Chechen leaders instrumentalized legal pluralism to fuel regional autonomy from the Russian federation, while legitimizing their rule locally.[40] This concept has also highlighted the importance of supranational juridical bodies in their linkages to national and local jurisdictions.[41] Finally, these works represent a political project of promoting otherness and recognizing the customary laws of minorities. More broadly, the success of this concept is evident from its inroads into everyday language and its recurrent use by international providers of expertise, development aid, and mediation in armed conflicts.[42] In these circles, the success of Taliban courts and the failure of the Western intervention are often explained by the attachment of Afghans—especially the Pashtuns—to tribal or customary norms.[43]

[36] Tobias Hagmann and Didier Péclard (eds), *Negotiating Statehood: Dynamics of Power and Domination in Africa*, Oxford, Wiley-Blackwell, 2011.

[37] For a detailed survey of the literature, see Kasper Hoffmann and Tom Kirk, *Public Authority and the Provision of Public Goods in Conflict-Affected and Transitioning Regions*, London, London School of Economics, 2013.

[38] Louis Assier-Andrieu, *Le droit dans les sociétés humaines*, Paris, Nathan, 1996; Baudoin Dupret, *Droit et sciences sociales*, Paris, Armand Colin, 2006.

[39] Jean Comaroff and John Comaroff, 'Law and Disorder in the Post-Colony: An Introduction' in Jean Comaroff and John Comaroff (eds), *Law and Disorder in the Postcolony*, Chicago, University of Chicago Press, 2006; Mark Fathi Massoud, *Law's Fragile State: Colonial, Authoritarian, and Humanitarian Legacies in Sudan*, Cambridge, Cambridge University Press, 2013.

[40] Egor Lazarev, *State-Building as Lawfare: Custom, Sharia, and State Law in Postwar Chechnya*, Cambridge, Cambridge University Press, 2023.

[41] Boaventura de Sousa Santos, *Toward a New Common Sense: Law, Science and Politics in the Paradigmatic Transition*, London, Routledge, 1995; Laura Nader (ed.), *Law in Culture and Society*, Berkeley, University of California Press, 1997; Shalini Randeria, 'The State of Globalization: Legal Plurality, Overlapping Sovereignties and Ambiguous Alliances between Civil Society and the Cunning State in India', *Theory, Culture & Society*, 2007, vol. 24, n° 1, pp. 1–33; Mireille Delmas-Marty, *Ordering Pluralism. A Conceptual Framework for Understanding the Transnational Legal World*, London, Hart Publishing, 2009.

[42] For instance, Deborah Isser, *Customary Justice and the Rule of Law in War-torn Societies*, Washington, US Institute of Peace Press, 2011.

[43] See especially Jennifer Brick Murtazashvili, *Informal Order and the State in Afghanistan*, Cambridge, Cambridge University Press, 2016. For a genealogy of this perspective and an analysis of its practical implications during the military intervention in Afghanistan, see chapter 4.

Although especially fertile for studying the entanglements between reconfigurations of power, property, and citizenship,[44] legal pluralism raises two obstacles to arriving at an understanding about civil wars. On the one hand, as Boaventura de Sousa Santos points out, in their desire to highlight and enhance the multiplicity of norms and conflict resolution bodies, some of these reflections are stamped with 'romantic biases'.[45] They minimize the dominance relationships that underlie the processes of incorporation, delegation, and thus hierarchization among the different entities. In a tribute to Georges Balandier, anthropologist Emmanuel Terray used the case of sociability spaces to highlight the power relationships lurking in the notion of plurality.[46] Similarly, Max Gluckman criticized analyses that distinguish between traditional and colonial societies, thus missing the integration of colonizers and colonized within one unequal social system.[47] In this regard, the frequently emphasized autonomy of the peripheries and subaltern groups should not make us forget that it is the centre—that is, the state or its elites—that produces the margin as a margin and the subalterns as subalterns. On the other hand, the insistence on coexistence and accommodation poses a major problem in the case of armed conflict. Such a perspective underestimates the violence and the rupture entailed by the existence of *competing* social orders all claiming to be the state. In other words, pluralism cloaks the war, making it impossible to account for the specific effects of the mortal struggle between antagonistic legal and institutional systems.

Actors which claim a legal authority are caught up in an implacable zero-sum game where the victory of one camp nullifies the legality of the competing legal systems. The belligerents in effect share the same public and the definition of the same good: *justice*. Even when operating in clearly distinct territories, their demand to exercise *exclusive* authority over the entire national territory—or at least part of it in the case of secessionist insurgencies—sustains a common arena of struggle. As we will see with the Afghan case, the warring parties may occasionally collaborate, share certain activities, and be bound by common conceptions of the criteria that define legal expertise, yet the sustainability of

[44] Shalini Randeria, 'Cunning States and Unaccountable International Institutions: Legal Plurality, Social Movements and Rights of Local Communities to Common Property Resources', *European Journal of Sociology*, 2003, vol. 44, n° 1, pp. 27–60; Jean-Pierre Jacob and Pierre-Yves Le Meur (eds), *Politique de la terre et de l'appartenance: Droits fonciers et citoyenneté locale dans les sociétés du sud*, Paris, Karthala, 2010, pp. 5–57; Christian Lund, 'Rule and Rupture: State Formation through the Production of Property and Citizenship', *Development and Change*, 2016, vol. 47, n° 6, pp. 1199–228.

[45] Boaventura De Sousa Santos, *Toward a New Legal Common Sense: Law, Globalization, and Emancipation*, Cambridge, Cambridge University Press, 2002, p. 91.

[46] Emmanuel Terray, 'Le climatiseur et la véranda' in *Afrique plurielle, Afrique actuelle: hommage à Georges Balandier*, Paris, Karthala, 1986, pp. 37–59.

[47] Max Gluckman, 'Analysis of a Social Situation in Modern Zululand. A. The Social Organization of Modern Zululand', *Bantu Studies*, 1940, vol. 14, pp. 1–30.

their actions depends on eliminating—or subjugating—other juridical systems. The ensemble of juridical actors in a civil war therefore remains caught up in the same field.

However, the functioning of a juridical field in civil war clearly differs from the conceptualization developed by Pierre Bourdieu for the peaceful France of the 1980s.[48] Under conditions of peace, legal professionals interact in institutions, and they struggle above all over their respective positions in the internal hierarchy of that same field and the definition of its boundaries. Even the extreme cases of challenges to the French judicial system, for example the 'rupture defence' strategy invented by Marcel Willard and applied by Jacques Vergès in the trials of FLN activists, or the political claim raised by the lawyers of the Red Army Faction, involved *at minimum* a recognition of the court as an arena.[49] By contrast, in a civil war, the key issue is defining the state, or more precisely who represents the state: the Taliban or the Kabul regime? The mere use of juridical terminology (law, court, judge, verdict) then makes an antagonistic statement. Even some academic works that profess a form of neutrality reject the nomenclature used by armed movements and affix to them the register of informality—calling them 'councils'—or put terms like judicial system or court in quotation marks. This contest over naming objects and persons denotes an acute awareness of the institutional power of 'acts of speech', the fact that naming things enables one to qualify or disqualify them.[50] In a civil war, the various juridical actors fight for the monopoly over organizing the law, i.e. the arranging of jurisdictions; personnel; material devices (courts, specific outfits, weapons); instruments of action (codes, legal texts); procedures; or legitimate practices which taken together constitute the law.

In addition, the recognition of the right to lay down the law is overdetermined by membership of one of the warring factions. Thus, positions in the field are informed by militant engagement: taking part in combat against the Western military for Taliban judges, membership in the PKK and PYD for Rojava judges in Syria, or by how the factions line up ideologically vis-à-vis the law, for example by privileging Islamic norms, as in the Syrian or

[48] Pierre Bourdieu, 'The Force of Law: Toward a Sociology of the Juridical Field', *Hastings Law Journal*, 1986, vol. 38, n° 5, pp. 814–53.

[49] Marcel Willard, *La défense accuse*, Paris, Éditions sociales, 1955; Jacques Vergès, *De la stratégie judiciaire*, Paris, Éditions de Minuit, 1981. For an analysis of the 'rupture defence' strategy, see Liora Israël, *L'arme du droit*, Paris, Presses de Sciences Po, 2009. For the defence strategy of the lawyers for the Red Army Faction, see Frédéric Audren and Dominique Linhardt, 'Un procès hors du commun?', *Annales. Histoire, Sciences Sociales*, 2008, vol. 63, n° 5, pp. 1003–34.

[50] John Austin, *How to Do Things with Words*, Oxford, Clarendon Press, 1962.

Taliban insurgencies. Moreover, the eventual recognition of legal competence depends on the military or diplomatic outcome of the war, which raises the question of the possible integration (rare, by all accounts) of the defeated camp's juridical personnel into the juridical system of the victorious side.[51] The political conditionality of juridical competence therefore leads to varying access to the juridical field according to the social orders and the vagaries of war. To use Bernard Lahire's distinction, the juridical field at war retains its distinct technical intricacies (demonstrating high 'autonomy-specificity') but legal institutions remains very dependent on armed factions (reflecting low 'autonomy-independence').[52] In simpler terms, in a civil war, the obviously political and partisan nature of juridical acts is constantly exposed, even if the procedures are standardized by a specialized institution.

Civil war thus results in a radical uncertainty about the validity of juridical acts. People caught up in the armed conflict face a tangle of contradictory norms, engendering uncertainty that plays out in two ways. On the one hand, far from the seductive idea that people would 'market shop' their jurisdiction,[53] confusion about who has authority to settle a dispute raises issues of affiliation and therefore of exposure to violence. On the other hand, in a context in which the warring parties instrumentalize disputes, the armed conflict blurs the line between private and public issues and raises the risk of politicizing personal conflicts. As long as the war continues, villages and neighbourhoods change hands, sometimes several times, leading to a succession of juridical systems, sometimes with obvious contradictions. As the military map changes and people move, some may live under the control of several successive authorities, up to a dozen for many Afghans. This revolving door of competing political authorities results in conflicting norms and verdicts, which profoundly destabilize social structures and aggravate disputes around certain issues, particularly property relations and ethnic, religious, class, age, and gender hierarchies.

[51] France after World War Two provides an example of the reintegration of judges who belonged to the Vichy regime. Liora Israël, *Robes noires, années sombres. Avocats et magistrats en résistance pendant la Seconde guerre mondiale*, Paris, Fayard, 2005, ch. VII.

[52] Bernard Lahire distinguishes 'autonomy-specificity', which refers to the gradual specialization of various social microcosms, and 'autonomy-independence' as designating the 'conquest of the independence of these microcosms with regard to the logics and powers that are external to them'. Bernard Lahire, *Monde pluriel: Penser l'unité des sciences sociales*, Paris, Le Seuil, 2012, p. 63.

[53] Keebet von Benda-Beckmann, 'Forum Shopping and Shopping Forums: Dispute Processing in a Minangkabau Village in West Sumatra', *The Journal of Legal Pluralism and Unofficial Law*, 1981, vol. 13, n° 19, pp. 117–59. For its use in analysing the Taliban, see Noah Coburn and John Dempsey, *Informal Dispute Resolution in Afghanistan*, Washington, United States Institute for Peace, 2010.

The force of law in a civil war

Talking about 'law' in a civil war is not self-evident. It requires measuring the gap between the representations commonly referred to by the terms 'judge', 'court', or 'verdict' in peacetime and the phenomena that I seek to account for here. This problem, stated in different terms, arose during a famous controversy between the anthropologists Paul Bohannan and Max Gluckman on whether the juridical phenomena observed in 'primitive societies' constitute law. While Bohannan advocated the exclusive use of indigenous terminology to capture the singularity of each practice, Gluckman argued for using equivalent terms in the service of comparative analysis, thus reflecting their juridical character and their specific features simultaneously.[54] Gluckman's position meets a theoretical requirement (unveiling social processes that go beyond ethnographic description) and allows critiquing of the intuitive presumption among his readers that these societies lack laws. My problem is similar: refusing to use the legal terminology even though my interviewees mobilized it would reinforce entrenched assumptions—on the absence of law in a civil war—thereby invisibilizing the juridical logics at work in the phenomena I seek to describe.

Such an approach requires a definition of the law as a practice. To this end, Gluckman draws inspiration from Bronislaw Malinowski's works in the 1930s: 'I personally believe that law ought to be defined by function and not by form, that is, we ought to see what are the arrangements, the sociological realities, the cultural mechanisms that entail the enforcement of law.'[55] In turn, Gluckman emphasizes the ambiguity and equivocality of the concept of law. To be observed in its concrete functioning, it must be defined as a set of rules that regulate social relations and of practices for enforcing it (physical, social, or symbolic constraints).[56] This approach to law as *an application of rules* makes it possible to conceptualize the regulation carried out by authorities other than the state and thus to document the juridical practices of armed factions. It also counteracts the positivist bias that leads the researcher to decide whether such

[54] Paul Bohannan, *Justice and Judgment among the Tiv*, Oxford, Oxford University Press, 1957; Max Gluckman, *The Judicial Process among the Barotse of Northern Rhodesia*, Manchester, Manchester University Press, 1955. For an analysis of the controversy and its stakes, see Laura Nader, 'The Anthropological Study of Law', *American Anthropologist, New Series*, 1965, vol. 67, n° 6, pp. 3–32; Sally Falk Moore, 'Certainties Undone: Fifty Turbulent Years of Legal Anthropology, 1949–1999', *The Journal of the Royal Anthropological Institute*, 2001, vol. 7, n° 1, pp. 95–116.

[55] See Bronislaw Malinowski, 'Introduction' in Herbert Ian Hogbin, *Law and Order in Polynesia: A study of Primitive Legal Institutions*, London, Christophers, 1934, p. lxiii.

[56] Max Gluckman, *Politics, Law and Ritual in Tribal Society*, Oxford, Blackwell, 1955, pp. 169–216; Max Gluckman, *The Judicial Process among the Barotse of Northern Rhodesia*, Manchester, Manchester University Press, 1955, p. 229.

practices are juridical or not in order to question the social determinants of their effectiveness.

Indeed, the specificity of the law, its 'force' (to take up Pierre Bourdieu's term), is its ability to institute social relationships and to naturalize domination:

> The law is the quintessential form of 'active' discourse, able by its own operation to produce its effects. It would not be excessive to say that it creates the social world, but only if we remember that it is this world which first creates the law. It is important to ascertain the social conditions—and the limits—of the law's quasi-magical power.[57]

This performativity of the law—its 'mystic foundation' to quote Montaigne—arises from *social recognition*, both by those who practise it and those to whom it is applied, of the juridical character of acts and words, that is, the particular form of neutrality that implies certainty of procedures and uncertainty of verdicts:

> As the quintessential form of legitimized discourse, the law can exercise its specific power only to the extent that it attains recognition, that is, to the extent that the element of arbitrariness at the heart of its functioning (which may vary from case to case) remains unrecognized. The tacit grant of faith in the juridical order must be ceaselessly reproduced. Thus, one of the functions of the specifically juridical labor of formalizing and systematizing ethical representations and practices is to contribute to binding laypeople to the fundamental principle of the jurists' professional ideology—belief in the neutrality and autonomy of the law and of jurists themselves.[58]

This specific logic of the law constrains its use and conditions its symbolic effectiveness. On the one hand, its agents must master and respect a language and codes specific to juridical activity to be able to use it; on the other hand, its technical nature facilitates the 'naturalization' of social hierarchies and thus legitimizes the domination exercised.[59] This conception of the law as speech that is both *instituting* and *naturalizing* thus opens the possibility of accounting

[57] Pierre Bourdieu, 'The Force of Law', *Hastings Law Journal*, 1986, vol. 38, n° 5, p. 839.

[58] Ibid., p. 844.

[59] In Pierre Bourdieu's sociology, 'naturalization' refers to the process by which social structures, norms, and practices become accepted and unquestioned as natural or common sense by individuals within a particular society. This process contributes to the reproduction of social inequality by discouraging individuals from challenging the existing social order and working towards social change.

sociologically for the 'quasi-magical effectiveness' of the law: 'These performative utterances […] are magical acts which succeed because they have the power to make themselves universally recognized. They thus succeed in creating a situation in which no one can refuse or ignore the point of view, the vision, which they impose.'[60]

However, this performativity of the law, because it depends precisely on the social recognition of those who are subject to it, requires its practitioners to consider, at least formally, the perceptions and interests of the former: 'This efficacy […] is exercised only to the extent that the law is socially recognized and meets with agreement, even if only tacit and partial, because it corresponds, at least apparently, to real needs and interests.'[61] It is useful here to keep in mind Edward Thompson's warning that the law would have no effectiveness as an instrument in the service of the dominant if it failed to mete out justice, at least marginally:

> If the law is evidently partial and unjust, then it will mask nothing, legitimize nothing, contribute nothing to any class's hegemony. The essential precondition for the effectiveness of the law, in its function as ideology, is that it shall display an independence from gross manipulations and shall seem to be just. It cannot seem to be so without upholding its own logic and criteria of equity; indeed, on occasion, by actually being just.[62]

Therein lies the ambiguity of the law: if it is to serve any project of domination, it must at least minimally do justice and thus transcend the social identities and interests of those who implement it.

In a civil war, political confrontation distorts the social hierarchies that undergird the law, weakening its claim to impartiality. More than elsewhere, here the force of the law is conditioned by the ability to have judges' decisions socially recognized as legal—not political—acts, even though they have an eminently political dimension. This social recognition of the judge *as a judge* requires the perception of his verdicts as objective, impartial as to the parties involved in the case, but above all detached from what is at stake in the warring context (but which they never are). In these contexts, the formation of a juridical system therefore makes clear how the *mechanisms for objectivizing* social relations render possible the appropriation of this symbolic efficacy.

60 Ibid., p. 838.
61 Ibid., p. 840.
62 Edward P. Thompson, *Whigs and Hunters: The Origin of the Black Act*, New York, Pantheon Books, 1975, p. 263.

Following Max Weber, the concept of objectivization (*Versachlichung*) refers to the impersonal mediatization in social relations and the exercise of authority, most notably via formalized and rationalized rules and procedures.[63] As in any institution, the objectivization of a juridical system happens through 'material devices' (buildings, courtrooms, police stations, vehicles); 'strictly codified instruments of action' (books, attributes, weapons); 'specialized training channels'; and 'monitoring bodies that allow everyone—and foremost the leaders—to verify the right practice of members, i.e. the correctness of their practices'.[64] In a context of legal uncertainty, the systematic nature of the decision-making procedures and their application becomes essential, bringing predictability to verdicts and the use of coercion, thus facilitating conflict resolution.

Instituting and naturalizing domination therefore requires establishing procedures and rules for exercising justice and coercion, even though the legal constraints on the belligerents seem, at first glance, weak or even absent. Armed actors are caught in a contradiction between their immediate interest in discretionary use of their juridical system and the legitimizing effects of having their law recognized as the law. In a context of civil war, where the future is uncertain and resources are precarious, the horizon of action tends to be limited. However, by refraining from manipulating judicial processes, a movement can naturalize its domination and its social project.[65] On the other hand, armed movements that deny any autonomy to the law mechanically weaken their own legitimacy.

Moreover, the introduction of rules in a juridical system also influences the wider structuring of the armed movement's political and administrative apparatus. Pierre Bourdieu points out that one of the contradictions for jurists is having to wrest a power of control from the rulers, which, however, only

[63] In the English translation of *Economy and Society*, *Versachlichung* is translated by the term 'impersonality', losing the processual nature of Weber's concept, as well as his insistence on the objectivity of rules and procedures in the rationalization of authority. Following Pierre Bourdieu, I translate the term as objectivization. Max Weber, *Economy and Society*, Berkeley, University of California Press, 1978, pp. 294 and 586.

[64] Jacques Lagroye, *La vérité dans l'Église catholique: Contestations et restauration d'un régime d'autorité*, Paris, Belin, 2006, p. 13.

[65] Pierre Bourdieu highlights the centrality of restraint in legitimizing violence through law:

> Force cannot assert itself as such, as brute violence, an arbitrariness that is what it is, without justification; and it is a fact of experience that it can only perpetuate itself under the colours of legitimacy, and that domination succeeds in imposing itself durably only in so far as it manages to secure recognition, which is nothing other than misrecognition of the arbitrariness of its principle. In other words, it wants to be justified (and therefore recognized, respected, honoured, considered), but its only chance of being so lies in declining to be exercised.

Pierre Bourdieu *Pascalian meditations*, Stanford, Stanford University Press, 2000, p. 104.

becomes legitimate when recognized by the latter.[66] The nub of the problem for judges is to have their autonomy recognized by those whom they control and whose power they thus limit, but to whom they in turn render the form of legitimacy proper to the law. Thus, by renouncing too direct a control over the actors of the law, political and military leaders extend the 'circuits of legitimation' between institutions and boost their effectiveness.[67] So long as judges remain independent, they become guarantors of respect for rules within the political and military apparatus. In a context where the primacy of the military and the blurring of the boundary between private and public affect the functioning of institutions, an autonomous juridical system constitutes a resource for an authority that seeks to consolidate its institutional network and thus its grip over the various social fields. The juridical field thus appears as a space which determines the relations between the other fields.

However, this domination remains extremely precarious, as it depends on the fortunes of war and competes with other social orders. While the establishment of a juridical system makes the penetration of a society possible, a civil war eventually must end with the victory of one side over the others. A military defeat or loss of control over a territory nullifies an armed actor's judicial decisions, a calling into question that can be seized upon by the losers under the now-defunct order. Moreover, the existence of an alternative juridical system encourages stratagems like delay and circumvention. These are all ways of *not recognizing* the authority of a juridical system, revealing the difficulty of imposing law as long as a rival is capable of challenging it.

The courts of the Taliban insurgency

This book deals with Taliban courts as a case study of how an armed movement gets its judges recognized as such in the midst of civil war. This research is underpinned by both my comparative experience and my field-based approach. Afghanistan furnished both the terrain from which I developed many of my hypotheses and a context that I have sought to disorientalize through comparison. Because this country drains so many fantasies and because of the

[66] Pierre Bourdieu, *On the State: Lectures at the Collège de France, 1989–1992*, Stanford, Stanford University Press, 2014, p. 321.

[67] Speaking of 'circuits of legitimation', Pierre Bourdieu writes: 'the legitimating efficacy of an act of recognition (homage, a mark of deference, a token of respect) varies with the degree of independence of the agent or institution that grants it.' Pierre Bourdieu, *Pascalian Meditations*, Stanford, Stanford University Press, 2000, p. 104.

heuristic value of the comparative approach, I conducted fieldwork in Syria, Iraq, and the Democratic Republic of the Congo in parallel to my stays in Afghanistan, and I studied there the juridical institutions of the various belligerents.[68] The insights gained from Afghanistan initially guided my research in the three other war-torn countries. Later, these cases allowed me to put into perspective the data collected during my fieldwork in Afghanistan. The comparison also offered a complementary mode of testing, allowing me to identify the most decisive processes and confirm or demolish the hypotheses I had constructed in the course of my investigations in Afghanistan. The analysis of the similarities and specificities of the juridical system of each of these armed movements constituted the empirical basis for generalizing the Afghan case.

Between 2010 and 2016, I undertook annual one- to three-month field stays in Afghanistan, conducting interviews in Kunar, Nangarhar, Laghman, Paktya, Kandahar, Ghazni, and Kunduz provinces in the East, South, and North. I conducted my research using a qualitative approach, inserting myself into several social networks, and combining interviews and observations. I had to adapt my investigation to the constraints of the armed conflict and to the mistrust and suspicion my endeavours aroused. If the encounters could not be as casual as in other contexts, I nevertheless had the chance to build relationships of trust over the years. These allowed me to stay in the territories held by the insurgency, which called for the taking of certain precautions (ways of dressing, growing a beard, modes of travel, choice of houses in which to sleep). I had to cope with setbacks, in particular the impossibility of attending a Taliban court in session and the inability to interview women. Nevertheless, I was able to gather empirical data on multiple cases of legal conflict, gain a general overview of the functioning of the Taliban courts, as well as sussing out elements concerning their public reception. In this way, I studied how the Taliban set up their courts and how the inhabitants related to this justice system in the wider context of war.[69]

The Western intervention, which installed a new regime, and the Taliban insurgency produced two social orders, with competing institutional and juridical systems. The law was indeed one of the key stakes in the ensuing armed struggle, creating drastic legal uncertainty. The Taliban courts have two

[68] The research in Syria was conducted collectively with Gilles Dorronsoro and Arthur Quesnay. For an exposition of our results, see Adam Baczko, Gilles Dorronsoro, and Arthur Quesnay, *Civil War in Syria: Mobilization and Competing Social Orders*, Cambridge, Cambridge University Press, 2018. For an account of the methodology adopted in this collaborative research, see Adam Baczko, Gilles Dorronsoro, and Arthur Quesnay, 'The Epistemological Privilege of Fieldwork: A Collective Investigation in War-Torn Syria', *Bulletin of Sociological Methodology*, 2021, vol. 151, no. 1, pp. 96–116.
[69] For further development of this, see the methodological appendix.

distinctive features compared to the other armed movements I investigated. First, the Taliban set up their courts in a social and political context marked by an unprecedented degree of internationalization. The US-installed Kabul regime governed the country in conjunction with Western donors and international organizations. While similar dynamics could be observed in other cases of external intervention (Somalia since 1990, the former Yugoslavia since 1990, Democratic Republic of the Congo since 1996, Iraq since 2003, Mali since 2012), the sums invested in Afghanistan and the degree of involvement in its administration created a radical version of these dynamics of fragmenting, overlapping, outsourcing, and privatizing the state.[70] In contrast to the situations in which the latter acts as a buffer between transnational operators and the society,[71] the various external actors intervening in Afghanistan enjoyed broad autonomy and imposed their views within the state apparatus. This transnational government fragmented the regime's juridical system and increased uncertainty in judicial matters, giving the Taliban an opportunity to step in and regulate social relations.

Secondly, although most armed groups set up legal institutions, the focus of the Taliban on the provision of justice is exceptional. The centrality of law derives from the sociology of the movement formed in the mid-1990s by mullahs and ulama and that recruited its leaders among the Deobandi madrasas of the Afghan-Pakistan border region.[72] The armed movement could count on a steady and costless influx of Islamic law and theology graduates for its justice system, which exploited the dual membership of its judges: they acted both as magistrates in the juridical field and as ulama in the religious field.[73]

[70] For analyses of the contemporary and global transformations of the state, see Shalini Randeria, 'The State of Globalization: Legal Plurality, Overlapping Sovereignties and Ambiguous Alliances between Civil Society and the Cunning State in India', *Theory, Culture & Society*, 2007, vol. 24, n° 1, pp. 1–33; Christian Lund, 'Fragmented Sovereignty: Land Reform and Dispossession in Laos', *The Journal of Peasant Studies*, 2011, vol. 38, n° 4, pp. 885–905; Lars Buur, 'The Sovereign Outsourced: Local Justice and Violence in Port Elizabeth' in Thomas Blom Hansen and Finn Stepputat (eds), *Sovereign Bodies: Citizens, Migrants, and States in the Postcolonial World*, Princeton, Princeton University Press, 2005, pp. 192–217; Béatrice Hibou, 'Retrait ou redéploiement de l'Etat?', *Critique internationale*, 1998, n° 1, pp. 151–68; Alessandro Monsutti, 'Fuzzy Sovereignty: Rural Reconstruction in Afghanistan, between Democracy Promotion and Power Games', *Comparative Studies in Society and History*, 2012, vol. 54, n° 3, pp. 563–91; Mariella Pandolfi, 'Une souveraineté mouvante et supracoloniale', *Multitudes*, 2000, vol. 3, n° 3, p. 97.

[71] For a conceptualization of some states as being able to use international pressures to pursue their own policies, see Shalini Randeria, 'Glocalization of Law: Environmental Justice, World Bank, NGOs and the Cunning State in India', *Current Sociology*, 2003, vol. 51, n° 3–4, pp. 305–28.

[72] Deobandism is a reform movement born in India in 1867 around a religious school, Dar ul-Ulum, founded in the city of Deoband. It is structured around a network of madrasas and theologians, preaching both a return to the foundations of Islam and an application of the precepts of the Hanafite school of jurisprudence. For a history of the movement, see Barbara Metcalf, *Islamic Revival in British India: Deoband, 1860–1900*, Princeton, Princeton University Press, 2014.

[73] The Taliban movement builds on the intertwining of legal and religious developments in Afghan history, a dynamic that echoes Somalia and other muslim postcolonial countries' legal politics. Mark

The independent mechanism for granting them the status of ulama promoted social recognition of their legal competence on top of their being appointed by the Taliban. While the essential problem of this recognition derived from the judges being simultaneously members of an armed movement and lawyers, legal certification by a third-party institution allowed the Taliban to circumvent this difficulty: judges were socially recognized as competent to decide disputes and impose sentences both because of their appointment to a judicial system and because their knowledge of Islamic law was vouched for by an independent institution. Thus, by virtue of their status as ulama, they legitimately decided the cases before them, and, as Taliban-appointed judges, they had the means to enforce their verdicts.

The organization of the book

The formation of the Taliban court system reflects a movement dominated by clerics in a context of civil war,[74] as well as the consequences of the Western intervention in law and justice. In 2001, Afghan society lived in a radical legal uncertainty created by twenty-three years of civil wars. The uprising sparked by the Communist coup d'état of 1978 led to a revolution in the juridical field alongside the armed clashes. Law and justice became an issue both in the confrontation between the Communist government and the insurgency, and in the underlying competition between elites (notables, university graduates, and ulama) over who would regulate social relations. While the Afghan state during the twentieth century had gradually secularized the judicial system, the insurgency's victory gave the ulama a monopoly on the legitimate exercise of law. After the fall of the Najibullah regime in 1992, armed factions, all claiming to uphold Islamic law, fought for power. This configuration favoured the Taliban, a clerical movement that relied on law and religious legitimacy to penetrate society (see Chapter 1). These two decades of civil war profoundly affected social structures, reshaping social

Fathi Massoud, *Shari'a, Inshallah: Finding God in Somali Legal Politics*, Cambridge, Cambridge University Press, 2021.

[74] I use the terms 'cleric' and 'clerical' to denote the existence of a body of religious professionals, the ulama, which claims a monopoly on interpreting the sacred texts. In South Asia, the organization of ulama around networks of religious institutions since the nineteenth century has structured autonomous religious fields in states. For an analysis of the organization of ulama in South Asia as a clergy, see Muhammad Qasim Zaman, *The Ulama in Contemporary Islam: Custodians of Change*, Princeton, Princeton University Press, 2002. On the notion of religious field, see Pierre Bourdieu, 'Genesis and Structure of the Religious Field', *Comparative Social Research*, 1991, vol. 13, pp. 1–44.

hierarchies, property, and gender relations. Furthermore, the armed movements instrumentalized the ensuing turmoil brought about by these shifts. These transformations thus led to a surge in the number of disputes, fuelled by the succession of competing judicial authorities, and thus the imposition of contradictory verdicts (see Chapter 2).

In 2001, Western intervention revived the struggle over law and justice between the regime it installed and the Taliban movement it had ousted from power. On the one hand, the juridical system gradually introduced by Western countries resulted in increasing uncertainty for the Afghan population. A maladapted corpus of laws, largely dictated by the cyclical priorities of the various financial backers, as well as the police and the judiciary undermined by nepotism, led to an unbalanced juridical system favouring the elites and inaccessible to the majority of the population. Western lawyers, experts, humanitarians, military personnel, and diplomats worked to have laws enacted that conflicted with the other Afghan laws, influenced appointments to key institutions, invented ad hoc committees, and interfered in court cases. Moreover, the judiciary's lack of independence favoured the regime's strongmen, the former commanders from the 1990s who seized entire sections of the state apparatus. These violent entrepreneurs exploited a system for appropriating resources by force, in which the courts lent a legal veneer to often violent de facto situations (see Chapter 3).

On the other hand, Western forces, starting with the US military, systematically circumvented Afghan law. In carrying out their operations against Al Qaeda and the Taliban, including through a campaign of targeted killings that sharpened local rivalries, they exempted themselves from any Afghan legal framework. Moreover, the Western military set up so-called 'customary' or 'traditional' councils that issued conflicting verdicts. With their uncertain legal status, these further undermined the regime's judicial institutions. Finally, in forming their own militias, the Western militaries handed various potentates the means for opposing the central state and eliminating their local rivals. Through its tribal and ethnic vision in Afghanistan, the US military contributed to a polarization of private conflicts along identity lines, making their resolution more intractable. The primordialist interpretations by American soldiers promoted strategies of ethnic or tribal instrumentalization. They allowed entrepreneurs of violence posing as community representatives to obtain weapons, occupy positions of power, and insinuate themselves as indispensable intermediaries, at the expense of official institutions. The alleged aversion of Afghans to the state ultimately became a self-fulfilling prophecy. It caused the US military to empower strongmen they regarded as local when these individuals in fact derived their power largely from international support (see Chapter 4).

Driven from power in 2001, the Taliban gradually re-established themselves in the countryside, village by village. Although the movement was transnational, it claimed the mantle of a legitimate state forced into exile by a foreign invasion. This allowed it to mobilize the population by painting the Western troops as occupiers. Despite their limited resources and the constraints of having to operate clandestinely, the Taliban nevertheless went about setting up courts in most of the country. They put in place mechanisms to extract judges and their verdicts from the war and its fallout on the local level. Yet several dynamics were at work hindering Taliban judges from being recognized as judges: military operations; the dependence of judges on fighters; and the tension between, on the one hand, the military imperatives of keeping on the move and, on the other, the appearance of objectivity that judges had to cultivate to remain credible. Nevertheless, the integration of judges into a bureaucratic system, the recruitment of clerical personnel schooled in hierarchical functioning, and the establishment of standard procedures allowed the Taliban to produce, even under wartime conditions, a relatively predictable court system. First, the movement integrated judges into a centralized judicial organization that was inspired by the institutional architecture of the Taliban regime of the 1990s. A rotation and monitoring system was designed to ensure judges' good practices and their detachment from local issues related to the conflicts they were called on to adjudicate (see Chapter 5).

Secondly, the recruitment of judges in the Deobandi madrasas let the Taliban set up a particularly economical system because of not having to train specialized staff or draft a legal code. In this way, the movement benefited from the education and ideological indoctrination performed by madrasas on young Afghans from rural areas and refugee camps. After ten years in religious schools, far from their families and villages, the ulama shared a range of theological and legal skills, a bureaucratic *habitus*, and a worldview that set them apart from their home environment. The education acquired in the Deobandi madrasas underpinned the coherence as well as the Islamic character of their verdicts, which were based mainly on the Hanafite case law that the judges were trained in.[75] This socialization also engendered individual inclinations that reinforced the effectiveness of the institutional arrangements into which the

[75] Hanafism is a school of Sunni jurisprudence based on the teachings of the theologian Abu Hanifa, who lived in Iraq in the eighth century. Dominant in Afghanistan, Hanafite jurisprudence has strongly influenced Afghan state law. Mohammad Hashim Kamali, *Law in Afghanistan: A Study of the Constitutions, Matrimonial Law and the Judiciary*, Leiden, Brill, 1985.

movement inserted them as judges. The Deobandi ideology, which accommodates a role for clerics in social regulation while denying the political character of their actions, fed into a particularly effective claim of judicial objectivity (see Chapter 6).

Finally, unlike most contemporary armed movements, the Taliban discarded the usual modes of objectivizing the judicial system with places (buildings, courtroom configuration) or attributes (specific dress, symbols, objects), because doing so would have increased the risks of Western troops honing in on the judges. They instead adopted the devices and rituals of rural social life, blending into the population while remaining accessible to their users.[76] The formalization of the Taliban judicial system relied on rudimentary but regular and therefore predictable procedures. In this it contrasted sharply with the regime's judicial system that, while conspicuously mobilizing the visible attributes of state justice, fostered legal uncertainty by frequently breaking its own rules. In the context of war and given the movement's limited resources, adherence to a procedural organization—from complaint to verdict and sentencing—conditioned the production of the Taliban judges' utterances as 'acts of naming or of instituting' (see Chapter 7).

The Taliban judicial system participated in the production of a social order at three levels: in structuring other branches of the armed movement, in legitimating the law, and in imposing a social project. First, the system was one of the elements of a broader administration, which incorporated the formal principles of state functioning. Within this clandestine government, Taliban judges were part of a system of cross-recognition and legitimization based on a differentiation between political, military, and judicial functions. Taliban leaders employed judges to buttress the hierarchy within the movement and thus maintain a centralized authority. However, judges depended on combatants to carry out their activities in their jurisdiction, which transferred to the relationship between leaders and commanders the latter's respect for judicial authority. But while subordinate commanders were forced to close ranks, the most important ones had the means to resist, forcing the political leadership of the movement to make deals (see Chapter 8).

Secondly, the judicial system was an essential part of the Taliban's claim that they *were* the state in Afghanistan. In practice, the political and strategic effectiveness of the courts is difficult to assess, although there are many indications that they facilitated the movement's implantation in previously hostile regions.

[76] This replication of the usual interactional layouts of Afghan society partly explains the confusion among observers who describe Taliban courts as customary courts.

The Taliban judges operated in a juridical field polarized by the transposition of political confrontation into law and justice. Therefore, users' assessments of the competing judicial systems directly impacted the ongoing struggle to impose a monopoly on the law's application. The legitimization of the Taliban courts can only be accounted for in contrast to the regime's courts and the legal practices of the international forces. In comparison, Taliban judgments were considered more effective, first because they were better respected locally than the government's. They were felt as a source of predictability in daily life, helping to establish the legal nature of the Taliban verdicts and thus the legal nature of their hold over the population. However, the international recognition enjoyed by the Kabul regime gave its courts an official—and therefore more lasting—character, which the Taliban judicial system never achieved (see Chapter 9).

Finally, the Taliban judicial system participated in the production of an alternative social order characterized by social conservatism and moral rigour. As a whole, its verdicts show the movement's plan to preserve—that is, to reproduce—the property structures and social hierarchies of the pre-war period. Thus, as had happened during the 1990s, the judges imposed an identity regime, which followed the main lines of the pre-war regime in favouring the Pashtuns by denying the ethnic question and relegating the Shiites to second-class status. In addition, they guaranteed private property by combating the violent land grabs by 1990s commanders and regime strongmen, but in the process they also ensured the reproduction of economic inequalities around land. When it came to gender issues, while the Taliban appeared to be more flexible than in the 1990s with respect to certain practices (music, mobile phones, films, games), quite the opposite was the case. Here, the judges ruled with particular severity: they guaranteed a system of patriarchal domination based on repressing deviance in the public sphere and on delegating the resort to violence in the domestic space to the heads of families. This conservative programme legitimized the social rise of religious elites. Indeed, the judges' attending to the public good concealed a work of universalizing the special interests of the ulama. By reshaping the state and society through the application of Islamic law, judges promoted an order in which religious status would determine access to positions of power, at the obvious expense of non-religious elites (see Chapter 10).

PART I
LEGAL UNCERTAINTY

1

A revolution in the juridical field

Introduction

The formation of the Taliban insurgency's judicial system harked back to the clerical movement's beginnings in the context of the war in the 1980–90s. The uprising fomented by the Communist coup d'état of 1978 brought with it, in parallel with the armed strife, a revolution in the juridical field. The confrontations between the Communist regime and the mujahideen, followed by the struggle among commanders during the 1990s, led to the emergence of competing legal systems. The war for control of the state was compounded by ulama, Kabul University graduates, and notables competing to craft the law, a process that ended up consolidating religious legitimacy. Far from the archaism and irrationality commonly attributed to the Taliban, the movement organized around ulama entering the juridical and political fields. The structuring of the Taliban around jurists and aspiring jurists translated into a legal and moral vision of politics, an insistence on the restoration of law and order that aimed to put an end to deviance and disorder and thus to war.

Religious versus secular jurists

Following the 1978 coup d'état, Communists and Islamists questioned the foundations of the juridical order: namely, what role the central state should play in regulating social relations, who was entitled to lay down the law, and from what sources. Law and justice thus became a battleground in the confrontation between the regime and the insurgency, as well as a key issue in the struggle for power between different elites.

On the eve of the Communist takeover, the Afghan judicial system was relatively centralized and secularized. During the reign of Abdul Rahman Khan (1880–1901), the great tribal notables lost their judicial prerogatives to ulama appointed by the emir.[1] Beginning in the 1920s, in the context of the

[1] Ashraf Ghani, 'Disputes in a Court of Sharia, Kunar Valley, Afghanistan, 1885–1890', *International*

The Taliban Courts in Afghanistan. Adam Baczko, Oxford University Press. © Adam Baczko 2023.
DOI: 10.1093/oso/9780198896777.003.0002

modernization enterprise led by the successive emirs, the state administration appointed judges to supplant the ulama and apply texts mixing Hanafite jurisprudence and imported legal norms. Between 1919 and 1923, King Amanullah called on Turkish and Indian jurists to draft the first constitution in Afghan history, a penal code and a civil code.[2] The new Basic Law explicitly affirmed the monopoly of the state courts, stripping the ulama of any legal prerogatives unless they performed official duties in the judicial system (Article 55).[3] However, the clergy remained dominant in the juridical field, as illustrated in the 1930s by the appointments as Minister of Justice of Fazl Omar Mojaddidi and later his son Fazl Ahmad Mojaddidi, members of one of the country's most important ulama families.[4]

The secularization of the Afghan juridical field accelerated from the 1960s onwards. The Constitution of 1964 established a Parliament charged with legislating but without violating Islamic principles (Article 64)—a relatively flexible formula—and it permitted recourse to Hanafite jurisprudence in the absence of enacted or adopted laws (Article 69). It also provided for the formation of an independent Supreme Court to oversee the judicial system and ensure compliance with the Constitution. (Article 98).[5] That same year, jurists from Kabul University's Faculty of Law and Political Science began staffing the Ministry of Justice, until then a stronghold of theologians.[6] In 1965, the writing of a Code of Criminal Procedure largely inspired by Egypt's, and the creation of the post of Attorney General (*saranwal*) strengthened the position of graduates from the Faculty of Law and Political Science. In 1968, the Jurisdiction and Organizing of Courts of Afghanistan Act provided for the establishment,

Journal of Middle East Studies, 1983, vol. 15, n° 03, pp. 353–67; Asta Olesen, *Islam and Politics in Afghanistan*, London, Routledge, 1995, pp. 61–94; Amin Tarzi, 'Islam, Shari'a, and State Building under 'Abd al-Rahman Khan' in Nile Green (ed.), *Afghanistan's Islam: From Conversion to the Taliban*, Berkeley, University of California Press, 2016, pp. 129–44.

[2] Until 2016, following Leon Poullada, researchers on Afghanistan agreed that French lawyers were present to advise on drafting the 1923 Constitution. Historian and lawyer Faiz Ahmed disputes this thesis, pointing out the lack of sources on the drafting process. Relying on sources of the Basic Law and the biography of the known drafters, he argues instead that it was done exclusively with Turkish and Indian Islamic jurists, and thus constituted, with the Ottoman Constitution of 1876 and Iran's of 1906, one of the essential stages of the Islamic modernist current. Leon Poullada, *Reform and Rebellion in Afghanistan, 1919–1929: King Amanullah's Failure to Modernize a Tribal Society*, Ithaca, Cornell University Press, 1973, pp. 92–4; Faiz Ahmed, *Afghanistan Rising: Islamic Law and Statecraft between the Ottoman and British Empires*, Cambridge, Harvard University Press, 2017, pp. 207–35.

[3] Leon Poullada, *Reform and Rebellion in Afghanistan, 1919–1929: King Amanullah's Failure to Modernize a Tribal Society*, Ithaca, Cornell University Press, 1973, p. 75.

[4] Asta Olesen, *Islam and Politics in Afghanistan*, London, Routledge, 1995, p. 185.

[5] Abdul S. Sirat, 'The Modern Legal System of Afghanistan', *The American Journal of Comparative Law*, 1968, vol. 16, n° 4, pp. 563–9.

[6] Louis Dupree, *Afghanistan*, Princeton, Princeton University Press, 1973, pp. 579–87.

under the supervision of the Supreme Court, of a Court of Cassation, a High Court of Appeals, provincial courts, and district courts. In addition, to integrate the graduates of the faculties of Sharia and of Law and Political Science, the Supreme Court created a legal training centre.[7] The presidency of Daoud Khan (1973–8) saw a particularly intense period of codification, including the enactment of new versions of the Penal Code and the Civil Code. In the 1977 Civil Code, personal status law largely remained the province of Islamic judges, who, however, now had to hand down fixed sentences.[8] On the eve of the 1978 coup d'état, the majority of judges still came from a religious background, and the juridical field became embroiled in a fierce competition between the two types of jurists.[9]

While notables and ulama no longer enjoyed prerogatives in state courts, they retained certain judicial functions in rural areas. In theory, each of the 220 districts had at least one sitting district judge and, in each provincial capital, a provincial court composed of three judges served as both a trial and appeals court.[10] Still, nearly half of the districts lacked a prosecutor and the courts struggled to adjudicate disputes in areas remote from district capitals. Many disputes were therefore brought to the ulama for a legal opinion *(fatwa)* or to councils (*jirga*) in which notables applied collective procedures of conciliation, negotiation, and occasionally arbitration. These bodies based on custom and Islam were de facto inserted into the judicial system, whose courts would handle conflicts when the latter failed to resolve them. Customary justice in the 1970s was not a parallel justice system, but a form of delegation by the state for managing local conflicts.[11] As in the colonial contexts of 'decentralized despotism', the use of custom strengthened the local authority of the notables while inscribing it in the enterprise of pacifying the margins led by the central state.[12]

[7] Mohammad Hashim Kamali, *Law in Afghanistan: A Study of the Constitutions, Matrimonial Law and the Judiciary*, Leiden, Brill, 1985, p. 207.

[8] Personal status encompasses all legal issues that directly concern the individual, including marital status, capacity, matrimonial regime, and inheritance. Regarding the transformations of personal status in the Civil Code of 1977, see Mohammad Hashim Kamali, *Law in Afghanistan: A Study of the Constitutions, Matrimonial Law and the Judiciary*, Leiden, Brill, 1985; Marvin Weinbaum, 'Legal Elites in Afghan Society', *International Journal of Middle East Studies*, 1980, vol. 12, n° 1, pp. 39–57.

[9] Marvin Weinbaum, 'Legal Elites in Afghan Society', *International Journal of Middle East Studies*, 1980, vol. 12, n° 1, pp. 40–2.

[10] Ibid., p. 40.

[11] On the concept of delegation, see Béatrice Hibou, 'Retrait ou redéploiement de l'État?', *Critique internationale*, 1998, n° 1, pp. 151–68.

[12] Mahmood Mamdani, *Citizen and Subject: Contemporary Africa and the Legacy of Late Colonialism*, Princeton, Princeton University Press, 1996. In Pakistan's Northwest Frontier province, there was a similar incorporation of local judicial practices, labelled as 'traditional', even though they operated in the Raj colonial system and then in the postcolonial legal system. See Benjamin Hopkins, 'The Frontier

Starting in 1978, the Communist regime pushed to a climax the centralizing and secularizing of the law, sweeping away the fragile compromises developed over several decades of reforms. For the first time in Afghanistan's history, the 1980 Constitution did not recognize Islam as an official religion and as the source of law. Communist leaders excluded notables and the religious from the judiciary—and more generally from the administration.[13] In the months following the 1978 coup, these two social groups were violently repressed. In a party state logic, judges were stripped of most judicial powers and, as early as 1978, the Revolutionary Committee, the new regime's executive body, created special courts under its own authority. With the Soviet occupation (1979–89), these were moved under the intelligence service, the KHAD (Khadamat-i Atalat-i Dawlati or State Information Service), causing the judicial system to atrophy.[14]

By contrast, in the regions controlled by the insurgency, ulama acquired a monopoly on the power to exercise the law. Graduates of the Faculty of Law and Political Science and notables in tribal bodies saw themselves quickly marginalized. Thus, in the early 1980s, in the campaign around Herat, a judge who switched sides was put in charge of propaganda, while a madrasa teacher was appointed to a judgeship.[15] The ulama were able to form a monopoly within the insurgency for several reasons. First, the framing of war as a jihad, which only the ulama were able to proclaim, eclipsed the secular jurists and tribal notables. The Islamist parties that imposed themselves at the head of the insurgents advocated the application of Islamic law and thus the recognition of the legal functions of the ulama. Starting in the early 1980s, Olivier Roy observed:

> The resistance movement has brought with it a strengthening of Islam's role in shaping the social order: everywhere the shari'at has been superseding common law and sometimes even the legislation enacted by the parties, who in any case are careful to leave civil law well alone. Muslim law, which is complex and intentionally casuistic, requires lengthy study: only the 'ulama have

Crimes Regulation and Frontier Governmentality', *The Journal of Asian Studies*, 2015, vol. 74, n° 2, pp. 369–89.

[13] Marvin Weinbaum, 'Legal Elites in Afghan Society', *International Journal of Middle East Studies*, 1980, vol. 12, n° 1, p. 39.

[14] Chantal Lobato, *Un islam conservateur au service du communisme: Kabul 1980–1985*, DEA d'histoire, EHESS, 1986, pp. 29–32; Barnett R. Rubin, *The Fragmentation of Afghanistan: State Formation and Collapse in the International System*, New Haven, Yale University Press, 2002, pp. 133–4.

[15] Olivier Roy, 'État et société en Afghanistan', *Revue française de science politique*, 1985, vol. 35, n° 3, p. 417.

mastered this law, whose authority is now accepted by the whole resistance movement.[16]

In addition, ulama were more accessible than regime judges in remote rural areas, causing many people to turn to them.[17] Finally, unlike judges, ulama did not depend on the existence of a legal system in Kabul for the recognition of their judicial competence and were therefore less affected when the state administration withdrew from most of the countryside. Despite repeated attempts throughout the twentieth century, the Afghan state had never managed to take control of ulama training and appointments.[18] Many mullahs and ulama had studied in private religious schools linked to Pakistani madrasa networks in Afghanistan or Pakistan instead of those run by religious dignitaries close to the regime. This state of affairs only became more pronounced with the war, the rising prestige of the religious vocation leading to an increase in private madrasas among refugees in Pakistan and in areas held by the insurgency.[19]

In this respect, the notables, who performed de facto judicial functions in the outlying regions, constituted an intermediate case. The recognition of their legitimacy to exercise law did not depend directly on the central state, but they ultimately relied on its presence and potential involvement for enforcing their decisions. How dependent on the state these tribal modes of conciliation were became evident in hindsight when these bodies collapsed the moment the Communist regime lost control of the periphery. To be sure, there were exceptions, especially in parts of the Southeast (Loya Paktya, Logar), where commanders brought together tribal elites and ulama in resolving disputes by combining customary norms and sharia.[20] The uniqueness of this region is largely explained by its marginality, away from major roads and infrastructure projects, which helped preserve the autonomy of the local tribal elites from the central state.[21]

[16] Olivier Roy, *Islam and Resistance in Afghanistan*, Cambridge, Cambridge University Press, 1990, p. 152.

[17] Ibid., pp. 211–16.

[18] Gilles Dorronsoro, 'Les oulémas afghans au XXe siècle: Bureaucratisation, contestation et genèse d'un État clérical', *Archives de sciences sociales des religions*, 2001, n° 115, pp. 63–79.

[19] On the Shiite jurisconsults' side, their religious and legal skills have never been officially recognized—the monarchy and the republic proclaimed themselves as Sunni—and many trained in Iran and Iraq. See Fariba Adelkhah, 'Religious Dependency in Afghanistan: Shia Madrasas as a Religious Mode of Social Assertion?' in Keiko Sakurai and Fariba Adelkhah (eds), *The Moral Economy of the Madrasa: Islam and Education Today*, London, Taylor & Francis, 2011, pp. 103–29.

[20] Barnett R. Rubin, *The Fragmentation of Afghanistan: State Formation and Collapse in the International System*, New Haven, Yale University Press, 2002, pp. 230–3; David Edwards, *Before Taliban Genealogies of the Afghan Jihad*, Berkeley, University of California Press, 2002, pp. 251–2.

[21] For example, in the mid-1970s, anthropologist Alef-Shah Zadran carried out a conflict resolution ethnographic study in Almarah, a village in present-day Khost province, and estimated

However, despite the ulama rapidly monopolizing justice, legal practices varied considerably within the insurgency. On the one hand, the absence of a unified hierarchy within the Sunni clergy left leeway for judicial interpretation in the application of Islamic law. Most Sunni-affiliated commanders followed recommendations like those found in *Mufti Sangar*, a pamphlet published in Peshawar in the 1980s that detailed the mujahid's legal obligations. For example, in it they would find guidance for resolving conflicts between combatants and between combatants and the population.[22] On the other hand, no party or structure succeeded in imposing its authority on the national level, and commanders remained free to administer their territories as they saw fit.[23] Starting from the diversity of local situations, it is possible to distinguish three models for organizing the law, which corresponded to differing relationships between commanders and ulama: first, in a patrimonial logic, some commanders—especially those who claimed religious competence—resolved disputes themselves; secondly, most allowed the population to consult ulama who remained outside their armed group; finally, some, notably the Hizb-i Islami, hired ulama to serve them or even, like Ahmad Shah Massoud and Ismael Khan, set up an entire juridical system with trial courts, an appeals court, and prisons.[24] These different practices corresponded to the manner in which commanders organized the territories under their control, ranging from a patrimonial model that drew no distinction between the personal budget of the chief and that of the armed group to one with specialized functions for administering the population.[25]

Moreover, in the absence of a single political authority controlling the whole insurgency, the various judicial instances could not arbitrate conflicts between commanders revolving around personal rivalries, the seizing of humanitarian aid, and the control of strategic points (roads, passes) and resources (mines,

that three-quarters of the disputes were resolved by tribal authorities. See Alef-Shah Zadran, *Socio-Economic and Legal-Political Processes in a Pashtun Village, Southeastern Afghanistan*, State University of New York, New York, 1977.

[22] Interview with Mullah Mohammed Osman Tariq, September 2012. See also the analysis of this booklet by David Edwards in *Caravan of Martyrs: Sacrifice and Suicide Bombing in Afghanistan*, Berkeley, University of California Press, 2017, pp. 66–8.

[23] Gilles Dorronsoro, 'Désordre et légitimité du politique en Afghanistan', *Cultures & Conflits*, 1997, n° 24–25.

[24] Olivier Roy, *Islam and Resistance in Afghanistan*, Cambridge, Cambridge University Press, 1990, pp. 153–6. For the judicial system of Ahmad Shah Massoud and Ismaël Khan, see respectively Jérome Bony and Christophe de Ponfilly, 'A Valley Against an Empire', *Central Asian Survey*, 1983, vol. 1, n° 4, pp. 133–48; Gilles Dorronsoro, *La ville d'Hérat dans la guerre*, DEA d'histoire, EHESS, Paris, 1987.

[25] Gilles Dorronsoro, *Revolution Unending: Afghanistan, 1979 to the Present*, New York, Columbia University Press, 2005, pp. 123–8.

lumber). Ulama were also powerless to settle disputes with a collective tribal or ethnic dimension. A few independent authorities—highly respected ulama or tribal *jirgas* from the Southeast, for example—at times did manage to play a conciliating or even arbitrating role.[26] In Kandahar, while there was still no conclusive winner, ulama under the leadership of Mawlawi Nazar Mohamad and then Mawlawi Mohamad Pasanai set up an independent Islamic tribunal near Kandahar City that most commanders recognized.[27] Subsequently, other courts were established in the surrounding districts by Mullah Naqib in Arghandab, Mullah Abdul Samad *Akhund* in Panjwai, and Mullah Akhtar Jan in Spin Boldak.[28] However, lacking the coercive power to enforce their verdicts, Islamic judges had to rely on recognition by local commanders. If, in a context of jihad against a foreign occupation, these courts were able to adjudicate many disputes, they saw their authority diluted after the Soviet withdrawal as infighting spread within the insurgency.

The Soviet withdrawal in the late 1980s enshrined the ulama monopoly on the juridical field. The new strongman in Kabul, Mohamad Najibullah, engaged in a policy of reconciliation, which entailed erasing Marxist symbols and re-establishing Islamic legitimacy. In 1990, a new constitution proclaimed an Islamic state and made sharia the ultimate authority.[29] The capture of Kabul in 1992 by the mujahideen and the fall of the Najibullah regime further consolidated the extension of the theologians' judicial monopoly over the entire country. Recognition of this jurisdiction became so compelling that even Abdul Rachid Dostum, a former Communist militia leader, established Islamic courts in the stronghold he had carved out in the North.

The theologians move into politics

The Taliban, essentially a grouping of clerics, systematized the new role of ulama or theologians in regulating social relations and integrated them into a centralized administration. The victory of a clerical party relates to the

[26] For example, Mawlawi Mohamad Hanif played such a role at Garmsir, in Helmand, see Carter Malkasian, *War Comes to Garmser: Thirty Years of Conflict on the Afghan Frontier*, Oxford, Oxford University Press, 2013, p. 32.

[27] Barnett R. Rubin, *The Fragmentation of Afghanistan: State Formation and Collapse in the International System*, New Haven, Yale University Press, 2002, pp. 244–5; Abdul Salam Zaeef, *My Life with the Taliban*, New York, Columbia University Press, 2010, p. 22.

[28] Alex Strick van Linschoten and Felix Kuehn, *An Enemy we Created: The Myth of the Taliban-al Qaeda Merger in Afghanistan*, Oxford, Oxford University Press, 2012, pp. 46–7.

[29] Barnett R. Rubin, *The Fragmentation of Afghanistan: State Formation and Collapse in the International System*, New Haven, Yale University Press, 2002, p. 166.

evolution of social structures in the war, during which religious capital gave access to legal and political positions.[30]

The move of the ulama into politics played out gradually throughout the 1980s. Against the background of their legitimacy in making law, clerics became key players in political parties. In the late 1980s, movements associated with madrasa networks emerged in several regions: in 1986, the Jama'at ud-Dawa in Kunar relied on the networks of the Salafist Panjpir madrasa; in 1988, in Hazarajat, Iranian-trained ulama played a key role in the founding of Hizb-i Wahdat;[31] in Ghazni, following the Soviet withdrawal, the commander *Qari* Baba set up a clerical administration to consolidate his power;[32] while *Rais* Abdul Wahid 'Baghran' in northern Helmand established his own madrasas and relied on mullahs and ulama to govern.[33] Born in 1994 in Kandahar province, the Taliban movement took the structuring of a political movement around networks of ulama a step further by making clerical status a condition for access to political positions. All senior Taliban officials were mullahs or ulama, often trained in Pakistani madrasas. By contrast, the ulama linked to the pre-war regime, followers of Sibghatullah Mojaddidi and Ahmad Gaylani, were excluded from the movement's ruling circles.[34]

The Taliban's clerical structure played a decisive role in their ascent to power. To begin with, it gave rise to the charismatic tale of a revolt against disorder and chaos. Indeed, the context in which the Taliban formed, in the Kandahar of 1994, was marked by particularly violent clashes between commanders. In the previous decade, the Russian KGB, though a skilful policy of manipulation and cooptation, had engineered a local fragmentation of the insurgency and stoked rivalries between commanders. After its departure, a dozen armed groups divided up Kandahar's only city; in the countryside, dozens more clashed daily for what were sometimes inane reasons. They set up roadblocks, extorted money

[30] Gilles Dorronsoro, 'Dynamiques entre champs religieux et politique. Le cas de l'Afghanistan', *Purusartha*, 2012, n° 30, pp. 363–76.

[31] However, unlike the other movements mentioned, the Hizb-i Wahdat resulted from a coalition of religious dignitaries, and its local administration depended on the political balance within its various branches. Interviews with Mualim Aziz, an intellectual close to Hizb-i Wahdat and Ali Amiri, political cadre of Hizb-i Wahdat, September 2012.

[32] Interviews with *Qari* Abdul Malik, son of *Qari* Baba; Khial Mohamad, *Qari* Baba's former deputy; Shah Jahan Noori, commander of Jabha-yi Nijat-i Milli and allied with *Qari* Baba; Mullah Wazir, a commander of *Qari* Baba's, September 2012.

[33] E-71, Abdul Wahid, Baghran's political representative in Kabul, September 2012.

[34] Gilles Dorronsoro, *Revolution Unending: Afghanistan, 1979 to the Present*, New York, Columbia University Press, 2005, pp. 276–8.

from residents, and caused schools to be shut as early as 1992.[35] Kandaharis refer to this time as the era of the 'gunmen' (*topakian*).[36]

As Taliban key figures and some residents of the province tell it, the movement was born out of moral shock.[37] The accounts of the initial expansion are invariably peppered with descriptions of corrupt and criminal commanders. Thus, the Taliban creation story has it formed by mullahs and seminarians (*taliban*) from the madrasa of Singesar village, veteran anti-Soviet fighters all, who took up arms against the wanton abuses, including sexual transgressions, of a commander named Saleh. After his defeat, people from the surrounding villages reportedly appealed to them against other commanders. Similarly, the attack on Kandahar City was justified by the abduction of several dozen truckers by a local commander.[38] These narratives remobilized the prophetic register, linked to the revolts against the British Empire and the state, of the charismatic, pious mullah who, in a context of moral and social crisis, reunifies a divided society.[39] They thus included the classic themes of Mullah Omar's initial hesitations, his submission to God, and the dreams in which Allah and the prophet Muhammad spoke to him.[40] Moreover, the motif of abuses echoed the situations experienced by most Afghans. As anthropologist David Edwards explains:

> Whether apocryphal or not, the story is believable within the experience of average Afghans, who came to see the Taliban as a deliverance from the

[35] Ibid., p. 246.

[36] Residents of Kandahar also used the term to describe police operations in villages. The parallel is significant. Abdul Salam Zaeef, *My Life with the Taliban*, New York, Columbia University Press, 2010, p. 59.

[37] James M. Jasper, *The Art of Moral Protest: Culture, Biography, and Creativity in Social Movements*, Chicago, University of Chicago Press, 1997, p. 106. The author defines moral shock thus: 'An unexpected event or information that arouses such a sense of indignation in a person that he becomes inclined to political action, with or without the network of personal contacts on which the theories of social movements insist.'

[38] Anthony Davis, 'How the Taliban Became a Military Force' in William Maley (ed.), *Fundamentalism Reborn? Afghanistan and the Taliban*, London, Hurst, 1998, p. 43; Abdul Salam Zaeef, *My Life with the Taliban*, New York, Columbia University Press, 2010, pp. 60–2; Ahmed Rashid, *Taliban: Militant Islam, Oil and Fundamentalism in Central Asia*, New Haven, Yale University Press, 2000, pp. 21–2; Alex Strick van Linschoten and Felix Kuehn, *An Enemy we Created: The Myth of the Taliban-al Qaeda Merger in Afghanistan*, Oxford, Oxford University Press, 2012, pp. 114–15.

[39] Milan Hauner, 'One Man against the Empire: The Faqir of Ipi and the British in Central Asia on the Eve of and during the Second World War', *Journal of Contemporary History*, 1981, vol. 16, n° 1, pp. 183–212; David Edwards, 'Mad Mullahs and Englishmen: Discourse in the Colonial Encounter', *Comparative Studies in Society and History*, 1989, vol. 31, n° 4, pp. 649–70.

[40] This articulation between bureaucratic personnel (ulama) and charismatic attributes partly explains the immense perplexity of journalists and researchers who have commented on the emergence of the Taliban movement. Yet, in his sociology of religions, Max Weber already pointed out that the rapprochements between clerical and prophetic logics were common. Max Weber, *Economy and Society*, Berkeley, University of California Press, 1978, vol. 1, pp. 452–67. For a description of Mullah Omar's dreams and their place in the movement's structure, see Ian R. Edgar, *The Dream in Islam: From Qur'anic Tradition to Jihadist Inspiration*, New York, Berghahn, 2011, pp. 79–94.

> anarchy that had befallen Afghanistan after the Soviet withdrawal. Even before people knew who the Taliban were or what they represented, they were willing to give the Taliban the benefit of the doubt, and even if they were suspicious, they weren't willing to risk their own lives to defend those in charge against the Taliban assault.[41]

The Taliban's discourse of restoring order and their effectiveness against commanders attracted the attention of local and foreign sponsors interested in ending the looting and creating a unified national market.[42] In particular, traders, whose businesses were heavily affected by roadblocks and racketeering, welcomed this new movement as a force for reopening the roads and restoring security.[43] The financing of an armed group by merchants to restore order and protect their activities recurs frequently in contemporary civil wars. In Somalia, the Union of Islamic Courts gained a hold in the 2000s thanks in part to funding from Mogadishu traders who wanted to end extortion by warlords and reopen the roads to Yemen and Kenya.[44] Similarly, in the Democratic Republic of the Congo's North Kivu province, Butembo traders and local Catholic Church officials subsidized Mai-Mai militias to secure the route to Goma and access to the Rwandan border.[45]

Pakistan likewise wanted to reopen the road to Central Asia. Journalist Ahmed Rashid highlighted the role played by the truckers' corporation in the southwestern Pakistani city of Quetta in funding the Taliban to restore free movement in Afghanistan.[46] Islamabad was also on the lookout for a candidate to succeed its protégé, Gulbuddin Hikmatyar's Hizb-i Islami, who had failed to seize Kabul. The Inter-Services Intelligence (ISI), Pakistan's CIA, trained the Taliban, provided them with technical advisers, and gave the green light to their recruiting

[41] David Edwards, *Before Taliban Genealogies of the Afghan Jihad*, Berkeley, University of California Press, 2002, pp. 293–4.

[42] Anthony Davis, 'How the Taliban Became a Military Force' in William Maley (ed.), *Fundamentalism Reborn? Afghanistan and the Taliban*, London, Hurst, 1998, pp. 43–71; Milan Hauner, 'One Man against the Empire: The Faqir of Ipi and the British in Central Asia on the Eve of and during the Second World War', *Journal of Contemporary History*, 1981, vol. 16, n° 1, pp. 183–212.

[43] Abdul Salam Zaeef, *My Life with the Taliban*, New York, Columbia University Press, 2010, p. 67.

[44] Cedric Barnes and Harun Hassan, 'The Rise and Fall of Mogadishu's Islamic Courts', *Journal of Eastern African Studies*, 2007, vol. 1, n° 2, pp. 151–60; Ken Menkhaus, 'Governance without Government in Somalia: Spoilers, State Building, and the Politics of Coping', *International Security*, 2007, vol. 31, n° 3, pp. 74–106; Aisha Ahmad, *Jihad & Co: Black Markets and Islamist Power*, New York, Oxford University Press, 2017.

[45] Interviews in North Kivu, Democratic Republic of the Congo, May–June 2012. See also Timothy Raeymaekers, *Violent Capitalism and Hybrid Identity in the Eastern Congo*, Cambridge, Cambridge University Press, 2014.

[46] Ahmed Rashid, *Taliban: Militant Islam, Oil and Fundamentalism in Central Asia*, New Haven, Yale University Press, 2000, pp. 189–91.

in Pakistan's madrasas with their many Afghan students. Saudi Arabia also financed the Taliban, which it regards, along with others—Hizb-i Islami (before it supported Saddam Hussein), Jama'at ud-Dawa, and Ittihad-i Islami—as vehicles for exporting its vision of Islam and advancing its interests in Afghanistan.

Finally, the Taliban's clerical composition kept them out of the personal, political, and communitarian strife between commanders in the mid-1990s. This allowed them to better exploit these rivalries as they conquered the country. It let them seize Kandahar City while Mullah Naqib remained passive, Helmand by allying themselves with *Rais* Abdul Wahid Baghran against Ghaffar Akhoundzada, Ghazni by supporting *Qari* Baba against Gulbuddin Hikmatyar, next *Qari* Baba's second-in-command Khial Mohamad against *Qari* Baba, and finally take Kunar by enlisting the defeated fighters of Jama'at ud Dawa against Hizb-i Islami. Similarly, in 1994, President Rabbani and Commander Massoud, who had few allies in the South, supported them in the hope of weakening the Hizb-i Islami besieging Kabul.

However, in February 1995, after the Taliban had crushed Hizb-i Islami, they turned on President Rabbani and Ahmad Shah Massoud. By this time, they had become a national force to be reckoned with, fielding tens of thousands of fighters, their discourse of order and justice resonating in both the cities and the countryside. The great commanders remained divided to the end: Ismael Khan attacked the Taliban without waiting for Massoud's troops. His defeat caused Herat to fall to the clerical movement in September 1995. Then, competition between Hizb-i Islami and Jamiat-i Islami and the choice by Jumbesh-i Melli to remain neutral played a key role in the Taliban's capture of Kabul in September 1996. Even as they advanced in the North, when the confrontation took on an ethnic tenor (Pashtuns versus minorities), rivalries between commanders persisted. The Taliban first seized Mazar-i Sharif in May 1997 thanks to the defection of the city's governor, Abdul Malik Pahlawan, who was in open conflict with Dostum. They had to give it up again, only to recapture it in August 1998 when the Jumbesh-i Melli and Hizb-i Wahdat alliance fell apart. In the fall of 2001, the commanders coalesced in the United Front, also known as the Northern Alliance, which continued to battle the Taliban, but only held on in a few valleys in Panjshir and Badakhshan.

The Islamic Emirate of Afghanistan

While the clerical nature of the Taliban played a decisive role in the movement's formation and in its victory, their regime, the Islamic Emirate of Afghanistan, did not merely transpose the clerical hierarchy to the state. The mullahs and ulama fit into the Taliban administration according to a largely partisan logic. Here, a comparison with other regimes applying sharia law is instructive for understanding the Islamic Emirate's workings. In Saudi Arabia, often referenced by pundits and scholars when writing about the Taliban, it is based on a strict separation between religious and political fields, with two distinct elites, the ulama and the Royal Family, who respectively hold a monopoly on interpreting the sacred texts and on governing the country.[47] Conversely, in a logic reminiscent of the Iranian theocracy of the 1980s, Islamic law as interpreted by the Islamic Emirate's ulama formed the basis for political decisions with the clerics occupying executive, judicial, and legislative positions. The Taliban forbade elections and parties, which they accused of fomenting division and disorder.

The movement's strength rested on this fundamental ambiguity: it was a political party whose moral discourse and demands for restoring order proclaimed it as eschewing any political ambition while also denying the eminently ideological dimension of its actions. However, unlike the Iranian ayatollahs, many Taliban leaders were mere mullahs on the lowest rung of the religious hierarchy. In particular, Mullah Omar, who signed most of the decrees and concentrated important legislative powers in his hands, had only studied in a village madrasa and was not even an alim. His authority derived not from his knowledge or his place in the clerical hierarchy but from his charisma. He was installed in the state by an assembly of ulama in Kandahar in the weeks following the capture of Kabul. The 1,500 religious dignitaries gathered there proclaimed him 'Commander of the Faithful' (*amir al-mouminin*) at a ceremony during which the Prophet's robe, a relic kept in the Kherqa Sharif shrine, was displayed in public for the first time since 1935.[48] The position of the other mullahs or ulama in the political apparatus was not a function of the clerical hierarchy, but of their early engagement with the movement and closeness to Mullah Omar.

In the context of war, the law provided the Taliban with an instrument of social penetration. In newly conquered provinces, the courts were the first institutions they got running. While in most ministries the movement relied on

[47] Stéphane Lacroix, *Les islamistes saoudiens: Une insurrection manquée*, Paris, Presses Universitaires de France, 2015.

[48] Mullah Omar's proclaiming himself Commander of the Faithful was less about establishing a leadership position in the global umma, as Islamic State leader Abu Bakr al-Baghdadi would do in June 2014, than about legitimizing his reign in the manner of the Afghan kings, as did Dost Mohamad Khan (1826–39, 1843–63) and Abdul Rahman Khan (1880–1901), who also held that title.

employees from the former Communist regime, it recruited its judges exclusively from among the ulama. As one former senior Taliban leader recounted:

> All the judges that were appointed had to have graduated from Islamic institutions, and needed to be verified in the Hanafi shari'a school of law and its principles. They also were required to be able to distinguish between weak and strong points of Islamic jurisprudence. All judges were to set an example themselves in spirit and appearance, and should not have been accused of any crimes, and not be addicted to drugs. These were the key criteria every judge needed to pass, but even the Taliban with their highest aspirations contained individuals whose standards fell short of what they should have been.[49]

Judges were under the sole jurisdiction of the Supreme Court, whose members Mullah Omar appointed, making them independent of the rest of the administration. They received the highest salaries, 5.4 million afghanis per month, or $1,150 in the values of the year 2000, which was almost twenty times what a senior civil servant was paid.[50] In addition, the Taliban reactivated the prewar jurisdictional organization consisting of district courts, provincial courts, the Supreme Court, and a Court of Cassation.[51] Although Taliban officials repeatedly emphasized in the media that the regime needed no fundamental law other than Islam and the Quran, Mullah Omar's 1998 decree ordered the Supreme Court to revise the 1964 and 1992 Constitutions.[52] When the Taliban regime collapsed in 2001, the draft constitution had still not been ratified, but in the meantime decrees had been issued ordering the Ministry of Justice to draft laws, submit them for approval to the Council of Ministers, and then implement them.

Law under the Taliban was part of a project to moralize society. The movement blamed the corruption of morals and the breakdown of the social order for war and factionalism. Controlling conduct and punishing deviance were therefore the means of bringing about a lasting peace. From this vision grew the transformation in 1996 of the Committee for the Promotion of Virtue and the Prevention of Vice. Already organized as a ministry under the Islamic State

[49] Cited by Alex Strick van Linschoten, *Mullah Wars: The Afghan Taliban between Village and State, 1979–2001*, Ph.D., King's College London, London, 2016, p. 194.

[50] Interview with Mullah Mohammed Osman Tariq, official in the Ministry of Foreign Affairs during the Islamic Emirate of Afghanistan, September 2012.

[51] Decree 105 of 10 September 1999.

[52] Alex Strick van Linschoten, *Mullah Wars: The Afghan Taliban between Village and State, 1979–2001*, Ph.D., King's College London, London, 2016, pp. 202–3.

of Afghanistan (1992–6), it had now its own police, the *mohtasebor amr bil-maruf*. As its former minister, *Mawlawi* Qalamuddin, put it:

> I was responsible for enforcing the Constitution, that is, sharia law. Applying it to everyday life is the purpose of this ministry, which seeks to spread the good word and prevent people from misbehaving. This cuts across multiple areas. We were a separate organization from the Department of Justice because justice cannot stop people from small deviations. It requires a quick reaction that is directly anchored in the distinction between good and evil.[53]

This ministry, which was independent of the judicial system, unceasingly regulated diverse aspects of daily life: appearance (clothing, beards) and adherence to religious rules. Prohibited as violating Islam were: equipment for listening to music; watching movies; playing games (chess, billiards, kites); as well as practising usury, consuming drugs and alcohol—and lobsters. Also forbidden were images of human beings, sales of birds for entertainment, and celebrations of the Persian New Year (*nawruz*).[54] Music furnishes a particularly telling example of what motivated the Taliban's coercion. As musicologist John Baily has shown, the ban did not apply to music in general, but to playing instruments (with the exception of some percussion instruments not regarded as making music). More than a rejection of music, the Taliban's prohibition was another means of prosecuting the war through culture: they made it a competition between different types of music, with the sung recitations of poetry (*tarana*) being widely encouraged by the Islamic Emirate. The Taliban thus continued the political instrumentalization of music started by the Communist regime in the 1980s, which employed artists and musicians to denounce first the archaism of Islamist insurgents, and then the mujahideen's wholesale ban on the use of instruments because of jihad.

Moral control targeted the public space, as *Mawlawi* Qalamuddin explained to Egyptian journalist Fahmi Huwaidi in the late 1990s:

[53] Interview with Mawlawi Qalamuddin, July 2011. It is interesting to note the consistency of what Qalamuddin said to me during my interview compared to what he had told Ahmed Rashid fifteen years earlier. Ahmed Rashid, *Taliban: Militant Islam, Oil and Fundamentalism in Central Asia*, New Haven, Yale University Press, 2000, p. 106.

[54] John Baily, 'Music and Censorship in Afghanistan, 1973–2003' in Laudan Nooshin (ed.), *Music and the Play of Power in the Middle East, North Africa and Central Asia*, London, Ashgate, 2009, pp. 143–63. For a collection of Taliban poems, see Alex Strick van Linschoten and Felix Kuehn, *Poetry of the Taliban*, New York, Columbia University Press, 2012.

> We do not spy on people. That is a matter forbidden by the divine law. Likewise, we do not enter anyone's house. Everyone is free in his home. God will punish him for any vice he commits there. What concerns us is open vice in the streets or public places. We see it as our responsibility to combat these vices because they harm the Islamic society we are seeking. In addition, our silence about them would be tantamount to encouraging the spread of vice.[55]

Singled out as targets of this moral order were the major cities, the erstwhile strongholds of the Communist regime. Kabul and Kandahar had been the scene of the infighting between mujahideen and some of the worst excesses of the war. This reading mobilized the classic register of the city as a place of depravity, as this statement by a Taliban spokesman made crystal clear:

> Our culture has been greatly changed over the past 40 or 50 years, particularly in Kabul. In the villages the culture has not changed much. [...] The Taliban are trying to purify our culture. We are trying to re-establish a purist Islamic culture and tradition.[56]

In contrast, the countryside was less in the regime's crosshairs for these measures, because much of the social life there took place in private spaces into which Taliban militants, themselves products of a rural upbringing, did not intrude.

The Islamic Emirate also pursued a state policy of marginalizing customary norms, for example those dealing with women's right to property and marital relations. In 1998, a series of Mullah Omar decrees recognized that under Islamic law half an inheritance share belonged to the deceased's wife and to unmarried or widowed descendants, which customary norms denied them. It also put an end to levirate marriage and forbade the practice of swapping women to settle vendettas.[57] While in some provinces, such as Kunar, these decrees appear to have been largely ignored or locally circumvented, other provinces saw them enforced effectively. For example, in the Alishang Valley of Laghman province, an unmarried woman fought her brothers for the half

[55] Cited by Juan Cole, 'The Taliban, Women, and the Hegelian Private Sphere' in Robert D. Crews and Amin Tarzi (eds), *The Taliban and the Crisis of Afghanistan*, Cambridge, Harvard University Press, 2009, p. 134.

[56] David B. Edwards, 'Learning from the Swat Pathans: Political Leadership in Afghanistan, 1978–97', *American Ethnologist*, 1998, vol. 25, n° 4, p. 725.

[57] Levirate is a practice whereby the brother of a deceased person has a duty to marry the widow if the widow does not have a son who can take care of her financially. Pierre Centlivres, 'Tribus, ethnies et nations en Afghanistan' in Hosham Dawod (ed.), *Tribus et pouvoirs en terre d'Islam*, Paris, Armand Colin, 2004, pp. 115–43.

share of inheritance now recognized under Islamic law. In the early 1990s, she appealed to the local emir of Hizb-i Islami, Mohamad Alim Qarar, who rejected her request. In the late 1990s, she won her case in an Islamic Emirate court.[58] However, the Taliban administration, its resources still limited, at that time still prioritized the ongoing war in the North. The regime therefore delegated administration in the back country to religious figures better established locally, for example Jalaluddin Haqqani in Loya Paktya and Mohamad Akbari, a Shiite alim, in Hazarajat.

[58] E-10, interview with complainant's nephew, April 2011. A female interlocutor of Torunn Wimpelmann related a similar case, in Torunn Wimpelmann, *The Pitfalls of Protection: Gender, Violence, and Power in Afghanistan*, Berkeley, University of California Press, 2017, p. 40.

2

The social upheavals of a war-torn society

Introduction

Far from the myth of local communities running themselves,[1] the Afghan civil war stirred up private conflicts that laid bare the place of the state in settling disputes and regulating social relations. When the United States intervened militarily in 2001, the twenty-three-year civil war had created deep legal uncertainty. Afghan villages had to cope with the transition from the judicial system of Daoud Khan's Afghan Republic to that of the Communist regime in 1978. They might have been taken over by a mujahideen commander, then wound up again in the hands of the government, only to be lorded over by a different commander a few years later. Then, during the 1990s, they would have eventually ended up under Taliban control until 2001, when the Western intervention established a new regime, only to have the Taliban insurgents move in. Cities, on the other hand, were relatively untouched by the fighting until the fall of Najibullah's regime in 1992, but then the neighbourhoods also passed from hand to hand, with city dwellers particular targets of Taliban-imposed measures.

The succession of different authorities shook social structures deeply. It put in play social hierarchies, property, and gender relations, especially as the belligerents exploited them. In the 1980s, Marxist parties, like the Islamist parties, espoused a revolutionary agenda to rebuild society on a new footing. The programme of the People's Democratic Party of Afghanistan (PDPA) called for the recognition of minorities, land redistribution, and gender equality. These reforms, only partially implemented by the time the state's authority over a large swath of territory evaporated, stirred up private disputes involving multiple and contradictory demands for social, economic, and political rights. Interpersonal disputes centring on property and gender relationships proliferated. They took on an ethnic-confessional colouration

[1] Nazif Shahrani advances the most explicit version of this vision which permeates many of the writings on Afghanistan. Nazif M. Shahrani, 'War, Factionalism, and the State in Afghanistan', *American Anthropologist*, 2002, vol. 104, n° 3, pp. 715–22.

The Taliban Courts in Afghanistan. Adam Baczko, Oxford University Press.
DOI: 10.1093/oso/9780198896777.003.0003

as the parties to these disputes mobilized their respective affiliations in the conflict. Insurgency commanders also stoked these conflicts, using them to impose their authority locally, to grab resources, and to enforce their vision of social relations.

The denaturalization of identity hierarchies

The war caused a denaturalization of the ethnic, tribal, and denominational hierarchies that determined who accessed what resources, especially those of the state.[2] Armed actors, insurgent commanders in particular, instrumentalized this transformation in the value of religious and ethnic identities, fuelling an ethnicization of private conflicts in the process.

Until the 1970s, the monarchy of Zaher Shah (1933–78) followed by the republic of Daoud Khan (1973–8) fostered an identity regime favouring the Pashtuns at the expense of minorities.[3] The state apparatus, born of the Pashtun conquests of the eighteenth and nineteenth centuries, pursued an ambiguous policy, obscuring any reference to ethnicity in official texts.[4] Thus, in continuity with the 1964 Constitution, the 1977 Constitution did not recognize any ethnicities, affirming only the unity and indivisibility of state and nation. Identity cards did categorize the population, but according to predominantly heterogeneous linguistic macrocategories: Pashtun, Tajik (Persian-speaking), and Turkmen (Turkish-speaking). Similarly, the lack of a reliable census left the impression that the Pashtuns, a politically dominant group, were also the majority. In reality, on the eve of the coup, the Pashtuns probably only represented some 40 per cent of the population. Their preeminent position in the ethnic hierarchy is reflected in the double meaning of 'Afghan': both demonym and ethnonym, it designates not only the Afghan nationality but also being

[2] To account for differentiated access to resources related to identity hierarchies and the mobilization processes that play out around them, I look only marginally at the (self-)identification of individuals in a category or a relational network. When I refer to an ethnic or religious category, I am interested in categorization, that is, the more or less objectified assignment to a category by others. Rogers Brubaker and Frederick Cooper, 'Beyond "Identity"', *Theory and Society*, 2000, vol. 29, n° 1, pp. 1–47.

[3] By 'identity regime', I mean all practices and discourses that prioritize, define, and organize relations between ethnic and religious groups. In this sense, identity, ethnic or religious, takes on the properties of a collective capital. In effect, identities are not just principles of territorial or social affiliation, categories of ethnographic description or popular perception; they are also affiliations that signal a rank in accessing different resources in the context of competition or unequal collaboration between groups. Gilles Dorronsoro and Olivier Grojean (eds), *Identity, Conflict and Politics in Turkey, Iran and Pakistan*, New York, Oxford University Press, 2018.

[4] Pierre Centlivres, 'Exil, relations interethniques et identité dans la crise afghane', *Revue du monde musulman et de la Méditerranée*, 1991, vol. 59, n° 1, pp. 70–82.

a Pashtun, a member of the dominant social group. As ethnologist Pierre Centlivres points out, '[t]his ambiguity tends to suggest that among the citizens, some, namely the Pashtuns, are more Afghan than others, or even are the Afghans par excellence.'[5]

The identity regime surfaced in administrative practices, particularly in land redistributions, law, education, and territorial redistricting. The Pashtuns were the principal beneficiaries of the land redistribution: they received the newly irrigated plots in the northern provinces, to the detriment of Tajiks and Uzbeks, and, in the middle of the country, took over the richest pastures at the expense of the Hazaras. Moreover, the law was based on Hanafite (Sunni) jurisprudence, which did not recognize communal particularisms, including the sizeable Shia minority.[6] Judges enforced the ethnic hierarchy, for example by compensating complainants differently according to their ethnicity.[7] Even though Persian was the language of administration, the state pursued an active policy of teaching Pashto to minorities.[8] Finally, the carving up of the provinces systematically disadvantaged the Hazaras, Uzbeks, and Turkmens, who were left divided and locally outnumbered.[9]

The impossible definition of ethnicities

Before the war, the ambiguity of state policy was fuelled by the fact that there were no clear-cut linguistic, religious, or geographical criteria for classifying Afghan social groups, commonly grouped by ethnologists into Pashtuns, Hazaras, Tajiks, Uzbeks, and Turkmens, not to mention the smaller groups, like the Aymaqs, Baloch, Qizilbashes, and Nuristanis. In a classic text, anthropologists Pierre Centlivres and Micheline Centlivres-Demont highlighted the problems posed by maps purporting to show the ethnic distribution of the Afghan population.[10] Indeed, the definition of ethnic groups is relational and

[5] Ibid., p. 71.

[6] Mohammad Hashim Kamali, *Law in Afghanistan: A Study of the Constitutions, Matrimonial Law and the Judiciary*, Leiden, Brill, 1985.

[7] For a case, see Sayed Askar Mousavi, *The Hazaras of Afghanistan: An Historical, Cultural, Economic and Political Study*, Basingstoke, Palgrave Macmillan, 1998, p. 160.

[8] Hafizullah Emadi, 'The Hazaras and their Role in the Process of Political Transformation in Afghanistan', *Central Asian Survey*, 1997, vol. 16, nº 3, pp. 363–87.

[9] Ibid., p. 370.

[10] Pierre Centlivres and Micheline Centlivres-Demont, *Et si on parlait de l'Afghanistan? Terrains et textes, 1964–1980*, Paris, Les Éditions de la MSH, 1988, pp. 53–63.

its usage often conceals the complexity of collective identifications.[11] Anyone who settles in a large city and speaks Persian in everyday life is then generally referred to as Tajik, regardless of ancestry and geographical origin.[12] Similarly, the various populations in the middle of the country are often considered Hazaras, provided they are Shia, but Sunni Hazaras may also be described as Farsiwan under certain circumstances. This amalgamating of ethnicity and denomination leads to an interchangeable use of the terms Hazara and Shia. In reality, the territorial distribution of social groups in Afghanistan is the result of a political history of displacement and upheavals, which produced mixed villages and regions, with populations of multiple and complex identifications.[13] In this context, ethnicity is only one of the many situational affiliations that Afghans mobilize, enshrining 'the overlap and pluralism of collective identities'.[14] As Pierre Centlivres shows:

> [T]he indigenous term for ethnic group is *qawm*, but the word has a much wider ambit: it actually refers to the whole group in relation to what is external to it; in its narrowest sense, it is used for the extended patrilineal family but can designate people of the same street, the same trade, the neighborhood where one lives, *qawm-e guzar*; the natural region, *qawm-e Turkestan*, the ethnic group, *qawm-e Uzbek*, *qawm-e Arab*, and finally sometimes nationality.[15]

Thus, individual and collective identifications obey relational and contextual rules: you call yourself a Pashtun (rather than a member of a tribe or as being from a place) before a Turkish-speaking interlocutor, but identify as a Shia in a Sunni environment.

Decades of war have led to a questioning of this identity regime and an affirmation of minorities. Whereas in 1978, the new Communist regime

[11] Gilles Dorronsoro, 'Politique et ethnicité en Afghanistan: le cas tadjik', *Cahiers d'Études sur la Méditerranée Orientale et le monde Turco-Iranien*, 1994, n° 18, pp. 131–47; Alessandro Monsutti, *War and Migration: Social Networks and Economic Strategies of the Hazaras of Afghanistan*, London, Routledge, 2005, pp. 59–62.

[12] Pierre Centlivres and Micheline Centlivres-Demont, *Et si on parlait de l'Afghanistan? Terrains et textes, 1964–1980*, Paris, Les Éditions de la MSH, 1988, p. 48.

[13] Louis Dupree, 'The Changing Character of South-Central Afghanistan Villages', *Human Organization*, 1955, vol. 14, n° 4, pp. 26–9; Robert L. Canfield, 'The Ecology of Rural Ethnic Groups and the Spatial Dimensions of Power', *American Anthropologist*, 1973, vol. 75, n° 5, pp. 1511–28.

[14] Pierre Centlivres and Micheline Centlivres-Demont, *Et si on parlait de l'Afghanistan? Terrains et textes, 1964–1980*, Paris, Les Éditions de la MSH, 1988, p. 38.

[15] Pierre Centlivres, *Un bazar d'Asie centrale: Forme et organisation du bazar de Tashqurghan (Afghanistan)*, Wiesbaden, Dr. Ludwig Reichert Verlag, 1972, pp. 158–9.

categorized the population by social classes, based on exclusively economic criteria, Soviet advisers, who developed state policy from 1979 onwards, envisioned it as a multinational society. Applying the evolutionist paradigm in vogue among Soviet anthropologists—one that progresses from 'tribe' to 'nationality' and then to 'nation'—these advisers classified Afghans into 'tribes' and 'nationalities' (*qawm* and *millat*, translated from the Russian *plemja* and *narodnost*).[16]

This vision informed ethnicized public policies. For most of the 1980s, Sultan Ali Kishtmand, a Hazara, served as Prime Minister—a first. In 1981, a Turkmen cultural committee was established 'to strengthen and improve the knowledge of Turkmen and the culture of Turkmen nations'.[17] In 1984, a Hazara Nationality Council (Shura-i Melli) was established under the aegis of the Ministry of Tribal Affairs and recognized—in another first for the Afghan state—the existence of a Hazara community. A year later, the establishment of the Grand Jirga for the border tribes, with one-third Pakistani Pashtuns, reactivated the rhetoric of the Pashtun nation and demands for sovereignty over Pakistan's border regions.[18] In 1987, a predominantly Uzbek province, Sar-i Pul, was established.[19]

In prosecuting the war, the KGB and its Afghan counterpart, KHAD (Khadamat-i Atalat-i Dawlati), responsible for counterinsurgency, also exploited identity, albeit at a more local level, as they sought to break up the insurgency by rallying commanders and sowing discord among them. Then, with Soviet troops preparing to withdraw in the late 1980s, the KGB and KHAD prioritized the formation of militias by recruiting minorities, including Ismailis and Uzbeks in the North and Pashais and Tajiks in the East.[20] This attempt to splinter the insurgency along ethnic and tribal lines failed almost from the start. The religious and nationalist framing of jihad tamped down the communal tensions that the regime and its Soviet sponsor tried to stoke. However, over the long term, this identity strategy set the stage for more strife among the

16 Olivier Roy, 'Afghanistan: Modèles anthropologiques et pacification', *Cahiers du monde russe et soviétique*, 1990, vol. 31, n° 2, pp. 405–11.

17 Alexandre Bennigsen, *The Soviet Union and Muslim Guerrilla Wars 1920–1981: Lessons for Afghanistan*, Santa Monica, Rand, 1981, p. 7.

18 Kristian Berg Harpviken, *Political Mobilization among the Hazara of Afghanistan: 1978–1992*, Oslo, Department of Sociology, University of Oslo, 1996, pp. 81–2.

19 Olivier Roy, 'Ethnic Identity and Political Expression in Northern Afghanistan' in Jo-Ann Gross (ed.), *Muslims in Central Asia: Expressions of Identity and Change*, Durham, Duke University Press, 1992, pp. 73–87.

20 Gilles Dorronsoro and Chantal Lobato, 'The Militia in Afghanistan', *Central Asian Survey*, 1989, vol. 8, n° 4, pp. 95–108.

mujahideen once the Soviets had departed and the war stopped being a jihad against a foreign occupier.

On the insurgency side, if the parties did not mobilize on the basis of ethnic rhetoric, ethnic membership was nevertheless one of the factors driving political affiliation. Many commanders joined parties whose leaders they were closest to from a communal—but also ideological, geographic, social, and religious—standpoint. Party leadership was often based on ethnic and regional origin: Jamiat-i Islami's was three-quarters Tajiks, in Hizb-i Islami Hikmatyar's two-thirds were non-Durrani Pashtuns, and Hizb-i Islami Khalis' was majority eastern Pashtuns. Still, Gulbuddin recruited for the same Hizb-i Islami without regard to any regional and ethnic base: Tajiks in Badakhshan, Sunni Hazaras and Uzbeks in Kunduz. Similarly, the Harakat-i Enqelab had a presence throughout the territory. Many commanders joined a party to differentiate themselves from their local rivals: the affiliation of Mullah Naqibullah and *rais* Abdul Wahid, two southern Pashtuns, with the Jamiat-i Islami, which consisted mostly of Tajiks, is thus rooted in their local rivals adhering to other parties.[21]

The uprising also challenged the popular anthropology underpinning the pre-war ethnic hierarchy.[22] In particular, it put to rest the historical narrative of the Pashtuns as uniquely capable of bearing arms and thus of ruling the country.[23] In the North and West, Tajik and Farsiwan commanders cast doubt on the notion of Pashtun military superiority. Even more patently, among the most stigmatized minority, the Hazaras, the emergence of armed movements composed of Shiite Hazaras challenged the ethnic and denominational hierarchy.[24] Starting in 1981, the regime withdrew from the mountainous Hazarajat regions in Afghanistan's middle. For the first time since the end of the nineteenth century, Shiite Hazara organizations now came to dominate the region, resulting in fierce competition along both ideological and social lines (between notables, sheikhs, intellectuals, and *sadat* [who claim descent from the

[21] Gilles Dorronsoro, *Revolution Unending: Afghanistan, 1979 to the Present*, New York, Columbia University Press, 2005, p. 168ff.

[22] On popular anthropology on the eve of the war, see Pierre Centlivres, 'Identité et image de l'autre dans l'anthropologie populaire en afghanistan', *Revue européenne des sciences sociales*, 1980, vol. 18, n° 53, pp. 29–41.

[23] Mike Barry, 'Afghanistan: Les séminaristes de la guerre', *Politique internationale*, 1997, n° 74, pp. 60–96.

[24] Sayed Askar Mousavi, *The Hazaras of Afghanistan: An Historical, Cultural, Economic and Political Study*, Basingstoke, Palgrave Macmillan, 1998; Robert L. Canfield, 'New Trends among the Hazaras: From "The Amity of Wolves" to "The Practice of Brotherhood"', *Iranian Studies*, 2004, vol. 37, n° 2, pp. 241–62.

Prophet]).[25] Amid this power struggle, a communal political field formed that was detached from the other rivalries of the insurgency. In areas they controlled, Hazara armed groups toppled the existing ethnic hierarchy and applied Jafarite jurisprudence. As Robert Canfield explains:

> The Shi'a Hazaras regained dominance of the region in spring 1979 when Sayyid Bihishti refused to allow the Pushtun pastoralists to enter their summer pasture lands. Also, the new predominance of Hazaras and possibly the intense internecine warfare seems to have driven the Tajiks out of the region, or at least forced them into a lower profile. The Bamian Markaz (center), once dominated by Tajiks, has become the capital of the Hazara organizations.[26]

This intercommunal violence ratcheted up due to fear of reprisals should the former dominants return (Pashtun nomads, Tajiks of Bamiyan) and fanned autonomist demands.

In the late 1980s, the Soviet withdrawal led to an upsurge in confrontations between parties increasingly framed along ethnic lines. The exclusion of Shiite parties from the negotiations, held in Peshawar (Pakistan) with a view to forming an interim government, impelled them to unite in a new organization, the Hizb-i Wahdat.[27] Despite the Shiite rhetoric, it in effect became the party of the Hazara community and standard bearer of its demand for political representation. Moreover, to keep from being marginalized, the Hizb-i Islami of Gulbuddin's Hikmatyar, notwithstanding its heterogeneous composition, positioned itself as representing the Pashtuns. In the case of Abdul Rachid Dostum's Jumbesh-i Melli, which presented itself as a defender of the 'Turks', ethnic mobilization was largely a strategy of instrumentalization by former Communist cadres. The movement, which had emerged from a militia that turned against the regime in 1992, explicitly played the pan-Turkic card. It tried to recruit Uzbek and Turkmen commanders, renamed villages and streets, and introduced Turkic languages into curriculums. This ethnicization of the parties was reinforced by the break-up of the Communist Party with Najibullah's fall in 1992. Many Pashtuns from the Khalq branch of the Communist Party defected to Hizb-i Islami; Uzbeks and Tajiks, many in the Parcham branch,

[25] Jan-Heeren Grevemeyer, 'Ethnicity and National Liberation. The Afghan Hazara between Resistance and Civil War' in Jean-Pierre Digard (ed.), *Le fait ethnique en Iran et en Afghanistan*, Paris, Éditions du CNRS, 1988, pp. 211–18.

[26] Robert L. Canfield, 'New Trends among the Hazaras: From "The Amity of Wolves" to "The Practice of Brotherhood"', *Iranian Studies*, 2004, vol. 37, n° 2, p. 254.

[27] Sayed Askar Mousavi, *The Hazaras of Afghanistan: An Historical, Cultural, Economic and Political Study*, Basingstoke, Palgrave Macmillan, 1998, pp. 192–6.

joined Jumbesh-i Melli and Jamiat-i Islami, and Hazaras went over to Hizb-i Wahdat.[28]

This ethnic framing was imposed on the two remaining actors, the Jamiat-i Islami and the Taliban, despite their political programmes explicitly disavowing any community references. Both had to deal with the complexities of their movement's composition, the population living in their territory, the effects of the strategies of rival movements, and how they were categorized. On the one hand, the gradual loss of Jamiat-i Islami's hold on the South and West ended up confining the movement to its Tajik stronghold in the Northwest. Territorial divisions between the Jumbesh-i Melli and the Taliban thus aligned with ethnic cleavages. Yet, the top leaders of Jamiat-i Islami—Ismael Khan, Burhanuddin Rabbani, and Ahmad Shah Massoud—defined themselves as nationalist Islamists and systematically rejected federalism.

On the other hand, the Taliban, who claimed a religious ideology that broke with the factionalism of the war, ended up recruiting mostly Pashtuns.[29] Following the movement's capture of Kabul in 1996, local alliances with Northern Pashtun commanders (Badghis, Kunduz) fed this ethnicization of partisan division. The Taliban seemed to show a willingness to compromise by installing Mohamad Akbari, a Shiite leader of a breakaway branch of Hizb-i Wahdat, as head of the Hazarajat administration, but then the movement brutally reinstated the pre-war identity regime by massacring thousands of Hazaras in 1998 and 2000–01 and reimposing Sunni law on the Shia. The new regime taking power after 2001 supported by the United States accelerated the questioning of this hierarchy. Tajiks held many positions of power within it and Hazaras benefited greatly from the international presence, particularly the investment in education.[30] These changes contributed to reviving certain conflicts along ethnic lines, for example between Pashtun nomads and Hazara farmers in the middle of the country or between Tajiks and Pashtuns in Kunduz.[31]

[28] In 1967, two years after its formation, the Afghan Communist Party split into two main branches, the Khalq (the Masses) and the Parcham (the Banner). Throughout the 1980s, the Soviet Union exploited the rivalry between the two factions, fanning internal dissension. These multiplied in the early 1990s, with the fragmentation of the Najibullah regime leading to an increased ethnicization of institutions and political movements. See Louis Dupree, 'Afghanistan under the Khalq', *Problems of Communism*, 1979, vol. 28, n° 4, pp. 34–50.

[29] The movement appointed some Tajiks, Uzbeks, Turkmens, and even Sunni Hazaras to civilian and military command positions. Nevertheless, the movement's leadership and the strategic positions remained mostly in the hands of the South Pashtuns.

[30] Fariba Adelkhah, 'War and State (Re)Construction in Afghanistan: Conflicts of Tradition or Conflicts of Development?', *International Development Policy*, 2017, vol. 8.

[31] Pashtun nomads saw their identity homogenized in the war, and especially with the post-2001 Western intervention. As Richard Tapper shows, the generic name 'kuchi', until then an exonym in use among the elites in Kabul, was now claimed by the nomads themselves. Remarkably, during the 1960 or

The commanders used this reification of tribal, ethnic, and denominational classifications to impose themselves locally. In the 1990s, anthropologist Bernt Glatzer noted that 'organisers and leaders of conflicts use ethnic and tribal emotions and the feelings of honor and shame connected with them as a tool or weapon as efficientely as a Stinger or Kalashnikov'.[32] In constant rivalry with each other, commanders hijacked disputes over private, interpersonal matters to give them a political and community dimension. This confusion between private and public interests was fed by the patrimonial model of some commanders who personally intervened in private litigation. As both judges and parties in the conflict, their interventions in land or marital disputes often inflamed the situation, raising the level of violence and the number of people involved.

This ethnicization of disputes proved particularly effective as the armed conflict challenged established hierarchies, whether through land redistribution, the assignment of economic responsibilities to minorities, or unconventional marriages (such as those between a Hazara man and a Pashtun woman). On the other hand, as long as disputes were part of a community logic, the evolution of the political map translated very directly into expropriations.[33] The land disputes between Pashtun nomads and sedentary Hazaras illustrated this. Captured weapons allowed the Hazaras to seize land they had claimed since Emir Abdul Rahman (1880–1901) distributed it to Pashtun nomads who had supported him in the conquest of Hazarajat. In the 1980s, Hazara factions banned nomads from entering their territory and redistributed land to Hazara peasants. In the 1990s, first the Ittihad-i Islami then the Taliban exploited this conflict, enlisting the nomads to fight against Hizb-i Wahdat to recover the lands from which they were now excluded. After 2001, the conflict persisted,

1970s, no anthropologist had encountered it among his nomadic interlocutors. In the 2000s, the term 'Kuchi' found a place in the new Constitution (Article 14) and the name became a collective identifier in the context of conflicts between nomads and farmers, allowing the nomads to gain media attention and attract funding from Western development aid agencies. Richard Tapper, 'Who Are the Kuchi? Nomad Self-Identities in Afghanistan', *The Journal of the Royal Anthropological Institute*, 2008, vol. 14, nº 1, pp. 97–116.

32 Bernt Glatzer, 'Is Afghanistan on the Brink of Ethnic and Tribal Disintegration?' in William Maley (ed.), *Fundamentalism Reborn? Afghanistan and the Taliban*, New York, New York University Press, 1998, p. 190.

33 Although the logics differed, there was an overdetermination of local situations in Afghanistan, as in the former Yugoslavia. For an ethnographic description of these transformations in a Croatian village and Sarajevo, see respectively Mary Kay Gilliland Olsen, 'Bridge on the Sava. Ethnicity in Eastern Croatia, 1981–1991', *Anthropology of Eastern Europe Review*, 1993, vol. 11, nº 1 & 2, pp. 54–62; Ivana Macek, *Sarajevo Under Siege: Anthropology in Wartime*, Philadelphia, University of Pennsylvania Press, 2009.

and political actors, both on the regime side and the Taliban, added fuel to the fire by instrumentalizing it.[34]

Uncertainty over land rights

The multiplicity and rapid succession of legal authorities in the war aggravated land uncertainty rooted in insecure land tenure rights and the failure of pre-war attempts at setting up a land registry.

In the 1970s, the agricultural sector sustained 90 per cent of Afghanistan's 11 to 12 million sedentary people. However, only 12 per cent of the country's 650,000 km^2 area was arable, with only half actually under cultivation with either irrigated or rainfed crops.[35] Afghan farmers remained poor, with incomes that stagnated between 1935 and 1966 and actually dropped in the years which followed, notably during the drought of 1970–71 and the famine of 1972.[36] On the eve of the war, more than a third of farmers did not own the land they tilled and a fifth worked as sharecroppers.[37] The lives of these poor farmers depended on relationships of reciprocity and notability structures which organized social life in the countryside. Indeed, the sharecroppers receiving even a small share of the harvests (sometimes a fifth) made them part of the clientele, or even the extended family of the *khan* or *bay* who was 'simultaneously master, exploiter and protector'.[38] The socio-economic transformations of the 1950–70s, including the advent of commercial farming and the weakening of the notables, worsened the lot of this peasantry.[39]

Pre-war Afghanistan was an extreme case of the dynamics observable in postcolonial societies, in which the social and legal recognition of land was

[34] Fariba Adelkhah, 'War and State (Re)Construction in Afghanistan: Conflicts of Tradition or Conflicts of Development?', *International Development Policy*, 2017, vol. 8.

[35] Pierre Centlivres and Micheline Centlivres-Demont, *Et si on parlait de l'Afghanistan? Terrains et textes, 1964–1980*, Paris, Les Éditions de la MSH, 1988, p. 11.

[36] On agriculture in Afghanistan, see Gilbert Andienne, *L'Afghanistan ou les aléas de la coopération*, Paris, Presses universitaires de France, 1972; Pierre Centlivres, *Paysannerie et pouvoir en Afghanistan: De la fin de la monarchie à l'intervention soviétique*, Geneva, Institut universitaire de hautes études internationales, 1985.

[37] Liz Alden Wily, *Land Rights in Crisis: Restoring Tenure Security in Afghanistan*, Kabul, Afghanistan Research and Evaluation Unit, 2003, p. 18.

[38] Pierre Centlivres and Micheline Centlivres-Demont, 'Les réformes agraires en Afghanistan, de la fin de la monarchie à la chute des talibans', *Revue des mondes musulmans et de la Méditerranée*, 2013, n° 133, p. 49.

[39] Jon Anderson, 'There Are no Khans Anymore: Economic Development and Social Change in Tribal Afghanistan', *Middle East Journal*, 1978, vol. 32, n° 2, pp. 167–83.

particularly fluid and depended on the ability to have ownership recognized.[40] In Afghanistan, in contrast to most countries in Latin America, Africa, and Asia, large properties were rare—only about thirty owners could claim over 200 hectares[41]—so that tensions crystallized around the precariousness of land tenure. Liz Alden Wily, who conducted the most detailed study on land in Afghanistan in the early 2000s, explains:

> Land holding in Afghanistan is not a simple question of owning or not owning. The most striking aspect of rural Afghan tenure is the high degree of uncertainty in land ownership, primarily in the sharecropping sector and the closely intertwined element of land mortgaging. This involves a web of relationships in which it is difficult to distinguish creditors/debtors from owners/sharecroppers, or to know precisely who is the legal or accepted right-holder over the property.[42]

Land tenure uncertainty stemmed from the compounding of legal and social problems, resulting in insecure land ownership. First, the legal descriptions of parcels were often ambivalent or even conflicting, and accepted practice might depart from what the law stated. Several ownership regimes coexisted in Afghanistan: governmental; public (state-controlled, but nationally owned and inalienable); private (which in practice includes shared forms of use); as well as communal and religious *(awqaf*, mortmain property managed by pious foundations). However, the state administration classified some lands used by local communities under customary practice as public lands; other private lands owned by an individual were collectively exploited; some communal lands, such as pastures, had been appropriated by individuals and planted with crops. If enclosure and state ownership of communal lands were typical processes of state formation in modern times,[43] in Afghanistan resistances had resulted in entangling the extension of public and private property and forms of communal use or possession.

Secondly, land was governed by a multiplicity of often conflicting legal regimes—customary norms, civil law, religious law, and state law. Throughout

[40] Jesse Ribot and Nancy Lee Peluso, 'A Theory of Access', *Rural Sociology*, 2009, vol. 68, nº 2, pp. 153–81; Thomas Sikor and Christian Lund, 'Access and Property: A Question of Power and Authority', *Development and Change*, 2009, vol. 40, nº 1, pp. 1–22.

[41] Louis Dupree, *Afghanistan*, Princeton, Princeton University Press, 1973, p. 153.

[42] Liz Alden Wily, *Land Rights in Crisis: Restoring Tenure Security in Afghanistan*, Kabul, Afghanistan Research and Evaluation Unit, 2003, p. 2.

[43] Karl Polanyi, *The Great Transformation: The Political and Economic Origins of Our Time*, New York, Farrar & Rinehart, 1944; Edward P. Thompson, *Whigs and Hunters: The Origin of the Black Act*, New York, Pantheon Books, 1975.

the twentieth century, judges and rural elites played an important role in resolving conflicts, with their rulings effectively used to attest to ownership. They might also issue certificates for transferring ownership, particularly in the case of sales and inheritances, but these were expensive documents. As a result, the types of documents used to certify a parcel's ownership and its map contours varied widely. They could include an Amir's *firman*, a recognition of debt, a certificate of a land transaction signed by the parties and witnesses, documents detailing a right to use water, or a proof of a property tax payment. Still others had only documents of dubious legal value drawn up between the parties directly concerned. Many transactions and *jirga* decisions were strictly verbal.

Thirdly, ambiguity also lay in the confusion between usufruct and property. Thus, in the 1970s:

> the dividing line between legitimately occupied land and land appropriated through prolonged use was unclear, and the subject gave rise to numerous trials and challenges. Often, in the minds of the owners, there was a confusion between the lender's debt and the title to the property, between the mortgage and the right to the field given in antichresis, confusion that the powerful profited from.[44]

This was one of the most critical problems in the countryside in the 1970s, where borrowing was a common way of meeting major expenses (marriage, medical treatment, clothing purchases) or crisis situations (drought, poor harvests). Migration to the city or abroad led to similar situations: the leavers let those who stayed behind use their part of the family land, a practice that with time could make it their property either through a transaction or inheritance.

The insecurity of legal guarantees had two consequences: the centrality of social capital and the difficulty in registering land. Legal uncertainty was compounded by recognition based on inter-knowledge. Indeed, plots were often demarcated on documents by neighbouring ones or by landscape features (streams, trees, rocks), a system that relied on collective memory. Many landowners did not have, or no longer had, documents and, in that case, a buyer or judge might rely on neighbours and relatives to certify the possession and boundaries of a plot. However, the precariousness of the guarantees on the demarcation of plots and the delimitation of individual and collective

[44] Pierre Centlivres and Micheline Centlivres-Demont, 'Les réformes agraires en Afghanistan, de la fin de la monarchie à la chute des talibans', *Revue des mondes musulmans et de la Méditerranée*, 2013, n° 133, p. 52.

access (irrigation, pastures, forest) in parallel implied having to preserve one's rights against those same neighbours or relatives, who might be tempted to usurp them. Individual and collective deterrence, through the mobilization of one's social capital, was the *prerequisite* for possession.[45] As the anthropologist Whitney Azoy explained in the 1970s:

> Everyone in a local community has some sense of whose land is whose. The absence, however, of precise survey and standardized documentation leads to disputes that are pursued through self-help. For all landowners, large and small alike, there is a constant need for vigilance against encroachment. Only such watchfulness and a forceful appearance of potential response can prevent predation. [. . .] Boundary lines are vague, irrigation barrages are flimsy, sheep are easily led away, and women are considered wild cards because of their innate sexuality. Virtually everyone, even more to the point, is a potential predator. Obviously some sort of deterrence is necessary.[46]

This socialization of the property guarantee implied tensions between neighbours. Land became a major stake and mounting a defence was essential, both to protect one's good, to assure one's position with one's relatives, and to deter any and all aggression. Land-related disputes, even benign ones, could quickly escalate into a cycle of mutual retaliation involving the relatives and allies of each party.[47]

While the lack of a land registry played a decisive role in land disputes, the uncertainty made surveying especially conflict-prone. Beginning in 1965, with funding and expertise from the US Agency for International Development, the monarchy began a programme of registering and issuing certified titles to end the confusion in the forms of proving ownership. The difficulties and costs involved caused the project's initial goals to be abandoned in 1971, only to be replaced by simple name registration without topographical references and without issuing titles. Even under these conditions, only 20 per cent of arable land had been registered when the Communist Party took power in 1978. In

[45] The Afghan situation is similar to the four African societies analysed by Sara Berry. As negotiation underpins possession, farmers therefore invest their resources in the means of negotiations, in particular the maintenance of a clientele, more than in the means of production. Sara Berry, *No Condition is Permanent: the Social Dynamics of Agrarian Change in Sub-Saharan Africa*, Madison, University of Wisconsin Press, 1993, p. 15.

[46] G. Whitney Azoy, *Buzkashi, Game and Power in Afghanistan*, Philadelphia, University of Pennsylvania Press, 1982, pp. 31–2.

[47] Louis Dupree, 'Tribal Warfare in Afghanistan and Pakistan: a Reflexion of the Segmentary Lineage System' in Akbar S. Ahmed (ed.), *Islam in Tribal Societies: From the Atlas to the Indus*, London, Routledge, 1984, pp. 266–86.

addition, the programme placed the millions of hectares of land for which no owner had been identified under the formal control of the state.[48] Thereafter, the state was no longer merely the guarantor of property, it also owned most of the land. In 1975, based on the early survey data, Daoud Khan implemented a first land reform to limit the size of land holdings but without significant effects. For one thing, large owners circumvented the law by registering plots above the limit in the name of their relatives; for another, the reforms were greatly diminished by entangled rights and imprecise boundary lines. The Daoud Khan regime was stymied by a classic difficulty in land rights registration policies: formalizing property involved making rights and practices explicit and was therefore a highly contentious process.[49]

Since 1978, the uncertainty surrounding land had been aggravated by land reforms, land grabs by commanders, the compounding of acts and decisions by successive authorities, and the undermining of social guarantees of ownership.[50] First, the Communist regime launched a series of contradictory reforms. Decrees 6 and 8 of 1978 attacked land seizures by creditors and again sought to redistribute land from the notables to farmers by limiting the size of land holdings. While these initiatives were meant to benefit the landless and heavily indebted farmers, they failed to acknowledge the social relations in which agricultural work was grounded. The regime did not distribute seeds, fertilizers, and tools normally provided by local notables, preventing the new owners from putting in crops on their parcels. Moreover, land reform was sometimes hijacked by local supporters of the regime who implemented it in a way that let them appropriate the confiscated land.[51] Because of the uprising, the reform was applied only to part of the territory and then amended following the Soviet intervention. Afghanistan's new leader, Babrak Karmal (1979–86), guaranteed private ownership and then banned the confiscation of *awqaf* and land owned by the great notables and economic entrepreneurs. Under Najibullah (1986–92), the reform was effectively scuttled by a multitude of exceptions granted to the regime's supporters.

[48] Liz Alden Wily, *Land Rights in Crisis: Restoring Tenure Security in Afghanistan*, Kabul, Afghanistan Research and Evaluation Unit, 2003, pp. 41–2.

[49] Jean-Philippe Colin, Pierre-Yves Le Meur, and Éric Léonard, 'Identifier les droits et dicter le droit: La politique des programmes de formalisation des droits fonciers' in Jean-Philippe Colin, Pierre-Yves Le Meur, and Éric Léonard (eds), *Les politiques d'enregistrement des droits fonciers: Du cadre légal aux pratiques locales*, Paris, Karthala, 2010, pp. 12–13.

[50] On this, see Fariba Adelkhah (ed.), 'Guerre et terre en Afghanistan', *Revue des mondes musulmans et de la Méditerranée*, 2013, n° 133, pp. 19–41.

[51] Mike Martin, *An Intimate War: An Oral History of the Helmand Conflict, 1978–2012*, Oxford, Oxford University Press, 2014, p. 44.

Subsequently, as the mujahideen seized territory they rescinded the reforms. Micheline Centlivres-Demont and Pierre Centlivres recount what a commander told them: 'At first, he tells us, the government shared the domains of the *bays* (*khans*, great landowners), but when the mujahideen took power, they cancelled the distributions, burned the certificates and returned the land confiscated from the *bay*; it is God who wants there to be rich and poor!'[52] In reality, rather than an impossible step backwards, these measures constituted a new redistribution, often to the benefit of commanders leveraging their position of power. The entire period saw a brutal rush to seize the country's land and resources. Thus, Massoud and his commanders instrumentalized the reinstatement of Islamic justice for justifying the abolition of state monopolies and the private takeover of lapis lazuli and emerald mines in Badakhshan. Similarly, in the early 1990s, Karim Khalili's brother, then one of the leaders of Hizb-i Wahdat, seized an entire district west of Kabul. Sayyaf, for his part, grabbed the Paghman archaeological site west of Kabul so that he could sell its antiquities in Pakistan.[53] In Kunar and Nouristan, commanders of the Salafist movements and Hizb-i Islami appropriated forests that they systematically logged to export noble wood varieties to Pakistan.

The succession of competing authorities moreover led to the enactment of a series of contradictory statutes of dubious legal value. The insurgents of the 1980s mobilized Islamic law pragmatically but at the cost of long-term uncertainty over land tenure. For example, judges used the sharia principle of vivification of fallow lands (*ihya*) to allow new owners to recultivate plots belonging to the state or abandoned by refugees,[54] but leaving the ownership by the new farmers in question for the future. Similarly, in accord with Islamic law, they reaffirmed collective rights to pasture or water taken away during the land surveys of the 1970s. However, judges from both the Taliban and the regime still relied on documentation from that era. Moreover, verdicts in land disputes and even normal transactions, in the context of a succession of legal authorities and land reforms, generated increased property claims and created difficulty in determining ownership. Each overthrow of an authority allowed those penalized by the previous legal regime to reopen their cases. As a resident of Asadabad explained:

[52] Pierre Centlivres and Micheline Centlivres-Demont, 'Les réformes agraires en Afghanistan, de la fin de la monarchie à la chute des talibans', *Revue des mondes musulmans et de la Méditerranée*, 2013, n° 133, pp. 45–61.

[53] Fariba Adelkhah, 'Afghanistan: La guerre des *qumandan* pour le contrôle des terres', *Moyen-Orient*, 2012, vol. 14, p. 76.

[54] Olivier Roy, *Islam and Resistance in Afghanistan*, Cambridge, Cambridge University Press, 1990, p. 156.

> Land ownership claims are multiplying. It is corruption that allows that. The government was looking for land and, at the same time, people were paying public servants to acquire new land. For example, this plot belonged to people who left after Kerala [a massacre committed by the Communist regime in 1980]. The Communist government made it an airport for helicopters. Then other people came back and occupied the place. And today the government is trying to get it back. And so it goes. Each time the governor changes, disputes that have been resolved are reopened, then resolved again, then reopened, and then resolved again. This is one of the weaknesses of this government.[55]

Finally, the war undermined the system of inter-knowledge that previously guaranteed land ownership and use. Alain de Bures, who worked on rural development in the areas of the uprising in the 1980s, explained that, at first, few disputes broke out: 'At that time, there were few conflicts over land. Most of the people were still in Pakistan and the intensity of the fighting made these issues secondary to jihad and survival.'[56] But, with the Soviet withdrawal and the gradual return of refugees in the 1990s, the blurring of ownership rights and boundary lines provided fertile ground for dispute: 'The ongoing fighting and the need to survive led many Afghans to pull old deeds of ownership and rights to share in the harvest from their cupboards, setting off conflicts.'[57] Moreover, through exiles and war-related deaths, memories were lost of who owned what, and the hostilities greatly altered the landscape, which had formerly helped orient property lines. 'The problem was that the one who signed, the mirab, demarcated the plots in relation to the domains of such, such and such, but as everyone had fled, such, such and such were untraceable, it was impossible to reproduce the boundaries.'[58] In some areas, hundreds of thousands of Afghans, who had mainly lived in refugee camps, inherited plots whose property lines they had trouble defining. In the meantime, the disputed properties had sometimes been sold, developed, shared out for inheritance, or mortgaged, with an enormous potential number of contending parties. For example, a farmer from Logar province, who fled with his family to Pakistan in 1990 and returned to Afghanistan in 2001 (he was fourteen at the time), discovered that his uncles who had looked after his family's plot of land had sold it:

[55] E-18, elected official in Kunar province, July 2011.

[56] Interview with Alain de Bures, humanitarian zootechnician working in Afghanistan since the 1980s, April 2011.

[57] Ibid.

[58] Ibid.

> When we went to Pakistan, I left the land to my uncle. We stayed there for 10 years, and my father died there in a car accident. I was alone with four sisters and had all the responsibility to work for them and find food for them. I did not return to the land, I was sure that my two uncles were there and they would take care of the land. But when we came back in the start of Karzai's government, my uncles had sold my inheritance.[59]

Reciprocity circuits and customary conflict resolution bodies, dependent on the state and rural elites, were also undermined by war and the rise of the commanders. These transformations minimized the possibility of resolving conflicts by conciliation, particularly those revolving around pastures, water, or forests, which involved entire communities.

In 2000, the Taliban regime tackled this situation with Decree 57, which put in place a complex system of compensation and repayments in consideration of subsequent parcel sales, transmission by inheritance, land development, including building construction, and more generally the many land claims of returning refugees. It specified the validity of documents according to their type, origin, and whether or not there were competing ownership claims on the land in question.[60] However, Hamid Karzai upon taking power invalidated the Taliban's land laws with a new decree annulling all rights and decrees that contravened the 1964 Constitution, further fuelling legal uncertainty. In this context, which favoured the questioning of the status quo, and saw the return of refugees, conflicts over land rose to become the number one source of litigation in the early months of the Western intervention. As early as 2002, these cases overwhelmed the new courts still struggling to rebuild, and even forced the establishment of special courts.[61]

The instrumentalization of gender relations

Decades of war, displacement, regime change, and external intervention profoundly changed gender and intergenerational relationships. These transformations affected urban and rural people differently, those who had experienced exile or the camps, and the others engaged in an armed movement or whose loved ones had died or were disabled. This diversity and the difficulty of

[59] I-37, resident of Baraki Barak district (Logar), 2013.
[60] Liz Alden Wily, *Land Rights in Crisis: Restoring Tenure Security in Afghanistan*, Kabul, Afghanistan Research and Evaluation Unit, 2003, p. 54.
[61] Ibid., pp. 62–3.

collecting data explain why it has been argued that the war has both disrupted Afghan family structures and that the family is the only stable structure surviving in Afghanistan.[62]

Rather than a hypothesized characterization of the transformations of the family institution and its role, the comparison with other civil wars suggests that it is more relevant to focus on intra-familial dynamics, including changes in intergenerational and gender hierarchies. On the one hand, war is an opportunity for social promotion for young men in a society typified by a marked hierarchy between generations. In times of peace, sons are expected to serve their fathers, and transgressions against this generational order are emblematic of the great tales of social success.[63] In Afghanistan, as elsewhere, the war led to a sudden reversal of this hierarchy. Indeed, committing to the regime side or to the insurrection offered the younger generations opportunities for social ascent, while the older ones were often humbled by the measures enacted by the Communist regime and the hardship of exile.[64]

On the other hand, war transformed gender relations, but in an ambivalent way. For example, fighting and migration forced many women to take paid employment for the first time, with increased visibility in the public space. Wives of combatants, the disabled, or widows often had to support themselves. Some were taken in by their extended families, but other women had to work, for example for humanitarian organizations, or turn to sex work. In addition, since the 1980s, non-governmental organizations (NGOs) and international organizations had been contributing to the evolution of family relations, imposing their own hierarchies through aid triage.[65] By imposing categories of 'vulnerabilities' (disabled, single women, children, the elderly) and thereby setting priorities for accessing the resources and services provided by NGOs, they set the stage for conflicts, which in fact sometimes turned out to the disadvantage of populations singled out by the humanitarians.[66]

[62] Nancy Dupree, 'The Family during Crisis in Afghanistan', *Journal of Comparative Family Studies*, 2004, vol. 35, nº 2, pp. 311–31.

[63] David Edwards, *Heroes of the Age: Moral Fault Lines on the Afghan Frontier*, Berkeley, University of California Press, 1996.

[64] David Edwards, *Before Taliban Genealogies of the Afghan Jihad*, Berkeley, University of California Press, 2002. Mats Utas, Henrik Vigh, and Danny Hoffman, in their ethnography of groups of young fighters in Liberia, Guinea Bissau, and Sierra Leone, describe the same dynamics. Mats Utas, *Sweet Battlefields: Youth and the Liberian Civil War*, Uppsala, Uppsala University, 2003; Henrik Vigh, *Navigating Terrains of War: Youth and Soldiering in Guinea-Bissau*, New York, Berghahn Books, 2006; Danny Hoffman, *The War Machines: Young Men and Violence in Sierra Leone and Liberia*, Durham, Duke University Press, 2011.

[65] Pierre Centlivres and Micheline Centlivres-Demont, 'The Afghan Refugee in Pakistan: An Ambiguous Identity', *Journal of Refugee Studies*, 1988, vol. 1, pp. 141–52.

[66] In this respect, Afghanistan furnishes a typical case of the practices of transnational NGOs. See Michel Agier, 'Le camp des vulnérables: Les réfugiés face à leur citoyenneté niée', *Les Temps Modernes*,

One of the defining features of the war in Afghanistan was how political actors exploited gender relations and how these exacerbated private conflicts. Indeed, from the first months of the war, women—their role, their behaviour, their rights, and their duties—became a determining factor in the engagement and discourse of political parties. They fought on behalf of women, their liberation, their protection, their chastity. The classic questions in revolutionary situations of the autonomy of the private and public spheres and the moralization of traditions would largely play out in Afghanistan around the place of women.[67] In such an atmosphere, intimate and family conflicts were immediately tainted by the ideological stakes of the struggle, from then on becoming an object that crystallized other social, religious, and political problems.

Starting with the coup d'état of April 1978, the new regime made women and private life a battleground. On 17 October 1978, the regime promulgated Decree 7, which promised to 'eliminate feudal and patriarchal relations between husband and wife'. Legislation outlawed forced unions, set a minimum age for marriage, and limited the bride price and compensation for the bride's family.[68] Women were appointed to family court judgeships and defended women's rights to divorce, obtain custody of children, or receive alimony.[69] These measures were accompanied by a greater visibility of unveiled women in the media and in the streets of cities, but also in rural areas, where Communist activists and women civil servants took charge of enforcing the reforms.

This policy of the Democratic Republic of Afghanistan was part of a long history of state formation by imposing greater visibility of women in the public space.[70] In the 1920s, the marriage reforms of Emir Amenullah and

2004, n° 627, p. 120; Vinh-Kim Nguyen, *The Republic of Therapy: Triage and Sovereignty in West Africa's Time of AIDS*, Durham, Duke University Press, 2010. For a case of a policy of promoting women that has the opposite effect, Simon Turner, 'New Opportunities: Angry Young Men in a Tanzanian Refugee Camp' in Philomena Essed, Georg Frerks, and Joke Schrijvers (eds), *Refugees and the Transformation of Societies: Agency, Policies, Ethics, and Politics*, New York, Berghahn Books, 2004, pp. 94–105.

[67] Hannah Arendt, *On Revolution*, New York, Viking, 1963; Jürgen Habermas, *The Structural Transformation of the Public Sphere: An Inquiry into a Category of Bourgeois Society*, Cambridge, Polity, 1989.

[68] Nancy Dupree, 'Revolutionary Rhetoric and Afghan Women' in Robert L. Canfield and M. Nazif Shahrani (eds), *Revolutions & Rebellions in Afghanistan: Anthropological Perspectives*, Berkeley, University of California Press, 1984, pp. 306–40. According to practices that vary by region and by social group, the payment of a bride price is a common practice. Nancy Tapper, *Bartered Brides: Politics, Gender and Marriage in an Afghan Tribal Society*, Cambridge, Cambridge University Press, 1991.

[69] Valentine Moghadam, 'A Tale of Two Countries: State, Society, and Gender Politics in Iran and Afghanistan', *The Muslim World*, 2004, vol. 94, n° 4, p. 455.

[70] As Deniz Kandiyoti has shown, the extension of women's rights and citizenship has been a key element in the formation and development of the state in the Global South. See Deniz Kandiyoti (ed.), *Women, Islam and the State*, London, Macmillan, 1991. For an extension of her analyses to the Afghan context, see Deniz Kandiyoti, 'Old Dilemmas or New Challenges? The Politics of Gender and Reconstruction in Afghanistan', *Development and Change*, 2007, vol. 38, n° 2, pp. 169–99.

the adoption by the royal family of Western clothes stirred up strong protests and contributed to his overthrow in 1929.[71] His successors pursued these reforms more circumspectly. The wives of the royal family and ministers stopped wearing the veil in public spaces in 1959, women were recruited into various government departments, and the 1964 Constitution formally guaranteed women the right to education, the choice of their husbands, and equality in work.[72] This policy, as evidenced by the 1970s photos of unveiled women in skirts at the university or hospital, was largely limited to Kabul and its elite.[73] It raised tensions considerably in families and fuelled the Islamist opposition in the 1960s and 1970s.[74] In the late 1970s, the reforms of the Communist regime were denounced in the countryside as an attack on religion, morality, and customs.[75] As Nancy Dupree reports:

> The DRA [the Democratic Republic of Afghanistan] was perceived as unlawfully interfering with Islamic values and violating social traditions, which were seen to be the provenance of Islam and beyond the competence of secular law. The unladylike public activities were viewed as undignified and detrimental to family honour. As proof that sexual anarchy was imminent, they pointed to women who expressed their new-found freedoms by flaunting their sexuality. Even their male supporters were embarrassed![76]

While Communist elites and activists despised rural Afghans, openly describing them as ignorant and archaic, women became essential stakes in the struggle to be liberated, to modernize society, or to be protected as an embodiment of the honour of men.

[71] Nancy Dupree, 'Behind the Veil in Afghanistan', *Asia*, August 1978.

[72] Louis Dupree, *Afghanistan*, Princeton, Princeton University Press, 1973, pp. 530–4.

[73] Moreover, visibility in the public space generally did not necessarily translate into power in the private sphere; on the contrary, women wearing *chadri* in the countryside sometimes had more prerogatives and autonomy in daily life. Pierre Centlivres and Micheline Centlivres-Demont, *Et si on parlait de l'Afghanistan? Terrains et textes, 1964–1980*, Paris, Les Éditions de la MSH, 1988, p. 22.

[74] Hasan Kakar, 'The Fall of the Afghan Monarchy in 1973', *International Journal of Middle East Studies*, 1978, vol. 9, n° 2, p. 202; Valentine Moghadam, 'Patriarchy, the Taleban, and Politics of Public Space in Afghanistan', *Women's Studies International Forum*, 2002, vol. 25, n° 1, p. 22.

[75] Particularly Decree 7 caused great indignation in rural areas, as the drastic limitation of the bride price put in question the material and symbolic economy around marriages. According to Nancy Tapper, the limitation of the bride price paradoxically led to a social devaluation of women, with marriage and reproduction being seen then as their essential modes of value production, which was measured by the amount of the bride price. See Nancy Tapper, 'Causes and Consequences of the Abolition of Brideprice in Afghanistan' in M. Nazif Shahrani and Robert Canfield (eds), *Revolutions and Rebellions in Afghanistan*, Berkeley, University of California Press, 1984, pp. 291–305.

[76] Nancy Dupree, 'The Family during Crisis in Afghanistan', *Journal of Comparative Family Studies*, 2004, vol. 35, n° 2, p. 317.

The insurgency thus waged jihad in the name of women and made their behaviour a political issue. Women played an important role in challenging the regime by demonstrating against repression and committing assassinations or acts of sabotage.[77] However, they participated more marginally in combat, usually in logistics and intelligence functions. Their mobilization was accompanied by a demand for moral probity and sobriety in a context of political parties competing for the monopoly of the Islamist cause.[78] Social control was generalized (bans on music, movies, and celebrations during weddings), but singled out women. In addition, the monitoring of morals was exacerbated by the unprecedented promiscuity of the camps in Pakistan, with extended families living under the same roof and close to other dwellings.[79] If men were held liable for women's behaviour in public, women also participated in imposing this moral order, a division of tasks that some anthropologists had already observed before the war.[80]

The measures taken became more radical as the war continued. In 1989, a group of mullahs banned women from working and threatened resisters with severe punishment. Another edict circulated the same year required the wearing of the full-face veil and, the following year, a *fatwa* was issued: 'The United Ulama of the Islamic Leaders of the Afghan resistance required that Afghans not permit women to attend schools or become educated or else the Islamic movement will meet with failure […] this is not the right time for women and girls to become educated. Therefore, learning and writing is religiously prohibited for women.'[81] Peshawar's main high school for Afghan women was attacked by gunmen. Once in power (1992–6), the mujahideen transposed this vision of women's seclusion into law. On 27 August 1993, a year before the emergence of the Taliban movement, a *fatwa* from the Supreme Court of the Islamic State of Afghanistan prescribed the following:

[77] Nancy Dupree, 'Revolutionary Rhetoric and Afghan Women' in Robert L. Canfield and M. Nazif Shahrani (eds), *Revolutions & Rebellions in Afghanistan: Anthropological Perspectives*, Berkeley, University of California Press, 1984, pp. 332–4.

[78] Audrey C. Shalinsky, 'Women's Roles in the Afghanistan Jihad', *International Journal of Middle East Studies*, 1993, vol. 25, n° 4, pp. 661–75. Julie Billaud analyses the reproduction during the 2000s of these same discourses. See Julie Billaud, *Kabul Carnival: Gender Politics in Postwar Afghanistan*, Philadelphia, University of Pennsylvania Press, 2015, pp. 177–81.

[79] Nancy Dupree, 'The Demography of Afghan Refugees in Pakistan' in Hafeez Malik (ed.), *Soviet-American Relations with Pakistan, Iran and Afghanistan*, Basingstoke, Palgrave Macmillan, 1987, pp. 366–94; Inger Boesen, 'What Happens to Honour in Exile? Continuity and Change among Afghan Refugees' in Bo Huldt and Erland Jansson (eds), *The Tragedy of Afghanistan: The Social, Cultural and Political Impact of the Soviet Invasion*, London, Croom Helm, 1988, pp. 219–39.

[80] See, for example, Inger Boesen, 'Women, Honour and Love: some Aspects of the Pashtun Woman's Life in Eastern Afghanistan', *Afghanistan Journal*, 1980, vol. 7, n° 2, pp. 50–9.

[81] Jan Goodwin, *Price of Honor: Muslim Women Lift the Veil of Silence on the Islamic World*, London, Penguin, 2002, pp. 212–13.

> Women need not leave their homes at all, unless absolutely necessary, in which case, they are to cover themselves completely; are not to wear attractive clothing and decorative accessories; do not wear perfume; their jewellery must not make any noise; they are not to walk gracefully or with pride and in the middle of the sidewalk; are not to talk to strangers; are not to speak loudly or laugh in public; and they must always ask their husbands' permission to leave home [...] government organs and officials are to oust all female employees from their jobs and get female students out of schools for, in reality, schools are whorehouses and centers of adultery and fornication.[82]

In this context, accusations of fornication and refusal to submit to marriages arranged by parents took on an immediate political connotation, attracting suspicions of indifference to jihad or even of treason.[83] These deviances were already violently punished before the war, but in the context of the struggle against the Soviet occupation punishments such as stoning and amputation returned, though they had rarely been inflicted since the 1920s and had been banned in 1971.[84]

While the defence of private space and public probity had been two of the uprising's watchwords, abuses by the mujahideen following the Soviet withdrawal seemed to signal a radical breakdown of the social order. The most transgressive practices, such as fighters bursting into homes or raping women, traumatized many Afghans. In this respect, Afghanistan presents an interesting contrast to the wars in the former Yugoslavia, Sierra Leone, Uganda, or the Democratic Republic of the Congo, where rape throughout these wars was extremely common.[85] In the Afghanistan of the 1980s, the political use of rape of women was rare, which could be linked to the preponderance of some social deterrence in war. This practice remained systematically presented as the absolute worst transgression, that parents, brothers, husbands, and sons had a duty to avenge or risk the loss of their social standing.[86] The few cases reported

[82] Quoted by Helena Malikyar, 'Development of Family Law in Afghanistan: The Roles of the Hanafi *Madhhab*, Customary Practices and Power Politics', *Central Asian Survey*, 1997, vol. 16, n° 3, pp. 395–6.

[83] Nancy Dupree, 'Revolutionary Rhetoric and Afghan Women' in Robert L. Canfield and M. Nazif Shahrani (eds), *Revolutions & Rebellions in Afghanistan: Anthropological Perspectives*, Berkeley, University of California Press, 1984, p. 334.

[84] Martin Lau, *Afghanistan's Legal System and its Compatibility with International Human Rights Standards*, Geneva, International Commission of Jurists, 2002, pp. 29–30.

[85] Véronique Nahoum-Grappe, 'La purification ethnique et les viols systématiques. Ex-Yougoslavie 1991–1995', *Clio. Femmes, Genre, Histoire*, 1997, n° 5, pp. 163–75; Zoe Marks, 'Sexual Violence in Sierra Leone's Civil War: "Virgination", Rape, and Marriage', *African Affairs*, 2014, vol. 113, n° 450, pp. 67–87.

[86] Inger Boesen, 'Conflicts of Solidarity in Pakhtun Women's Lives' in Bo Utas (ed.), *Women in Islamic Societies: Social Attitudes and Historical Perspectives*, London, Curzon Press, 1983, pp. 104–23; Kathleen Howard-Merriam, 'Afghan Refugee Women and their Struggle for Survival' in Grant Farr and John Merriam (eds), *Afghan Resistance: The Politics of Survival*, London, Westview Press, 1987, pp. 103–25.

in the 1980s took place in a context that emphasized the transgressive dimension of this practice. Thus, when Babrak Karmal took power in 1980, the official press reported cases of sexual abuse to discredit Amin, his predecessor.[87] However, in the 1990s, thousands of women were raped and abducted; some committed suicide to escape the disgrace that befell them.[88] Repeated rapes of women played a key role in the story of the genesis of the Taliban uprising against the commanders in Kandahar.[89] The breakdown of the social order in the mid-1990s was also evident in the practices of humiliation, animalization, and desecration, whose cruelty, inserted into daily life, accentuated their transgressive character. Thus, a commander holding the heights of the road between Jalalabad and Kabul became notorious for keeping a man on a leash who barked and bit like a dog. In Kabul's Kart-e Seh district, gunmen collected the eyes of the people they executed as spies.[90] In Kandahar, between 1992 and 1994, processions accompanied celebrations of the unions of commanders with male youngsters (*bacha*). While having a *bacha* was a widespread prewar practice among some elites, but also among truck drivers, its staging in the open was a show of strength, of the power to break social rules and Islamic norms with impunity.

The regulation of women's behaviour also was a key point in the Taliban Islamic Emirate (1996–2001) project to moralize society. Continuing the measures taken by the Burhanuddin Rabbani government (1992–6), the Taliban banned women from working; they had to wear the *chadri* and be accompanied by a relative (*mahram*). Under the pretext that ensuring the safety of women was impossible, public baths and girls' schools were closed.[91] Women were regularly caned by the morality police, especially in Kabul, and adulterers were sometimes punished by stoning.[92] To act as a deterrent, sentences were both brutal and public.[93] This crackdown specifically targeted cities and

[87] Nancy Dupree, 'Revolutionary Rhetoric and Afghan Women' in Robert L. Canfield and M. Nazif Shahrani (eds), *Revolutions & Rebellions in Afghanistan: Anthropological Perspectives*, Berkeley, University of California Press, 1984, p. 328.

[88] *Women in Afghanistan: A Human Rights Catastrophe*, London, Amnesty International, 1995.

[89] The founders of the Taliban movement say they rose up following the serial rapes by a commander west of Kandahar; see, for example, Abdul Salam Zaeef, *My Life with the Taliban*, New York, Columbia University Press, 2010.

[90] *Women in Afghanistan: A Human Rights Catastrophe*, London, Amnesty International, 1995, pp. 10–11.

[91] Nancy Dupree, 'Afghan Women under the Taliban' in William Maley (ed.), *Fundamentalism Reborn? Afghanistan and the Taliban*, London, Hurst, 1998, pp. 154–5.

[92] In practice, this sentence is rarely applied: to prove guilt, the accuser is supposed to present witnesses who can attest to the sexual act. The judge's interpretation is decisive because he may require either that these persons had to have directly observed penetration between the lovers or that they are simply able to certify that the woman was alone with a man.

[93] Nancy Dupree, 'Afghan Women under the Taliban' in William Maley (ed.), *Fundamentalism Reborn? Afghanistan and the Taliban*, London, Hurst, 1998, p. 152; Juan Cole, 'The Taliban, Women,

public spaces. In the countryside, many women did not cover their faces when working in the fields, and nomadic women did not wear the *chadri*. Thus, in the East:

> [in the valley of] Alishang, women do not wear the chadri; they wear only the veil and they are the ones who do the work in the fields while the men look after the animals. At the time, the Taliban never prevented women from working and never asked them to wear the chadri. It's the same today. They did this mostly in the bazaar, in Mihtarlam or Jalalabad. The women of the valley only put on their chadri when they went down to the city and removed it as soon as they returned to the valley.[94]

In practice, it was mostly women from educated urban backgrounds who did not previously wear the *chadri* in public spaces and were forced to wear it on a daily basis. Similarly, the ban on salaried employment probably affected between 40,000 and 150,000 women: it did not impact most women who farmed the land and produced handicrafts at home.[95]

Western discourse towards the Taliban also played a role in turning Afghan women into a symbolic and political issue. In the late 1990s, state and non-state actors put the status of Afghan women under the Taliban regime on the media and political agenda in the West, notably through the efforts of the 'Campaign to Stop Gender Violence in Afghanistan'.[96] The US intervention was also justified on behalf of Afghan women. On 17 November 2001, Laura Bush, wife of the President of the United States, addressed the American nation on radio: 'Civilized people throughout the world are speaking out in horror, not only because our hearts break for the women and children of Afghanistan, but also because in Afghanistan, we see the world the terrorists would like to impose on the rest of us.'[97] In 2002, Christine Delphy, Lila Abu-Lughod, Charles Hirchkind, and Saba Mahmood analysed how these public campaigns were reconstructing recent Afghan history and instrumentalizing the status of women. Disregarding two decades of armed conflict, the poverty,

and the Hegelian Private Sphere' in Robert D. Crews and Amin Tarzi (eds), *The Taliban and the Crisis of Afghanistan*, Cambridge, Harvard University Press, 2009, pp. 118–54.

94 E-57, a veterinarian in Laghman province, April 2011. See also Parwin Ali Majrooh, 'Afghan Women between Marxism and Islamic Fundamentalism', *Central Asian Survey*, 1989, vol. 8, n° 3, pp. 91–4.

95 Nancy Dupree, 'Afghan Women under the Taliban' in William Maley (ed.), *Fundamentalism Reborn? Afghanistan and the Taliban*, London, Hurst, 1998, p. 155.

96 www.helpafghanwomen.com/.

97 www.whitehouse.gov/news/releases/2001/l 1/20011117.html.

misery, and insecurity that had impacted Afghan women since the start of the war was blamed on the Taliban's religious fundamentalism.[98] Anthropologist Anila Daulatzai points to similar biases among researchers who wrote about Afghanistan at the time.[99] For example, in 1998, an influential report, followed by an article in a medical journal, blamed the Taliban for the deterioration of women's health in Afghanistan, again without mentioning the preceding two decades of armed conflict.[100]

This discourse grew as images of a woman's public execution in Kabul's stadium and the stories of women beaten for not covering themselves in the capital sparked considerable outrage.[101] The anonymous figure of the woman in the burqa stood out as the symbol of the Afghan situation, as justification *a posteriori* of a decision already taken to intervene, and her uncovering as the means for 'liberating' Afghanistan.[102] After the fall of the Taliban Emirate, this figure of 'the Afghan woman' was also mobilized in the growth and promotion of development programmes that were just as disconnected from the material conditions in which Afghan women lived.[103] This objectification of Afghan women hence posed them as a stake in the struggle between civilization and barbarism, law and terrorism, modernity and obscurantism, as well as liberalism and fundamentalism, thereby fuelling the instrumentalization of gender relations throughout the intervention.

[98] Christine Delphy, 'Une guerre pour les femmes afghanes?', *Nouvelles Questions Féministes*, 2002, vol. 21, nº 1, pp. 98–109; Charles Hirschkind and Saba Mahmood, 'Feminism, the Taliban, and Politics of Counter-Insurgency', *Anthropological Quarterly*, 2002, vol. 75, nº 2, pp. 339–54; Lila Abu-Lughod, 'Do Muslim Women Really Need Saving? Anthropological Reflections on Cultural Relativism and Its Others', *American Anthropologist*, 2002, vol. 104, nº 3, pp. 783–90.

[99] Anila Daulatzai, 'The Discursive Occupation of Afghanistan', *British Journal of Middle Eastern Studies*, 2008, vol. 35, nº 3, pp. 419–35.

[100] Vincent Iacopino et al., *The Taliban's War on Women: A Health and Human Rights Crisis in Afghanistan*, Boston, Physicians for Human Rights, 1998; Zohra Rasekh et al., 'Women's Health and Human Rights in Afghanistan', *JAMA: Journal of the American Medical Association*, 1998, vol. 280, nº 5, pp. 449–55.

[101] Nancy Dupree, 'Afghan Women under the Taliban' in William Maley (ed.), *Fundamentalism Reborn? Afghanistan and the Taliban*, London, Hurst, 1998, pp. 306–40; Sippi Azerbaijani-Moghaddam, 'Afghan Women on the Margins of the Twenty-First Century' in Antonio Donini, Norah Niland, and Karin Wermester (eds), *Nation-building Unraveled? Aid, Peace and Justice in Afghanistan*, Bloomfield, Kumarian Press, 2004, pp. 95–116.

[102] For an analysis of this figure of the woman in a blue burqa who regularly makes headlines, see Judith Butler, *Precarious Life: The Powers of Mourning and Violence*, New York, Verso, 2004; Zillah R. Eisenstein, 'Feminisms in the Aftermath of September 11', *Social Text*, 2002, vol. 20, nº 3, pp. 79–99.

[103] Julie Billaud, *Kabul Carnival: Gender Politics in Postwar Afghanistan*, Philadelphia, University of Pennsylvania Press, 2015; Torunn Wimpelmann, *The Pitfalls of Protection: Gender, Violence, and Power in Afghanistan*, Berkeley, University of California Press, 2017.

3

Regime justice

Rubberstamping the balance of power

Introduction

On 11 September 2001, with Northern Alliance commanders cornered in the Panjshir Valley, the Taliban were on the verge of winning the war when Al Qaeda commandos hijacked four US airliners and crashed three of them into the Twin Towers of the World Trade Center and the Pentagon. Mullah Omar's regime refused to extradite the leader of Al Qaeda, Osama bin Laden, and the United States intervened militarily in Afghanistan on 7 October 2001 at the head of a broad international coalition. Washington launched a bombing campaign, dispatched several thousand Special Forces troops, and distributed $70 million and 767 tons of military equipment to Northern Alliance commanders.[1] Within weeks, its fighters entered Kabul, forcing Taliban leaders and al-Qaeda militants to take refuge in Pakistan.

The US intervention installed a new regime under the leadership of Hamid Karzai, who administered the country jointly with Western donors and international organizations. This transnational government was particularly important in the legislative and judicial domains. Western lawyers, experts, humanitarians, military officers, and diplomats had laws enacted that contradicted existing Afghan law, influenced appointments to key institutions, conjured up customary justice councils, and interfered in cases before the courts. Inadequate law and a lack of a coherent policy in the judicial sector at the time explain why courts were inaccessible to most Afghans and had incompetent judges. The judicial system built by the 'international community' was incapable of settling conflicts; on the contrary, it fuelled legal uncertainty.

[1] The US military refused to accede to the request of the leader of the Northern Alliance, Marshal Mohamad Fahim, to distribute the money through the structures of the coalition. By paying the various commanders directly, the US military secured more control over its factions, but at the cost of fragmenting the Northern Alliance. Peter Tomsen, *The Wars of Afghanistan: Messianic Terrorism, Tribal Conflicts, and the Failures of Great Powers*, New York, Public Affairs, 2013, p. 597; Conor Keane, *US Nation-Building in Afghanistan*, London, Routledge, 2016, pp. 105–10.

The Taliban Courts in Afghanistan. Adam Baczko, Oxford University Press. © Adam Baczko 2023.
DOI: 10.1093/oso/9780198896777.003.0004

The regime's strongmen took advantage of a situation in which the head of state held on to power thanks to a laissez-faire system that allowed them to enrich themselves through violence. Against this background, the courts lent a veneer of legality to situations of fact and thus appeared to merely rubberstamp the balance of power. Contrary to the classic model of 'statemaking as organized crime', developed by Charles Tilly and reworked to account for the 'criminalization of the state' in Africa or Brazil, Western intervention prevented the formation of a political elite which might have formed the core of a functioning state apparatus.[2] Unable to secure their capital for the long run, the regime's strongmen funnelled money from aid diversion, land speculation, and drug trafficking into deposits abroad, draining resources from the economy and from the state machinery.

A transnational government

Born in backroom international negotiations, the new Afghan regime was characterized by an unprecedented degree of transnational government. A multitude of external actors and commanders' networks returning to power coproduced public policies in an administration fissured by cronyism. Hamid Karzai himself as head of state was a creature of this transnational government. The United States brought considerable pressure to bear to put him into power during the various stages of the political transition that took place between 2001 and 2004. Having lived in the United States and being relatively unknown in Afghanistan, Karzai possessed two essential qualities in the eyes of the Bush administration: as the son of a Pashtun notable from the South, he belonged to the dominant ethnic group, and he was a known quantity to American neoconservative circles, including Zalmay Khalilzad, the special representative of President George W. Bush in Afghanistan.[3]

At a conference held in Bonn under the United Nations umbrella, the United States brought together the leaders of the Northern Alliance and

[2] Charles Tilly, 'War Making and State Making as Organized Crime' in Dietrich Rueschemeyer, Peter B. Evans, and Theda Skocpol (eds), *Bringing the State Back In*, Cambridge, Cambridge University Press, 1985, pp. 169–91; Jean-François Bayart, Stephen Ellis, and Béatrice Hibou, *Criminalization of the State in Africa*, Bloomington, Indiana University Press, 2009; Christian Geffray, 'État, richesse et criminels' in Yann Guillaud and Frédéric Létang (eds), *Du social hors la loi: L'anthropologie analytique de Christian Geffray*, Marseille, IRD Éditions, 2009, pp. 243–70.

[3] Hamid Karzai has been close to Zalmay Khalilzad since the late 1990s, after working with him on a white paper on the Afghan situation for the Afghanistan Foundation. Zalmay Khalilzad, a former collaborator of Albert Wohlstetter and Zbigniew Brzezinski, a member of the second Reagan administration, promoted an anti-Taliban policy within the US administration.

representatives of the main exiled factions. On 5 December 2001, they signed an agreement establishing an interim administration under the leadership of Hamid Karzai. He was given the task of assembling an 'emergency Loya Jirga' within six months to set up a transitional administration with a view to writing a new constitution in within eighteen months. The Loya Jirga convened in June 2002, with US officials taking a direct hand in its deliberations. In particular, they forced Karzai's main rival, former King Zahir Shah, to withdraw, which—the ultimate humiliation—none other than Zalmay Khalizad announced at a press conference.[4] In addition, the emergency Loya Jirga tilted in Karzai's favour when he packed it at the last minute with a hundred local administrators personally appointed by him some months earlier. Finally, members of the new intelligence services controlled by the Northern Alliance networks in attendance openly intimidated delegates during the deliberations.[5]

Once Karzai was appointed president of the transitional authority, he became the main intermediary for the United States and the United Nations. He held weekly talks with President Bush and was in daily contact with Khalilzad (nicknamed 'the Viceroy') as well as Lakhdar Brahimi and Jean Arnault who in succession steered the United Nations Assistance Mission in Afghanistan (UNAMA).[6] Chosen as president in 2004 by a large majority in an election with 70 per cent voter turnout and boosted by the expectations generated by the international intervention, Karzai initially enjoyed a honeymoon period. However, his popularity was short-lived: as early as 2005, the irregular parliamentary elections only brought 35 per cent of the electorate to the polls. His re-election in 2009 took place under a cloud of widespread fraud, which, however, did not prevent the international actors from recognizing the results.

Parachuted into the country's leadership without a popular or military base, Hamid Karzai accommodated himself to the potentates of the 1990s in building his administration. They took advantage of the limited nature of American involvement in the early years. A United States intent on limiting its commitment to fighting Al Qaeda delegated Kabul's security to the International Security Assistance Force (ISAF), a multinational force under a United Nations mandate. Besides, the 2003 invasion of Iraq by the United States and the vicious fighting that followed the fall of Saddam Hussein diverted international attention from Afghanistan. Profiting from these circumstances, former

[4] M. Jamil Hanifi, 'Editing the Past: Colonial Production of Hegemony through the "Loya Jerga" in Afghanistan', *Iranian Studies*, 2004, vol. 37, n° 2, pp. 295–322.

[5] *The Afghan Transitional Administration: Prospects and Perils*, Brussels, International Crisis Group, 2002, pp. 3–4.

[6] E-23, UN political officer, May 2013.

commanders wasted no time in taking back control: Ismael Khan in Herat, Gul Agha Shirzai in Kandahar, Abdul Rashid Dostum in Shiberghan, and Mohamad Fahim in the Northeast.

President Karzai integrated them into his administration through a neopatrimonial system that worked largely to their benefit:[7] the ex-commanders obtained ministries or governorships which allowed them to appropriate the resources of the state whose budget was entirely sourced from international aid. Successive vice-presidents were informally granted the authority to appoint local administrators (a presidential responsibility according to the constitution) in Hazarajat by Karim Khalili (2002–14) and in a large part of the North by Ahmad Zia Massoud (2004–9) and Mohamad Fahim (2002–4, 2009–14). The President also bargained with these strongmen for the key ministries: they informally agreed that the Shura-i Nazar, the movement created by Ahmad Shah Massoud, who took Kabul in November 2001, would keep two of the three key posts (Interior, Defence, and Intelligence). Applying a clientelist logic, Hamid Karzai bypassed or hamstrung all institutions that could possibly constitute countervailing powers (Parliament, the judicial system, political parties) but which, in turn, might have provided his regime with legitimacy and a social base. In the ensuing years, timid reform attempts supported by the United Nations and the United States, including the creation of supervisory authorities, failed, Hamid Karzai having managed to gut them all. The weakening of the institutions deepened further when Ashraf Ghani succeeded Karzai in another blatantly fraudulent election. The new president, a PhD graduate from Columbia University, former senior World Bank official, and author of a book entitled *Fixing Failed States*, was a paragon of Western modernization.[8] However, when he took over the reins of the country, he continued to bypass the institutions and his attempts at reform came too late in a context of accelerated state decay.

The Western countries, which fully financed the budget, divided the responsibility for the country's reconstruction among themselves. At the Tokyo Donor Conference in January 2002, a 'lead country' was designated for each portfolio: the United Kingdom for the fight against narcotics, Italy for the

[7] The concept of neopatronialism, developed in postcolonial African contexts to describe political systems that take on legal-rational forms of administration while following a logic of patrimonial functioning, is particularly appropriate for describing the relationship between the presidency and the networks of former commanders. For the concept of neopatronialism, see the pioneering work of Shmuel Eisenstadt and its extension by Jean-François Médard. Shmuel Eisenstadt, *Traditional Patrimonialism and Modern Neopatrimonialism*, Thousand Oaks, Sage Publishing, 1973; Jean-François Médard, 'L'État néo-patrimonial en Afrique noire' in Jean-François Médard (ed.), *États d'Afrique noire: Formations, mécanismes et crises*, Paris, Karthala, 1991, pp. 323–53.

[8] Ashraf Ghani and Clare Lockhart, *Fixing Failed States: A Framework for Rebuilding a Fractured World*, Oxford, Oxford University Press, 2009.

judicial system, the United States for the army, Japan for disarming combatants, and Germany for the police. As a government was forming with ministries, Parliament, and local governments, Western countries pursued a variety of reforms in the areas of foreign policy, the civil service, the budget, and the judiciary. Implementation of public policies was variously delegated to Western development agencies (USAID, AUSAID, GTZ, AFD, DFID); international organizations (IMF, World Bank, UNDP, UNHCR); private companies (Adam Smith International, Pacific Architects and Engineers, Development Alternatives Incorporated, Checchi and Company Consulting); and NGOs. Inside ministries and local governments, Western countries and the World Bank employed private foreign and binational consultants, who were paid tens of thousands of dollars a month, to drive the reforms.

The various operators of the intervention rejected any form of regulation and coordination, defended the independence of their programmes, and regularly bypassed the Afghan administration. The opaque process of awarding contracts and the widespread practice of subcontracting resulted in significant embezzlement of aid funds.[9] With a few exceptions (e.g., the International Committee of the Red Cross and Doctors Without Borders), the various organizations maintained collusive relationships, built through professional networking and during social gatherings reserved for expatriates of the 'Kabubble'. This term ironically encapsulated the foreign bubble within Kabul, which escaped the direct fighting between the Taliban and Western forces. Typical of the international response, humanitarian personnel routinely took jobs with international organizations, then moved to private companies and even went to work for the Western armed forces. To maximize their take from the aid windfall, employees of these different organizations set up their own businesses and consulting firms offering audits and monitoring services to help donors document the effectiveness of the programmes they were funding.[10]

[9] In this regard, the denunciation of corruption in Afghan institutions is part of a broader dynamic of transforming the fight against corruption into a global issue, in a game with variable geometry to the advantage of Western countries that arbitrarily define what constitutes corruption or does not. While the outsourcing system of Western development agencies and companies causes most of the diversion of aid from its advertised objectives, it is the Afghan practices that are described as corruption by international organizations and NGOs. The case of Afghanistan resembles, on a considerable scale, the dynamics observed by Olivier Vallée in Nigeria and Cameroon. See Olivier Vallée, *La police morale de l'anticorruption: Cameroun, Nigeria*, Paris, Karthala, 2010.

[10] I observed the same practices of social closure by expatriates vis-à-vis the residents on the Turkish-Syrian border in 2012–13, in Iraqi Kurdistan between 2009 and 2015, and in North Kivu, in the Democratic Republic of the Congo in 2012. The movement between war zones of personnel from humanitarian organizations, international institutions, the armed forces, and private companies partly explains the similarity of practices. To account for these bubbles, anthropologist Raymond Apthorpe talks about the 'aidland', an ironic reference to *Alice in Wonderland* by Lewis Carroll. David Mosse (ed.),

This way of operating was not unique to Afghanistan, but there it reached an unprecedented scale because of the sums invested.[11]

'Legal transplant' or ungrounded law

In the midst of this war in all but name, the various donors and international experts embarked on a complete redrafting of Afghan law. They did so by systematically circumventing legislative bodies and failing to give extant legislation and legal practices their due. While Western actors described their work in this area as 'assistance for legal reform' or as a 'legal transplant',[12] in reality they took on a legislative role and set priorities that were often detached from the sociopolitical problems facing Afghan society.

The explanation for the preponderant weight of the donors lay in the weakness of the new Afghan regime's legislative institutions. The presidency preempted the drafting of the constitution and concentrated power in the executive branch. In October 2002, Hamid Karzai, as head of the transitional administration, appointed the commission to draft the constitution. Its membership consisted mainly of veterans of the 1990s armed groups, which were assisted by foreign experts, in particular a French constitutionalist, Guy Carcassonne; a United Nations official, Eckart Schiewek; and an American political scientist, Barnett Rubin.[13] Drafted between 2002 and 2003, the first version of the Constitution sealed a compromise between armed groups and international actors. Afghanistan was defined as an Islamic Republic (Article 1) whose laws could not conflict either with sharia (Article 3) or the Universal Declaration of Human Rights and international treaties (Article 7). Judges had to apply laws

Adventures in Aidland: The Anthropology of Professionals in International Development, New York, Berghahn Books, 2011; Anne-Meike Fechter and Heather Hindman (eds), *Inside the Everyday Lives of Development Workers: The Challenges and Futures of Aidland*, Sterling, Kumarian Press, 2011. For a similar argument in the context of peacekeeping interventions, see Séverine Autesserre, *Peaceland: Conflict Resolution and the Everyday Politics of International Intervention*, Cambridge, Cambridge University Press, 2014.

[11] On the eve of the war in Afghanistan, Mark Duffield already pointed to the fusion between the security and development worlds. Mark R. Duffield, *Global Governance and the New Wars: The Merging of Development and Security*, London, Zed Books, 2001. For an analysis of the role of private companies in this articulation between military and humanitarian logics, see Vijay Kumar Nagaraj, '"Beltway Bandits" and "Poverty Barons": For-Profit International Development Contracting and the Military-Development Assemblage', *Development and Change*, 2015, vol. 46, n° 4, pp. 585–617.

[12] The term was created by Alan Watson to describe the importation of a law or system of laws by one country from another. Alan Watson, *Legal Transplants: An Approach to Comparative Law*, Athens, University of Georgia Press, 1974.

[13] E-70, UN political officer, April 2013.

and decrees in making decisions and rely on Hanafite jurisprudence in the absence of any other legal requirement (Article 130).[14] Inspired by the 1964 constitutional monarchy, the original version of the Constitution also provided for a prime minister responsible to the lower house.

However, between the time the commission's work on the document ended in September 2003 and its publication on 3 November 2003, Khalilzad allowed President Karzai and his advisers to rewrite the document. They greatly strengthened presidential power, abolished the post of prime minister, and pared back the prerogatives of Parliament and the judiciary.[15] According to Barnett Rubin, who had a hand in drafting the Constitution, this shift to a presidentialist regime ensured that 'there would be no uncertainty about who held legitimate executive power in Kabul, and Washington would retain the benefit of having a clearly identifiable Afghan partner whom it would know well and indeed preferred'.[16] In the final version of the Constitution, the President disposed of much broader legislative prerogatives than did Parliament (Articles 94, 95, and 97). He could veto the laws it passed, and, most importantly, if Parliament was not in session, he could in the name of 'urgent necessities' (Article 79) issue decrees that carried the force of law, except in budgetary matters. In addition, this new version of the Constitution reserved to the head of state and judges the right of appeal to the Supreme Court, stripping Parliament of any chance to challenge the executive power (Article 121).[17]

In the years following its adoption, the imbalance enshrined in the Constitution was compounded by the rapid decline of Parliament. It was bypassed as laws were written outside it and promulgated by presidential decrees. Not until 2007 did the legislature pass its first law; it provided for amnesty for crimes committed during the 1980s and 1990s, the main perpetrators of which now sat in Parliament or were members of the government.[18] This

[14] If both sides are Shia, Jafarite (Shia) jurisprudence can be invoked in place of Hanafite (Sunni) jurisprudence (Article 131). This article of the Constitution legally recognizes the Shiite minority, but grants it a lower status, since a case involving a Shia faith with a Sunni will be judged according to Hanafite jurisprudence. For a detailed analysis of Article 130 and the application of Islamic law by the Islamic Republic's judges, see Lutforahman Saeed, *Islam, Custom and Human Rights: A Legal and Empirical Study of Criminal Cases in Afghanistan After the 2004 Constitution*, New York, Springer, 2021.

[15] *Afghanistan's Flawed Constitutional Process*, Brussels, International Crisis Group, 2003; Astri Suhrke, 'Democratizing a Dependent State: The Case of Afghanistan', *Democratization*, 2008, vol. 15, n° 3, pp. 630–48.

[16] Barnett R. Rubin, 'Crafting a Constitution for Afghanistan', *Journal of Democracy*, 2004, vol. 15, n° 3, p. 12.

[17] Rainer Grote, 'Separation of Powers in the New Afghan Constitution', *Zeitschrift für ausländisches öffentliches Recht und Völkerrecht*, 2004, vol. 64, pp. 897–915; John Dempsey and J. Alexander Thier, *Resolving the Crisis over Constitutional Interpretation in Afghanistan*, Washington, United States Institute of Peace, 2009.

[18] On the presence of commanders in Parliament, see Andrew Wilder, *A House Divided? Analysing the 2005 Afghan Elections*, Kabul, Afghanistan Research and Evaluation Unit, 2005, p. 14.

parliamentary atrophy had several causes: first, the electoral voting system discouraged members from legislating and representing their constituents among the population. As the Special Representative of the European Union Francesc Vendrell (2002–8) explained: 'When in the autumn of 2005 elections for parliament took place, they were held, at president Karzai's insistence, under a rarely used electoral system called the single non-transferable vote (SNTV),[19] which discourages the development of political parties and led to a fragmented parliament in which majorities have often been built through bribery.'[20] Indeed, party membership was neither a legal requirement nor an asset in running for office. The voting system encouraged a multiplicity of candidates and fostered the building of personal clienteles, thus bypassing political parties. The four one-time dominant formations (Hizb-i Wahdat, Hizb-i Islami, Jamiat-i Islami, and Jumbesh-i Melli) each splintered into several factions. Moreover, popular support was not necessary for winning a seat in the lower house—all it took was patronage from the machinery of state, the ability to manipulate elections, and, in a highly fragmented system, occasional dumb luck. Vote scattering was the rule, so that in the first election of 2005, some MPs were elected with just 1–2 per cent of the vote, amounting in one case to less than 2,000 votes. As a result, the majority of parliamentarians had no political affiliation and sold their votes. Moreover, if the President did not like the way a parliamentary vote turned out, he could circumvent it by appealing to the Supreme Court, thus further weakening the Parliament. In 2007, when Parliament approved a motion of no confidence against Foreign Minister Rangin Dadfar Spanta, Hamid Karzai manoeuvred to have the vote declared unconstitutional by the Supreme Court. Finally, as foreign countries funded almost the entire budget, the Parliament's budgetary prerogatives were largely constrained by donor countries, which often had the final say over how funds would be allocated.

Western countries imposed their agendas, implemented their visions of the law, and bypassed the relevant Afghan institutions. In the eyes of coalition members, especially the United States, Afghanistan was a 'failed state' that had to be rebuilt from the ground up. Inspired by post-1945 German and Japanese precedents, donors viewed the Afghan institutional system as a *tabula rasa*. In doing so, they disregarded history, legal practices, and the fallout from

[19] Under a single non-transferable voting system, each voter chooses a candidate from a list of candidates, but several seats must be filled in each electoral constituency. Candidates who received the most votes are elected. This can result in seats being won with few votes, making it difficult for any partisan strategy at the national or even at the constituency level.

[20] Francesc Vendrell, 'The International Community's Failures in Afghanistan' in Whit Mason (ed.), *The Rule of Law in Afghanistan: Missing in Inaction*, Cambridge, Cambridge University Press, 2011, p. 58.

two decades of armed conflict.[21] As two Western jurists who participated in the development of many of the major laws of the 2000s explained in retrospect: 'Laws are drafted and implementation planned by foreigners as if in a vacuum, inevitably setting the new law on a collision course with the old law, the legal culture and Afghan legal circumstances, creating mounting confusion and resentment among the Afghan professionals who are expected to implement it.'[22] In the early years of the intervention, it was routine for an American or European body to finance the drafting of an ad hoc bill, sometimes without even checking the existing legislation, transpose its own legal concepts and procedures in the process, and then implement the law without first consulting the various Afghan institutions concerned. In the absence of a coherent project, legal reform programmes produced a contradictory law that Afghan lawyers could not apply.

To begin with, donors would set about drafting legislation based on their priorities. The ability of international actors to impose their agendas, the lack of coordination, and the high turnover among Western experts and lawyers produced multiple pieces of legislation, *leges speciales* that were at odds with each other. The choice of Italy—the 'lead country' for justice issues—to write an Interim Code of Criminal Procedure was mainly due to the fact that the head of the Italian legal mission, Giuseppe di Gennaro, a former anti-mafia judge, had helped revise Bosnia's and Albania's Codes of Criminal Procedure in the 1990s. Similarly, in the autumn of 2004, USAID and the US Department of Justice drafted three different laws geared to their priorities in the 'war on terror': corruption, money laundering, and terrorist financing. In 2005, the United Kingdom, chosen as the 'lead country' in the fight against drugs, developed the Counter Narcotics Drug Law because it was set on having a newly created drug war ministry as its sole interlocutor for all related police and legal activities. Germany and the United States, both funding police reform, drafted a police law that failed to tie in with the Interim Code of Criminal Procedure, which Italy had managed to promulgate the previous year.

The ad hoc dimension of this legal engineering was also evident in the proliferation of courts with fuzzy jurisdictions. For example, the United

[21] For such perspectives, see James Dobbins, *America's Role in Nation-Building from Germany to Iraq*, Santa Monica, Random House, 2003; Francis Fukuyama, *Nation-Building: Beyond Afghanistan and Iraq*, Baltimore, Johns Hopkins University Press, 2008.

[22] Michael Hartmann and Agnieszka Klonowiecka-Milart, 'Lost in Translation: Legal Transplants without Consensus-based Adaptation' in Whit Mason (ed.), *The Rule of Law in Afghanistan: Missing in Inaction*, Cambridge, Cambridge University Press, 2011, p. 273. This text, co-authored by two lawyers who participated in the rewriting of Afghan law in the 2000s, represents the most detailed testimony and is therefore an essential source for the following paragraphs.

Kingdom-sponsored Counter Narcotics Drug Law of 2005 created special courts to try crimes that, under the Penal Code, fell within the jurisdiction of the courts of appeal. Similarly, the US-sponsored law against bribery and corruption of 2004 established an independent anti-corruption commission tasked with 'investigating the affairs related to bribery and corruption in offices' contrary to Article 134 of the Constitution, which stated that this responsibility rested with the Attorney General's Office. In addition, the law defined the crime of corruption so broadly that it overlapped with many other types of crimes in the Penal Code. This commission, headed by a convicted drug trafficker, was so inefficient that the Western donors pressed to have this system overhauled and replaced with ad hoc tribunals to handle corruption issues, which, however, also failed to meet expectations.[23]

Secondly, Western donors largely ignored the important pre-2001 Afghan legal production and transposed instead Western legal syntax and concepts. The various countries involved in reforming Afghan law prioritized drafting new laws over collecting, studying, and revising existing legislation. Thus, Italian legal experts specializing in organized crime developed the Interim Code of Criminal Procedure in consultation with American military lawyers. The Italian project did not pull in Afghan legal practitioners and failed to consider the legal history and political situation of the country. In producing a new code by transposing Italian concepts, legal syntax, and procedures, Italian legal experts ignored in particular both the Afghan 1976 Penal Code and the 1974 Code of Criminal Procedure.[24] Modelled on the Italian one, the new Code provided for a judicial police force, which Afghanistan did not have, and gave prosecutors the power to ratify police acts, in contravention of constitutional mandates. Without citing a rationale, it replaced the legal concept of absolute or relative reasons for quashing a judgment used in the 1974 Code with that of *nullity* derived from Italian law and which Afghan lawyers were not trained in. Finally, it set a maximum twenty-four-hour time limit between detection, investigation, and prosecution of cases, an unrealistic limit in a country whose roads and institutions had been devastated by two decades of armed conflict.[25] Because of both its brevity—eighty-nine articles against 500 for the 1974 version—and the lack of definition of many terms used, the new Code lent itself to highly varied interpretations and was therefore difficult to

[23] *Reforming Afghanistan's Broken Judiciary*, Brussels, International Crisis Group, 2010, p. 17.

[24] Michael Hartmann and Agnieszka Klonowiecka-Milart, 'Lost in Translation: Legal Transplants without Consensus-based Adaptation' in Whit Mason (ed.), *The Rule of Law in Afghanistan: Missing in Inaction*, Cambridge, Cambridge University Press, 2011, p. 272.

[25] *Reforming Afghanistan's Broken Judiciary*, Brussels, International Crisis Group, 2010, p. 10.

apply. For Afghan judges and prosecutors trained in the 1974 Code of Criminal Procedure, it created tremendous confusion, particularly compounded by the fact that the new Code was not provided to them until 2007, three years after completion.

Similarly, the 2004 laws on financing of terrorism and money laundering, drafted by World Bank and USAID consultants, was incompatible with existing legislation setting out specific criminal procedures that overlapped with the newly established Code of Criminal Procedure. Legal concepts transplanted from US law (freezing, seizure of assets, mutual legal assistance) and introduced without being defined ended up conflicting with the rest of Afghan criminal law. Moreover, without explanation or justification, entirely different procedures were prescribed for similar measures. Thus, while the law against money laundering allowed the Central Bank to freeze funds for seven days, the law on the financing of terrorism required a request from the prosecutor and a court authorization. A year later, the Justice Department prosecutor at the US Embassy in Kabul even proposed a terrorism bill directly inspired by the US Patriot Act. The use of a syntax foreign to Afghan law drew fierce criticism from Afghan and foreign lawyers. They recognized the magnitude of the resulting legal chaos, but were unable to stop the enactment of an amended version in 2008.

Finally, the donor countries relied on—and thus fed—the weaknesses of the Afghan legislative system so they could circumvent the institutions concerned. Between the adoption of the Constitution in January 2004 and the first session of Parliament on 19 December 2005, Western agencies tabled their bills at the Ministry of Justice. Once the Constitution was in force, they had President Karzai promulgate these laws under the aforesaid Article 79, which, as we have seen, gave the force of law to his decrees if Parliament was not in session. Invoking the need to enact legislation rapidly, and with parliamentary elections not slated until 2005, all laws passed in 2004 and 2005 were enacted under Article 79. Thus, the Interim Code of Criminal Procedure was adopted in February 2004 by a Hamid Karzai decree over the protests of Afghan lawyers.[26] In late 2005, faced with the prospect of having the newly elected Parliament in business for the first time, the United States and the United Kingdom silenced the many critics of their draft Counter Narcotic Drug Law and accelerated its drafting so that Karzai could promulgate it two days before Parliament's

[26] Faiz Ahmed, 'Judicial Reform in Afghanistan: A Case Study in the New Criminal Procedure Code', *Hastings International and Comparative Law Review*, 2005, vol. 29, pp. 93–134; *Reforming Afghanistan's Broken Judiciary*, Brussels, International Crisis Group, 2010, p. 10; Laurel Miller and Robert Perito, *Establishing the Rule of Law in Afghanistan*, Washington, United States Institute for Peace, 2004.

opening session. In the end, this haste proved unnecessary: President Karzai would continue to enact most new laws under Article 79.[27] For example, during the parliamentary break from December 2006 to February 2007, Karzai passed eight laws, including reforms to the labour and trade laws.[28] One summer, the US Embassy even sent an email to agencies involved in legal reform asking if they had any suggestions for laws to be enacted by presidential decree before Parliament returned from its break.[29]

Other tactics for sidelining Afghan institutions included donors paying the salaries of some key department officials. For example, the Afghan Ministry of Interior legal adviser who worked with the US and British embassies on the Counter Narcotic Drug Law was paid $3,000 a month by the United Kingdom on top of his civil servant's salary of a few dozen dollars. No surprise then that he supported the bill drafted by the two embassies despite the opposition it met with from other international and Afghan organizations. Similarly, Italy threatened to end its legal assistance as leverage in getting Karzai to enact the Interim Code of Criminal Procedure, which Afghan jurists also strenuously opposed.

Faced with the problems posed by imported legislation disconnected from Afghan society, in the late 2000s, the main actors in the intervention tried to legislate in more restrained ways. The criminal law reform working group sponsored by the United Nations Office on Drugs and Crime (UNODC) and the US State Department brought together Afghan and international lawyers, members of various Afghan institutions, and major donors. The working group embarked on a review of ad hoc legislation, including the Interim Code of Criminal Procedure, the poster child for failed legal transplants. Revising it took a year's work: for the first time, Persian replaced English as a working language and Afghan lawyers and parliamentarians participated in the editorial process.[30] However, with the fighting intensifying and under pressure from

[27] Michael Hartmann and Agnieszka Klonowiecka-Milart, 'Lost in Translation: Legal Transplants without Consensus-based Adaptation' in Whit Mason (ed.), *The Rule of Law in Afghanistan: Missing in Inaction*, Cambridge, Cambridge University Press, 2011, p. 274; Salima Ahmadi, '2015 Performance of the Wolesi Jirga: Low Attendance, Nominal Oversight', *Afghan Analyst Network*, 2016, www.afghanistan-analysts.org/en/reports/political-landscape/2015-performance-of-the-wolesi-jirga-low-attendance-nominal-oversight/.

[28] Ali Wardak, Daud Saba, and Halima Kazem, *Afghanistan Human Development Report. Bridging Modernity and Tradition: Rule of Law and the Search for Justice*, Kabul, Center for Policy and Human Development, 2007, p. 87.

[29] Torunn Wimpelmann, *The Pitfalls of Protection: Gender, Violence, and Power in Afghanistan*, Berkeley, University of California Press, 2017, p. 73.

[30] Michael Hartmann and Agnieszka Klonowiecka-Milart, 'Lost in Translation: Legal Transplants without Consensus-based Adaptation' in Whit Mason (ed.), *The Rule of Law in Afghanistan: Missing in Inaction*, Cambridge, Cambridge University Press, 2011, pp. 293–7.

international donors, the experiment, which suffered from the reputation of being too slow and too costly, was not repeated. In any event, President Karzai blocked the revised Code of Criminal Procedure. Lacking legitimacy, he was by that time playing an ambiguous game, arousing nationalist sentiments against the foreign presence while simultaneously presenting himself to the donors as the indispensable intermediary.

A judicial system undermined by nepotism

The judicial system that the Islamic Republic and its international sponsors were installing was not only inaccessible to the rural population but also undermined by nepotism and incapable of enforcing its verdicts. In principle, the 2004 Constitution and the 2005 Law on the Organization and Authority of the Courts provided for the establishment of an independent judicial system, largely inspired by the pre-war one.[31] The judicial system therefore consisted of trial courts (Mahakim-i Ibtidaia), whose jurisdiction spanned a district, courts of appeal (Mahakim-i Istinaf) located in provincial capitals, and a Supreme Court (Stara Mahkama). Seating a president and eight judges, the latter served as both a court of last resort and the ultimate administrative authority for all judicial personnel below it. The appeals courts amended, approved, or overturned rulings by trial judges. Judges had to have a law degree or a degree in Islamic law and to have completed practical training.

However, in practice, the establishment of this new judicial system depended on Western donors, who initially neglected it. Between 2003 and 2005, 3 per cent of reconstruction funds went to justice, while 60 per cent were spent on the army and 6 per cent on demining.[32] USAID's funding for justice between 2002 and 2007 represented a mere 1 per cent of its budget for the country.[33] Italy was appointed 'lead country' in the judicial sector despite its lack of Afghanistan expertise or experience with legal reform in Muslim countries. Italy initially interpreted the role of 'lead country', which was nowhere explicitly defined, as a simple task of coordinating international assistance. In late 2002, the subcontractor of the Italian aid agency, the International Development Law Organization (IDLO), had only one full-time envoy for Afghanistan and produced zero results. Facing a storm of criticism, IDLO hastily organized a donor

[31] Matteo Tondini, *Statebuilding and Justice Reform: Post-Conflict Reconstruction in Afghanistan*, London, Routledge, 2010, pp. 51–4.

[32] *Reforming Afghanistan's Police*, Brussels, International Crisis Group, 2007, p. 6.

[33] Ibid., pp. 11–12.

conference and a two-day seminar for judges, prosecutors, and members of the Judicial Reform Commission.[34]

In 2003, a highly critical report published by the International Crisis Group forced Italy to become more actively involved with legal reform programmes, financial support for the new Ministry of Justice, and the establishment of a legal training centre. At the same time, other countries involved themselves in the reconstruction of the judicial system without coordinating with one another: the German development agency GTZ did so by producing a study assessing the needs of the legal sector and offering assistance from the Max Planck Society; the United Nations Development Program (UNDP) pitched in by developing its own roadmap for rebuilding the judicial sector; the United Nations Office on Drugs and Crime (UNODC) and the US and British embassies each also launched their separate initiatives. Between 2003 and 2005, a series of reports denounced the ineffectiveness of Western programmes, the drastic lack of infrastructure and training, and the impunity of local commanders in rural areas.[35] In 2007, almost a quarter of the 1,400 judges existed on paper only, 45 per cent of those on the bench did not have the required law degree, and nearly 60 per cent did not complete the practical training prior to their appointment. In addition, 57 per cent of court still lacked buildings and 40 per cent were in need of significant restoration: most trial courts outside provincial capitals were inoperative.[36]

If the judicial system was neglected until quite late in the war, it is worth noting by contrast the considerable attention paid by the actors of the intervention to transitional justice. For example, as of June 2002, a specialized institution, the Afghan Independent Human Rights Commission (AIHRC), was given the mandate to conduct national consultations and to identify war crimes committed since 1978. Human Rights Watch and the United Nations Office of the High Commissioner for Human Rights were simultaneously writing their reports on the same subject. However, in response to the publication of the Human Rights Watch report,[37] Parliament, with a majority of the seated representatives being ex-members of armed groups in the 1980s and 1990s, passed a law in 2007 conferring immunity on all Afghans involved in previous decades

[34] *Afghanistan: Judicial Reform and Transitional Justice*, Brussels, International Crisis Group, 2003, p. 8.

[35] Ibid.; Amnesty International, *Afghanistan: Re-establishing the Rule of Law*, London, Amnesty International, 2003.

[36] Ali Wardak, Daud Saba, and Halima Kazem, *Afghanistan Human Development Report. Bridging Modernity and Tradition: Rule of Law and the Search for Justice*, Kabul, Center for Policy and Human Development, 2007, pp. 70–1.

[37] *Afghanistan: Blood-Stained Hands*, New York, Human Rights Watch, 2005.

of conflict.[38] Similarly, the report of the Office of the High Commissioner for Human Rights, completed in 2005, was never officially issued, even after its release in 2010.[39] Finally, after several years of blocking the more than 800-page report produced by AIHRC, President Karzai in 2009 terminated the action plan for transitional justice.[40] Since the Bonn Agreement of 2001 and the emergency Loya Jirga of 2002, individuals responsible for war crimes in the 1980s and 1990s had been among the main interlocutors of the United States and the United Nations. Moreover, the fight against Al Qaeda continued to have priority for Washington, and in hunting down its militants, the US military relied on these same commanders, stymieing behind the scenes any moves that could have led to their indictment.[41]

In the late 2000s, with the insurgency and its parallel administration on the advance, the United States took over the reform of the judicial system. In 2008, it allocated $92 million to 'establishment of the rule of law' activities, as much as for the entire 2002–7 period.[42] The United States alone spent nearly $1 billion on the judicial sector between 2008 and 2014.[43] This resulted in a spectacular upgrade to the system: courts were built in all district capitals, salaries multiplied tenfold, and thousands of staff were trained. However, the effectiveness of successive US programmes was limited, as the various agencies involved worked independently and outsourced most tasks to US private companies, including to the development heavyweights Checchi and Company Consulting and Pacific Architects and Engineers. As a former US Ambassador to Afghanistan, Ronald Neumann (2005–7), admitted:

> Our own plunge into judicial assistance was chaotic. USAID ran some programs through contractors. State (Department) had its own contracts but was also paying for several experienced prosecutors on loan from the Department of Justice who often seemed to operate independently. The U.S. military was funding some work on its own, but neither we nor they

[38] Amin Tarzi, 'Afghanistan: Amnesty Bill Places Karzai In Dilemma', *RFE/RL*, 23 February 2007.
[39] Thomas Ruttig, *No Nobel Price (yet) for Sima Samar*, 2010, www.afghanistan-analysts.org/en/reports/rights-freedom/no-nobel-price-yet-for-sima-samar/.
[40] 'Justice Action Plan Heading for Oblivion', *IRIN*, 14 April 2010.
[41] Francesc Vendrell, 'The International Community's Failures in Afghanistan' in Whit Mason (ed.), *The Rule of Law in Afghanistan: Missing in Inaction*, Cambridge, Cambridge University Press, 2011, p. 54.
[42] Matteo Tondini, *Statebuilding and Justice Reform: Post-Conflict Reconstruction in Afghanistan*, London, Routledge, 2010, p. 84.
[43] *Rule of Law in Afghanistan*, Washington, Special Inspector General for Afghanistan Reconstruction, 2015, p. 7.

knew what the other was doing. Coordination among our elements was weak and relations were strained.[44]

Outsourcing posed problems in the judiciary identical to those that plagued other sectors: collusion, turnover of foreign experts, mismanagement, lack of coordination, and lack of independent evaluations.[45] With no coherent vision for and knowledge of the Afghan system, subcontractors were unable to spend their budgets and complete the tasks for which they were hired.[46] For example, USAID outsourced the training of thousands of judicial agents to Checchi and Company Consulting; this consisted of two- to four-week seminars at the conclusion of which they handed out certificates without a final examination. The consultants who taught the courses would fly in, stay a few days, pay no attention to local legal and political developments, and, in some cases, were not trained in the law.[47] For example, a constitutional law professor at a major American university explained to me in 2010 that he and his colleagues were invited by Checchi and Company Consulting to stints in-country lasting a few days, for which they received tens of thousands of dollars and were housed in the Serena Hotel (the most luxurious palace in Kabul) for the sole purpose of holding a seminar for Afghan judges. He admitted being unfamiliar with the Afghan legal system and therefore taught them American constitutional law.[48] A former US State Department employee was recruited by Adam Smith International to review the Afghan Ministry of Justice procedures, an area in which she admitted to me that she lacked expertise.[49] Such practices were widespread, leading the Attorney General, Abdul Jabar Sabit, to remonstrate with a United Nations executive: 'I will not have my prosecutors taught their criminal procedure and penal codes by lawyers from Australia and Argentina who fly in for six weeks and then fly out.'[50] In 2010, the International Crisis Group denounced the fact that 'judicial institutions have withered to near

[44] Ronald E. Neumann, *The Other War: Winning and Losing in Afghanistan*, Lincoln, Potomac Books, 2011, pp. 95–6.

[45] When the Special Inspector General for Afghanistan Reconstruction (SIGAR), the US government's dedicated oversight authority, conducted an audit of development programmes in the justice sector in 2015, the agencies concerned were unable to document a large part of their expenditures, and half of the programmes had never been subject to independent monitoring. *Rule of Law in Afghanistan*, Washington, Special Inspector General for Afghanistan Reconstruction, 2015, pp. 10–11.

[46] *Support for Afghanistan's Justice Sector*, Washington, Special Inspector General for Afghanistan Reconstruction, 2014.

[47] *Reforming Afghanistan's Broken Judiciary*, Brussels, International Crisis Group, 2010, pp. 10–11.

[48] E-15, professor of constitutional law, consultant for Checchi and Company Consulting, July 2010.

[49] E-49, consultant for Adam Smith International, attached to Ministry of Justice, September 2012.

[50] Michael Hartmann and Agnieszka Klonowiecka-Milart, 'Lost in Translation: Legal Transplants without Consensus-based Adaptation' in Whit Mason (ed.), *The Rule of Law in Afghanistan: Missing in Inaction*, Cambridge, Cambridge University Press, 2011, p. 278.

non-existence', destroyed by the lack of qualified personnel, extortion, lack of resources, and confused functioning.[51] The judges were still underqualified, as illustrated by a case reported to me that same year by a resident of Laghman province: 'The current judge of Mihtarlam is the brother of Judge Jawar. His name is Judge Sharazi. Previously, he worked in a hospital and had no legal training. Judge Sharazi is just a judge's brother, he is not a real judge.'[52]

These shortcomings put the judicial system out of reach of the majority of the population and benefited those who could afford to bribe judges to advance their cases.[53] Absent from the countryside, favouring the powerful, unable to enforce their verdicts, the courts served more to legalize situations of fact than to settle disputes. First, the regime's courts never really became accessible to rural residents. In the early years, inaccessibility was due to a lack of resources, but even with the considerable boost in funding of the late 2000s, the expansion of the judicial system in rural areas was hampered by the Taliban's advance. For example, the Supreme Court's director of human resources estimated in 2010 that 69 of the 364 courts were closed due to insurgency operations—most likely an underestimate. Out of a theoretical complement of ninety judges, only twelve were active in Kandahar province and these were confined to holding court in the city, away from their assigned districts. In Wardak province, a few dozen kilometres from Kabul, half of the courts were shuttered and judicial staff also retreated to the provincial capital of Maidan Shahr in 2009 after two judges and two prosecutors were kidnapped by the Taliban.[54] In Paktya, in 2014, only three judges were posted for fourteen districts.[55] In Kunar, a resident explained: 'Judges never leave Asadabad, the Chaghan checkpoint [at the city limits] for them is like a boundary.'[56] Another resident of this province confirmed to me that the judicial services of his district (Ghaziabad) were now concentrated in the provincial capital, Asadabad. Some judges had even taken refuge outside the province, in Kabul or Jalalabad.[57] As a result, the only alternative for people was to make the long, costly, and often dangerous journey to provincial capitals, or even further afield. Moreover, as the insurgency gradually deployed its own judges, it kept inhabitants of the regions under its control from resorting to regime courts.

[51] *Reforming Afghanistan's Broken Judiciary*, Brussels, International Crisis Group, 2010.
[52] E-57, veterinarian in Laghman province, April 2011.
[53] Antonio De Lauri, 'Access to Justice and Human Rights in Afghanistan', *Crime, Law and Social Change*, 2013, vol. 60, n° 3, pp. 261–85.
[54] *Reforming Afghanistan's Broken Judiciary*, Brussels, International Crisis Group, 2010, p. 18.
[55] E-64, Afghan analyst for UNAMA, specializing in Paktya province, September 2014.
[56] E-37, resident of Kunar province, July 2011.
[57] E-6, resident of Ghaziabad district (Kunar), July 2011.

> Everyone feels threatened by the Taliban in Said Abad district if we secretly go to the Afghan government court. If Taliban capture someone with a document from an Afghan government court, the Taliban give a very severe punishment. Here, no one even tries to go to Afghan government court in Maidan Shar.[58]

Secondly, obtaining a favourable decision in the regime's courts was conditioned by the economic and social resources of the parties involved. The majority of Afghans who used the judicial system told of having to bribe their way in and, even then, only a small minority (10–20 per cent, depending on the year) expressed confidence that they would prevail in a dispute.[59] The entire system was undermined by corruption and nepotism, with the going rates, from the basic policeman to the Supreme Court judge, common knowledge.[60] The judges enjoyed pervasive impunity, despite the successive anti-corruption bodies created under pressure from donors. Since their inception, they had only handed down a few convictions—and their staff members themselves were guilty of graft. For example, in 2009, it surfaced that 90 per cent of the anti-corruption unit's prosecutors had been bribed.[61] The nepotism of the judicial system aggravated land and matrimonial conflicts that became bogged down in the various jurisdictions, with judgments that often depended on money or relationships mobilized by each of the parties. It was not uncommon for a judge or a simple court clerk to delay a case for months or even years to extort money from the parties at trial. For example, a woman who was seeking a divorce for her daughter who was suffering abuse by her husband recounted:

> First I went to the [court of] the government in Mohamad Agha district and I wanted to resolve this matter with the government. But the court judge demanded 100,000 afghanis [$2,000] and said: 'I will try to release your daughter through a divorce.' After this, I agreed and mortgaged my property

[58] I-32, resident of Sayid Abad district (Wardak), 2011.

[59] In this regard, the various surveys show surprisingly similar and stable results until 2015. See the Afghanistan profile on Transparency International's website, the annual surveys conducted by the Asia Foundation, and the regular reports of Integrity Watch Afghanistan, especially Yama Torabi, *Afghan Perceptions and Experiences of Corruption: A National Survey*, Kabul, Integrity Watch Afghanistan, 2010. For an analysis of how judges talk about corruption, see Antonio De Lauri, 'Corruption, Legal Modernisation and Judicial Practice in Afghanistan', *Asian Studies Review*, 2013, vol. 37, n° 4, pp. 527–45.

[60] For testimonies collected by NGOs on this question, see Yama Torabi, *Afghan Perceptions and Experiences of Corruption: A National Survey*, Kabul, Integrity Watch Afghanistan, 2010; Manija Gardizi, Karen Hussmann, and Yama Torabi, *Corrupting the State or State-Crafted Corruption?*, Kabul, Afghanistan Research and Evaluation Unit, 2010.

[61] *Reforming Afghanistan's Broken Judiciary*, Brussels, International Crisis Group, 2010, p. 26.

> and gave the sum to the judge. I started this case in 2010 and it dragged on for a year, but the judge did not want to finish our case. The person we had problems with gave more money to the judge and he decided the case in favor of the opposite party. The judge said: 'your daughter is not being mistreated.'[62]

The simplest procedures, such as registering the transfer of a parcel of land in court, could cost hundreds or even thousands of dollars in commissions.[63] In 2012, a man told me that he paid the judge and the chief of police a third of the value of 30 hectares of disputed land to have it recognized as his property.[64] In the same year, an Afghan female journalist secretly recorded a judge to whom she had brought her case. As she pleaded for a divorce, the judge, after unsuccessfully trying to extract $2,000 from her, asked for her hand in exchange for a legal ruling in her favour.[65] The parties in court cases had to pay large sums or use highly placed persons to move the proceedings along and to obtain a favourable verdict.[66] This benefited political entrepreneurs who wielded significant economic, social, and coercive resources.

Moreover, procedures were rarely followed, as a senior official of the Ministry of Justice explained:

> In most cases, court sessions aren't held. Instead a group of judges sit together in a room. There is no defense lawyer there. There is no prosecutor there. The defendant is rarely allowed to participate. If the family members of the accused are there, they are barred from speaking. When we ask these judges why they are conducting court this way they say: 'We called the prosecutor. We called the defense lawyer. But we couldn't reach them'. Or they say, 'The prosecutor has done his job and we know what our job is so we don't need him there' ... The problem is that our judges and prosecutors believe they personally are the highest authority in the land, not the law, and they abuse the law as a result of this thinking.[67]

[62] I-38, interview with a female resident of Mohamad Agha district (Logar), 2013.

[63] For an example, see Livingston Armytage, 'Justice in Afghanistan: Rebuilding Judicial Competence after the Generation of War', *Heidelberg Journal of International Law*, 2007, vol. 67, p. 198.

[64] E-34, landowner in Kunduz province, September 2012.

[65] Emal Pasarly, 'Afghan Judge Zahorudin Recorded on Tape Seeking Bribe', *BBC News*, 12 December 2012.

[66] For cases, see Martina Van Biljert, *Stories People Tell (1): An Attempted Land Grab, a Fabricated Case and an Expensive Release*, 2011, www.afghanistan-analysts.org/en/reports/political-landscape/stories-people-tell-1-an-attempted-land-grab-a-fabricated-case-and-an-expensive-release/; Bilal Sarwary, 'Why Many Afghans Opt for Taliban Justice', *BBC News*, 2 December 2013.

[67] Quoted in *Reforming Afghanistan's Broken Judiciary*, Brussels, International Crisis Group, 2010, p. 17.

Lack of due process and the possibility of overturning the trial by overbidding resulted in an appeals rate of 80 per cent from trial courts to courts of appeal and 70 per cent from appeals courts to the Supreme Court.[68] Many lawsuits in practice resembled auctions between the parties, with the amounts paid sometimes exceeding the value of the object being litigated, especially when something of special symbolic value, such as land or marital relations, was at stake.[69] Sometimes, judges mobilized the legal pluralism between positive law, Islamic jurisprudence, and tribal custom to avoid ruling.[70] This translated into trials that could drag on for years, if not decades, accompanied by rising tensions and violence around festering disputes.

Finally, because of the weakness and corruption of the police, judges lacked the means of enforcing their verdicts. As early as 2001, many local Northern Alliance cadres assumed the title of chief of the district police and incorporated their men into it, which allowed them to keep their weapons in spite of the disarmament policy. The commanders of the Shura-i Nazar seized key executive positions in the new Ministry of the Interior, leaving the technical positions to the former policemen from the Communist era. From then on, they would maintain control over successive reforms.[71] The police quickly established themselves as the most corrupt institution in Afghanistan. 'Forget about the Taliban. Our biggest problems are with the police', explained a truck driver in 2007.[72] Diversion of funds allocated to salaries and equipment was commonplace, and police were systematically involved in drug trafficking, extortion, and kidnapping.[73] The collusion between the police and the entrepreneurs of violence provided them with impunity in the (rare) cases when a judge went after them. A judge in Nangarhar, speaking on condition of anonymity, described how he was threatened and forced to change his verdict:

[68] Livingston Armytage, 'Justice in Afghanistan: Rebuilding Judicial Competence after the Generation of War', *Heidelberg Journal of International Law*, 2007, vol. 67, p. 188.

[69] These problems concern civil disputes in the first place, but also criminal justice trials. For a case of gross manipulation of a trial resulting in the death sentence of the two accused, see Frank Ledwidge, 'Justice in Helmand: The Challenge of Law Reform in a Society at War', *Asian Affairs*, 2009, vol. 40, n° 1, pp. 80–4.

[70] Antonio De Lauri, 'Between Law and Customs: Normative Interconnections in Kabul's Tribunals', *Diogenes*, 2015, vol. 60, n° 3–4, p. 52ff.

[71] *Reforming Afghanistan's Police*, Brussels, International Crisis Group, 2007.

[72] Chris Sands, 'Afghan Truck Drivers Quiver from Lawlessness, not Taliban', *San Francisco Chronicle*, 28 May 2007. A report by the Integrity Watch Afghanistan NGO deals at length with this problem. *On Afghanistan's Roads: Extortion and Abuse against Drivers*, Kabul, Integrity Watch Afghanistan, 2013.

[73] *Policing in Afghanistan: Still Searching for a Strategy*, Brussels, International Crisis Group, 2008; Andrew Wilder, *Cops or Robbers? The Struggle to Reform the Afghan National Police*, Kabul, Afghanistan Research and Evaluation Unit, 2007.

> One day, I made a decision against the interests of a powerful man in the district. When I announced the decision, the man who lost the case asked me how could I go safely home now? As I am not from this area and have no one to protect me, I was very frightened; I had to change my decision.[74]

The United States rebuilt the police as a paramilitary force, not civilian law enforcement, so they could deploy it against the Taliban insurgency. Indeed, in 2003, the State Department and the US military trained police officers in parallel with Germany, which was supposed to be the 'lead country' for this dossier. The United States blamed Berlin for its slow pace and exclusive focus on the senior ranks. Because of its financial investment, the US military's views prevailed: criminal and investigative functions were discontinued in favour of militarizing the police (with Kalashnikovs, machine guns, military vehicles, and combat training).[75] In addition, as in other sectors, the Pentagon outsourced the training to private companies. In the mid-2000s, the salary cost of the 500 DynCorp trainers, each paid more than $100,000 a year, exceeded the total salaries of Afghanistan's 62,000 police officers.[76] Concurrently, Western troops deployed in the provinces pursued their own initiatives in training local police officers, or even raising more or less legal local militias but with police powers (see Chapter 4).

Selective passivity and violent accumulation

The selective passivity practised by the courts was a key element in the laissez-faire system that allowed strongmen to appropriate the country's resources through violence.

Since its formation in 2002, the judicial system had been undermined by dependence on various Afghan and international actors. In the first months of the intervention, the reconstruction of the judicial system became the stakes in a competition between the different political movements that emerged out of the preceding civil war. The Judicial Commission set up in May 2002 to coordinate the rebuilding of the judicial system was paralysed by conflicts between

74 Quoted in Ali Wardak, Daud Saba, and Halima Kazem, *Afghanistan Human Development Report. Bridging Modernity and Tradition: Rule of Law and the Search for Justice*, Kabul, Center for Policy and Human Development, 2007, p. 72.

75 Cornelius Friesendorf and Jörg Krempel, *Militarized Versus Civilian Policing: Problems of Reforming the Afghan National Police*, Frankfurt, Peace Research Institute, 2011.

76 Andrew Wilder, *Cops or Robbers? The Struggle to Reform the Afghan National Police*, Kabul, Afghanistan Research and Evaluation Unit, 2007, pp. 34–5.

conservative Islamists on the one hand and reformers associated with exile circles in the West and international organizations on the other. Compounding the problem, the Shiite parties protested at being left out of the commission. It was dissolved in August 2002 and reconstituted in November as the Judicial Reform Commission. Analogously, in the early years, the main judicial functions were split along ethnic and partisan lines: the Attorney General was a Tajik linked to the Shura-i Nazar network, the Minister of Justice was an Uzbek, and the President of the Supreme Court was a Pashtun ulama close to Sayyaf. The powers of the main judicial administrations were also structured and spelled out subject to similar struggles along ethno-denominational lines. Pressure on judicial institutions did not just come from Afghan actors: in 2006, under the pretext of 'professionalizing' the Afghan judicial system, several European embassies pressured the executive to eliminate the most conservative judges on the Supreme Court, starting with its president.[77]

Hamid Karzai exploited the weakness of the judicial system to keep the regime's strongmen in line. As with the rest of Karzai's system of government, he used the appointment of judges and prosecutors to establish a clientele. In 2005, the President allowed the Minister of Transport, Enayatullah Qasimi, to escape prosecution by the Attorney General. The latter's refusal to drop the charges cost him his job.[78] His successor, Abdul Jabar Sabit, suffered a similar fate when he indicted Dostum for attacking his former deputy, Akbar Bai, in Kabul in February 2008.[79] Karzai vetoed Dostum's prosecution and, after rumours began circulating about Sabit as a potential presidential candidate in the coming elections, forced him to resign. His successor, Mohamad Ishaq Aloko, was careful to squelch any investigations into Dostum's war crimes and the corrupt affairs of other senior regime officials.[80] In 2010, Deputy Attorney General Fazel Ahmad Faqiryar was fired as he was about to indict several ministers, governors, and ambassadors.[81]

By regularly interfering in trials, Karzai protected his allies or made new ones who depended on him to block any moves to reopen their cases. Emblematic of the presidency's blatant clientelism was the case of five drug traffickers linked to Haji Din Mohamad, the ex-governor of Nangarhar, who were arrested in

77 Astri Suhrke, *When More is Less: The International Project in Afghanistan*, London, Hurst, 2011, p. 197.

78 Tanya Goudsouzian and Helena Malikyar, 'From Words to Deeds', *RFE/RL*, 18 November 2009.

79 Ron Synovitz, 'Afghanistan: Prosecutor Suggests "Some People" Cannot Be Tried', *RFE/RL*, 6 February 2008.

80 Greg Miller and Ernesto Londoño, 'U.S. Officials Say Karzai Aides Are Derailing Corruption Cases Involving Elite', *Washington Post*, 28 June 2010.

81 Dexter Filkins and Alissa J. Rubin, 'Graft-Fighting Prosecutor Fired in Afghanistan', *The New York Times*, 28 August 2010.

April 2009 with 60 kilos of heroin in their possession. Karzai ordered their release, thereby securing Haji Din Mohamad's support for his presidential campaign.[82] The president also weakened his opponents by putting pressure on them through the judicial system. For example, Ismael Khan, a strongman in the West, had been accused since 2004 of grabbing properties and land belonging to the state and the Majid Zabouli Foundation. Despite an administration delegation having concluded that this was indeed the case, the Afghan prosecutor's office took no action. In 2012, when Hamid Karzai sought to marginalize Ismael Khan, by then a minister, he had the complaint against him resurrected.[83]

The judicial system's inertia allowed the few to plunder the country's resources. Since the methods were essentially illegal and violent, it was in fact inaction by the executive with its control over the courts that enabled them to do so. Hamid Karzai thus made commanders beholden to him by letting them enrich themselves and squirrel away their fortunes in the Gulf States, India, Turkey, and the West. Unlike the model of the 'big men', who spent a significant portion of their economic capital to maintain their political position, the regime's strongmen used their political position to accumulate economic capital, producing an extraordinarily unequal society.[84]

This dynamic also tied in with the pervasive legal uncertainty, since even these violent entrepreneurs could not safeguard their ill-gotten gains at home, causing them to send them out of the country. In October 2009, Vice President Ahmad Zia Massoud was arrested by Dubai Customs with a suitcase containing $52 million in cash.[85] In 2011, capital outflows through Kabul airport amounted to nearly $4.6 billion, equal to the state budget or to nearly one-third of the country's annual income. It was not until the Kabul Bank scandal, caused by the embezzlement of $1 billion by Hamid Karzai's relatives, and significant pressure from Western donors, that, in 2012, the Central Bank imposed a limit of $20,000 on cash transported through Kabul airport—which barely hampered the continuing capital flight.[86]

[82] Sayed Salahuddin, 'Karzai Pardons Five Afghan Heroin Traffickers', *Reuters*, 9 July 2009.

[83] Abasin Zaheer, 'Minister, Mayor Accused of 22m USD Landgrab', *RAWA News*, 9 June 2012.

[84] For the original conceptualization of the 'big man', see Marshall D. Sahlins, 'Poor Man, Rich Man, Big-Man, Chief: Political Types in Melanesia and Polynesia', *Comparative Studies in Society and History*, 1963, vol. 5, n° 3, pp. 285–303. For contemporary uses in African political systems, see Jean-François Médard, 'Le "big man" en Afrique: esquisse d'analyse du politicien entrepreneur', *L'Année sociologique*, 1992, vol. 42, pp. 167–92; Mats Utas, *African Conflicts and Informal Power: Big Men and Networks*, London, Zed Books, 2012.

[85] Jonathan Steele and Jon Boone, 'WikiLeaks: Afghan Vice-President Landed in Dubai with $52m in Cash', *The Guardian*, 2 December 2010.

[86] Matthew Green, 'Afghanistan Acts to Curb Flight of Capital', *Financial Times*, 18 March 2012.

This predatory accumulation essentially took three forms: the diversion of public money and aid, drug trafficking, and land grabs. First, entrepreneurs of violence enriched themselves by systematically diverting state resources, that is, international aid. Commanders were widely described as 'warlords' in the 2000s.[87] This was a misnomer, as these violent entrepreneurs did not exploit the resources of their fiefdoms only to subsequently distribute them among their clients. Quite the contrary: Mohamad Fahim, Mohamad Mohaqiq, Ahmed Zia Massoud, Ismael Khan, Abdul Rashid Dostum, Mohamad Ata Nur, and Gul Agha Shirzai enriched themselves in a parasite logic, which required obtaining a position in the government to gain access to a whole range of income streams.

A pyramid-like system was set up with the corruption trickling down from the top of the hierarchy to the bottom. These strongmen drew up price lists for purchasing lower positions under their control, which for Vice-President Mohamad Fahim meant all appointed positions in the Northeast and for Vice-President Karim Khalili in the Hazarajat. For example, in 2011, to be appointed police chief in a northeastern district cost some tens of thousands of dollars payable to Mohamed Fahim, with the price rising to $100,000 for the lucrative Badakhshan districts that were conduits for heroin shipments.[88] Police chiefs would recoup their costs and more by taking a slice of their men's budgets and salaries; by getting paid to turn a blind eye to illegal activity, especially the production or transport of drugs; or by extorting money from the population. Further down the ladder, positions were also sold according to how much income they could generate. For ordinary Afghans, it resulted in daily harassment and uncertain treatment by police officers demanding money at each roadblock, the necessity of greasing palms for any administrative matter, medical care, or education—even for simply paying the electricity bill. In 2009, the United Nations estimated that the entire population paid about $2.5 billion a year in bribes, an amount equal to almost a quarter of GDP.[89]

Similarly, government ministries were stakes haggled over by the President and the heads of the major clientelist networks. Ministers could then appoint their clients to key positions in Kabul and the provinces, offering a variety of benefits, not the least of which was overseeing contracts related to international assistance from which they would divert a share into their own pockets. The

[87] Antonio Giustozzi, *Empires of Mud: War and Warlords of Afghanistan*, London, Hurst, 2009; Dipali Mukhopadhyay, *Warlords, Strongman Governors, and the State in Afghanistan*, Cambridge, Cambridge University Press, 2014.

[88] E-21, analyst at an Afghan think tank, July 2011.

[89] This estimate is based on an extrapolation from 7,600 interviews conducted across the country. Enrico Bisogno, Anna Alvazzi del Frate, and Philip Davis, *Corruption in Afghanistan: Bribery as Reported by the Victims*, Vienne, UNODC, 2010.

sovereign ministries (Interior, Defence, Intelligence) were a key part of this system: they could be used to circumvent disarmament programmes and thus allow men to be kept under arms. The governorships of the provinces with border posts—Balkh in the North, Nangarhar in the East, Kandahar in the South, and Herat in the West—were special prizes because they provided lucrative access to customs revenues. In 2004, to consolidate the power of his half-brother Ahmad Wali Karzai and move Gul Agha Shirzai out of Kandahar, Hamid Karzai offered Shirzai the governorship of Nangarhar where he could tap the revenues from the Torkham border crossing, which he then split with Karzai's Finance Minister, Omar Zakhilwal.[90]

Secondly, while the war against drugs was a priority for Western countries, and therefore of the Karzai administration, the regime strongmen who derived most of the income from trafficking were exempted from the repression. The President's half-brother and president of the provincial council of Kandahar, Ahmad Wali Karzai, was the main drug lord in the South directly involved with drug trafficking, as were many of his police commanders.[91] International attention largely focused on poppy growers[92] that the West believed were the source of the Taliban insurgency's income. However, according to UNODC's 2007 report on opium culture, 76 per cent of the $3.1 billion in export revenues came from processing and transporting heroin out of the country, and this was controlled by the regime's potentates.[93] The eradication campaigns carried out under pressure from the United States and the United Nations exclusively targeted farmers. They were coordinated locally by some of the major drug traffickers: Haji Din Mohamad for the 2004–5 drug trafficking campaign and Gul Agha Shirzai for the 2007–8 campaign, both in Nangarhar province. When the Kabul customs chief caused a stir in the press by arresting five or six heroin smugglers a week, Attorney General Abdul Jabar Sabit fired him in October 2006. His successor got the message and saw to it that arrests dropped precipitously.[94]

Finally, in a context of accelerated urbanization, land became a highly lucrative resource that commanders grabbed, having been given carte blanche by Hamid Karzai. Nearly thirty-four laws and decrees on land issues were passed

[90] E-28, expert for an Afghan anti-corruption NGO, September 2014.

[91] Scott Baldauf, 'Inside the Afghan Drug Trade', *Christian Science Monitor*, 13 June 2006.

[92] For analyses of farming families' livelihoods, see Adam Pain, 'Land, Power and Conflict in Afghanistan: Seeking to Understand Complexity', *Revue des mondes musulmans et de la Méditerranée*, 2013, n° 133, pp. 63–81; David Mansfield, *A State Built on Sand: How Opium Undermined Afghanistan*, Oxford, Oxford University Press, 2016.

[93] Jonathan Goodhand, 'Corrupting or Consolidating the Peace? The Drugs Economy and Post-conflict Peacebuilding in Afghanistan', *International Peacekeeping*, 2008, vol. 15, n° 3, p. 410.

[94] Arthur Kent, 'Covering up Karzai & Co.', *Policy Options*, 1 July 2007.

and amended between 2002 and 2012 but not enforced by the administration.[95] The regime's inertia was all the more consequential because the 2002 decree put the state in de facto or *de jure* possession of 80 per cent of the country's surface area, including all land without registered claims. Many parcels converted to housing, cultivated by farmers, or used communally as pastures were legally the property of the state because of pre-existing land legislation, successive land reforms, and the landowners' lack of title documents. Karzai turned a blind eye to illegal land grabs by violent entrepreneurs and to their mobilizing contacts inside the administration to help carry these out.

In the eyes of many Kabulis, the villa district of Shirpur symbolized this systemic corruption. An Army-owned piece of land, it was subdivided into parcels by the Minister of Defence, former Vice-President and head of the Northern Alliance, Mohamad Fahim, and divvied up among the commanders, ministers, and the mayor of Kabul. The police evicted the 250 people living on it who had settled there as displaced persons in the 1990s. When the UN Special Rapporteur on Housing and Land Rights, Miloon Kothari, protested and called for the resignation of the ministers involved, it earned him a reprimand from his boss, the United Nations Special Representative for Afghanistan, Lakhdar Brahimi. Karzai's government denied any involvement and convened a commission whose report would never see the light of day. He sacked the Kabul police chief who led the eviction, only to secretly appoint him as police chief in Wardak. His replacement, General Baba Jan, was one of twenty-nine beneficiaries of the land distribution. A few years later, the villas with Greek colonnades that had sprouted up on the land were leased to international organizations for tens of thousands of dollars a month.[96]

This scenario was replayed in other major cities. In Kandahar, Hamid Karzai's half-brother and brother took over state-owned land to develop the Aino Mina neighbourhood with $3 million in funding from the Overseas Private Investment Corporation, a US development agency that channels private capital to advance US interests abroad.[97] In 2010, a local official gave me a tour of that still expanding gated community:

[95] For a list, see Liz Alden Wily, *Land, People, and the State in Afghanistan*, Kabul, Afghanistan Research and Evaluation Unit, 2013, pp. 41–2.

[96] Joanna Nathan, *Land Grab in Sherpur: Monuments to Powerlessness, Impunity, and Inaction*, 9 April 2012, www.mei.edu/publications/land-grab-sherpur-monuments-powerlessness-impunity-and-inaction.

[97] James Palmer, 'For Sale: Luxury Villa in Afghanistan with Balcony, Pool and Taliban Death Threat', *The Guardian*, 11 September 2008.

> The city was created by Ahmad Wali Karzai and Mahmud Karzai [the president's half-brother and brother]. […] The district is guarded at both gates by the security forces of Mahmud Karzai, the land belongs to him, around 1,000 *jaribs* [200 hectares] […]. There are shops, schools and a hospital as big as Karachi's Aga Khan Hospital in the planning stage. The land was worth $1,600 per *biswa* [100 m^2] a few years ago and is worth at least $10,000 per *biswa* now, to which must be added the houses. 800 houses have been built so far, another tranche is planned.[98]

This predation system also impacted the countryside. In Kunar, for example, Jahan Dad and Malik Zarin brazenly took over state-owned buildings and land when the Taliban fled in 2002. They later became two of the main intermediaries in the province for the US Army.[99] A 2014 report by the government's anti-corruption commission tallied 1.2 million *jaribs* (240,000 hectares) as having been seized throughout the country.[100]

Political entrepreneurs took advantage of the inflation in land prices linked to the rapid urbanization that was fed by a population explosion, a rural exodus, and the return of nearly six million refugees from Iran, Pakistan, and, marginally, from the United States and Europe. Between 2001 and 2015, the population of Afghanistan doubled from 15 million to more than 30 million.[101] On their return to Afghanistan, the millions of refugees often resettled in major cities, which were the safest areas after 2001, while the fighting flared up again in the countryside. Kabul's population exploded from a few hundred thousand in 2002 to nearly five million in 2014. Similarly, Herat, Jalalabad, Mazar-i Sharif, and Kandahar swelled with more than a million inhabitants each.

Afghanistan gradually became a country with a majority urban population, far from the rural image that still attaches to it.[102] Across the country, residential development gradually nibbled away at farmland, whose prices soared under the impact of population growth and the inflow of money from outside. Thus, around the city of Jalalabad, the Ministry of Agriculture in 2009 leased

[98] E-54, local administration official in Kandahar province, July 2011.

[99] Adam Baczko, 'Legal Rule and Tribal Politics: The US Army and the Taliban in Afghanistan (2001–13)', *Development and Change*, 2016, vol. 47, n° 6, pp. 1412–33.

[100] *Report of the Public Inquiry into Land Usurpation*, Kabul, Independent Joint Anti-Corruption Monitoring and Evaluation Committee, 2014, p. 9.

[101] In the absence of a census since 1979, the only demographic statistics available, produced by the Afghan statistical agency, the World Bank, and the United Nations, are approximations.

[102] The available statistics on cities are particularly problematic because they are based on outdated administrative limits, while cities have widely encroached on rural districts. The Afghan statistical agency estimated the number of urban dwellers at 6.7 million, or about a quarter of the population. Yet the country's five largest cities alone had 10 million residents, plus millions of residents in cities such as Khost, Taloqan, Kunduz, and Ghazni.

several thousand hectares of cultivated land to a few private entrepreneurs for ninety years. They subdivided the land into residential parcels and illegally sold them to developers, who in turn deeded them to private individuals. In this area, cultivated land yielded 2,400 dollars per *jarib* (2,000 m^2), while these parcels sold for around $30–40,000 dollars per *jarib*.[103] Near Kabul, in 2014, 'under the Taliban, a *jarib* of land in Bagram was worth $500, now you have to pay $70,000 for it.'[104] In and around the major cities, particularly lucrative block- or even neighbourhood-sized privately developed real estate projects sprouted. This construction boom inflated a real estate market bubble in Kabul's central neighbourhoods filled with the offices of foreign organizations and populated by their expatriate workers. At its height in 2012, the price of a *jarib* in the capital's central districts of Qala-i Fatullah and Wazir Akbar Khan, which had been a mere $60–80,000 in 2001, had reached respectively $1.2 million and $1.8 million.[105]

[103] Fabrizio Foschini, *Land Grabs in Afghanistan (1): Nangrahar, the Disputed O-Rangeland*, 2012, www.afghanistan-analysts.org/en/reports/economy-development-environment/land-grabs-in-afghanistan-1-nangrahar-the-disputed-o-rangeland/.

[104] E-25, head of an Afghan NGO in Kabul, September 2014.

[105] Nick Miszak and Alessandro Monsutti, 'Landscapes of Power: Local Struggles and National Stakes at the Rural-Urban Fringe of Kabul, Afghanistan', *The Journal of Peasant Studies*, 2014, vol. 41, n° 2, pp. 183–98.

4

The US Army

Reinventing the tribe, circumventing the courts

Introduction

The Western armed forces, particularly the US Army, systematically circumvented the official legal system, relying instead on strongmen and promoting bodies they called 'tribal'. In a seemingly paradoxical way, the United States and European countries were weakening with one hand what they propped up with the other. This contradiction between *state-building* and state circumvention was conspicuously based on two very different visions of governing: on the one hand, propping up the new regime responded to a logic of institutional engineering, the construction *ex nihilo* of political and legal institutions; on the other hand, the Western militaries installed a governmentality based on reinventing the tribe, an essentialist vision of an unchanged, immutable society, reliance on which they viewed as pragmatically essential for winning the war. This contradiction emerged from the sharp cleavage in American objectives as soon as hostilities began. The intervention in Afghanistan, launched to eliminate Al Qaeda and all its allies following the 9/11 attacks, was also justified by the defence of human rights, by the need to liberate Afghan women from Taliban oppression, and to export the democratic model.

The bypassing of the state by the US military was justified by an 'imaginary anthropology' which also was shared by other actors of the intervention.[1] On the eve of his appointment in 2009 as commander of the International Security Assistance Force (ISAF), General Stanley McCrystal could thus declare the following:

> An isolating geography and a natural aversion to foreign intervention further works against ISAF. Historical grievances reinforce connections to tribal or ethnic identity and can diminish the appeal of a centralized state. All

[1] Gilles Dorronsoro, *Le gouvernement transnational en Afghanistan. Une si prévisible défaite*, Paris, Karthala, 2021.

The Taliban Courts in Afghanistan. Adam Baczko, Oxford University Press. © Adam Baczko 2023.
DOI: 10.1093/oso/9780198896777.003.0005

> ethnicities, particularly the Pashtuns, have traditionally sought a degree of independence from the central government, particularly when it is not seen as acting in the best interests of the population. These and other factors result in elements of the population tolerating the insurgency and calling to push out foreigners.[2]

Some US Army men were blunter. In *One Tribe at a Time*, a book that two successive ISAF commanders, Stanley McCrystal and David Petraeus, recommended as a must-read to their officers, Major Jim Gant promoted a strategy of alliance with the 'tribes' against the 'terrorists':

> The central cultural fact about Afghanistan is that it is constituted of tribes. Not individuals, not Western-style citizens—but tribes and tribesmen. It is my deep belief—and the thesis of this paper—that the answer to the problems that face the Afghan people, as well as other future threats to US security in the region, will be found in understanding and then helping the tribal system of Afghanistan to flourish. [...] When one says the 'Afghan people' what I believe they are really saying is 'tribal member'. Every single Afghan is a part of a tribe and understands how the tribe operates and why. [...] Afghanistan has never had a strong central government and never will. That is a fact that we need to accept, sooner rather than later.[3]

More broadly, Jim Gant's book, which he based on his experience leading the US Special Forces in Kunar province in 2003, offers a stereotypical view of the population, mixing essentialism and caricature. Afghans were compared to Native Americans: his unit named its base 'Fort Navajo', and Jim Gant nicknamed an influential notable 'Sitting Bull'. In a similar vein, General David Petraeus declared in 2008, two years before taking over as head of ISAF: 'This is a country in which support of the tribes, of the local communities, for the overall effort is essential. It is a country that has not had a tradition of central government extending into the far reaches of its provinces and its districts.'[4]

Afghanistan was believed to have never existed as a state, and the Afghans were thought to be a primarily tribal people who zealously guarded their

[2] Stanley McCrystal, *COMISAF Initial Assessment (Unclassified)*, Washington, US Department of Defense, 2009.

[3] Jim Gant, *One Tribe at a Time: A Strategy for Success in Afghanistan*, Los Angeles, Nine Sisters Imports, 2009, pp. 8, 10.

[4] Roberto González, *Militarizing Culture: Essays on the Warfare State*, Walnut Creek, Left Coast Press, 2010, p. 154.

independence and had for centuries resisted all attempts at modernization. In an abundant literature amalgamating social sciences and strategy, the country was invariably characterized as an 'ungoverned space',[5] a 'graveyard of empires',[6] and thus always relegated to eternal otherness.[7] This reading of Afghanistan draws on the colonial and post-colonial era anthropology of Pashtun tribes across the border in Pakistan.[8] The observations of British colonial agents at the end of the nineteenth century largely shaped this vision of Afghanistan, which has since been dusted off even in social science books.[9] Following the dismemberment of the British Raj, Fredrik Barth, Akbar Ahmed, Louis Dupree, and Charles Lindholm, all anthropologists who worked on both sides of the Afghan-Pakistan border between the 1950s and 1970s, described a society that governed itself without the state, an 'ordered anarchy' as Lindholm phrased it.[10] Thomas Barfield, an American anthropologist specializing in Afghanistan and widely listened to in American military circles, called for using tribes to administer the country in a paper that opened with these words: 'The view from Kabul is often received with suspicion by rural Afghans. Rather than seeing themselves as part of a single nation with common interests, their primary allegiance is to local solidarity groups based on kinship or locality.'[11]

Hovering between idealized tribal democracy and Hobbesian dystopia, these primordialist interpretations ignored the state that had begun forming in the late nineteenth century.[12] Recent work by historians, anthropologists, and

[5] Anne Clunan and Harold A. Trinkunas, *Ungoverned Spaces: Alternatives to State Authority in an Era of Softened Sovereignty*, Stanford, Stanford University Press, 2010.

[6] Seth Jones, *In the Graveyard of Empires: America's War in Afghanistan*, New York, W. W. Norton & Company, 2010.

[7] Whit Mason, 'Introduction' in Whit Mason (ed.), *The Rule of Law in Afghanistan: Missing in Inaction*, Cambridge, Cambridge University Press, 2011, pp. 1–12; Jennifer Brick Murtazashvili, *Informal Order and the State in Afghanistan*, Cambridge, Cambridge University Press, 2016.

[8] Benjamin Hopkins, 'The Problem with "Hearts and Minds" in Afghanistan', *Middle East Report*, 2010, n° 255, pp. 24–9. Beyond Afghanistan, the counterinsurgency manual FM 3-24 illustrates the structural-functionalist vision of culture that permeates the US military. Roberto González, 'Towards Mercenary Anthropology? The New US Army Counterinsurgency Manual FM 3–24 and the Military-Anthropology Complex', *Anthropology Today*, 2007, vol. 23, n° 3, pp. 14–19.

[9] On the colonial origins of this vision, see Benjamin Hopkins, *The Makings of Modern Afghanistan*, Basingstoke, Palgrave Macmillan, 2008; Sana Haroon, *Frontier of Faith: Islam in the Indo-Afghan Borderland*, London, Hurst, 2011.

[10] Fredrik Barth, *Political Leadership among Swat Pathans*, London, Athlone Press, 1959; Akbar Ahmed, *Millennium and Charisma among Pathans: A Critical Essay in Social Anthropology*, London, Routledge, 2012; Louis Dupree, 'Tribal Warfare in Afghanistan and Pakistan: A Reflexion of the Segmentary Lineage System' in Akbar S. Ahmed (ed.), *Islam in Tribal Societies: From the Atlas to the Indus*, London, Routledge, 1984, p. 147.

[11] Thomas Barfield and Neamatollah Nojumi, 'Bringing More Effective Governance to Afghanistan: 10 Pathways to Stability', *Middle East Policy*, 2010, vol. 17, n° 4, p. 44. Thomas Barfield develops this thesis in his book, *Afghanistan: A Cultural and Political History*, Princeton, Princeton University Press, 2010.

[12] A new generation of Afghan historians has studied the historicity of the state in Afghanistan and its central place, as early as the nineteenth century, in both the economic and legal realms. Shah Hanifi, *Connecting Histories in Afghanistan: Market Relations and State Formation on a Colonial Frontier*,

sociologists who highlighted Afghanistan's transformations in the context of decades of war and intervention was neglected.[13] Their studies showed how the public policies of successive regimes, the emergence of a new elite of military commanders in the war, mass migration, and urbanization had contributed to a general weakening of tribal structures.[14] Only in the Southeast did a network of tribal institutions still play a decisive role in social relations.

Essentialist characterizations depoliticized the problem facing the Western military. The inability of judges and police to access rural areas due to the insecurity and dilapidated state of institutions was portrayed as a manifestation of cultural preference: Afghans, it was said, true to their culture would prefer to call on their tribal elites rather than state institutions. Similarly, the Taliban courts, which constituted a centralized legal system (see Part II), were generally described by the US military and Western analysts as an insurgency's exploitation of the public's preference for customary law. These considerations went beyond judicial issues: thus framed, the insurgency ceased to constitute a political movement and became the generic name for a congruence of various local interests in 'an accidental guerrilla', according to the title of a book influential in military circles.[15]

While the war in Afghanistan was waged by many organizations belonging to a coalition of countries, the US military was the dominant player. The American contingent represented about two-thirds of total foreign troops, and the US Army alone spent $718 billion between 2001 and 2014.[16] Until 2007, it operated independently of the rest of the Western contingents, which were grouped under ISAF. Subsequently, facing the escalating insurgency, the United States increased its presence in the country and took command of ISAF. In addition, the priorities and successive changes in strategy (the stationing

Stanford, Stanford University Press, 2011; Faiz Ahmed, *Afghanistan Rising: Islamic Law and Statecraft between the Ottoman and British Empires*, Cambridge, Harvard University Press, 2017.

[13] For a critique of Orientalism that permeates recent literature on Afghanistan and a review of social science research dealing with the transformations of Afghan society during the war, Alessandro Monsutti, 'Anthropologizing Afghanistan: Colonial and Postcolonial Encounters', *Annual Review of Anthropology*, 2013, vol. 42, n° 1, pp. 269–85.

[14] Gilles Dorronsoro, 'Le déclin de l'institution tribale en Afghanistan' in Hosham Dawod, *La constante 'tribu', variations arabo-musulmanes*, Paris, Démopolis, 2014, pp. 93–117.

[15] David Kilcullen, *The Accidental Guerrilla: Fighting Small Wars in the Midst of a Big One*, Oxford, Oxford University Press, 2009.

[16] This estimate, made by the Watson Institute's 'Costs of Wars' programme, only includes the costs directly budgeted for operations in Afghanistan. To measure the total cost of war to the United States, we must add nearly $2,150 billion, covering the costs of medical treatment and disability pensions and other military expenditures that have increased without being explicitly budgeted for Afghanistan, such as equipment purchases and additional salaries for recruitment or maintenance. Neta Crawford, *U.S. Cost of Wars through 2014: $4.4 Trillion and Counting*, Boston, Watson Institute, 2014.

of ISAF troops in Kabul in 2002–3, a troop surge in 2009, focus on the South, withdrawal of most troops in 2014, negotiation with the Taliban, complete withdrawal in 2021) were all decided in Washington, according to the internal balances of successive US administrations. Finally, American supremacy was all the more potent because other Western countries contributed to the military coalition foremost with a view to strengthening their alliance with the United States. Thus, the analysis of the US military's practices is of heuristic interest in understanding the effects of the intervention overall.

The US military in Afghanistan systematically relied on strongmen, justifying the strategy by calling them 'tribal elders' or 'local elites'. By doing so, they empowered the latter to oppose the central state and prevail over their local rivals, fuelling existing conflicts and sparking new ones. First, to conduct their operations against Al Qaeda and the Taliban, US troops exempted themselves from the Afghan legal framework, conducting a campaign of targeted killings that sharpened local rivalries. Secondly, the Western military set up 'customary' or 'traditional' bodies whose conflicting verdicts, with uncertain legal status, further undermined the official judicial system. Finally, the US military trained militias along tribal or ethnic lines, which reinforced entrepreneurs pursuing identity strategies and a community-based framing of private conflicts.

Targeted killings: violence outside the law

Beginning in October 2001, President Bush dispatched CIA agents and US Special Forces to track down members of Al Qaeda and the Taliban movement. The US intervention was initially framed as an international police operation by soldiers whose mission was killing or arresting 'terrorist' militants. This policing framework was reflected in a strategy of 'targeted killings' and the deeper involvement of lawyers to justify it as a legal use of force under international humanitarian law. Beyond the limited deference paid to this legal framework by the US military,[17] the attention to international standards concealed the lack of respect for the Afghan juridical system. In fact, the immunity from the Afghan justice system enjoyed by American soldiers put their violence outside

[17] Philip Alston, the United Nations Special Rapporteur on extrajudicial, summary or arbitrary executions, issued a particularly critical report and accused the United States of provoking 'the displacement of clear legal standards with a vaguely defined licence to kill, and the creation of a major accountability vacuum'. Philip Alston, *Report of the Special Rapporteur on Extrajudicial, Summary or Arbitrary Executions: Study on Targeted Killings*, Geneva, UN Human Rights Council, 2010, p. 3.

the law, an arbitrariness that heightened their preference for those who provided them with information and auxiliaries.

Targeted killings became the modus operandi of choice for three reasons. First, the intervention in Afghanistan was launched in the emotional good-versus-evil atmosphere that set in after the 9/11 attacks. The images of the collapsing towers, broadcast endlessly on television, brutalized American society, which had not experienced acts of war on its continental territory since the nineteenth century. The attacks led to an upwelling of patriotism and calls for sacred unity relayed by the media. On 14 September, President Bush visited the World Trade Center site and promised to avenge the victims of the attacks: 'I can hear you, the rest of the world can hear you and the people who knocked these buildings down will hear all of us soon.'[18] Three days later, he approved broad powers for the CIA to organize actions against the Taliban, which were lumped together with Al Qaeda as 'terrorists'. President Bush also approved the CIA's Extraordinary Rendition Program: tracking, kidnapping, and transferring captives to clandestine prisons, 'black sites' located in third countries where they could be interrogated under torture.[19] In his address to Congress on 20 September 2001, President Bush announced the Manichaeism that would characterize American actions in Afghanistan for years to come:

> Our war on terror begins with al-Qaida, but it does not end there. It will not end until every terrorist group of global reach has been found, stopped, and defeated [...] Our response involves far more than instant retaliation and isolated strikes. Americans should not expect one battle, but a lengthy campaign, unlike any other we have ever seen. It may include dramatic strikes, visible on TV, and covert operations, secret even in success. We will starve terrorists of funding, turn them one against another, drive them from place to place, until there is no refuge or no rest. [...] Every nation, in every region, now has a decision to make. Either you are with us, or you are with the terrorists. From this day forward, any nation that continues to harbor or support terrorism will be regarded by the United States as a hostile regime.[20]

[18] 'Bush: I Can Hear You', *LiveNow from Fox*, 2001, www.youtube.com/watch?v=z3YnAsOeUpA&t=3s&ab_channel=LiveNOWfromFOX

[19] Ahmed Rashid, *Descent into Chaos: How the War Against Islamic Extremism is Being Lost in Pakistan, Afghanistan and Central Asia*, London, Penguin, 2008, pp. 61–2; Tim Weiner, *Legacy of Ashes: The History of the CIA*, New York, Knopf Doubleday, 2007, p. 481. For an analysis of these extraordinary renditions, see Amrit Singh, *Globalizing Torture: CIA Secret Detention and Extraordinary Rendition*, New York, Open Society, 2013.

[20] *Address to a Joint Session of Congress and the American People*, 20 September 2001, https://georgewbush-whitehouse.archives.gov/news/releases/2001/09/20010920-8.html.

Secondly, the targeted killings strategy grew out of the wish by successive administrations to limit the number of troops deployed in Afghanistan and to minimize US casualties. A distant legacy of defeat in the Vietnam War, American military doctrine, known as the Weinberger doctrine after the Secretary of Defense who developed it in 1984, limited the commitment of regular troops to conventional military operations, mobilizing massive resources for a limited time to avoid prolonged interventions. During the 2000 presidential campaign, candidate Bush affirmed his commitment to this doctrine: 'I don't think our troops ought to be used for what's called nation-building. I think our troops ought to be used to fight and win war.' In line with this doctrine, the US administration resisted sending more than a few thousand Special Forces to Afghanistan and focused its resources on arresting and eliminating Al-Qaeda and Taliban militants. As the top US commander General Tommy Franks said: 'We don't want to repeat the Soviets' mistake. There's nothing to be gained by blundering around those mountains and gorges with armor battalions chasing a lightly armed enemy.'[21] With the fall of the Taliban Islamic Emirate, Washington handed over security of the new regime to ISAF. US Special Forces received orders to track down and eliminate jihadist militants, reporting up a separate chain of command from ISAF.

Thirdly, targeted strikes also corresponded to framing the war as a police action with decidedly vague legal contours. In 2001, the United States did not recognize the Islamic Emirate as a political authority or the Taliban movement as a belligerent. The intervention was not preceded by any declaration of war, and the US military targeted individuals and organizations that the United States accused of terrorist acts. Consequently, this framing of a military intervention as a police action denied any legal status to those targeted by the US military in Afghanistan. Indeed, three days after 9/11, Congress passed a resolution 'Authorizing Use of United States Armed Forces against Those Responsible For Recent Attacks Against the United States', stating:

> That the President is authorized to use all necessary and appropriate force against those nations, organizations, or persons he determines planned, authorized, committed, or aided the terrorist attacks that occurred on September 11, 2001, or harbored such organizations or persons, in order to prevent any future acts of international terrorism against the United States by such nations, organizations or persons.

[21] Tommy Franks, *American Soldier*, New York, Harper Collins, 2009.

Two months later, the President authorized the Department of Defense to detain individuals outside of any civilian jurisdiction.[22] Taken together, these legislative acts authorized the detention and execution of persons outside existing legal frameworks. On the one hand, those targeted by the US military were defined as criminals and therefore not accorded the status of combatants and the protections provided by the Geneva Conventions. On the other, they were treated as enemies who could be executed or detained without judicial process. In March 2002, a Bush administration lawyer coined the term 'enemy combatant' to avoid the possibility of appeal to a US or international court.[23] Mere proximity to a target was considered an indication of combatant status. As one Special Forces member said after a targeted killing that resulted in civilian casualties: 'if someone is a bad individual or someone is with that person, they are unlawful combatants.'[24] In this grey area of law, tens of thousands of Afghans were killed in night raids and airstrikes, and thousands of people were held without status in clandestine prisons that dotted Afghanistan, in the internment centre of the Bagram military base near Kabul, and in the Guantanamo prison camp in Cuba.[25] These thousands of detainees had no right to a lawyer or to visits by the International Committee of the Red Cross, which the United States treated with hostility during the early years of the conflict. It was not until the election of Barack Obama in January 2009 that 'personal representatives' were allowed, and systematic abuses and torture ceased in US detention centres. However, during his two terms in office, targeted killings massively increased in Afghanistan.

From 2002 onwards, targeted killings were also a tool for stemming the spread of the Taliban insurgency. A Special Forces unit, Task Force 373, was formed with the mission of eliminating individuals whose names were on the Joint Prioritized Effects List.[26] Its members usually conducted the raids, termed 'kill or capture missions', at night to benefit from their technological superiority (sensors, night vision). United States military personnel broke down doors, entered homes, and surprised people who were arrested or killed. At the same time, drone strikes were becoming a routine mode of operation on both sides of the Afghan-Pakistan border. This war from the air, waged by operators

[22] The text of the presidential decree *Detention, Treatment, and Trial of Certain Non-Citizens in the War Against Terrorism* is available on the official White House website, https://georgewbush-whitehouse.archives.gov/news/releases/2001/11/20011113-27.html.

[23] The Geneva Convention only recognizes 'legal' or 'illegal' combatants.

[24] Kate Clark, *The Takhar Attack*, Kabul, Afghanistan Analysts Network, 2011, p. 30.

[25] For one of the few reports on secret American prisons in Afghanistan, see Anand Gopal, 'America's Secret Afghan Prisons', *The Nation*, 28 January 2010.

[26] Nick Davies, 'Afghanistan War Logs: Task Force 37— Special Forces Hunting Top Taliban', *The Guardian*, 25 July 2010.

based in Nevada or Florida—who worked daily eight-hour shifts, broke for lunch, killed, and went home to sleep—was made possible by the rollout of new killer drones with evocative names like Predator and Reaper.[27] In 2009, the appointment of General Stanley McCrystal to lead ISAF endorsed this strategy. During the previous five years, he had commanded the Joint Special Operations Command (JSOC), the entity responsible for coordinating Special Forces, and thus for most targeted killings in Afghanistan and around the world. Officials of ISAF reported that between 2009 and 2011, targeted killings by Special Forces raids and precision airstrikes numbered in the thousands each year.[28]

However, the US military struggled to accurately identify individuals to be apprehended or eliminated. Being ignorant of local dynamics, inadvertently became entangled in local rivalries, effectively becoming a blind instrument in parochial conflicts. To obtain intelligence and auxiliaries, the military supported those who managed to present themselves as reliable allies. The US military's counterinsurgency manual, FM3-24, explicitly advocated this bias: 'Go with, not against, the grain of the local populace. First, win the confidence of a few villages, and then work with those with whom they trade, intermarry, or do business. This tactic develops local allies, a mobilized populace, and trusted networks.'[29] In the same vein, Jim Gant tells of how he helped the strongman he nicknamed 'Sitting Bull' in a land dispute while he led a Special Forces detachment in Kunar province in 2003:

> The highland people had taken and were using some land that belonged to the lowland people. The Malik told me the land had been given to his tribe by the 'King of Afghanistan' many, many years ago and that he would show me the papers. I told him he didn't need to show me any papers. His word was enough. [. . .] I made the decision to support him. 'Malik, I am with you. My men and I will go with you and speak with the highlanders again. If they do not turn the land back over to you, we will fight with you against them.'[30]

[27] Grégoire Chamayou, *A Theory of the Drone*, New York, The New Press, 2015.

[28] E-48, European officer attached to ISAF command, July 2011; E-52, US Special Forces officer, September 2012; E-58, United Nations political officer attached to ISAF, September 2014. In March 2011, before the US Congress, ISAF Commander David Petraeus spoke of 360 targeted killings per quarter. For the full text, see Bill Roggio, *Full Text of General Petraeus' Testimony to Congress*, 15 March 2011, www.longwarjournal.org/archives/2011/03/full_text_of_general_petraeus.php. Compiling ISAF press releases between December 2009 and September 2011, Alex Strick van Linschoten and Félix Kuehn counted 3,873 people killed and 7,146 arrested. Alex Strick van Linschoten and Felix Kuehn, *A Knock on the Door: 22 Months of ISAF Press Releases*, Kabul, Afghanistan Analysts Network, 2011.

[29] The United States Army and Marine Corps, *The U.S. Army/Marine Corps Counterinsurgency Field Manual*, Chicago, University of Chicago Press, 2007, section A-5.

[30] Jim Gant, *One Tribe at a Time: A Strategy for Success in Afghanistan*, Los Angeles, Nine Sisters Imports, 2009, p. 18.

Major Gant does not tell how this story ended; his offhand remark, 'suffice it to say that the dispute with the highlanders was resolved', suggests that he helped his 'friend' take over the contested lands.

In practice, behind the cloak of the village or tribe, American soldiers sided with local entrepreneurs of violence against their rivals. In November 2001 in Kandahar, Special Forces relied on one of the 1990s' feared warlords, Gul Agha Shirzai, to recapture Kandahar. He provided auxiliaries and translators and became their main interlocutor in the province. In exchange, the US military leaned on Hamid Karzai to appoint him governor of the province, which Shirzai took advantage of to favour his relatives and eliminate his rivals.[31] In 2003, a Special Forces operative in Kandahar declared, 'Everything that happens in this province goes through the governor. We don't trust the others.'[32] In the mid-2000s, when President Hamid Karzai succeeded in weakening Shirzai by appointing him governor in another province, the US military applied the same logic by banking on Abdul Raziq. Appointed chief of police, he effectively ruled the city by surrounding himself with members of his tribe, the Ashiqzai.

In neighbouring Uruzgan province, US Special Forces relied on the 1990s Popolzai commander Jan Mohamad Khan. His nephew, Matiullah Khan, was the only commander authorized to let his men keep their weapons because they operated directly with the Special Forces. Moreover, he was not given any trouble about his involvement in drug trafficking and extorting money from convoys on the Kabul-Kandahar highway. As Martine Van Bijlert explains, Jan Mohamad Khan 'used his relations with U.S. Special Forces and his reputation as an effective Taliban hunter to target a wide range of tribal leaders and former Taliban officials, particularly from the Ghilzai and Panjpai tribe.'[33] In 2006, the Netherlands in a rare exception made the departure of Jan Mohamad Khan a condition for their deployment to the province because the Dutch contingent wanted to strengthen the central government's structures and avoid taking sides in local conflicts. However, the US Special Forces continued to support Jan Mohamad Khan and Matiullah Khan, which allowed the pair to bypass state structures and stay on as the dominant actors in the province.[34]

[31] Matthieu Aikins, 'The Master of Spin Boldak', *Harper's Magazine*, December 2009; Peter Tomsen, *The Wars of Afghanistan: Messianic Terrorism, Tribal Conflicts, and the Failures of Great Powers*, New York, Public Affairs, 2013, pp. 615–17.

[32] Sarah Chayes, *The Punishment of Virtue: Inside Afghanistan after the Taliban*, New York, Penguin Press, 2006, p. 272.

[33] Martina Van Biljert, 'Unruly Commanders and Violent Power Struggles: Taliban Networks in Uruzgan' in Antonio Giustozzi (ed.), *Decoding the New Taliban: Insights from the Afghan Field*, New York, Columbia University Press, 2009, p. 158.

[34] For a detailed account of the relationship between Jan Mohamad Khan and the US Special Forces, see Deedee Derksen, *Transition in Uruzgan (2): Power at the Centre*, 12 June 2013, www.afghanistan-analysts.org/en/reports/war-and-peace/transition-in-uruzgan-2-power-at-the-centre/; Anand Gopal,

The US military, cut off from Afghan society, also could not verify and interpret the information it gathered. The troops had extremely limited contact with the population. Fearing attacks from all sides, the soldiers viewed their entire environment as hostile. A range of devices reinforced their isolation from the Afghan population: several lines of fortifications to prevent attacks, body searches, and frequent incidents of American soldiers opening fire. United States bases in the highlands launched salvos into the vicinity every other day. This shelling, known as 'suppressive fire', designed to keep the Taliban from taking up positions around the base, mainly killed or wounded many of the herders and livestock in the area.[35] Patrols in armoured vehicles or on foot allowed only limited interactions, a few hours or even minutes, by soldiers covered in protective gear and sensing equipment.

Troop rotations every six to twelve months prevented any adaptation processes. To paraphrase John Paul Vann, one of the figures of the Vietnam War, between 2001 and 2014 the US military did not wage thirteen years of war, but a year of war repeated thirteen times. The US military's rare regular contact with Afghan society was through the translators and auxiliaries they recruited. In this context, Afghans who managed to be recruited or to place their men in these jobs, took advantage of their position as interfaces between the US military and the population. As troop deployments to Afghanistan increased, the recruitment of translators was outsourced to private companies. In 2010, a complaint against one of the main subcontractors revealed that the company, which had a $1.4 billion contract, had falsified the tests and that 28 per cent of translators did not know the language they were supposed to translate.[36] Translators often spoke Persian, but not Pashto, while with decades of war and the collapse of the education system, mastery of Persian had declined among the Pashtuns of the South and East. In 2011, one of my interlocutors from the East told me about his cousin who worked at the prison on Bagram base:

No Good Men among the Living: America, the Taliban, and the War through Afghan Eyes, New York, Metropolitan Books, 2014.

[35] E-4, contractor conducting the civilian-military component of the American counterinsurgency in the East, July 2010.

[36] Matthew Mosk, Brian Ross, and Joseph Rhee, 'Exclusive: Whistleblower Claims Many *U.S. Interpreters* Can't Speak Afghan Languages', *ABC News*, 7 September 2010. Moreover, translators were often distrusted by the troops. E-27, Afghan translator for US Special Forces between 2003 and 2007, July 2010; E-65, Afghan translator of the US Army between 2002 and 2006, August 2010. See also this testimony by a translator for the US Army; Zabih Farhad, *How Hearts and Minds Were Lost in Afghanistan? A Personal Experience Working with the International Military*, 20 April 2012, www.mei.edu/publications/how-hearts-and-minds-were-lost-afghanistan-personal-experience-working-international.

> My cousin was translating during the interrogation of a man from Kandahar, who answered 'ya' with a slight nod, which in Kandahar means no. Yet each time, my cousin translated it as yes. As the questions followed one another, the interrogator was astonished to have before him someone who not only confessed to being a Taliban, but personally knew Osama bin Laden and Mullah Omar. It was the interrogator who finally caught on that something was out of whack.[37]

Language did not present the only barrier. American soldiers did not know enough of the historical and political context to analyse the information they collected or the denunciations lodged with them. In a report on intelligence in Afghanistan, ISAF's director of intelligence between 2009 and 2010, Major General Michael Flynn, minced no words when he said:

> Ignorant of local economics and landowners, hazy about who the powerbrokers are and how they might be influenced, incurious about the correlations between various development projects and the levels of cooperation among villagers, and disengaged from people in the best position to find answers—whether aid workers or Afghan soldiers—U.S. intelligence officers and analysts can do little but shrug in response to high level decision-makers seeking the knowledge, analysis, and information they need to wage a successful counterinsurgency.[38]

A strike that mistakenly hit civilians in Takhar province in September 2010 illustrates the inability of the Special Forces to accurately identify those they targeted.[39] Indeed, having confused the name of a member of a candidate's campaign team in the parliamentary elections with that of the province's Taliban deputy governor, the US Special Forces and Air Force had killed ten civilians and wounded seven in this operation. A thorough investigation by Kate Clark showed that the Special Forces relied exclusively on electronic surveillance and social network analysis, without inquiring about the individuals involved. Soldiers deduced people's political affiliation from who they socialized with, from their phone calls, and their locations. A simple check with local

[37] E-37, resident of Kunar province, July 2011.

[38] Michael Flynn, Matthew Pottinger, and Paul Batchelor, *Fixing Intel: A Blueprint for Making Intelligence Relevant in Afghanistan*, Washington, Center for a New American Security, 2010, p. 4. In 2011, when I corrected an American officer who had called the Pashai residents of the Dar-i Nur Valley in Nangarhar Pashtuns, he replied that 'it's easier to call them all Pashtuns', E-32, Rural Development Program Manager for the Provincial Reconstruction Team in Asadabad, July 2010.

[39] Kate Clark, *The Takhar Attack*, Kabul, Afghanistan Analysts Network, 2011.

and national Afghan authorities would have told them that they were mixing up two relatively well-known local figures. Relying exclusively on the wiretaps of the Taliban vice-governor and ignorant of the political and military context, the Special Forces soldiers were unable to interpret the discussions they intercepted.

With the US military unable to verify their information, many Afghans used them to get rid of an inconvenient cousin in an inheritance case, a neighbour over a disputed piece of land, or a local rival. Many of those arrested or killed had nothing to do with the Taliban. For example, a supplier to the American Chawkay base in Kunar was arrested in 2009, having been denounced as pro-Taliban by competitors. After fifteen months in prison, seven of them in solitary confinement, he was finally released without explanation. The informer was never confronted and walked away with the contract of the arrested supplier.[40]

By falling for denunciations like this, the US military fed rivalries. For example, in the same province, after a 2003 Taliban attack on a base in the Ganjgal Valley, the Americans received intelligence pointing them to a prominent member of the Shinwari tribe, Abdul Wali. On 21 June 2003, on the advice of the governor of the province, *sayid* Faizal Akbar, whom he knew personally, Abdul Wali accompanied by the governor's son went to the American base where he was arrested upon arrival. It took several days for the governor to find out that he had died during interrogation by David Passaro, a contractor working for the CIA. The Army's official version stated that he died of a heart attack. The victim's relatives meanwhile soon learned the source of the slanderous denunciation: Mahmud Miran, a Salarzai commander, Abdul Wali's personal enemy. Blood debt changed the nature of hostility. Shinwari notables decided to avenge him by informing on some Salarzai close to the Taliban to the Americans who then arrested them.[41] In 2007, David Passaro was convicted of murder by a US federal court and sentenced to eight years in prison. But it came much too late. When I conducted my interviews in 2011–12, the rivalry between Abdul Wali and Mahmud Miran had evolved into a conflict between Shinwari and Salarzai commanders that some of my interlocutors put down to tribal motives.[42]

[40] E-3, former US Army supplier in Kunar province, July 2011.

[41] Interview with Hyder Akbar, son of Faizal Akbar, the governor of Kunar province, who had delegated him to accompany Abdul Wali to the American base, July 2010; E-27, Afghan translator for US Special Forces between 2003 and 2007, deployed in Kunar province between 2003 and 2005, July 2010; E-31, notable in Kunar province, July 2010.

[42] For a development of these dynamics, see Adam Baczko, 'Legal Rule and Tribal Politics: The US Army and the Taliban in Afghanistan (2001–13)', *Development and Change*, 2016, vol. 47, nº 6, pp. 1412–33.

These practices by the US military generated a pervasive rise in uncertainty and mistrust between relatives and neighbours. When I would learn of slanderous denunciations from my interlocutors, they could finger, often with certainty, the person behind it. But in other cases, targeted killings resulted not from individual identification, but from behavioural tendencies or modelling social networks based on intercepted phone calls (so-called 'signature strikes'). Several of my interlocutors reported rumours to me and remarked on an atmosphere of paranoia. They repeatedly told me about the existence of bugging devices that people paid by the US military would slip under someone's seat or into their pocket, or about the use of paint invisible to the naked eye that these people could apply surreptitiously during conversations or in someone's home. They concluded that it was now difficult to trust people and that keeping a wider circle of acquaintances carried a certain risk. These discussions unveiled people's inability, despite decades of experiencing warfare, to ascertain the origins or rationale behind the targeting of individuals with no apparent connections to the Taliban. In this regard, the explanation offered one day by one of my closest interlocutors, who had lived most of his life in the United States, was particularly revealing. He speculated that the only plausible explanation would be that the US military and the Central Intelligence Agency struck at random as a way of generating mistrust and destroying the Afghan social fabric in their quest to slow the spread of the insurgency. Noticing my scepticism, he finally told me, practically beside himself, that otherwise the actions of the American military made no sense.

Reinventing customary justice

By the late 2000s, as the Taliban insurgency spread, the United States changed its approach in Afghanistan. Newly elected President Barack Obama announced a surge in the Western troop contingent to nearly 130,000 and appointed General Stanley McCrystal as head of ISAF. In his initial assessment, conducted just before taking office, the new top commander wrote:

> Our strategy cannot be focused on seizing terrain or destroying insurgent forces; our objective must be the population. In the struggle to gain the support of the people, every action we take must enable this effort. The population also represents a powerful actor that can and must be leveraged in this complex system. Gaining their support will require a better understanding of the people's choices and needs.[43]

[43] Stanley McCrystal, *COMISAF Initial Assessment (Unclassified)*, Washington, US Department of Defense, 2009.

For General McCrystal, the courts were a crucial factor in the progress made by the insurgency:

> The QST [the Quetta Shura Taliban] has a governing structure in Afghanistan under the rubric of the Islamic Emirate of Afghanistan. They appoint shadow governors for most provinces, review their performance, and replace them periodically. They established a body to receive complaints against their own 'officials' and to act on them. They install 'shari'a' courts to deliver swift and enforced justice in contested and controlled areas. They levy taxes and conscript fighters and laborers. They claim to provide security against a corrupt government, ISAF forces, criminality, and local power brokers. They also claim to protect Afghan and Muslim identity against foreign encroachment. In short, the QST provides major elements of governance and a national and religious narrative.[44]

Conversely, the government's lack of legitimacy was allegedly due to its inability to deliver justice:

> The people's lack of trust in their government results from two key factors. First, some GIRoA [Government of the Islamic Republic of Afghanistan] officials have given preferential treatment to certain individuals, tribes, and groups or worse, abused their power at the expense of the people. Second, the Afghan government has been unable to provide sufficient security, justice, and basic services to the people. […] These problems contribute to the Afghan Government's inability to gain the support of the Afghan population. ISAF errors also compound the problem.[45]

From now on, providing justice would no longer be a matter for development and reconstruction, but the military would make it its problem instead. Solving it now became an indispensable and urgent mission for winning the war. But, from this angle, the Afghan state now appeared to be so corrupt that it was beyond reform. Between the lines, General McCrystal was proposing to circumvent it by acting directly at the local level, through structures he described as 'informal':

[44] Ibid.
[45] Ibid.

> ISAF must work with its civilian and international counterparts to enable justice sector reform and locate resources for formal and informal justice systems that offer swift and fair resolution of disputes, particularly at the local level. The provision of local justice, to include such initiatives as mobile courts, will be a critical enhancement of Afghan capacity in the eyes of the people. ISAF must work with GIRoA to develop a clear mandate and boundaries for local informal justice systems.[46]

Beginning in 2009, the US military launched several initiatives to fund and establish what it conceived of as customary forms of conflict resolution, namely councils of notables commonly referred to as *jirga* in Pashtun and in Persian as *shura*.

By supporting the establishment of a system of informal justice, the US military became mired in an extremely tense debate that had pitted Western donors and experts against Afghan judges and human rights activists since 2002. An institute associated with the State Department, the United States Institute for Peace (USIP), began promoting the traditional form of justice. Its principal local partner, Tribal Liaison Office (TLO), an NGO founded by Afghan-Western dual nationals following the 2001 intervention, established '*jirgas*' in the East and Southeast. At the same time, an Afghan law professor in the United Kingdom, Ali Wardak, advocated a hybridization of the judicial system with the inclusion of forms of conciliatory and non-punitive justice. As a consultant to international organizations, he played a major role in promoting *shuras* and *jirgas*.[47] In the 2007 Human Development Report, Ali Wardak critiqued the weaknesses of the Afghan judicial system and the corruption of its judges and estimated that *shuras* and *jirgas* handled over 80 per cent of conflicts. He called for de-emphasizing state institutions and for including the councils as a court of first instance. The report enjoyed a wide circulation, and the figure of 80 per cent, at times inflated to 95 per cent, or even 99 per cent in one case, was taken as gospel in most reports from then on.[48]

The Chief Justice of the Afghan Supreme Court responded by censoring the report and threatening its author with legal action, causing Ali Wardak

[46] Ibid.

[47] Ali Wardak, 'Jirga: A Traditional Mechanism of Conflict Resolution in Afghanistan' in John Strawson (ed.), *Law after Ground Zero*, London, Cavendish, 2002, pp. 187–203; Ali Wardak, 'Building a Post-War Justice System in Afghanistan', *Crime, Law and Social Change*, 2004, vol. 41, n° 4, pp. 319–41.

[48] Frank Ledwidge, 'Justice and Counter-Insurgency in Afghanistan: A Missing Link', *The RUSI Journal*, 2009, vol. 154, n° 1, pp. 6–9.

to leave the country for the United Kingdom.[49] Afghan human rights activists also rejected these proposals, on the grounds that these bodies were biased against women in disputes over property or marriage: denying divorces, barring any inheritance by women, offering women as compensation in conflict, and forcing them into marriages. In addition, many human rights activists expressed reservations about the lack of qualifications for being a *jirga* member and leaving the door open to all manner of abuses given the lack of codification of customs. Some international actors, including the World Bank, also opposed this strategy and instead advocated more consistent support for official institutions.

Concurrently, the British Army set up its own councils in Helmand, selecting their memberships. Funded by the British Department for International Development (DFID), the councils were empowered to rule, among other things, on the release of people arrested by British soldiers, thus bypassing the judicial system and the local administration with which the British army did not see eye to eye. In collaboration with the American USIP institute and TLO, DFID became one of the main advocates of recognizing and strengthening the role of *shuras* and *jirgas*.

At the 2008 preparatory meetings for the National Justice Sector Strategy, a formal five-year plan for reforming the legal system, USIP and DFID lobbied to include customary bodies in the programmatic document. In the face of unyielding opposition from Afghan human rights activists and justice officials, defining the relationship between formal and informal justice was eventually delegated to the drafters of an official document on the subject.[50] A year later, a still-hostile Supreme Court convened a working group to draft the document. Discussions between Afghan human rights activists and officials on one side and USIP and DFID on the other dragged on for ten months. Finally, in 2010, faced with these competing pressures, the Ministry of Justice decided to cut the Gordian knot by writing its own bill—one that criminalized initiatives in the field of informal justice by making members of *shuras* and *jirgas* liable to prosecution if they failed to apply the prevailing legal code.[51]

[49] Astri Suhrke, *When More is Less: The International Project in Afghanistan*, London, Hurst, 2011, pp. 212–14.

[50] Matteo Tondini, *Statebuilding and Justice Reform: Post-Conflict Reconstruction in Afghanistan*, London, Routledge, 2010, p. 73; Astri Suhrke, *When More is Less: The International Project in Afghanistan*, London, Hurst, 2011, p. 215.

[51] Torunn Wimpelmann, 'Nexuses of Knowledge and Power in Afghanistan: The Rise and Fall of the Informal Justice Assemblage', *Central Asian Survey*, 2013, vol. 32, n° 3, pp. 408–11.

However, the US military simply brushed aside any reluctance to use the customary bodies, which it had by now added to its arsenal for winning the war. The military's involvement triggered a classic cycle familiar in the development world: increased funding led to proliferating reports and conferences which justified the increased funding for these programmes. In 2010, USAID split its judicial sector programme in two, henceforth budgeting half for informal institutions. The agency reproduced the processes which, however, had proved disastrous for the judicial system. For example, the private Checchi and Company Consulting firm once more received tens of millions of dollars a year to support the establishment of customary councils in Afghanistan. US Special Forces took the lead in this reinventing of tradition,[52] as the head of the United Nations Assistance Mission in Afghanistan (UNAMA) in the Southeast explained in 2010:

> Special forces are setting up their own *shuras* everywhere. For example, in Jani Khel district [Paktya province], they appointed commanders in a 'peace *shura*' that is associated with the existing 'tribal *shuras*'. It was the special forces that appointed the members, two representatives from the ten tribes they consider important. They are generally not real tribal leaders, but commanders from jihad [against the Soviets]. Establishing these jirgas is part of the attempt by the special forces to arm the tribes, to build up *arbakai* [militias] against the Taliban.[53]

The Provincial Reconstruction Teams (PRT), the US army's mixed civilian-military teams, also funded programmes. The American military's involvement prompted a wholesale reversal of positions, with the Afghan Ministry of Justice, local governments, UNAMA, various development agencies and Western military contingents each piling on with their own *shura* and *jirga* initiatives. To implement their conflict resolution programmes, Western donors distributed large sums to Afghan ministries of Justice and Women's Rights, NGOs, academic departments, and Western private companies.

In a seemingly paradoxical way, this call to heed Afghanistan's social structures justified importing models from the West and the development sector. While resorting to informal justice was supposed to allow consideration of local realities, it privileged Western experts who wrote the reports and made

[52] Eric Hobsbawm and Terence Ranger (eds), *The Invention of Tradition*, Cambridge, Cambridge University Press, 1983.

[53] E-39, UNAMA's head in the Southeast, July 2010.

the recommendations. The figures of 80 to 95 per cent of conflicts having been dealt with by informal bodies were bandied about from crisis situation to crisis situation, in reports covering African, Middle Eastern, and Central Asian countries without ever being validated.[54] Throughout, anthropological knowledge about Afghanistan was mobilized superficially.[55] The intervention's actors used the terms '*shura*' and '*jirga*' to describe informational meetings in a village as well as bodies that met regularly and issued legally recognized decisions. The words 'traditional', 'customary', 'community', 'tribal', or 'informal' were used interchangeably. On the side of operators in the development and humanitarian sectors, the use of the Persian and Pashtun terms (*shura, jirga*) concealed their importation of concepts, intangible technologies ('soft technologies') linked to alternative dispute resolution mechanisms and mediation. As the legal anthropologist Laura Nader notes, the establishment of informal bodies has been a widespread practice, resulting in a 'globalization of informal law', for which Afghanistan was a poster child. Far from respecting local cultural specificities, donor support for the establishment of informal bodies was really an export of alternative dispute resolution mechanisms developed in the West in the 1980s and 1990s.[56]

This reinvention of traditional justice ended up undermining the regime's courts and reducing people's access to a legal settlement. First, consensus was lacking on how such bodies should work, what standards to apply, and how to appoint their members. In particular, determining the criteria to qualify as 'tribal elites' or 'elders' proved highly controversial (lineage, local recognition, state appointment, religious education, secular education, military involvement), especially since foreigners generally were ignorant of the differences between different social statuses (*khan, bay, arbab, malik* ...). To be recognized as 'elders' became an issue since it meant getting access to positions of power

[54] Torunn Wimpelmann, 'The Informal Justice Paradigm and the Appropriation of Local Reality', *Northern Ireland Legal Quarterly*, 2013, vol. 64, n° 3, pp. 397–411. For a case of these figures circulating, see Leila Chirayath, Caroline Sage, and Michael Woolcock, *Customary Law and Policy Reform: Engaging with the Plurality of Justice Systems*, Washington, World Bank, 2005.

[55] The case of the Human Terrain System (HTS) is telling. In principle, these civilian teams embedded in military units were supposed to guide military action by applying ethnographic methods, inspired by the role anthropologists played in the colonial conquest. In reality, the Human Terrain Teams lacked trained anthropologists, and instead fielded people with a master's degree in any of the humanities and social sciences disciplines. They remained largely confined to the bases, where they conducted conventional intelligence work. Meanwhile, the critical work of anthropologists, showing detribalization under the blows of war, migration, and rapid urbanization, was systematically ignored. Roberto González, *Militarizing Culture: Essays on the Warfare State*, Walnut Creek, Left Coast Press, 2010; Alessandro Monsutti, 'Anthropologizing Afghanistan: Colonial and Postcolonial Encounters', *Annual Review of Anthropology*, 2013, vol. 42, n° 1, pp. 269–85.

[56] Laura Nader, 'The Globalization of Law: ADR as "Soft" Technology', *Proceedings of the Annual Meeting (American Society of International Law)*, 1999, vol. 93, pp. 304–11.

and to the international windfall. The commanders of the jihad against the Soviets, who had marginalized the lineage-based elites in the 1980s, presented themselves to the actors of the intervention as the custodians of a traditional legitimacy.

Secondly, the lack of coordination between these informal bodies increased the number of places for disputing and issuing property titles and contracts with uncertain legal status, which led to more disputes. As the head of UNAMA's Southeast office told me:

> In the province [of Paktya], there are four types of *jirgas* that each deal with private conflicts: those organized by USAID, by the U.S. Special Forces unit, by the provincial governor, and the district *shuras* associated with the central government. Per the Constitution, district shuras and village *shuras* should have been set up everywhere, but this has never been done systematically. Each type of council follows its own logic. Creating *shuras* makes it easier to control local actors, have local interlocutors and bypass the institutions set up by others.[57]

Jirgas and *shuras* proliferated to the point where in 2011 the main instigators of their establishment, USIP and TLO, started voicing their concern in meetings with the US military.[58] They raised the alarm about an epidemic of self-proclaimed notables whom Afghans called 'trader elders' (*tijarati*).[59] In the city of Ghazni, one notable, a member of one of the many customary institutions created by Western actors, parlayed his titles into forming his own conflict resolution body that handed down verdicts for a price.[60]

Finally, the informal conflict resolution bodies failed to fill in for the missing courts; quite the contrary in fact. In 1980, the jurist Richard Abel pointed out that this delegalization 'increases the level of contentiousness in society', lets 'the party with greater power, wealth, or status simply dominating his opposite' and 'tends to deprive those who are weaker, poorer, or of lower social status of whatever protection they had obtained from formal legal recognition of their

[57] E-39, UNAMA's head in the Southeast, July 2010.

[58] Torunn Wimpelmann, 'Nexuses of Knowledge and Power in Afghanistan: The Rise and Fall of the Informal Justice Assemblage', *Central Asian Survey*, 2013, vol. 32, nº 3, pp. 406–22.

[59] See, for example, the contribution by the Director of Research of TLO, Susanne Schmeidl, 'Engaging Traditional Justice Mechanisms in Afghanistan: State-Building Opportunity or Dangerous Liaison?' in Whit Mason (ed.), *The Rule of Law in Afghanistan: Missing in Inaction*, Cambridge, Cambridge University Press, 2011, p. 162.

[60] E-67, elder in Ghazni province who opened a conflict-resolution boutique, September 2014.

rights'.[61] He also explained how such bodies 'presuppose informal mechanisms of control that are adequate to secure conformity in the absence of state coercion'.[62] In the case of the United States, Laura Nader showed that the establishment of alternative dispute resolution mechanisms starting in the late 1970s brought with it the atrophying of the complainant's powers and disadvantaged the poorest Americans.[63] In Afghanistan, the war exacerbated the effects of these bodies that were cutting rural Afghans off from the chance for formalized legal proceedings and making them more vulnerable to local power relations. The conflict resolution bodies were generally unable to enforce their judgments. In principle, a party rejecting the verdict risked opprobrium; in practice, those who could afford it simply appealed to the regime or to the Taliban courts, or ignored the judgments entirely, since these bodies lacked the means of enforcement. A religious cleric living between Kabul and Logar explained: 'today's *jirgas* are not like the *jirgas* of the past. With the *jirgas* of the past, people could not disobey. What the *jirgas* decided, people accepted.'[64] In a rural society, where many own weapons and some can marshal fighters to support them, *jirgas* and *shuras* were constrained by the unequal balance of power resulting from war. In many cases, setting up these customary bodies further reduced access to the law for the majority of the population and favoured violent entrepreneurs.

Standing up the militias

To combat the Taliban insurgency, the US military armed violent entrepreneurs competing locally with the Kabul administration. Privatizing security has a long and fraught history in Afghanistan. Soviet-led militias in the 1980s had been relatively effective in countering the mujahideen and thus protecting the outskirts of cities. However, their empowerment in the early 1990s, following the Soviet withdrawal, was a key factor in the fall of the Najibullah regime in 1992. In the ensuing years, the armed groups which fought each other divided along ethnic lines. In the 2000s, militias formed mainly at the behest of Special Forces and the CIA inflamed local rivalries. Arming various segments

61 Richard Abel, 'Delegalization: A Critical Review of its Ideology, Manifestations, and Social Consequences' in Erhard Blankenburg, Ekkehard Klausa, and Hubert Rottleuthner (eds), *Alternative Rechtsformen und Alternativen zum Recht*, Opladen, Westdeutscher Verlag, 1980, pp. 32, 40, and 41.

62 Ibid., p. 40.

63 Laura Nader, *The Life of the Law: Anthropological Projects*, Berkeley, University of California Press, 2002.

64 E-26, cleric who regularly sits in *jirgas*, Logar province, May 2013.

from a perspective both tribal and ethnic fragmented the society and polarized communities.

From early in the intervention, the CIA and Special Forces trained, equipped, and helped exempt some commanders from successive disarmament campaigns in return for their support in operations against the Taliban and Al Qaeda. Formed in the utmost secrecy, these first militias gradually gained a reputation for abuses committed with impunity thanks to their American protectors. For example, the 3,000-strong Counter-Terrorism Pursuit Teams, deployed along the border, illegally conducted operations in Pakistan.[65] My interlocutors in Kunar province evidently lived in fear of them. Their existence was revealed in 2013 when seventeen civilians, including ten children, were killed under unknown circumstances during one of their operations in that province.[66] The Afghan Guard Force, recruited from elements of the 25th Division of the Northern Alliance and later renamed the Afghan Security Guard, ostensibly was trained by Special Forces and the CIA to protect their base in the Southeast. In reality, this militia accompanied the Special Forces on their operations and controlled strategic points in the region.[67] The atrocities committed by this militia, in particular those by one of its commanders accused of extortion, murder, rape of male youngsters, and desecration of bodies, was denounced in 2010 in United Nations reports—in vain.[68]

In another infamous case, the Khost Protection Force, named after the southeastern province where its men were recruited, was established in 2003. By 2014, it fielded nearly 5,000 militiamen who rampaged among the population with impunity and without state supervision because the US military praised their effectiveness against the Taliban and protected them.[69] In the same context, in 2004, the CIA recruited, and the Special Forces trained, 400 fighters to form the Kandahar Strike Force. Symbolically stationed in Mullah Omar's former compound, they accompanied the Special Forces during raids. Their sense of impunity was such that in 2009 they killed the province's police chief who belonged to a rival network and had jailed one of their men. However, in this case the police chief having been connected to senior regime officials, dozens of Kandahar Strike Force members were arrested. The journalist who

[65] Bob Woodward, *Obama's Wars*, New York, Simon and Schuster, 2010, p. 8.

[66] Rod Nordland, 'After Airstrike, Afghan Points to C.I.A. and Secret Militias', *The New York Times*, 18 April 2013.

[67] E-42, Afghan analyst in UNAMA, specializing in Paktika province, September 2014.

[68] Julius Cavendish, 'Afghanistan's Dirty War: Why the Most Feared Man in Bermal District Is a U.S. Ally', *Time*, 4 October 2011.

[69] E-77, Afghan analyst with UNAMA specializing in Khost province, September 2014. See also David Jolly, 'Civilian Deaths Raise Questions About C.I.A.-Trained Forces in Afghanistan', *The New York Times*, 3 December 2015.

reported on the case recalled the words of a member of the Special Forces who supervised the militia:

> The ugly reality, says Matt, a Green Beret captain who gives only his first name because of protocol security concerns, is that if the US wants to prevail against the Taliban and its allies, it must work with Afghan fighters whose behavior insults Western sensibilities. 'There are no good guys by our standards. There is no standard to begin with. There is no justice system or rule of law to hold people accountable', Matt says. 'The Taliban are not horribly bad and the Afghan farmer is not an innocent victim.' In this moral twilight, refusing to work with paramilitaries accused of rights abuses accomplishes nothing, he argues. Instead, as relationships develop, so do the possibilities for altering the 'moral calculus' of the Afghan fighters. 'I don't like this reality', says Matt. 'But I do not have the power to make Afghans conduct themselves like Americans in matters of politics and warfare. I can only influence it over time.' The alternative is to 'go home now'.[70]

The US military's ethnic and tribal perspective played a key role in the formation of these armed groups—and the parallel with the reinvention of customary justice is striking. Just as *jirga* and *shura* concealed a globalization of informal justice mechanisms, the use of the emic terms *arbaki* (tribal levy) and *lashkar* (army) justified local programmes that replicated the privatization of security in vogue in the development sector and reproduced the militia formation model from the Iraq War in 2006. Moreover, the same actors pushing the customary justice agenda promoted the establishment of militias. For example, a congruence of Western and binational experts, NGOs such as The Liaison Office (TLO) or Washington think tanks published reports and articles calling for the formation of militias described indiscriminately as 'tribal', 'traditional', 'local', or 'community'.[71] Once again, the United Kingdom led the way in Helmand in 2006. On 12 December 2007, Prime Minister Gordon Brown told the British Parliament that it was important to work 'with the grain of Afghan tradition' and went on to say: 'One way forward is to increase our support for community defence initiatives, where local volunteers

[70] Julius Cavendish, 'After the US Pulls Out, Will CIA Rely More on Afghan Mercenaries?', *Christian Science Monitor*, 16 November 2011.

[71] Mohammed Osman Tariq, *Tribal Security System (Arbakai) in Southeast Afghanistan*, London, Crisis States Research Centre, 2008; Shahmahmood Miakhel, *Advantages and Disadvantages of Supporting a Community Force: The History of the Arbaki System and its Use in the Present Context of Afghanistan*, Kabul, UNAMA, 2008; Greg Bruno, *A Tribal Strategy for Afghanistan*, Washington, Council for Foreign Relations, 2008.

are recruited to defend homes and families modelled on traditional Afghan *arbakai*.'[72] For that matter, the formation of militias was gradually implemented through a series of uncoordinated initiatives just as customary justice had been. Formed in 2006, the Afghan National Auxiliary Police (ANAP) was quietly dismantled in 2008, as local recruitment of fighters ended up rearming many commanders from the 1990s and diverting many weapons to the Taliban insurgency.[73] Despite the programme's manifest failure, Secretary of Defense Robert Gates still maintained that year: 'At the end of the day the only solution in Afghanistan is to work with the tribes and provincial leaders in terms of trying to create a backlash ... against the Taliban.'[74] From then on, the militia programmes increased in number: the Afghan Public Protection Program (AP3), the Community Defense Initiative (CDI), the Local Defense Initiative (LDI), the Interim Security for Critical Infrastructure (ISCI), Community Defense Forces (CDF), the Community-Based Security Solution (CBSS), and the Critical Infrastructure Program (CIP).[75] Some programmes were launched by the Afghan government in coordination with the US Army (ANAP), some were launched by the Special Forces (AP3, LDI), and others were improvised for an event, for example the 2009 presidential elections (CDI); still others were local initiatives, such as one set up by the US Marines newly deployed in Helmand in 2009 (ISCI). This rapid spread of uncoordinated programmes hampered supervision and resulted in arming or rearming existing networks of violent entrepreneurs.[76]

The recruitment and expansion of militia formations by the United States only accelerated nationally in the run-up to the American withdrawal in 2014. Appointed in 2010 to head ISAF, General Petraeus, the originator of Iraq's militia programme, created the Afghan Local Police (ALP), which he characterized as a 'community watch with AK-47s'. Mustering 30,000 men, this militia was presented as a popular mobilization, or even, in the context of the Arab Spring, as a popular uprising: 'This is an important program because no one protects their home like a homeowner and this really mobilizes a community.

[72] *House of Commons Hansard Debates for 12 Dec 2007*, 12 December 2007, https://publications.parliament.uk/pa/cm200708/cmhansrd/cm071212/debtext/71212-0004.htm.

[73] Mark Sedra, 'Security Sector Reform and State Building in Afghanistan' in Geoffrey Hayes and Mark Sedra (eds), *Afghanistan: Transition under Threat*, Waterloo, Wilfrid Laurier University Press, 2008, pp. 197–9.

[74] Greg Bruno, *A Tribal Strategy for Afghanistan*, Washington, Council for Foreign Relations, 2008.

[75] For a detailed account, see Matthieu Lefèvre, *Local Defence in Afghanistan: A Review of Government-backed Initiatives*, Kabul, Afghanistan Analysts Network, 2010; Aziz Hakimi, 'Getting Savages to Fight Barbarians: Counterinsurgency and the Remaking of Afghanistan', *Central Asian Survey*, 2013, vol. 32, n° 3, pp. 388–405.

[76] Rachel Reid and Sahr Muhammedally, *'Just Don't Call it a Militia': Impunity, Militias, and the 'Afghan Local Police'*, New York, Human Rights Watch, 2011, pp. 22–3.

When community representatives, shura council members, nominate their sons to defend their village, their valleys, this is them defending their community and showing their commitment to fight the Taliban.'[77] So they would not rampage like previous militias, the ALP in theory would report to the Ministry of the Interior, which would vet, register, and pay the recruits proposed by local notables. In fact, the many armed groups guilty of repeated abuses collaborating with the Special Forces in other programmes were simply transferred to the ALP. Thus, the ALP absorbed the Afghan Security Guard, implicated in 2010 by the United Nations report mentioned earlier. Its leader was appointed to the police so that he could legally command the ALP's operations in other districts.[78] Moreover, the Special Forces included in the programme any group likely to oppose the Taliban: dissident branches of the insurgency, competing Islamist groups (Hizb-i Islami), or local violence entrepreneurs. From the perspective of the US military leaders, the programme essentially was about withdrawing from a country where they had failed to produce stable institutions. It was a matter of exploiting any pocket of resistance to the Taliban, regardless of the cost to the official government and the population. As an advisor to the commander of Special Forces in Afghanistan explained in June 2011:

> The military and Afghan government began seeing pockets of local resistance to the Taliban in the south and southeast. ISAF and district Afghan government officials went to talk to the people. They were not always supportive of the central government and generally opposed to the Taliban. But these areas had no sustained security presence. They did not necessarily want or trust the police, who they see as corrupt, to play a permanent role. A local defense force was part of the answer, along with improving basic informal governance and development.[79]

A US Army contractor in the North more crudely confided to me that the aim was to use the militias he helped organize to embroil the Taliban in local rivalries between Pashtuns and non-Pashtuns. The assumption was that insurgents would side with the Pashtuns, setting back their progress among non-Pashtuns.[80]

[77] 'Petraeus Speaks about Troop Withdrawal, Battling Al-Qaida', *DVIDS*, 7 September 2011.
[78] E-42, Afghan UNAMA analyst specializing in Paktika province, September 2014.
[79] Quoted in Rachel Reid and Sahr Muhammedally, *'Just Don't Call it a Militia': Impunity, Militias, and the 'Afghan Local Police'*, New York, Human Rights Watch, 2011, pp. 54–5.
[80] E-38, private contractor in charge of civil-military activities related to the American counterinsurgency in the North, September 2014.

This privatization of violence fostered an increase in local conflicts according to ethnic, tribal, or partisan logics. From the outset, the militia system boosted the autonomy of local actors vis-à-vis the central government and its regular armed forces, which the militia groups often outnumbered. In Kandahar, Uruzgan, or Kunduz provinces, militia leaders even managed to appoint or place relatives in leadership positions in the police or local administration, often with a helping hand from the US military. These militia leaders usually took advantage of their positions to avenge themselves on their rivals. In Nangarhar province, Special Forces armed and financed members of a Shinwari tribe clan, who used their weapons to seize pastures and communal lands claimed by another clan. The conflict, exploited by provincial governor Gul Agha Shirzai and local rivals of the Arsala family, resulted in dozens of deaths and a lasting weakening of the notables, some of whom had to take refuge in the provincial capital of Jalalabad or even flee the country.[81]

Thus, by arming certain networks, the American military fuelled conflicts along lines that depended largely on which group they supported. By forming the Khost Protection Force and the Afghan Security Guards, the Special Forces armed former Communist networks of the 1980s which took advantage of their position to avenge themselves on ex-mujahideen.[82] In Baghlan and Ghazni, the recruitment of Hizb-i Islami members reignited conflicts between mujahideen factions dating back to the 1990s.[83] By arming Tajiks and Hazaras respectively in Urgun (Paktya) and Khas Uruzgan (Uruzgan), the Special Forces managed to polarize a predominantly Pashtun region along ethnic lines.[84] In Kandahar, they relied on tribal networks (Barakzai, Ashiqzai), thus abetting a

[81] E-35 and E-81, elders of the Shinwari tribe living in Achin district (Nangarhar), August 2015. For a detailed account of the events, see Fabrizio Foschini, *How Outside Interference Politicised the Achin Let Conflict*, 30 October 2011, www.afghanistan-analysts.org/en/reports/war-and-peace/how-outside-interference-politicised-the-achin-land-conflict/.

[82] Thomas Ruttig, 'The Haqqani Network as an Autonomous Entity' in Antonio Giustozzi (ed.), *Decoding the New Taliban: Insights from the Afghan Field*, New York, Columbia University Press, 2009, pp. 87–8.

[83] E-33, assistant to the governor of Ghazni province, September 2014; E-50, president of the Ghazni Provincial Council, September 2014; E-76, second in command of the Afghan Local Police unit in Andar district, militant of the Hizb-i Islami, in Ghazni province, September 2014. For a detailed account of each of these local configurations, see Emal Habib, *Who Fights Whom in the Andar Uprising?*, 10 August 2012, www.afghanistan-analysts.org/en/reports/war-and-peace/aan-reportage-who-fights-whom-in-the-andar-uprising/; Gran Hewad, *When the Police Goes Local; More on the Baghlan ALP*, 4 March 2011, www.afghanistan-analysts.org/en/reports/political-landscape/when-the-police-goes-local-more-on-the-baghlan-alp/.

[84] Julius Cavendish, 'Afghanistan's Dirty War: Why the Most Feared Man in Bermal District Is a U.S. Ally', *Time*, 4 October 2011; Martina Van Biljert, *Security at the Fringes: the Case of Shujai in Khas Uruzgan*, 6 April 2013, www.afghanistan-analysts.org/en/reports/war-and-peace/security-at-the-fringes-the-case-of-shujai-in-khas-uruzgan/.

tribal framing of political opposition.[85] Sometimes the contracts awarded by the US military were the stakes in these clashes, as in the case of two militia commanders in the Shindand district (Herat) that was reported on in detail in a US Senate investigation. Cynically, the executives of the British company that employed them nicknamed the two commanders 'Mr. White' and 'Mr. Pink', a reference to Quentin Tarantino's film *Reservoir Dogs* about gangsters fighting over the loot from a robbery.[86]

[85] E-1, militia commander in Dand district (Kandahar), August 2010; E-17, former NDS agent, executive of a private Afghan security firm, August 2010; E-19, notable of Arghandab district (Kandahar), July 2011; E-62, senior official in the Kandahar provincial administration, July 2011. See also Anand Gopal, 'The Taliban in Kandahar' in Peter Bergen and Katherine Tiedemann (eds), *Talibanistan: Negotiating the Borders between Terror, Politics, and Religion*, Oxford, Oxford University Press, 2013, pp. 1–69.

[86] See the detailed investigation by the United States Senate, *Inquiry into the Role and Oversight of Private Security Contractors in Afghanistan*, Washington, United States Senate Armed Services Committee, 2009.

PART II
THE TALIBAN COURTS

5
A bureaucratic system

Introduction

> Mujahideen should make honest efforts to maintain justice and security in areas under the rule of the Islamic Emirate. They should eliminate thieves, highway robbers, and saboteur elements and procure a conducive atmosphere of security and well-being for people.
>
> Mullah Omar[1]

Establishing a judicial system was part of the Taliban's strategy of regaining power through armed struggle. From their Pakistani sanctuary, the leaders posed as a legitimate authority that alone was capable of restoring the rule of law, uniting Afghan society, and thus bringing an end to the civil war. In words and deeds, they did not regard themselves as an 'armed opposition', as the Kabul regime and the Western armed forces characterized them, but claimed legal continuity with the Islamic Emirate of the 1990s. However, in rebuilding their judicial institutions, the Taliban now adapted them to the conditions of war and clandestinity.

To begin with, structuring the Taliban judicial system required formalizing decision-making processes. The movement's disorganization after its defeat in 2001 slowed the pace of reconstituting a judicial system. The first judges were often appointed in response to local demands, but by the late 2000s the Taliban operated a bureaucratic and centralized system. Inserting judges into the jurisdictional hierarchy required the creation of processes to appoint them and formalize their position and relationship with the Taliban institutions and the court users. Two mechanisms ensured that judges followed procedures: close supervision by Taliban leaders and regular rotation to guarantee their impartiality.

[1] Speech by Mullah Omar on the occasion of Eid al-Fitr, 2014. In fact, Mullah Omar had already died when this speech was published on the movement's previous website—now no longer functioning (www.alamarah.com).

The Taliban Courts in Afghanistan. Adam Baczko, Oxford University Press. © Adam Baczko 2023.
DOI: 10.1093/oso/9780198896777.003.0006

However, operations by Western armed forces hampered centralization of the judicial system by disrupting the Taliban administration. The judges, relentlessly pursued by Western Special Forces, were forced into hiding. Senior movement officials at times would also interfere in decision-making processes and prioritize strategic issues over procedural compliance. While such interventions appeared to be infrequent, they were reminders of the primacy of the movement's political objectives and of the constant tension between immediate needs and the advantage of having a legitimate judicial system.

Formation of a judicial branch

In the early years, reforming a judicial system was not a priority for the Taliban leaders, disorganized as they were after their defeat by the US military and the Northern Alliance. The movement's officials were arrested, including the ambassador to Islamabad, Mullah Zaeef, and the commander of the Kabul garrison, Mullah Abdul Rauf Khadem. Others, such as Foreign Minister Mullah Mutawakil, surrendered and others ceased all military activity, as did Mawlawi Qalamuddin, the head of the Taliban's moral police known as the Ministry for the Propagation of Virtue and the Prevention of Vice. However, Mullah Omar and several of the movement's top leaders, in particular Mullah Baradar, Mullah Dadullah, Mullah Osmani, and Mullah Obaidullah, fled to Pakistan where they set about rebuilding the movement. In the early years of the war, this meant overcoming a series of obstacles. Many Afghans had actually welcomed the Emirate's fall, having had enough of authoritarianism, puritanism, the banning of drug culture, and the lack of economic development. Moreover, defeat and exile once again made the Taliban beholden to the Pakistani state, which many Afghans reviled for its role in the civil war of the 1990s. Finally, while the leadership had remained relatively intact, most of the militants had laid down their arms and gone home.

Politically marginalized, Taliban leaders hesitated at first to resume the armed struggle and repeatedly offered to negotiate or even capitulate. In December 2001, a letter from Mullah Omar's circle offered to recognize the new regime in return for immunity.[2] In November 2002, Taliban leaders held a meeting in Pakistan in an attempt to open negotiations with the Afghan

[2] Anand Gopal, 'The Taliban in Kandahar' in Peter Bergen and Katherine Tiedemann (eds), *Talibanistan: Negotiating the Borders between Terror, Politics, and Religion*, Oxford, Oxford University Press, 2013, pp. 11–12.

government and to consider peaceful participation in political life. In the winter of 2003–4, the Taliban made new overtures for negotiation, having by then reconstituted their movement sufficiently to demand a place in the government.[3] However, neither the Kabul government nor the United States, which considered the Taliban movement as annihilated, responded to these offers. In the aftermath of the 9/11 attacks, captured militants did not enjoy the legal protections accorded combatants, and even if they had laid down their arms, they were still vulnerable to imprisonment, torture, or even killing by the US military and Northern Alliance commanders. The continuing violence saw many of the movement's supporters take up arms again, as a Taliban judge during the former regime recounted: 'During the Taliban ouster from Afghanistan, then I was in Kandahar and decided to live like a normal villager. But after around two or less than two years, the Afghan government persecuted me. The Americans were searching for ex-Taliban commanders, that's why I had no choice but to rejoin the Taliban.'[4] Another former Islamic Emirate judge joined the insurgency in the 2000s after Gul Agha Shirzai's men, US Special Forces auxiliaries, imprisoned and tortured him.[5]

Between 2002 and 2004, the movement re-established itself clandestinely from Quetta, Pakistan, where the Taliban leaders had found refuge. They dispatched militants to the South and East to mobilize former members and recruit new ones, and they organized secret meetings to reconnect with their contacts. A Taliban official from Helmand province told me that he had crisscrossed the southern provinces (Zabul, Helmand, Kandahar, and Uruzgan) starting in the spring of 2002. In private residences, he brought together former militants to discuss the foreign presence and the new regime and urged them to take up arms again.[6] The insurgency made the border regions its first targets, taking advantage of the rugged terrain to the East and in the desert expanses to the South. At first, the insurgents moved discreetly into the most isolated villages, far from the main lines of communication. They secured control over these areas before gradually tightening the noose around the cities. As they settled in the villages, they intimidated or assassinated the regime's representatives (civil servants, pro-government clerics, or notables).

[3] Alex Strick van Linschoten and Felix Kuehn, *Lessons Learnt, 'Islamic, Independent, Perfect and Strong': Parsing the Taliban's Strategic Intentions, 2001–2011*, Swindon, Arts and Humanities Research Council, 2012, p. 7.

[4] I-20, Taliban appeals court judge, Qarabagh district (Ghazni), 2011.

[5] Anand Gopal, 'The Taliban in Kandahar' in Peter Bergen and Katherine Tiedemann (eds), *Talibanistan: Negotiating the Borders between Terror, Politics, and Religion*, Oxford, Oxford University Press, 2013, pp. 12–13.

[6] E-60, Taliban commander in Kandahar province, April 2013.

Gradually, groups called 'fronts' (*mahaz*) multiplied and built up their ranks of fighters. As one resident of Ghazni province said, 'in 2003, the groups formed in Ghazni were made up of locals who picked up their weapons and took refuge in the mountains. In 2004, large quantities of weapons began to pour in and fighters from Quetta began to be seen.'[7] Similarly, in Helmand in 2004, groups of several dozen fighters roamed the province's isolated northern districts; a year later, they numbered several hundred men.[8] In the East, the sequence was repeated: In 2002–3, Quetta envoys reconnected with former militants who were gradually rebuilding the movement. In July 2005, a clash in Kunar province, which killed nineteen American soldiers, revealed how deeply anchored the insurgency was locally by then. The northern provinces, more difficult to access from their Pakistani sanctuary and better controlled by Northern Alliance commanders, saw the first Taliban presence later, between 2006 and 2008.

Little is known about how the Taliban judicial system began and when the first courts appeared. Several judges said their first activities dated back to 2003–4: 'We did not have court in the provinces for only two years after the ouster of the Taliban government and the establishment of Karzai government; in fact we had not yet started jihad. When we started jihad against the Americans and the Afghan Government, from that time until now, we have had a court.'[9] Residents of the remote southern and eastern districts also recalled the existence of judges in the early years of the insurgency:

> When the Taliban came back from Pakistan and started jihad against the Karzai government and American troops, that's when the Taliban started their activities in our district [Qarabagh, Ghazni province]; at that time, they gathered villagers in the mosque and told us that they set up a court and had judges and warned us to use their court instead of the government court.[10]

According to a notable from Achin (Nangarhar), the first Taliban judge arrived in the district in 2005: 'Until 2003, there were no Taliban. They returned after 2003, a few men who preached, recruited men and extorted money. From 2005 on, they became more numerous, they collected the ushr [Islamic tithe of one tenth of the crops] and a judge settled in a village nearby.'[11] That same year, the

[7] E-79, resident of Ghazni province, April 2013.

[8] Theo Farrell and Antonio Giustozzi, 'The Taliban at War: Inside the Helmand Insurgency, 2004–2012', *International Affairs*, 2013, vol. 89, nº 4, pp. 849–51.

[9] I-20, Taliban appeals court judge, Qarabagh district (Ghazni), 2011.

[10] I-31, resident of Qarabagh district (Ghazni), 2011.

[11] E-81, a notable of the Shinwari tribe in Achin district (Nangarhar), August 2015.

British media reported for the first time a statement by a Taliban spokesman, Lutfullah Hakimi, that a British kidnap victim would be 'tried'. However, journalists immediately questioned his credibility, calling Hakimi 'self-proclaimed spokesman and […] frequently inaccurate in his statements, although he is said to speak for the Taliban'.[12] Starting in 2008, foreign correspondents and Afghan journalists regularly reported on the existence of Taliban judges and described their activities among the rural populations.[13]

In 2010, when I began my research, the judicial system operated with several hundred judges and covered all rural areas except the central areas inhabited by Shia. Although difficult to assess, the activity of the Taliban courts appeared to be considerable, although varying by province. Several district trial court judges estimated that they received from ten to as many as twenty complaints on days they were in session. In the remote Alishang district (Laghman), the situation was different:

> Residents of Alishang don't flock to the Taliban courts. We receive only two or three complaints in a week. So, we have enough time to take a rest and study books. We have nothing more to do. However, there is great rush in the Taliban courts of the southern provinces. When I was serving in other districts, we would not receive applications after 10 am due to the influx of petitioners. But, here we happily receive a complaint even after 1 o'clock in the afternoon.[14]

Understandably, appeals courts received fewer petitions. 'The appeals court in Dahan-i-Ghori receives five to six appeals daily. People come and inform us about their judges. They also file appeals with us against verdicts of lower courts when they are not satisfied with them.'[15]

The Taliban established courts as part of forming an alternative government. In June 2003, the Taliban announced the formation in Quetta of a ten-member Leadership Council (Rahbari Shura) to coordinate the fight against Western troops and the government, which they dismissed as 'puppets'.[16] Initially, this council appointed governors for the southern provinces, where the insurgency

[12] Mitchell Prothero, 'Body of Missing Briton Found in Afghanistan', *The Observer*, 4 September 2005.
[13] 'Living under the Taleban', *Institute for War and Peace Reporting*, 11 April 2007; Tom Blackwell, 'Taliban Rule Returning to Kandahar Province', *National Post*, 26 October 2008; Chris Sands, 'Afghans Missing Taliban Justice', *The National*, 24 November 2008; Soraya Nelson, 'Taliban Courts Filling Justice Vacuum in Afghanistan', *National Public Radio*, 16 December 2008; Jason Straziuso and Amir Shah, 'As Taliban Nears Kabul, Shadow Gov't Takes Hold', *Associated Press*, 27 December 2008.
[14] I-19, Taliban trial court judge, Alishang district (Laghman), 2011.
[15] I-4, Taliban appeals court judge, Dahan-i Ghuri district (Baghlan), 2011.
[16] 'Taliban Names Anti-U.S. Leadership Council', *Reuters*, 24 June 2003.

was most entrenched. As its military fortunes improved, from 2006 onwards the movement tightened its grip by appointing district governors.[17] In 2008, at least two dozen districts were ruled by the Taliban, and half of them no longer saw representatives of the Kabul regime. At the same time, coordination bodies were multiplying at different administrative levels. In 2012, governors were appointed in all provinces except Panjshir, and in 150–200 districts out of 350.[18]

The setting up of courts accompanied the territorial expansion of this administrative apparatus. In the early years, the Taliban appointed judges only in areas where they had a firm foothold. For example, the provinces of Helmand, Kandahar, and Zabul, bordering the Pakistani province of Balochistan where the movement's leaders had taken refuge, were the first to have the insurgency control villages and appoint judges. Subsequently, the courts became part of the Taliban's arsenal for their territorial conquests. In the North in particular, as early as 2006–8, as the insurgency began to set up cells, judges went in with the first groups of fighters. A Taliban leader active in the insurgency since 2002–3, who led operations in Kabul against Western troops and then became a district administrator, explained to me that 'at first, the priority was to put all the men available in the military, but today it is in the judicial system that we put men, because our military structure is quite developed'.[19]

The jurisdictional structure

The Taliban integrated judges into a hierarchical system that helped rationalize its functioning. In the early years, it was common for commanders to act as magistrates.[20] The insurgency's first senior officials were ulama and they claimed legal competence by virtue of that title. Beginning in the mid-2000s, judges deployed by the movement were ordered to stay out of combat. 'A Taliban judge never goes out to fight, because the Taliban high-ranking officials are afraid

[17] Antonio Giustozzi, *Koran, Kalashnikov, and Laptop: The Neo-Taliban Insurgency in Afghanistan*, New York, Columbia University Press, 2008, p. 111.

[18] Antonio Giustozzi, 'Hearts, Minds, and the Barrel of a Gun: The Taliban's Shadow Government', *Prism*, 2012, vol. 3, n° 2, p. 73. Although the Taliban were not established in the areas populated by Shiite Hazaras, successive Afghan rulers have divided Hazarajat into several provinces (Bamyan, Parwan, Maidan Wardak, Ghazni, Uruzgan, Daikundi, Ghor), each time with a large Sunni population, which explains the appointment of Taliban governors in these provinces.

[19] E-60, Taliban commander in Kandahar province, April 2013.

[20] See, for example, the case of the Taliban commander Mullah Asadullah in Ghazni who, in 2006, on his own ruled on a case of adultery, Christoph Reuter and Borhan Yunus, 'The Return of the Taliban in Andar District' in Antonio Giustozzi (ed.), *Decoding the New Taliban: Insights from the Afghan Field*, New York, Columbia University Press, 2009, p. 111.

that judges will get killed in the fighting, it being so difficult to find a well-trained man to be a judge.'[21]

The Taliban replicated the institutional architecture of their judicial system from the 1990s based on the 1964 Constitution: trial or lower courts (Ibtidaia Mahkama); provincial appeals courts (also called executive courts, Ijraia Mahkama, or superior courts, Stara Mahkama); a Supreme Court (Mahkam-i Markazi); and a Court of Cassation (Mahkam-i Tamiz). By taking over the nomenclature of the Islamic Emirate's judicial institutions, the Taliban movement staked a claim to the continuity of its state authority, in this way lending its courts more official gravitas. One of its judges described how the legal process typically functioned under this scheme: 'In our judicial system, a case is first decided by a lower court. If a litigant has any objection to the verdict of the lower court, he goes to the appeals court. His petition is dealt with by the appeals court judge. Usually, the verdicts of appeals courts are not challenged unlike those of the lower courts.'[22] Jurisdictions generally overlaid the government's map of provinces and districts, which in turn conformed to those of earlier regimes. In principle, persons who disagreed with an appeals court's verdict could petition the Supreme Court, located in Helmand.

> The Taliban Supreme Court is currently in office in Nawzad district in Helmand province. People from all provinces of Afghanistan come to the Supreme Court. A large number of people visits it daily. Every day, about 20 to 25 persons come to the Supreme Court. […] It was already the Taliban's Supreme Court when the Islamic Emirate of Afghanistan was there. […] All Taliban judges are representatives of the Supreme Court and all Taliban courts in all districts are branches of the Supreme Court.[23]

To my knowledge, resort to the Supreme Court was rare. It was reserved for weightier matters that usually involved parties who were well-connected with the Taliban and could travel. In addition, to be effective, the prerogatives of the Supreme Court required practical adjustments: a branch of the Supreme Court had to be opened in Peshawar (Pakistan) for Afghans from the East or North who had difficulty in getting to Helmand.[24] In some places, it had to delegate its prerogatives to a Military Commission (Nizami Komisiun): 'In the remote provinces, the role of the Supreme Court is played by the Military Commission.

[21] I-9, judge in a Taliban court, Dawlat Abad district (Faryab), 2011.
[22] I-25, Taliban appeals court judge, Bala Mughab district (Badghis), 2011.
[23] I-3, Taliban trial court judge, Ab Kamari district (Badghis), 2011.
[24] E-8, resident of Shirzad district (Nangarhar), August 2015.

The Military Commission, which is functional in every province, works as the Supreme Court in the remote areas.'[25] Lastly, the Court of Cassation could review the verdicts of the Supreme Court: 'There is a department, called cassation, which can overturn the verdicts of the Supreme Court. It can ask the Supreme Court to revisit a verdict. The cassation department works in Sangin district in Helmand province.'[26] Formally, the Supreme Court and the Court of Cassation had their seats in two neighbouring districts in northern Helmand; in practice, they often held hearings in Pakistan, especially to avoid airstrikes and raids by the US Special Forces.

All judges were managed by the executive leadership as they had been in the 1990s. In 2007, a Judiciary Committee (Qaziano Komitah) was formed within the Leadership Council (Rahbari Shura), the movement's executive body headquartered in Quetta. It was composed of ulama, who were usually veteran leaders of the movement. 'The courts are established on the orders of a committee, based in Quetta, Balochistan province of Pakistan. This committee is comprised of ten members. All of them are religious scholars and they know Islamic law very well.'[27] The Judicial Committee appointed, assigned, and paid the judges. In 2011–12, their monthly salary amounted to 10,000–12,000 afghanis depending on their position, or about $200–$250—a high salary in rural areas.

Centralized supervision of all judges from Quetta soon proved unwieldy, however. Branches of the Judiciary Committee therefore opened in Peshawar and Miranshah, Pakistani cities from which the Taliban coordinated their military operations in the East and Southeast, respectively. In addition, the Military Commission in each province organized the armed struggle and the civil administration:

> The Taliban courts, operating in various districts of a province, work under the Military Commission of that province. In each province, there is a separate Military Commission. This commission is authorized to open or close Taliban courts in the province concerned. The Military Commission closes Taliban courts in a district in case of danger or threat. That's why the 10 members of the Quetta [Leadership] Council formed a Military Commission in every province to look after the Taliban courts. It is the duty

[25] I-13, head of the Military Commission in Laghman province, 2011.
[26] I-10, Taliban trial court judge, Tala wa Barfak district (Baghlan), 2011.
[27] I-5, Taliban trial court judge, Karagai district (Laghman), 2011.

of Military Commission to issue transfer orders to Taliban judges and district administrators.[28]

In Badghis, Baghlan, and Laghman provinces, the Military Commission met with the judges every Friday. A judge in Dushi district (Baghlan) explained: 'All Taliban judges, me included, hold a meeting in a court every Friday, changing the court each time. Members of the Military Commission along with its chief attend this meeting. On this occasion, the Military Commission issues new directives and advices for Taliban judges.'[29] The commissions were empowered to open and close courts and had to approve sentences before judges could hand them down. '[N]one of the judges can announce a verdict without the permission of the Military Commission. Every judge has to send his verdict to the Military Commission before announcing it. The members and head of the Military Commission validate the decision and then authorize a judge to pronounce it.'[30] The head of the Laghman Military Commission explained his role like this:

> As the head of a Military Commission, I am responsible for the whole province. I appoint all judges in the province on the advice of the [Judiciary] Committee. But, as I said, that does not mean that I control the minds of judges. There must be someone in charge, as in any organization, to run it and, in that case, this is me. And that is it. There is no question of control that would allow me to derive personal benefits or things like that.[31]

However, this control was also eminently political (see Supervision of judges).

In 2010–11, following a conflict within the Taliban administration of Zabul province, the insurgency split the provincial commission: on one side, the Military Commission assembled the province's senior leaders and led the movement at the local level; on the other, a new Implementation Council saw to the administrative tasks:[32]

> It is a council that works alongside the Taliban provincial council in every province of the country. It comprises 12 ulama. These members include ulama from the areas where the Taliban has courts. This council performs

[28] I-13, head of the Military Commission in Laghman province, 2011.
[29] I-8, Taliban trial court judge, Dushi district (Baghlan), 2011.
[30] I-21, Taliban trial court judge, Ghormach district (Badghis), 2011.
[31] I-13, head of the Taliban Military Commission in Laghman province, 2011.
[32] I-25, Taliban appeals court judge, Bala Mughab district (Badghis), 2011.

> the following tasks: one, it conducts tests to appoint new judges; two, it issues guidelines to new Taliban judges; three, it drafts leaflets and declarations on behalf of the Taliban; four, it reviews and, along with the members of provincial council, checks verdicts delivered by Taliban judges.[33]

A judge summarized the pyramidal hierarchy between the three institutions in this way:

> The Implementation Council is composed of ulama. It works under the supervision of the Military Commission. It hands over its decisions and orders to the Military Commission for implementation. The commission then sends them to the [Judiciary] committee. These decisions are implemented by the Military Commission after approval by the Quetta Shura.[34]

In practice, this layering applied only in provinces with the most centralized administrations, and often the prerogatives of both bodies overlapped, for example, when recruiting judges (see Chapter 6).

In areas which the regime functionaries and Western military no longer entered, the Taliban set up their administrative function in buildings known to the residents. Conversely, districts in which the insurgency's control was weak did not have appeals courts and instead the Military Commission fulfilled that function there. The degree of control exerted by the insurgency determined how the courts operated, as explained by another judge:

> Taliban courts operate only in districts that are Taliban strongholds. The Taliban do not establish their courts in areas they do not control. Because, you know, it is difficult to administer justice in an area you do not control at all. So how can you take decisions and enforce them? Because it's not just a matter of taking decisions, you have to enforce them as well.[35]

For example, in the summer of 2011, the Taliban Military Commission in Baghlan province refused to set up a court because the movement lacked a footprint on the ground: 'People have just requested the Military Commission to establish Taliban courts in Tala wa Barfak district so that poor residents of the district can easily resolve their problems. But the commission says it cannot set

[33] I-3, Taliban trial court judge, Ab Kamari district (Badghis), 2011.
[34] I-19, Taliban trial court judge, Alishang district (Laghman), 2011.
[35] I-26, Taliban appeals court judge, Alishang district (Laghman), 2011.

up courts in the district until there are enough local Taliban in Tala wa Barfak.'[36] The organization of the courts was also vulnerable to strategic adjustments by the Western armed forces. For example, the 30,000 troops the US poured into the southern provinces (Helmand, Kandahar) disrupted the Taliban justice system for several years. Conversely, in the East, the insurgency's continued progress was reflected in a more extensive court infrastructure.

The rotation of judges

The Taliban rotated its judges through the court system to achieve two ends: to keep them from being coopted by the populations and to enforce discipline. 'Like Taliban military commanders and other officials, Taliban judges are also transferred after a fixed period, usually after three months. If a judge is not transferred after three months, he must be transferred after six months. A six-month term is the longest period for a Taliban judge to serve in a position.'[37] A judge reflected on his series of assignments:

> I have served in five–six districts as a judge. My first appointment as a judge was in Shahr-i Naw district in Paktia. Then I was transferred to Mohamad Agha district in Logar. My third appointment was in Narkh district of Maidan Wardak province, from where I was transferred to Sayid Abad district in the same province. My fifth assignment took me to Khogiani district in Nangarhar province. Presently, I serve in Karagai district in Laghman province.[38]

This rotation system covered the entire country, with judges sent from East to West, from North to South: 'I have worked as a judge in nine provinces. These provinces include Ghazni, Zabul, Helmand, Khost, Kunduz, Uruzgan, Herat and Logar. Then I was transferred to Laghman.'[39] People living in areas controlled by the insurgency were aware of this practice. A resident of the district of Qarabagh (Ghazni) thus was able not just to name his current district judge and which province he came from, but also to recall the name of his predecessor and how long he had held the post.[40] However, contrary to reports of

[36] I-23, Taliban trial court judge, Dahan-i Ghuri district (Baghlan), 2011.
[37] I-6, Taliban trial court judge, Qala-i Naw (Badghis), 2011.
[38] I-2, Taliban trial court judge, Karagai district (Laghman), 2011.
[39] I-5, Taliban trial court judge, Karagai district (Laghman), 2011.
[40] I-36, resident of Qarabagh district (Ghazni), 2011.

Taliban judges being rotated every three to six months, this resident of Sayid Abad district, Wardak, described a more irregular schedule:

> Taliban have no system, but Taliban judges rotate when the Taliban high ranking officials want to rotate their commanders, judges or fighters. Sometimes Taliban judges change in three months, sometimes they change in six months and sometimes they change after one or two years. The rotation of Taliban judges depends on their work in the district or village, if the villagers are happy with a judge then he stays a long time. I've seen some Taliban judges rotate out after a very short time in Sayid Abad district.[41]

This rotation was coordinated by the movement's provincial and central institutions. 'There is an established mechanism for this. They are transferred from one province to another after the end of their term. They are not transferred from one district to another in the same province.'[42] Military Commissions supervised rotations of individual judges locally on instructions from the movement's leadership. 'The orders are issued by the [Leadership] Council in Quetta to the Military Commission. The Military Commission carries out these orders in all the departments of the province concerned. No one except the Taliban Military Commission can transfer a judge.'[43]

As noted earlier, this system for appointments and rotations was designed to prevent a judge from establishing links with the population under his jurisdiction and becoming susceptible to forms of pressure or bribery. The head of the Laghman Military Commission explained the rotation system thus:

> We have our policy. We do not want someone to stay longer in a position because, after becoming familiar with the area, people and the local norms and values, he might get in a corrupt way. He may become despotic. So, taking this policy into account, we are following the instructions from the council and of course Mullah Mohamad Omar the mujahid to transfer judges after at least six months. Sometimes, when the people are happy with the judge, then why would we transfer him? It depends on the judge and his integrity.[44]

The Taliban judges justified this transfer system in similar terms:

[41] I-32, resident of Sayid Abad district (Wardak), 2011.
[42] I-21, Taliban trial court judge, Ghormach district (Badghis), 2011.
[43] I-22, Taliban appeals court judge, Ghormach district (Badghis), 2011.
[44] I-13, head of the Taliban Military Commission in Laghman province, 2011.

> This is only to avoid any unpleasant incident. Sometimes you know when you remain in power for a longer time, you become used to everything, you come to know people very well but on the other hand you become despotic and there is a great possibility that you become corrupt. That's why Taliban have devised a system to transfer everybody after a fixed tenure so that there should be no possibility of that at all.[45]

The testimony of a resident of Qarabagh district, Ghazni, suggests that not only the Taliban but also the population saw it in that way: 'If there were a Taliban judge from Qarabagh district, there might be possibilities of passing an unfair judgment for the benefit of their family, friends, etc. Now these Taliban judges do not have family here and friends in this district to find for unfairly. That is why they can deliver fair verdicts and judge cases according to sharia law.'[46]

To compensate for the effects of frequent changes in jurisdiction, local ulama supported the magistrates. 'Taliban judges, both at lower and superior courts, are flanked by white-bearded and young ulama. Taliban judges seek suggestions from these religious scholars. The suggestions of these mullahs are essential to deciding a case.'[47] These local ulama—who were paid—fulfilled an advisory role and ensured continuity. 'They have complete information about all verdicts and guide the newly-appointed judge if a case is brought a second time before the court.'[48] They also have a memory of local conflicts and so can provide the judge with context: 'The new judge can easily get information about the case. There are elderly mullahs from the district in every court. The judges are transferred, but the mullahs stay. They can point out if a person files a case, which has been decided by the former judge.'[49] They could dissent from the judge's verdict and, while the final decision rested with the judge, their objection strengthened the cause when appealing the judge's verdict.

In addition, judges reported archiving practices for verdicts that varied by time period and province. They usually filed copies with the Military Commission. These archives served to verify past verdicts if a party appealed the decision or turned to Taliban judges for the same cause. 'It is easy for a judge because he knows if a case has already been decided. He knows that all verdicts are sent to the Military Commission where the members of the commission review them and then allow judges to pronounce them. So he can get

[45] I-6, Taliban trial court judge, Qala-i Naw district (Badghis), 2011.
[46] I-36, resident of Qarabagh district (Ghazni), 2011.
[47] I-25, Taliban appeals court judge, Bala Mughab district (Badghis), 2011.
[48] I-12, Taliban trial court judge, Nahrin district (Baghlan), 2011.
[49] I-1, Taliban trial court judge, Nahrin district (Baghlan), 2011.

information if a case has already been decided by the former judge.'[50] Despite several centralization projects, judicial records were retained at the provincial level because of wartime pressures. However, in some provinces, the Military Commission did not seem to require copies of verdicts, for example in Ghazni, where a judge said that he recorded his rulings in a notebook:

> When I was a judge in Kandahar province, Shah Wali Kot district, at that time we kept a record of most cases. But in here we do not keep a lot the record of the cases […] We don't keep a record of the issued sentences, but we take a short note in our notebook about every trial and sentences issued.[51]

In Logar province, another judge said he passed out copies of his verdicts to the parties and did not file them:

> We do not keep a record of our verdicts because what we say, people accept it. No one rejects it. We only give one copy of the verdict to one party and another copy of the verdict to the other party. Another reason is that we do not have an appropriate facility to keep these records, and we do not carry copies of verdicts from one place to another.[52]

In some provinces, due to a lack of qualified judges and a weak administration, judges were rarely if ever transferred. This seemed to reflect pragmatism on the part of the insurgency, as noted by a resident of Qarabagh district (Ghazni) who had a case before the Taliban court:

> The judges are not changing in a short time, because the Taliban don't have many judges to change them very quickly. While the Taliban change the fighters or commanders very quickly, because they have a lot of fighters and commanders, they don't have enough judges to change them every five or six months. But yes, if any judge tries to do something wrong, he will be changed very quickly, but if a judge works properly and according to the Taliban system and according Sharia law, they won't change him for one or two years.[53]

Contrary to the procedures as described by most judges, in some districts local ulama were appointed as judges. A US Army adviser, Carter Malkasian,

[50] I-17, Taliban appeals court judge, Dushi district (Baghlan), 2011.
[51] I-20, Taliban trial court judge, Qarabagh district (Ghazni), 2011.
[52] I-7, Taliban court judge, Logar province, 2013.
[53] I-31, resident of Qarabagh district (Ghazni), 2011.

reported that until 2008 in Garmsir district, Helmand, the Taliban governor Abdul Hadi Agha appointed judges from within the district.[54] In some districts of Kunar and Nouristan, Salafist groups in the insurgency installed their own judges.[55]

Supervision of judges

Holding judges accountable for their work relied on internal supervisory mechanisms. First in line were the Military Commissions to which judges had to submit their weightiest rulings before handing them down. A Taliban judge practising in Badghis province explained how it worked:

> Taliban judges don't decide cases like the judges of the puppet Karzai's government. Government judges issue different verdicts in similar cases. Government judges decide a case in your favor if you have money to bribe them. On the other hand, Taliban judges first send their proposed verdicts to the Military Commission along with the petitions and then make their verdicts public. So, the Military Commission receives complete information on all verdicts.[56]

Several other judges interviewed also pointed to the link between the commission's control and the impartiality of the judicial system. As the head of the Laghman Military Commission explained: 'If a verdict seems incorrect to us, then we summon the judge concerned and discuss it with him. After getting complete information and thinking about the verdict, we order the judge to either announce it or change it.'[57] He made clear that this review was not intended to alter the rulings but only to ensure that the verdict was impartially arrived at in conformity with Islamic law:

> This doesn't mean that we, as a commission, have an upper hand and can interfere in other's domain. We have our own limitations and we can't go beyond our limitations. But this is a set procedure to closely monitor all the decisions made in various cases to ensure that justice is served to each and every

[54] Carter Malkasian, *War Comes to Garmser: Thirty Years of Conflict on the Afghan Frontier*, Oxford, Oxford University Press, 2013.
[55] E-7, Taliban court judge, Kunar province, April 2013.
[56] I-22, Taliban appeals court judge, Ghormach district (Badghis), 2011.
[57] I-13, head of the Military Commission in Laghman province, 2011.

> one who seeks it from the Taliban. So that's why a case has to pass through us to make sure the judge has no personal interest in a particular case and that it has been decided totally on the merits.[58]

Commissions met regularly and residents could lodge complaints about judges with their members. 'The commission punishes judges for wrong decisions. The punishment includes termination of service and six months' imprisonment. The Commander of the Faithful [Mullah Omar] has empowered the Military Commission to punish judges.'[59]

The practical effect of this political control was to make sure that political affairs were handled as the movement's leaders wanted. For example, in a land dispute between two villages in Khogiani district (Nangarhar), successive jurisdictions of the Taliban judicial hierarchy referred their representatives to the Supreme Court branch in Peshawar, which stayed a judgment until the end of the war.[60] Similarly, in a conflict over land between two families, both with links to the Taliban, the documentary and testimonial evidence did not conclusively favour either party, causing the judge to refer the case to the provincial commission, which sent it up to the Supreme Court in Quetta. The person who told me about the case was a party to the disputes; he was convinced that the movement leadership held the judgment in abeyance because of the two families' connections in the insurgency.[61] In another case involving a dispute over a forest in Asmar district, Kunar, a Taliban judge was ordered to stay his verdict, as it had turned into an issue fought over by notables of the Salarzai and Mashwani tribes. The Taliban hierarchy ordered all logging in the forest stopped pending a decision, to avoid offending either party.[62]

As another device for keeping tabs on judges, the movement regularly sent undercover operatives to gauge the public's opinion about a district court or to investigate specific cases. 'I can be sent to monitor judges and commanders in their activities. They don't know me. I can be sent to any province or on any case by the Leadership Council [Rahbari Shura].'[63] The existence of these secret investigators of Taliban cadres' conduct was confirmed by journalists and interrogation notes of US Special Forces leaked in 2012 to the *New York Times*.[64]

[58] Ibid.
[59] I-18, Taliban appeals court judge, Alingar district (Laghman), 2011.
[60] E-8, resident of one of the two villages involved, Shirzad district (Nangarhar), August 2015.
[61] E-16, resident of Kunar province, April 2013.
[62] E-31, a notable of Kunar province, September 2012.
[63] E-69, Taliban official tasked with inspecting the courts for the Leadership Council, April 2013.
[64] Miles Amoore, 'Afghans Flock to Judge Dread and his Butcher Boys', *The Sunday Times*, 23 January 2011; 'State of the Taliban', *The New York Times*, 23 February 2012.

Similarly, members of the Military Commission regularly visited villages and kept themselves informed of how the locals felt about the judges. The head of the Laghman Military Commission explained:

> We have six functional courts in the province under my command. So it's not a big deal. My people inform me on all changes that happen in the area of my operation. […] I myself inspect the various courts and oversee the activities of the judges and courts. That's no problem at all. And that's how we used to run things during the era when we were in power.[65]

District governors also played a role in this monitoring system, even though court-related issues were not formally part of their portfolio. A notable from the district of Dawlat Abad (Faryab) recounted that 'Taliban district governor Mullah I. also sometimes observes the judging of Mullah M. Sometimes he comes in the villages and asks people about security and about the judging of Mullah M.'[66] He next brought up the case of a dispute over an unpaid debt, adding, 'the district governor Mullah I. came to our village and met with the elders. He then asked the elders: "last week Mullah M. solved a problem in here, how was it?" And he asked the people: "are you happy with his judgement?"'[67]

Finally, village notables could report a judge who abused his power to the Military Commission. As one judge explained: 'While we are resolving cases, there are also Taliban commanders, local notables attending the trial. So if we try to misuse our position or try to take a bribe or announce the decision in favor of one side on the basis of relations, then these people will inform the commission and there will be big problems.'[68] A resident of Wardak province confirmed that the most influential notables would take a complaint about a judge to the Military Commission:

> Sayid Abad district is a remote district and the Taliban have lots of activities in the villages of this district, but the Taliban also has a[n] [administrative] system in this district. If someone feels that this judge is not good enough and causes lots of problems, then there are some notables who can complain to the high ranking officials of Taliban about that judge. Most of the time, they complain to the Military Commission and then the Military Commission investigates that judge. If they find out that he is not a good enough judge, then

[65] I-13, head of the Military Commission in Laghman province, 2011.
[66] I-28, a notable of Dawlat Abad district (Faryab), 2011.
[67] Ibid.
[68] I-20, Taliban appeals court judge, Qarabagh district (Ghazni), 2011.

> they change him very quickly. It doesn't happen a lot, but sometimes influential notables have this ability to complain against the Taliban commander and Taliban judges to the Taliban high ranking authorities like the Military Commission or the Taliban district chief.[69]

Nevertheless, accusations of nepotism and malfeasance were still levelled at Taliban judges, as one resident of Ghazni province pointed out: 'Some of the local villagers are against the Taliban court and against the Taliban judges, because sometimes Taliban also judges on relations of friendship or sometimes Taliban judges get bribes from one side and solve for the benefits of that side. That's why some people are not happy with the Taliban court.'[70] Several of my interlocutors pointed out in the same vein that having connections inside the insurgency could be essential to winning at trial:

> We are caught up in a conflict over land ownership in Andar. We went to the government, but we lost the case. We don't know what to do, people have a choice between the government men, who want money, and the Taliban who demand to have relations (wasta), or to be on the side of the militiamen, but then you have to get in with them. Everyone's corrupt.[71]

I was told about instances in which corrupt judges favouring their relatives would invariably be fired. In 2012, a notable from Andar, often asked to facilitate the work of the Taliban courts, told me: 'A judge ruled against the person who should have won the case. The person complained to the Commission. They investigated and discovered that the judge had received a bribe. The judge was summoned to Quetta and dismissed. [...] Taliban judges are rarely corrupt, they are too afraid of their leaders and the Military Commission that regularly visits villages.'[72] In 2009, a similar case was reported to a Canadian journalist. A shopkeeper in Helmand told of a judge who 'was found taking a bribe and the Taliban put black all over his face and tied him to a tree, when he was released, he was fired'.[73] In 2015, a resident of Shirzad district, Nangarhar province, told me about another judge's dismissal: "They replaced the judge just before Ramadan, a month and a half ago [in June]. The Taliban

[69] I-33, resident of Sayid Abad district (Wardak), 2011.
[70] I-31, resident of Qarabagh district (Ghazni), 2011.
[71] E-78, user of a Taliban court in Andar district (Ghazni), September 2014.
[72] E-13, notable of Andar district (Ghazni), September 2012.
[73] Kathy Gannon, 'Despite U.S. Troops, Taliban Roam Freely in South', *Associated Press*, 18 August 2009.

were dissatisfied with the judge: he accepted gifts, not money, but gifts. After his decisions in particular, people offered him small gifts, clothes, shoes, worth around a hundred dollars. The Taliban didn't know the judge was accepting gifts.'[74] Finally, far from the exceptionalism associated with armed movements, the Taliban case showed the effectiveness of conventional institutional processes. As in any institution, the formation of the Taliban judicial system happened through the objectivization of social relations. Integrating judges into a bureaucracy allowed for both impersonal mediation and establishing rules and rationalizing procedures.[75] This is a common feature of contemporary insurgencies, although it is rare to see the degree of centralization that here ensured the regular transfer of judges. The uniqueness of the Taliban compared to other armed movements, however, lies elsewhere: in their connection with a network of madrasas providing them with jurists socially recognized as competent to interpret the law.

[74] E-45, student at Jalalabad University and resident of Shirzad district (Nangarhar), August 2015.

[75] Max Weber, *Economy and Society*, Berkeley, University of California Press, 1978, pp. 292–4 and 584–5.

6
The dual membership of judges

Introduction

The key to understanding the insurgency's juridical system is that the movement organized itself around a network of madrasas. While the Taliban shared the political agenda of other Islamist movements—the application of Islamic law—they differed from them on the question of how to institute sharia law. A comparison with the Islamic State in Iraq and Syria and the 2012–13 Syrian insurgency is instructive for characterizing the Taliban's relationship with the law. As is typical of most contemporary insurgencies, the Syrian insurgency used the regime's buildings, personnel, and procedures to build its juridical system. Looking towards Western powers and international institutions, whose support and recognition they hoped for, the Syrian insurgents also appropriated the formal trappings of judicial activity: the court building, the trial setting, the legal codes. The law they adopted was a product of negotiation among different stakeholders, including lawyers, regime judges who had switched allegiance, and religious scholars. This compromise was also shaped by the pressures of international recognition and their own political objectives. As a result, they picked up a readily available source from a public institution: a codified Islamic law found on the internet known as the Code of the Arab Union, created in the 1990s by an obscure Arab League commission and never before applied anywhere.[1]

In stark contrast, the Islamic State, breaking with an international order whose premises it rejected (borders, international recognition, multilateral institutions), did away with any formalization of Islamic law. Its judges asserted a radical version of Salafist ideology, applying a literal reading of precepts drawn from the Quran and the hadiths. In practice, the limited number of religious texts left the judges with a great deal of discretion, all the more so since the Islamic State only set up courts in areas where it had earlier achieved a

[1] For more on this, see Adam Baczko, Gilles Dorronsoro, and Arthur Quesnay, *Civil War in Syria: Mobilization and Competing Social Orders*, Cambridge, Cambridge University Press, 2018, pp. 118–32.

The Taliban Courts in Afghanistan. Adam Baczko, Oxford University Press. © Adam Baczko 2023.
DOI: 10.1093/oso/9780198896777.003.0007

monopoly on violence. Indifferent to the structures of the international system, this legal system was also detached from local issues, essentially carrying out a programme of moral edification and political repression.[2]

The Taliban positioned themselves differently, however. On the margins of the international system, because of their association with Al Qaeda in particular, they also craved international recognition. Thus, in continuity with their practices of the 1990s, the Taliban juridical system in essence oriented itself to handling Afghan issues—but without rejecting international norms. Its specificities lay in the multipositionality of the judges: as ulama, they belong to the religious field, and, as magistrates, to the juridical field, a dual positioning made possible by their recruitment from Deobandi madrasas on the Afghan-Pakistan border, which also produced the movement's top leaders.

This pool of recruits furnished the insurgency with a homogeneous body of candidates who already shared the social profile of its leaders. In this way, the Taliban benefited from the ideological work the madrasas did with young Afghans from rural areas and refugee camps. After a decade in religious schools, far from their families and villages, the graduates shared a range of theological-legal skills, a bureaucratic *habitus*, and a worldview that set them apart from their home environment. In addition, many fought for the movement, usually during their student years. The passage through the Deobandi madrasas provided the Taliban with trained staff. It created individual dispositions in judges that reinforced the effectiveness of the institutional arrangements into which the movement inserted them. This system also facilitated the recruitment of loyal militants who, by the sole fact of their recruitment and appointment, were presented—and perceived themselves—as impartial.

While Deobandi religious schools actively supported the Taliban movement, they retained their independence. Having the status of *alim* conferred by external institutions reinforced their legitimacy. By relying on an independent training body, the Taliban responded in part to the difficulties of ascertaining legal competence in a war context. The ulama's technical competence in Islamic law, certified by external institutions commonly recognized in the religious field, countered the suspicion that political affiliations swayed judicial actions. Judges derived their authority both from being appointed by the Taliban and from the madrasas certifying their competence. In effect, as ulama they had credibility in deciding the cases before them and as Taliban judges they had the means of enforcing their verdicts.

[2] Ibid., pp. 199–221.

Recruitment by examination

Candidates for Taliban judgeships had to pass an examination that tested their competence in Islamic law. A judge in Baghlan province justified this method of recruitment as both simple and quick: 'We have a very simple mechanism for selecting judges. We can't afford lengthy and complicated procedure. Taliban leaders conduct tests for judicial appointment.'[3] Another judge outlined the standard test procedure in the following way:

> Taliban judges are appointed by the 10-member Quetta council via the Military Commission. The 10-member council sends a sample of legal cases through the Military Commission, which is then used to examine the candidate judges. They are asked to decide the cases. The candidates write down their decisions. Then the papers are sent to the council along with three photos and photocopies of the candidates' identity cards. The council forwards the photocopies of the identity cards of successful candidates to the Military Commission, which announces the names of the candidates appointed as Taliban judges.[4]

Only madrasa graduates could take the exam. This eligibility criterion underlines the importance accorded by the movement to this qualification, which is explained by the Taliban's clerical composition. This attention to the objectivized form of religious knowledge can also be explained by the transformations the Afghan juridical field underwent during the war. To graduate from a madrasa became an essential qualification for applying the law. The testing by the movement in effect established a barrier to the conversion of religious capital into a legal appointment. It marked the key moment in the formation of an institution: it installed the *alim* as a judge. If being an *alim* was a precondition for being appointed judge, the Taliban movement granted itself the prerogative of determining which ulama qualified for judicial appointment. In principle, they had to have completed at least eight years of higher education (*fazilat*) before being allowed to interpret religious texts (*ijaza*), at which point they earned the title of *alim*. According to a senior official of the movement, responsible for inspecting magistrates, 'Judges cannot be ordinary people. After obtaining a religious education, they must have completed the Daura-i Hadith [final year of the graduate cycle] and have completed a specialization in jurisprudence.'[5]

[3] I-12, Taliban trial court judge, Nahrin district (Baghlan), 2011.
[4] I-14, Taliban trial court judge, Alingar district (Laghman), 2011.
[5] E-2, senior Taliban official, April 2013.

In practice, rare was the candidate who specialized in jurisprudence (*Takmil Ifta*) or in the hadiths (*Takhassus fil Hadith*) during his schooling and was therefore a highly sought after commodity.

The exam was overseen by the Military Commissions—the insurgency's executive bodies in the provinces—acting on instructions from the movement's leadership. For example, as described by the head of the Military Commission in Laghman province in 2011: 'Taliban judges are appointed by us, but tests for their selection are conducted by Implementation Councils, both bodies are composed of religious scholars. These two councils conduct tests for the appointment of judges. The successful candidates are appointed as judges regardless of their ethnic and linguistic background.'[6] Candidates were then evaluated by the Judicial Committee based on their answers to the test. 'We test [candidates] by giving them cases to solve, we let them do it and observe them', according to a Taliban official attached to the Quetta Judicial Committee.[7]

The test consisted of a series of cases that the candidate had to decide. 'There were 20 questions in the paper and I was asked to answer these questions within the given three hours. We were not allowed more time. Though I was not very satisfied with how I did on the test, I finally got the good news on a piece of paper. And now I am happy with this profession.'[8] Most judges agreed that knowledge of Islamic law was essential for passing the examination. 'Any person having comprehensive knowledge of religious books can appear for the test. There is no experience requirement for becoming a judge. A judge only needs religious knowledge and fulfillment of Islamic obligations.'[9] Book learning from the classic sources recognized by Hanafite jurisprudence was essential. Judges therefore had to master the instructions of the Quran, the handed-down actions and statements of the prophet (hadiths), and the commentaries by the jurists who, since the eighth century, had compiled the legal sources that constitute contemporary Islamic law. Several judges pointed out the particular importance of inheritance law (*qanoun-i wizarat*), with which many questions on the exam dealt, because their case load as judges would include many complaints relating to this area of the law.

However, some judges stressed the role that other elements might play, such as right conduct, or observance of the precepts of sharia law: 'The examiners keep some standards in mind as well. For example how pious is the person? What is his past history? This also means that council consider his social

[6] I-13, head of the Military Commission in Laghman province, 2011.
[7] E-2, senior Taliban official, April 2013.
[8] I-21, Taliban trial court judge, Ghormach district (Badghis), 2011.
[9] I-4, Taliban appeals court judge, Dahan-i Ghuri district (Baghlan), 2011.

reputation and character before conferring this sacred duty on him.'[10] Others, however, put the stress on the casuistic form of the test and therefore on legal experience as the key. However, only the older ones could claim to have experience, like this judge: 'Before that, I was a prayer leader in Daychopan district of Zabul. The villagers would bring their disputes to me and I would resolve them according to Sharia. I became known in the area.'[11] Candidates who had previously practised Islamic law were extremely rare commodities:

> Education and experience both are necessary. You must have a good understanding of the law of the land. […] Experience is not a necessary criteria to qualify but it is an added advantage. But how could you gain experience if you did not practice as a judge? There is no such forum where you get this experience. This is experience you get on the job.[12]

Before sitting for the examination, the candidate underwent an informal screening relying on what the ulama knew about each other. The mention of social capital, both religious and militant, came up regularly when the interviewed judges recalled how they presented themselves:

> After completing my studies at a seminary, one of my colleagues offered to include me in the Taliban provincial council. I went with him to the house of the governor, who told us that all the members of the provincial council were already selected. He told me to contact the Military Commission. I contacted the Military Commission and they asked me whether I could take a test to become a judge. I took the examination and they appointed me as a judge.[13]

One judge pointed to the role his family played, including his cousin, a former Minister of Education under the Islamic Emirate and still a leading official in the movement, and his brothers, who were commanders in the insurgency.[14] Another mentioned a friend, also a judge, who encouraged him to apply. 'I have a very good friend. […] He was instrumental in getting me appointed as a judge. He brought me here. Finally I took the test, conducted by the Taliban provincial council.'[15] A third judge was screened by his former teacher, who had joined a Military Commission:

[10] I-5, Taliban trial court judge, Karagai district (Laghman), 2011.
[11] I-4, Taliban appeals court judge, Dahan-i Ghuri district (Baghlan), 2011.
[12] I-10, Taliban trial court judge, Tala wa Barfak district (Baghlan), 2011.
[13] I-14, Taliban trial court judge, Alingar district (Laghman), 2011.
[14] E-63, Taliban court judge, Ghazni province, May 2013.
[15] I-21, Taliban trial court judge, Ghormach district (Badghis), 2011.

> It was my desire for a long time to become a judge. Allah Almighty fulfilled my desire. I took an exam meant for the judges. Luckily, my teacher Mawlawi Abdul Haq, who is deputy chief of the Logar provincial council, gave me the test. This was by chance, not as a favor. Then he handed me a letter to produce it before the Implementation Council, which conducted a second test. I passed the second test also. So now you can see me here.[16]

In a similar vein, another judge told me how a friend, a member of the Laghman Military Commission, introduced him to the insurgency's networks. 'I had a friend, who was a member of the Military Commission. He helped me to become a judge. He summoned me to the Implementation Council [...]. I was successful and after one month, he asked me to meet him again on Friday in Alishang district. I went there and he introduced me to people as a Taliban judge.'[17]

For some judges, relationships with Commission members also helped propel them through the screening. 'I was appointed a Taliban judge on the basis of the test, conducted by the Implementation Council. I showed up for the test and learned 45 days later that I had passed. I had a friend, who was also a member of the council. He basically pushed me to get admitted to the justice system.'[18] However, the movement's central leadership reserved the final say over the nominations for itself. Thus, a judge recounted how he was forced to requalify because of suspicions of favouritism:

> I appeared in the test, conducted by the provincial council. I passed the test but the Implementation Council raised some objections at some of my answers. It alleged that members of the provincial council had helped me write those answers. I was asked to take another examination. I again appeared for the examination and passed it. Thus I was appointed judge.[19]

Finally, a judge was tested by his commander instead of the Military Commission, but the commander in the end confirmed his appointment:

> The group commander gave me a test before my appointment as a judge. I passed the test and became a judge. Our group commander was Mawlawi Ihsanullah, a resident of Kolangar district in Logar. He helped me to become

[16] I-25, Taliban appeals court judge, Bala Mughab district (Badghis), 2011.
[17] I-19, Taliban trial court judge, Alishang district (Laghman), 2011.
[18] I-10, Taliban trial court judge, Tala wa Barfak district (Baghlan), 2011.
[19] I-4, Taliban appeals court judge, Dahan-i Ghuri district (Baghlan), 2011.

a judge as he knew about my family problems. He sent my application to the Military Commission. I was first appointed as a judge in the Shahr-I Nau district of Paktia province.[20]

In a category of their own were former judges of the Islamic Emirate of Afghanistan: taken in directly, they were appointed to strategic positions:

I knew many high ranking Taliban from the Emirates time. I went to Pakistan, I found my friends in Quetta and they recruited me as a judge in Shah Wali Kot district of Kandahar province. In the time of the Emirate, I was working for the Taliban as judge. As I had a lot of experience of judging, Taliban didn't require any exam from me and they sent me directly to Shah Wali Kot district.'[21]

Starting in the late 2000s, stepped-up Special Forces operations targeting judges required the Taliban to replace killed or captured judges. For example, a judge in Logar province was appointed in 2009 without evaluation: 'I had not worked as a judge but I took part in solving disputes of various people. I took part as a mullah, as a village notable. So I was appointed as judge by the Peshawar Council four years ago.'[22] To keep their judgeship pipeline filled, the Taliban encouraged students to quit their studies early and appointed them even absent the ulama title. A Taliban judge proudly admitted to a British journalist in 2011 that he had interrupted his studies to join the movement: 'The Taliban told me that the time was right for me to serve my nation. I was reluctant at first to leave my studies but after they spoke to me, it quickly became clear that this was my calling.'[23]

A body of ulama

Contrary to the prevailing assumption that the Taliban underwent a radical transformation in 2001—a notion that would henceforth gain currency as the 'neo-Taliban'[24]—the organic relationship between the movement and religious

[20] I-2, Taliban appeals court judge, Karagai district (Laghman), 2011.
[21] I-20, Taliban appeals court judge, Qarabagh district (Ghazni), 2011.
[22] I-11, Taliban court judge, Logar province, 2013.
[23] Quoted in Miles Amoore, 'Afghans Flock to Judge Dread and his Butcher Boys', *The Sunday Times*, 23 January 2011.
[24] Antonio Giustozzi, *Koran, Kalashnikov, and Laptop: The Neo-Taliban Insurgency in Afghanistan*, New York, Columbia University Press, 2008.

schools from which the movement derived its strength in the 1990s remained an essential part of its functioning. As noted earlier, the Taliban recruited their judges from among the students and graduates of the Deobandi madrasas of the Afghan-Pakistani border regions, from which, historically, the movement had also drawn its cadres. This transnational network of religious schools turned out ulama who shared a *habitus*, a worldview, fighting experience, and a range of theological-legal skills.

A large majority of the judges interviewed were thus trained in Pakistani madrasas belonging to the Deobandi school, a clerical revivalist Hanafite movement that emerged in India in the nineteenth century. One madrasa in particular, Dar ul-Ulum Haqqania, located in Akora Khattak, near Peshawar, repeatedly came up in the interviews. 'I received religious education in Afghanistan, except for the final course, which I completed in Dar ul-Ulum Haqqania, situated in Akora Khattak near Peshawar in Pakistan. It is a great seminary and a branch of Dar ul-Ulum Deoband.'[25] Founded in 1947 by *mawlana* Abdul Haq, a disciple of Dar ul-Ulum Deoband, and led by his son *mawlana* Sami ul-Haq, this madrasa fulfilled a key role during the war. With Pashto as the language of instruction, the school attracted many Afghan refugees, who by 1985 accounted for nearly 60 per cent of the student body.[26] Over two decades, several thousand Afghans passed through the madrasa, including at least eight ministers of the Islamic Emirate and numerous Taliban judges, governors, senior officials, and military commanders.[27] The school figured prominently in the training of the insurgency's judges. Many mentioned the links between it and the Taliban, as did this appeals court judge in Laghman province: 'All Taliban judges and other members of Taliban movement are linked to Dar ul-Ulum Deoband. Dar ul-Ulum Haqqania in Pakistan, where most of our people come from, is also a branch of Dar ul-Ulum Deoband.'[28] A former official in the Islamic Emirate's religious police resumed his studies in the madrasa after the fall of the regime, only to be subsequently recruited as a judge by the insurgency. 'I worked in the Ministry of the Promotion of Virtue and the Prevention of Vice in the Taliban government. I also led the prayer in Kabul. I completed my religious education after the fall of the Taliban government in Dar ul-Ulum Haqqania.'[29]

[25] I-8, Taliban trial court judge, Dushi district (Baghlan), 2011.

[26] Jamal Malik, *Colonialization of Islam: Dissolution of Traditional Institutions in Pakistan*, New Delhi, Manohar, 1996, pp. 202–9.

[27] Ahmed Rashid, *Taliban: Militant Islam, Oil and Fundamentalism in Central Asia*, New Haven, Yale University Press, 2000, p. 90.

[28] I-26, Taliban appeals court judge, Alishang district (Laghman), 2011.

[29] I-8, Taliban appeals court judge, Dushi district (Baghlan), 2011.

Other judges studied in Afghanistan, especially in the madrasas of the Southern Pashtun regions also associated with the Deobandi movement. Most of them were trained in Nur ul-Mudaris, Afghanistan's most prestigious religious school located in Ghazni. It was founded in the 1930s by Fazl Omar Mojaddidi, a member of an illustrious religious family and a disciple of Dar ul-Ulum Deoband. The importance of southern madrasas (Kandahar, Helmand, Zabul) was also due to the proliferation of Deobandi religious schools. However, there were exceptions: in the provinces of Kunar and Nuristan, several locally recruited Taliban judges were educated in the madrasas of the Ahl-i Hadith movement, linked to Pakistan's Panjpir madrasa.[30] One judge I interviewed had imbibed the teachings of an Ahl-i Hadith school in Kunar followed by attending a Panjpir madrasa, but he downplayed the legal implications of these theological differences:

> The differences between us and the other [Taliban] judges are small. We disagree on small things, how to hold hands when praying, how to dress, but these are questions related to faith (*aqida*), not jurisprudence (*fiqh*). On the case law, our disagreements are minor, for instance on how to determine that a girl is marriage material, no more than that.'[31]

Moreover, in 2010 a report on the Taliban's northern advance mentioned the case of a Taliban judge in Khwaja Ghar district (Takhar) who had studied at Balkh University's Law Faculty.[32]

Many judges, for example in Nahrin district, were quick to claim and champion the movement's roots in Deobandism and Hanafite jurisprudence: 'Our teachers and former clerics of Afghanistan were educated in Deoband. The graduates of Deoband belong to Hanafite school. The Commander of the Faithful, Mullah Mohamad Omar the Mujahid, had decided twice at the time of

[30] The Ahl-i Hadith movement ('the people of tradition') was a reform movement born in India in the second half of the nineteenth century. Its disciples rejected all practices that did not come directly from religious texts, thus denying the interpretations and prescriptions of the classical jurisprudence schools and advocating a literal reading of the Quran and hadiths. The scripturalism of the Ahl-i Hadith movement explained its members' relationships with the Saudi Wahhabi currents that financed the Panjpir madrasa, founded after Pakistan's independence. Its proximity to the provinces of Kunar and Nouristan explains the attendance by many of the movement's followers. No reference studies have been produced on the movement, but Barbara Metcalf traces its genealogy in her history of Deobandism. Barbara Metcalf, *Islamic Revival in British India: Deoband, 1860–1900*, Princeton, Princeton University Press, 2014, pp. 264–96.

[31] E-7, Taliban court judge, Kunar province, April 2013.

[32] Antonio Giustozzi and Christoph Reuter, *The Insurgents of the Afghan North*, Kabul, Afghanistan Analysts Network, 2011, p. 19.

the Islamic Emirate of Afghanistan to construct a large seminary in Kandahar with the name of Dar ul-Ulum Deoband.'[33]

These transnational madrasa networks had welcomed Afghan students since the nineteenth century and formed the historical crucible of the Taliban movement. Two researchers on the South Asian Sunni clergy, Barbara Metcalf and Muhammad Qasim Zaman, pointed out this linkage and recalled the Taliban movement's continuity with the evolution of the Deobandi movement since the mid-nineteenth century.[34] Unlike the Islamist movements that emerged from the Muslim Brotherhood, whose cadres graduated from universities (as in the Hizb-i Islami or the Jamiat-i Islami in Afghanistan), the Taliban as a primarily clerical movement reflected the essential role of madrasas in South Asia's political Islam. Dar ul-Ulum Deoband was founded in 1866 in the northern Indian city of Deoband during the British colonial era. Ulama faced with the loss of their social and judicial prerogatives there at the time established a modern curriculum, combining theological and scientific disciplines with which to train a new generation of clerics. They republished and wrote religious and legal works, with the aim of educating Muslims under British rule on how they should live and act.[35] A transnational network of madrasas formed around Dar ul-Ulum Deoband, advocating strict adherence (*taqlid*) to the legal precepts of classical Hanafite authors and producing a political theology that infused contemporary Pakistani and Afghan political life. My judge interlocutors regularly alluded to this heritage:[36] 'All religious scholars of Afghanistan, living or dead, arrested and free, and all members of the Taliban are followers of the Deobandi school of thought. […] Dar ul-Ulum Deoband imparted religious education to Afghan scholars when Pakistan did not yet exist.'[37]

This Deobandi grounding partly explains the ideology of the Taliban movement and of its judges. The Deobandi encouraged clerics to enter politics as guides for the community of believers, a pervasive trait of the Taliban movement. In Pakistan, this clerical network founded a political party, the Jamiat Ulema-e-Islami, to promote its vision of society and federated Deobandi madrasas in the Wifaq ul Madaris al-Arabia. The latter ensures the conformity

[33] I-12, Taliban trial court judge, Nahrin district (Baghlan), 2011.

[34] Barbara Metcalf, *'Traditionalist' Islamic activism: Deoband, Tablighis, and Talibs*, Leiden, ISIM, 2002; Muhammad Qasim Zaman, *The Ulama in Contemporary Islam: Custodians of Change*, Princeton, Princeton University Press, 2002.

[35] Barbara Metcalf, *Islamic Revival in British India: Deoband, 1860–1900*, Princeton, Princeton University Press, 2014.

[36] Dietrich Reetz, 'The Deoband Universe: What Makes a Transcultural and Transnational Educational Movement of Islam?', *Comparative Studies of South Asia, Africa and the Middle East*, 2007, vol. 27, nº 1, pp. 139–59.

[37] I-18, Taliban appeals court judge, Alingar district (Laghman), 2011.

of curricula and diplomas and defends their interests before the state.[38] In several interviews, the judges affirmed their membership in this network with reference to the scholars under whom they studied. For example, a judge in Ghazni mentioned an illustrious Deobandi *alim*, the former vice-president of Wifaq ul Madaris al-Arabia and close to one of the historical Jamiat Ulema-e-Islami cadres, Fazl-ur-Rahman: 'I attended a madrasa here in Ghazni for my primary education, then I continued my studies and finished the course of Daura-i Hadith in Pakistan, at the Darwish Masjid, in Peshawar, with Mawlana Hassan Jan Madani. Then I studied the case law in Karachi.'[39]

The compilations of hadiths and the legal commentary the judges referenced were those by the classical Hanafite jurists who were taught in the Deobandi madrasas. Since the 1990s, these books have been widely available in Pakistan in photocopied editions. Originally intended as discussion and training guides for jurisconsults, they see wide use as handbooks.[40] The judges refer to six classical compilations of hadiths in particular: the *Sahih* of al-Bukhari but also the *Sahih* of Muslim ibn al-Hajaj, and the *Sunan* of al-Nassa'i, the *Sunan* of Abu Daud, the *Sunan* of Ibn Majah, and the *Sunan* of al-Tirmidhi.[41] 'My religious studies included the illustrious Quran, the hadiths, the illustrious Bukhari, the illustrious Muslim, the illustrious Abu Daud and the illustrious Tirmidhi.'[42] In case law, judges relied on Hanafite works, starting with those personally written by the founder of this school of jurisprudence: 'For example, we use *Fiqa*, whose author is Imam Abu Hanifa the Merciful. [. . .] We also use a book called *Fatawa [Dar ul-Ulum] Deoband*.'[43] *Fatawa Dar ul-Ulum Deoband*, a compilation of legal opinions written by Mufti Aziz al-Rahman Uthmani at the Dar ul-Ulum Deoband madrasa in the second half of the twentieth century, got several mentions in my interviews. Legal commentary was also vital,

[38] Jamal Malik, *Colonialization of Islam: Dissolution of Traditional Institutions in Pakistan*, New Delhi, Manohar, 1996, pp. 124–38 and 211–16; Masooda Bano, *The Rational Believer: Choices and Decisions in the Madrasas of Pakistan*, Ithaca, Cornell University Press, 2012, pp. 87–93.

[39] E-63, Taliban court judge, Ghazni province, May 2013.

[40] However, contrary to Joseph Schacht's classical thesis regarding the end of the jurists' reasoning role at the close of the Middle Ages (*ijtahid*), Muhammad Qasim Zaman shows the ambiguity of the application by Deobandi theologians of the injunction to imitate (*taqlid*) the medieval jurists. The choice of books and the way they are used reveal a constant reinterpretation of texts in the light of the social, economic, cultural, and political transformations facing the clerics. See Joseph Schacht, *An Introduction to Islamic law*, Oxford, Clarendon Press, 1964; Muhammad Qasim Zaman, *The Ulama in Contemporary Islam: Custodians of Change*, Princeton, Princeton University Press, 2002, pp. 17–37. During the 1980s, Wael Hallaq had already questioned the thesis of a closure of interpretation by jurists in Islamic law. Wael Hallaq, 'Was the Gate of Ijtihad Closed?', *International Journal of Middle East Studies*, 1984, vol. 16, n° 1, pp. 3–41.

[41] E-2, senior official of the Taliban movement, April 2013.

[42] I-7, Taliban court judge, Logar province, 2013.

[43] I-24, Taliban court judge, Logar province, 2013.

starting with that by the twelfth-century jurist Burhan al-Din al-Marghinani, *al-Hidaya* (the guide), often singled out by judges as the most useful work for resolving disputes. A judge from Qala-i Naw district explained why:

> I have already told you that religious education is essential for becoming a judge. Likewise, understanding religious books is also a must. The knowledge of jurisprudence is the most important compared to other branches of religious education for becoming a judge. Most cases are discussed in *al-Hidaya*. But the knowledge of inheritance law is also necessary for a judge.[44]

The centrality of *Al-Hidaya* for the Deobandi movement formed part of the initial confrontation between the madrasa's clerics and the British colonizers. Indeed, the book was translated into English and in the late eighteenth century became one of the foundations of the British codification of Islamic law that gave rise to Anglo-Muhammadan law.[45] At about the same time, the British also translated *al-Sirajiya*, the work of the eleventh-century jurist Siraj al-Din al-Sajawind, a frequent reference for the founding ulama of the Deobandi movement and still used today by the Taliban for ruling on inheritance issues.[46] Similarly, many judges mentioned *Fatawa al-Hindiyal al-Alamgiriya*, a pre-colonial compilation of Mughal-era Hanafite authors widely studied in Deobandi madrasas.

Because of the historical link between the Deobandi madrasas and the Taliban movement, religious training was also a time for militant and combatant socialization. Since the mid-1990s, with the permission, if not encouragement, of their teachers, seminarians between class semesters have fought shoulder to shoulder with the Taliban. In 1997, as the Taliban suffered setbacks against the Northern Alliance, Dar ul-Ulum Haqqania and other Pakistani Deobandi madrasas temporarily closed and exhorted their students to join the Taliban, providing thousands of fighters to the movement. The intermingling of religious studies and jihad continued with the Western intervention. Most judges fought for the movement during their religious training in the 1990s or 2000s: 'When I was a student of a seminary, I would go on vacation to take

[44] I-6, Taliban trial court judge, Qala-i Naw district (Badghis), 2011.

[45] Muhammad Qasim Zaman, 'Tradition and Authority in Deobandi Madrasas of South Asia' in Robert W. Hefner and Muhammad Qasim Zaman (eds), *Schooling Islam: The Culture and Politics of Modern Muslim Education*, Princeton, Princeton University Press, 2007, pp. 21–31; Wael Hallaq, *Shari'a: Theory, Practice, Transformations*, Cambridge, Cambridge University Press, 2009, pp. 371–95.

[46] Muhammad Qasim Zaman, 'Tradition and Authority in Deobandi Madrasas of South Asia' in Robert W. Hefner and Muhammad Qasim Zaman (eds), *Schooling Islam: The Culture and Politics of Modern Muslim Education*, Princeton, Princeton University Press, 2007, pp. 21–31.

part in jihad with the Taliban in Logar province. We were seven roommates in the seminary. Now only we three are alive, as the other four were killed in a battle on the border between Khost and Paktia provinces.'[47] Some continued fighting for a few years before becoming judges. 'I have taken part in many offensives. I also even worked as leader of a Taliban group when I was a seminarist. I fought alongside the Taliban in Zabul under Mullah Ahmadzada Aqa when the US-led NATO forces attacked us back in late 2001.'[48]

Recruiting the graduates of the Deobandi madrasas allowed the movement to appoint loyal supporters who embedded their judgeship in a broader commitment to jihad. According to this judge, the experience of jihad is even a practical test of disinterestedness, a quality he considered to be essential in a judge:

> I was taking part in jihad when I was studying in a seminary. I would go with my friends and classmates to the Taliban bases during vacations to take part in jihad. I have cordial relations with commanders of different Taliban groups. I spent days and nights with them. May Allah accept our jihad, which we waged with sincerity! Unless and until you are a mujahid, you could hardly be trusted by the Taliban to become a judge. This is a test. If you can fight a jihad, it means you are sincere with the cause and hence you could be trusted that you are not a greedy man but a pious man with a sacred cause.[49]

For many judges, the fighting and activist experience seems to have been decisive in their decision to become a judge. Here is one who said he became a judge because of people he met in his fighting unit:

> I have taken part in many battles under the leadership of Mullah Abdul Razaq Akhund [Minister of the Interior during the Islamic Emirate, a senior leader of the insurgency]. I was fond of the battlefield but my friends forced me to become a judge. [. . .] I passed the test and was appointed judge. I believe this is the best service I can provide to society to the best of my ability.[50]

While fighting Western troops, another judge met the son of Jalaluddin Haqqani, a prominent leader of the movement, who ordered him to become a judge:

[47] I-25, Taliban appeals court judge, Bala Mughab district (Badghis), 2011.
[48] I-15, Taliban appeals court judge, Qala-i Naw district (Badghis), 2011.
[49] I-19, Taliban trial court judge, Alishang district (Laghman), 2011.
[50] I-12, Taliban trial court judge, Nahrin district (Baghlan), 2011.

> Initially, I started my career as a madrasa teacher in Charsadda district [Khyber Pakhtunkhwa, Pakistan], but later I left Charsadda for Afghanistan to fight against the NATO forces alongside my brothers in Afghanistan. This brought me in close contact with Khalifa [Sirajuddin Haqqani] at the Mamba ul-Ulum seminary in Miranshah in the tribal areas of Pakistan. Khalifa introduced me to the right people and now, as you can see me, I am a judge.[51]

A veteran of many firefights in the vicinity of Kabul and a Taliban militant since the early years, this judge explained how conversations with other fighters, fellow mullahs, pointed him towards a career as a judge:

> I had never thought about becoming a judge. I just wanted to become a good religious scholar, but one day when I was sitting with a military commander, Mullah Abdul Salam Haqqani, along with some of my colleagues over a cup of tea, I was impressed by the discussion they were having amongst them. It made me realize that a judge can serve his community by standing for justice, to what extent one can play his role in a society that had gone wrong and was in need of justice. This changed my life. Hence, I chose to become a judge.[52]

Islamic law

The Taliban judges sought to apply Islamic law based on the classic authors of the Hanafite school of jurisprudence, unlike the Syrian insurgency in 2012 or the many Islamic regimes that codified or incorporated Islamic law into their legal codes. The Islamic character of the verdict is based on references to the Quran, hadiths, and commentary by renowned jurists:

> When we make decision, we tell the punishment of this sin in the name of Almighty Allah [by saying that] 'it is in the holy and illustrious Quran, in this sura and in this verse.' For example, if someone kills another person without any reasons, it is mentioned in holy Quran that that person must be killed. For example, if someone steals something, whether it is a man or a woman, his or her hand must be cut off.[53]

[51] I-18, Taliban appeals court judge, Alingar district (Laghman), 2011.
[52] I-1, Taliban appeals court judge, Nahrin district (Baghlan), 2011.
[53] I-24, Taliban court judge, Logar province, 2013.

Many judges, forced to move frequently to avoid being spotted by Western troops, relied in particular on a few essential, highly portable texts, usually the Quran and compilations of hadith.[54] With the advent of laptops in rural Afghanistan, some Taliban judges compiled digital libraries with thousands of books on Islamic law. One judge showed me a computer program that allowed him to conduct keyword searches that let him directly access pages with the relevant hadiths and commentary. The reference works could be indexed by category to facilitate search or to filter search results.[55]

In principle, the edicts of Mullah Omar, who bore the title of 'Commander of the Faithful', still applied, including the new ones he continued to issue after 2001. However, the movement's legal output remained limited. In 2005, on its official website the Taliban published the constitution that the Supreme Court of the Islamic Emirate had been tasked with drafting in the late 1990s. The gesture was mostly symbolic: the twenty-three-page document, signed by several of the movement's senior officials, while it supported the claim to represent the state, then was a dead letter because it was unenforceable.[56] In communications to its militants, the Taliban leadership acknowledged this situation. The 2009 version of *The Instructions to Mujahideen*, the fighter's code of conduct (see Chapter 8), prohibited the reopening of cases tried by the courts of the Islamic Emirate before 2001: 'The renewal and reviewing of cases that were resolved correctly during the rule of the Islamic Emirate of Afghanistan is forbidden. This is the case even if one side is not satisfied with the verdict, because more justice was possible then than now' (Article 45).

Mullah Omar's legal authority was evident from the directives he issued in the late 2000s covering changes in the treatment of non-combatants. This newfound concern for civilians was part of a campaign for international recognition that was reflected in the increasing attention paid to international humanitarian law. This shift appeared in the later of two versions of the movement's Code of Conduct: marginally discussed in the 2006 version, it was covered at length in the 2009 version in several articles dealing with the treatment of prisoners or the respect fighters owed to the chain of command. The Code stressed the obligations of the mujahideen under Islamic law and, though it made no mention of international humanitarian law, it took up some

[54] Ashley Jackson and Florian Weigand refer to an internal document instructing judges to consult the Ottoman codification of Hanafi jurisprudence on civil matters (*al-Majala al-Ahkam al-Adliya*). Ashley Jackson and Florian Weigand, *Rebel Rule of Law: Taliban Courts in the West and North-west of Afghanistan*, London, ODI, 2020, p. 5.

[55] E-55, Taliban judge, Ghazni province, May 2013.

[56] Alex Strick van Linschoten, *Mullah Wars: the Afghan Taliban between Village and State, 1979–2001*, Ph.D., King's College London, London, 2016, p. 203.

of the latter's essential principles. Concurrently, Mullah Omar ordered a stop to attacks on schools and clinics, which, because of the involvement of Western organizations, the Taliban had until then regarded as legitimate targets.[57] Humanitarian organizations were now allowed to operate in Afghanistan, conditional upon staying out of the war and on consulting regularly with the insurgency.[58] Judges enforced these directives in several cases involving Taliban fighters (see Chapter 8).

These edicts were promulgated against a background of dialogue between the movement's senior leaders and international organizations on the definition and use of legal categories. In 2012, when UNAMA's Human Rights Department accused the Taliban of responsibility for 70 per cent of the civilians killed, its spokesperson and official website challenged the impartiality of UNAMA's criteria and its statistical methods. Specifically, the Taliban objected to counting police and regime officials as civilians—the United Nations under international law did not count them as belligerents unless they were visibly engaged in military operations. The Taliban claimed that the military role of the police, and more broadly of the state's agents, made them legitimate targets. In addition, it tried to justify the many civilian casualties its fighters caused in the South when they deployed improvised explosive devices that were set off by pressure plates by citing the fact that the US military had the capability to detect remote detonators. The argument is legally weak but indicates a bid for international legitimacy.[59]

Conversely, the movement mobilized human rights rhetoric to criticize the abuses it attributed to the American armed forces and the Kabul regime. In 2010, Mullah Omar declared:

> I call on the Islamic Conference and all organizations that have been established under the name of human rights protection to take steps for the prevention of civilian casualties caused by the invading forces of America and the coalition and to raise their voice for the punishment of the perpetrators of

[57] The 2006 version of the *Instructions to the Mujahideen* called international humanitarian organizations 'tools of the infidels. In the guise of serving, they are destroying Islam, so all their activities are banned, whether it is [building] roads or anything else, or clinics or schools or a madrassa or anything else. If a school fails to heed a warning to close, it must be burned' (Article 26). For the edict banning attacks on schools, see 'Government Hails Taliban Decree on Schools', *IRIN*, 29 March 2011.

[58] Officials of several humanitarian organizations in Afghanistan confirmed to me that they could operate in the country provided they consulted locally with the insurgency. Notably, E-66, head of an Aga Khan Foundation programme in Baghlan province, August 2010; E-80, senior official with Madera, September 2012; E-24, senior official with the Afghan mission of Doctors Without Borders, September 2014.

[59] E-5, director of UNAMA's Human Rights Department, September 2012.

> this crime. Similarly, the invading forces under the leadership of America and the surrogate regime of Kabul have erected prisons under different names in all parts of the country in contravention to international principles. A great number of our miserable and innocent countrymen are brutally tortured there. All human rights organizations who claim being advocates of human rights should promptly and as per their responsibility take steps to prevent occurrence of such brutal acts. Many of our prisoners have been martyred and maimed as a result of harsh conduct and torture in these prisons.

In the years that followed, the movement regularly denounced misinformation that it said would lead to overestimating abuses by the insurgency and underestimating those caused by the coalition and the regime. Thus, in a 2012 speech, Mullah Omar acknowledged the legitimacy of human rights organizations, calling on them to investigate the abuses by Western troops:

> We urge all universal organizations working for the protection of human rights not to rely only on reports of the foreign forces and western media outlets. Carry out your own impartial and on site investigation about the ground realities in the area, by fulfilling your responsibility in this regard. The civilian casualties that occur as a result of the American blind bombardment, unsanctioned raids on houses, letting loose dogs on children and women to bite them; urination on dead bodies, torture of prisoners in prisons, rape of women at the hands of soldiers, police and *arbakis*; violation against the honor and property of people are no more something hidden from the eyes of people.

This human rights rhetoric fed into the Taliban's policy shift on noncombatants. For instance, in the Southeast, movement officials were now cooperating with UN officials in verifying the status of the victims and the identity of those responsible.[60] The UN report on the situation in Afghanistan took note of this attention to the treatment of civilians, which had become an issue of legitimacy in the war:

> In 2012, the Taliban released 53 public statements on their website, 25 of which addressed issues relating to civilian casualties and human rights protection. These statements appeared to indicate a continued public awareness of civilian protection concerns. The statements also claimed that the vast

[60] E-46, head of UNAMA's Human Rights Department in the Southeast, September 2014.

> majority of civilian casualties in Afghanistan resulted from the operations of Pro-Government Forces. In seven statements, the Taliban claimed that their followers and Mujahedeen always tried to protect civilians during operations, as part of their Islamic responsibility and obligation.[61]

The consistency of verdicts mainly derived from the homogeneity of the education received by these judges. Once appointed, judges no longer received training on interpreting legal sources or laws and decrees issued by the Islamic Emirate. They relied in their deliberations on the religious references they had absorbed during their madrasa education. A Taliban judge from the district of Ab Kamari (Badghis) explained: ‘No special training. You know we don’t have a dedicated academy for such kind of trainings. We get on the job training. We get instructions and pamphlets from time to time as guiding principles from the top that help us a lot in deciding the cases. We learn from the company of the seasoned judges as well.’[62] The instructions mentioned by this judge were booklets printed under the name of Mullah Omar and distributed to the newly appointed judges: ‘Six guidelines are issued for the new judges, who are required to study them and implement them. They must perform their duty according to these guidelines. In most cases, these guidelines are included in the instructions issued from time to time by Mullah Mohamad Omar the Mujahid.’[63] The judges invariably pointed out that these guidelines did not deal with Islamic law but distilled a set of principles on how judges should comport themselves and interact with those who come before them:

> The guidelines are personally issued for the judges. They are not meant to be included in Sharia Law. Judges are instructed through such guidelines that they shouldn’t take bribes. They are asked to keep common people happy by treating them politely. They are directed to win people’s hearts. They are directed to keep in line with the Islamic teachings and that’s all.[64]

Moreover, contrary to the commonly held notion of the Taliban applying customary Pashtun norms (*pashtunwali*), another Mullah Omar decree explicitly barred judges from referring to them when deciding cases:

[61] *Afghanistan Annual Report 2012: Protection of Civilians in Armed Conflict*, Kabul, UNAMA, 2012, p. 25.
[62] I-3, Taliban trial court judge, Ab Kamari district (Badghis), 2011.
[63] I-8, Taliban trial court judge, Dushi district (Baghlan), 2011.
[64] I-26, Taliban appeals court judge, Alishang district (Laghman), 2011.

> There are strict orders for all Taliban courts to decide cases in the light of Islamic laws. They are directed not to care for the customs and traditions of anyone but to uphold Sharia Law. These directives are issued by the Military Commissions to all Taliban courts throughout Badghis province. […] Taliban judges don't care about the culture and traditions of Pashtuns. They decide all cases under Sharia Law. This is an order of The Commander of the Faithful [Mullah Omar] for the Military Commissions and the Supreme Court to decide all cases according to Islamic laws and not to follow the words of any tribal notable. Taliban judges are required to follow Islamic laws.[65]

The judges generally appeared to respect this instruction, nearly all of them insisting they did not refer to customary norms in their decisions. They also tended to justify their exclusion by painting them as unfairly favouring one ethnic group over the rest of the population and thus fomenting dissension:

> We have not waged jihad for the sake of Pashtunwali. We have left our homes to defend our honor, implement the orders of Allah Almighty and enforce Sharia Law. If we would care for who speaks Pashto and who speaks Dari, then we should have joined Hezb-e-Islami because its leader Gulbudin Hikmatyar is a Pashtun. Doctor Najibullah [President of Afghanistan from 1986–92], a Communist, was also a Pashtun.[66]

Hanafite jurisprudence is ambiguous on the place of custom (*adat*), with some commentators denying it any legal character, but with others, notably Ibn Nujaim and Ibn Abidin, according it a subsidiary role where the religious texts are silent.[67] In the Afghan case, Pashtun customary norms and Islamic law diverge on several key issues, notably those involving marriage and property. For example, several Taliban judges in Logar and Ghazni provinces insisted on the ban on exchanging women to end a blood debt (*baad*), even if, in the absence of complaints, they did not oppose its application. As in the 1990s, the half-share of inheritance that the Quran attributes to women, but which was often denied to them on the grounds that it is not prescribed by custom, was a particularly delicate issue (see Chapter 10). In a sign of the difficulty this question

[65] I-21, Taliban trial court judge, Ghormach district (Badghis), 2011.
[66] I-18, Taliban appeals court judge, Alingar district (Laghman), 2011.
[67] Noel Coulson, 'Muslim Custom and Case-Law', *Die Welt des Islams*, 1959, vol. 6, n° 1-2, pp. 13–24; Wael Hallaq, *Authority, Continuity and Change in Islamic Law*, Cambridge, Cambridge University Press, 2001, pp. 213–31.

poses, most judges were eager to explain the differences between Islamic and *pashtunwali*:

> The Military Commission does not allow judges to decide a case in the light of traditions and customs of any tribe. Tribal customs and traditions are a different story and Islamic laws remain sovereign when it comes to deciding a case in a court. You can settle cases on that basis in the context of a family dispute or in such instance as a *jirga*, but here you have no choice but the path of Islam. All our decisions are Islamic. There is a lot of difference between sharia and Pashtun culture and customs. Someone who wants to get his case decided according to the customs of the Pashtuns does not go to the Taliban court.[68]

Only one judge denied the conflict of norms between Islamic law and custom: 'We are Pashtuns but, after all, we are all Muslims. We don't do anything in our social set-up that is repugnant to Islam. *Pashtunwali* is totally in line with Islamic values. So I don't think there is any clash between Islamic laws and our own cultural values.'[69]

However, some judges did admit to using customary norms on an ad hoc basis to decide cases. Questioned on this subject, a judge in Baghlan province provided this example:

> I will never forget a case from the time I was newly appointed in Arghandab (Kandahar). A case involving two persons had been brought to my court. The two persons, good friends, one of them rich and the other poor, had promised in the presence of other villagers that their as-yet unborn children would marry each. After some time, a son was born to the poor man and the rich one fathered a daughter. But the rich man broke his promise and refused to marry off his daughter to the son of his poor friend. This case was brought to my court. This was a case where I followed our cultural values instead of deciding the case in the light of sharia because the nature of the case did not allow me to ignore the social structure and, of course, the cultural values of a traditional society.[70]

This judge, who imposed respect for a customary marriage contract, which carries no weight in Islamic law, had to be aware of prohibition from the

[68] I-3, Taliban trial court judge, Ab Kamari district (Badghis), 2011.
[69] I-26, Taliban trial court judge, Alishang district (Laghman), 2011.
[70] I-23, Taliban trial court judge, Dahan-i Ghuri district (Baghlan), 2011.

leadership on applying custom. Nevertheless, he justified his decision by reference to the local culture and the social stakes that underlie this type of conflict:

> A decree by the Commander of the Faithful Mullah Mohamad Omar the Mujahid is displayed in every Taliban court. The decree orders Taliban judges not to be prejudiced and not to favor a notable or governor. They are asked to decide all cases in the light of sharia. But, as I told you, in some of the cases you can't just ignore your social and cultural values.[71]

Falling back on customary norms gave some judges leeway for pragmatism in applying the harsh punishments prescribed by a literal interpretation of Islamic law:

> We refer the cases to tribal justice if it is appropriate, to *pashtunwali*. For instance, if there is a boy and girl, and they are friends with one another and they run away from their houses. When they come back before the court, we take some money from the boy and use it for marriage expenses. In short, we're marrying them off.[72]

Users of the Taliban courts confirmed the application of custom-based verdicts, in the following case involving *baad* (exchange of women to compensate a blood debt):

> I, myself also solved my problem or my case through Taleban judges in our village, the case was a murder that happened around 6 years ago. One of our villagers fought with my son over water sharing. He killed my son with his knife and escaped from the village to an unknown place. [After arresting him and putting him to trial,] the Taliban judges condemned him to be hanged, but his father came to me, begging me to forgive him. He was ready to pay any price to compensate for the loss of my son. When I saw that his father was crying a lot, and I myself also had to overcome the loss of my son, because he was killed 6 years ago, I told the Taliban judges that I forgave him, but on condition that his father should give his daughter to my other son for free. My son would marry his daughter but he would not get money from us [for the bride price]. On the spot Taliban Judges announced their decision and told him and his father that they should give their sister and daughter to my son.

[71] Ibid.
[72] I-24, Taliban court judge, Logar province, 2013.

> Both sides agreed and within one week, my son married her and now we are living in peace.[73]

All the cases involving customary norms that the judges told me about were family matters. This one-off use of custom was due to the distinction that judges drew between public and private affairs, relegating marital issues to a domestic sphere where the priority was to find a solution that suited the dominant actors, i.e., the heads of families (see Chapter 10).

Moreover, if a dispute did not result in deaths and was of limited scope, if none of the plaintiffs files a complaint with a Taliban court, the insurgents often let people informally negotiate out-of-court settlements. A judge told me: 'We do respect the opinions of the elders and religious scholars in the district. Sometimes we submit them a few minor cases to resolve [. . .] in a way that satisfies both parties. If the local elders couldn't solve the case, then they refer the case back to us and we try our best to resolve it.'[74] Some judges also admitted referring people to a conciliation body, for example, if their interpretation of Islamic law would result in severe punishment when a *jirga* could work out a settlement instead. In a case reported by the press of a woman demanding justice for the death of her son, who had been killed by a neighbour in a quarrel, she received a letter signed by the Taliban governor and addressed to the notables: 'Tell us if there is a tribal solution to the woman's complaint. If not, we will resolve the dispute our way.'[75] In these types of cases, the litigants knew that if they failed in the conciliation process, the case would end up before the Taliban judges and the verdict would be difficult to challenge. For example, a veterinarian working in Laghman told me how locals dealt with irrigation conflicts: 'In the Alishang Valley, there are frequent water shortages at the end of the summer. First the problem is managed by a *shura*, with the *mirab* and the local mullah. But if that fails, in areas that the Taliban control, people turn to them to enforce water sharing.'[76] A cleric close to the Taliban explained to me the intertwining of the conciliation bodies, in which he participated, and the Taliban judicial system:

> Taliban judges and notables are two sides of the same coin. They are not different systems. Taliban judges let the notables solve the problems and it is

[73] I-39, resident of Arghandab district (Kandahar), 2011.
[74] I-20, Taliban appeals court judge, Qarabagh district (Ghazni), 2011.
[75] Bilal Sarwary, 'What Happened after the Americans Left Afghan Hotspot?', *BBC News*, 3 December 2011.
[76] E-57, veterinarian in Laghman province, April 2011.

> only when the latter fail that they take charge of the case with their men. It's simple, because the notables don't want problems and don't want to use violence. The Taliban, on the other hand, judge on sharia law and enforce their verdict by violence.[77]

This description is of course a biased one: it speaks of a system at peace, where the Taliban supported the social ascent of the religious, often at the expense of the notables (see Chapter 10). Nevertheless, it illustrates the ultimate deterrent function performed by the Taliban, one that, until the late 1970s, was a state prerogative conditioning the authority of local elites.

[77] E-43, a religious scholar living in Logar province, May 2013.

7
The trials

Introduction

Unlike most contemporary armed movements, the Taliban did not rely on traditional modes of objectivizing the legal system with places (buildings, courtroom configuration) or attributes (special attire, objects, symbols), since these increased the risk of being targeted by Western troops. They adopted instead the usual physical patterns and forms of rural Afghan social life, which allowed them to blend in with the population while remaining accessible to their users. The formalization of the Taliban judicial system took place through rudimentary, but regular—and therefore predictable—procedures. It was in stark contrast to the regime's marshalling of the visible attributes of state justice while feeding uncertainty by frequently skirting its own rules.

While the movement had limited resources, keeping to a procedural regimen, from complaint to verdict and sentencing, conditioned the Taliban judges' decisions as 'acts of naming or of instituting'.[1] Respect for procedures allowed the individualizing of disputes and defining the parties as litigants, as persons with *rights*, able to present evidence in support of their claims and bound to abide by the judge's *ruling*. From this perspective, the use of conspicuous but predictable violence, to the extent that it could be justified as an outcome of a judicial process, played a determinative role in the legal nature of the decision.

However, the accessibility of judicial procedure, particularly in light of the lack of legal representation, concealed power relationships that helped individuals linked to the insurgency. Moreover, the positioning of judges—simultaneously fulfilling the role of impartial third parties adjudicating disputes and of agents for moralizing society—had them alternating between a rigorist application of Islamic law and informal settlements. Last but not least, this was a judicial system caught up in a war: summary and arbitrary proceedings by judges undermined the force of the law that the Taliban laid

[1] Pierre Bourdieu, 'The Force of Law: Toward a Sociology of the Juridical Field', *Hastings Law Journal*, 1986, vol. 38, n° 5, p. 838.

The Taliban Courts in Afghanistan. Adam Baczko, Oxford University Press. © Adam Baczko 2023.
DOI: 10.1093/oso/9780198896777.003.0008

claim to—and the durability of their decisions remained closely linked to the fortunes of war.

Using the Taliban courts

To reduce the risk of attacks, the courts never held sessions in buildings marked as such, as a Nahrin district judge described:

> We don't have buildings like the superior courts and high courts where it would be written in black letters 'Supreme Court' or 'High Court'. We operate from simple buildings that cannot be targeted by the NATO forces, because of being located in the middle of a village inhabited by the people. So it is difficult to target that.[2]

In many cases, Western troops or Afghan army operations kept the Taliban from setting up courts in a fixed location. For example, in the Maywand district of Kandahar, the Taliban court sat in a dedicated building in the village of Garm Abak until the American troop surge in 2010. From then on, to help them elude Special Forces raids, the judges were reintegrated with groups of Taliban fighters that roamed from village to village. Similarly, in the Pech Valley (Kunar), the judge moved constantly with a commander and his unit to which he had been attached.[3]

In Dawlat Abad district, Faryab province, the judge made the rounds on a motorcycle, escorted by two fighters, and never stayed long in the same place:

> It's almost two years that I have been a judge in Dawlat Abad district and, before me, there was a Judge, who was called Mawlawi Akhtar from Pashtun Kot district of Faryab province, he has been killed by an ISAF bombing. [. . .] When people have problems, sometimes they call me directly or they ask the Taliban who are based in their villages to call me. Before I had a permanent place in the district and people came over there directly, but now, due to security concerns and ISAF airstrikes, we have changed our system to a mobile judge, because a lot of our friends have been killed by these airstrikes. Now,

[2] I-1, Taliban appeals court judge, Nahrin district (Baghlan), 2011.

[3] Pal Refsdal, *Behind the Taliban Mask: The Other Side of Afghanistan's Front-line*, Thames Ditton, Journeyman Pictures, 2010.

> most of the times, I travel to the villages, talk to the notable and ask them if they have problems in their village. This is how people reach me.[4]

In Qarabagh district (Ghazni), the judge also had to go into hiding in 2010, after his two predecessors were killed in airstrikes. He explained:

> The Taliban have changed their court system and became mobile for over a year. We all know that before the Taliban had permanent places for their court in most of the districts of Ghazni provinces. But now, due to the orders we receive from our high-ranking officials to protect our life, not only the judges or court became mobile, even the Taliban commanders move quite regularly. We fear the American airstrikes and bombings and night raids. That's why we changed our plan and became a mobile court. If we stay in one place for a long period, someone may report us to the foreign troops or ANA soldiers so they can quickly target us. […] it has caused a lot of problems for the local villagers and also for the Taliban judges. But we are giving our phone numbers to the village notables and the local Taliban commanders find us very easily.[5]

When judges did not conduct court in the same place for any length of time, they tried to remain accessible. As this testimony illustrates, in areas well covered by Afghan cell phone carriers, the judges' numbers were widely shared with Taliban sympathizers and notables. Alternatively, people could contact the judge through militants who visited villages regularly. Some judges took the initiative and travelled to villages to hear complaints. A resident of Ghazni who appealed to a Taliban judge recalled:

> Before, it was very easy for the villagers to lodge their complaints to the Taliban judges, because the Taliban had a permanent court in the district. But after the Taliban judges moved from place to place, it became difficult for the villagers to find out the Taliban judges's whereabouts in the district. […] Of course, it creates problems for the villagers, because in Qarabagh district without the Taliban court, they don't have access to the government court. That's why villagers have to seek out the Taliban judges.[6]

[4] I-9, Taliban court judge, Dawlat Abad district (Faryab), 2011.
[5] I-20, Taliban appeals court judge, Qarabagh district (Ghazni), 2011.
[6] I-31, resident of Qarabagh district (Ghazni), 2011.

Another Ghazni user concluded that 'the transformation of the Taliban courts has caused problems for the villagers, but not too much. Simply, people have to look for Taliban judges for two or three days before finding them.' Yet, while sometimes it could take several days to find a judge, the most isolated villages often had no alternative to resort to.

Nothing in the Taliban judicial process required special accommodations different from rural social life:

> Taliban courts operate in a very simple way. The Taliban judge sits in front of a cup of green tea that got cold and hears people's complaints. The judge himself receives the petition. Then he calls a member of the Taliban movement and tells him to go and ask the people against whom a complaint was filed to appear the next day.[7]

With no specialized buildings, Taliban judges would sit in a mosque or in the private houses of sympathizers:

> Most of the times, the Taliban hold their trials in the mosques of Sayid Abad district. But they don't care what kind of place, they just want a place safe for them. In fact, Sayid Abad district is a safe place for Taliban, who can move easily and can set up their court easily, but still they want a safe place, be it in the mountain, the desert, or a mosque.[8]

In 2011, in the Taliban-controlled district of Wardak province, judges moved constantly but retained their freedom of movement. On the other hand, in 2013, in Logar, people had to go off-road to look for judges in the mountains, as one resident explained: 'There are a lot of Taliban and judges in Surkhaw Mountains. I walked there for three hours and I asked people where are the Taliban [...] I saw with the judge in the mosque in a mountain village, in the mountain. [...] there were ten fighters with him as bodyguards for protection.'[9] In 2011, in Ghazni, some trials took place at night to evade Western and Afghan security forces, as described by a resident of Qarabagh district:

> Taliban judges hold their courts in different areas, because they seek to protect themselves from the foreign troop attacks, as well as the Afghan army and

[7] I-14, Taliban trial court judge, Alingar district (Laghman), 2011.
[8] I-33, resident of Sayid Abad district (Wardak), 2011.
[9] E-72, user of a Taliban court in Mohamad Agha district (Logar), May 2013.

police. Therefore, Taliban judges always try to hold their court in the safest places in the village and it doesn't matter if it is in a village, the mountains, or forests. Sometimes the Taliban also hold their trial during the night in the mosques.[10]

The path of litigation

Litigation followed a brief sequence of essential steps. While Taliban judges could take up certain cases themselves, particularly those relating to political justice (see Chapter 8), a complaint (*aghiza*) to a judge appears to have been the most common method of filing a case. An investigation would ensue, during which the judge conducted an investigation, collected testimonies, and examined written evidence. The judge would then submit his verdict to the Military Commission for approval before announcing it. As required in Islamic law, witness statements were given preponderant weight. 'Taliban judges do not decide cases without interviewing witnesses and reviewing the documents. The presence of three witnesses is a must in deciding any case. Judges make their decision after recording statements of witnesses.'[11] The weight given to the spoken word also allowed judges to factor in the social status of witnesses in assigning value to their testimony. Thus, in a conflict over land boundaries in Kunar province, the Taliban judge conducted one-on-one interviews with the village's fifteen notables, questioning them about the past location of the boundaries and letting themselves be guided by the majority opinion.[12] This emphasis on verbal corroboration was also a pragmatic response to the difficulties of conducting trials in the midst of a civil war. Many documents were lost or forged, and those issued by successive regimes were of uncertain validity. In addition, certain crimes, such as illicit sexual intercourse (*zina*) had to be corroborated by eyewitness accounts. Such a restrictive evidentiary regime in general limited convictions for crimes that usually carried the death penalty but sometimes also caused cases to take a surprising turn. Residents of Washir district in Helmand reported the following case to a British Army adviser on judicial affairs:

[10] I-31, resident of Qarabagh district (Ghazni), 2011.
[11] I-4, Taliban appeals court judge, Dahan-i Ghuri district (Baghlan), 2011.
[12] E-73, a mullah living in Kunar province, August 2015.

> A woman was raped. No recourse to governmental authority was available. So the case was taken before the Taliban judges. They ruled that the necessary four witnesses for a rape case were not available and that therefore no crime could be proved. The victim's family were unhappy with this, and took matters into their own hands. They kidnapped the perpetrator and raped him themselves. In turn he brought his own rapists before the Taleban Court. The ruling was the same. He could produce no witnesses and therefore the crime could not be proved.[13]

Paradoxically, in this particular case, the response of the raped woman's family points out the predictability of the Taliban court procedure for them to subvert.

However, while verbal testimony was the primary evidentiary regime, written records were essential for supporting a defence. A man, who claimed to have paid the bride price by wire transfer while he was living in England, had to furnish the receipt issued by Western Union before the judge in the case would rule in his favour.[14] Land titles and marriage certificates were taken as evidence, but judges usually checked their validity with neighbours or elders. The value of the legal documents issued by the Kabul regime was a matter of dispute among judges. Several judges considered that the titles issued by state institutions, despite the recurrence of fraudulent practices, were stronger than the traditional titles issued by the *jirgas*. Some judges said they recognized the former. 'We recognize official titles on land. We also recognize the divorces granted by the government courts.'[15] One judge drew a distinction between civil and political decisions of the regime's courts:

> We can take into account some judicial decisions from the courts and the law of the government provided that they refer to Islam. Not all of them. For example, not in denunciations. But we recognize the official land titles if they are genuine, we recognize divorces pronounced by the government courts. If a person brings us a case dealt with by the government court and that case has not been contrary to Islam and the Quran, we are happy to accept it.[16]

[13] Frank Ledwidge, 'Justice in Helmand: The Challenge of Law Reform in a Society at War', *Asian Affairs*, 2009, vol. 40, n° 1, p. 87.
[14] E-72, user of a Taliban court in Mohamad Agha district (Logar), May 2013.
[15] I-11, Taliban court judge, Logar province, 2013.
[16] I-24, Taliban court judge, Logar province, 2013.

A different judge recognized the titles issued by earlier regimes, but not by the contemporaneous one, which he accused of corruption and of imposing divorces on men:

> Yes we recognize [the land titles], but not from this government, we recognize these from the other governments, from previous governments. We do not recognize the divorce pronounced by the government courts, we recognize it only when the husband of the women accepted the divorce. Because nowadays, the women appeal to human rights saying that 'I want to divorce my husband', then that women is sent to the government court and the husband can do nothing whether he agrees or not. So such cases are not accepted by us. We do not consider such judicial decisions because they are decisions made by money. We do not recognize the government courts.[17]

Generally, verbal and written evidence were reviewed concurrently. For example, a resident of Kandahar province told me how he won his case:

> I received a letter that this person had filed a complaint against me, and I was summoned to Garm Abak court. The court was in a house, with two judges sitting at the back, me and my witnesses on one side, my opponents on the other. I showed my title, the [recent] decision of the [regime court] judge in Kandahar. I had with me three witnesses who confirmed that the plot belonged to me. It was a Saturday, the hearing lasted from 8 a.m. to 1 p.m. and I won, the judge decided in my favor.[18]

The speed with which cases were resolved was an important issue: it came up regularly in interviews, as a marker demonstrating the Taliban system's superiority over that of the regime:

> We try to go as quickly as possible, because this is something that we can offer to the people which the government run courts simply cannot.[19]

> Taliban judges try their best to decide in the shortest possible time. However the process still takes about a week. Complicated and more important cases are discussed with the Military Commission. In some cases it may take longer, but usually cases are decided in the shortest possible time. That's why

[17] I-7, Taliban court judge, Logar province, 2013.
[18] E-74, a notable from Maywand district (Kandahar), August 2010.
[19] I-17, Taliban appeals court judge, Dushi district (Baghlan), 2011.

> people are coming to us for their cases instead of going to the government-run courts.[20]

In the less problematic cases, the standard procedure—including getting the Military Commission's approval for announcing the verdict—could be jettisoned in favour of a swift inquiry, as one Logar judge stated: 'An ordinary case takes no more than three days.'[21] The Taliban judge would summon the parties and announce the verdict right after questioning them. Sometimes the procedure was even sketchier: in a dispute over a woman's half-share of inheritance in Logar province, the Taliban judge, instead of holding a hearing, went to the house of the complainant's brothers. After questioning them, he announced the verdict and had them flogged.[22] In another case, to extract a confession the judge had a man beaten who was accused of stealing two cows.[23] Taliban judges took responsibility in interviews for meting out quick justice, presenting it as a response to popular demand in keeping with the Taliban's discourses on justice of the 1990s. Speaking about their rule then in Laghman province, an intellectual close to Hizb-i Islami, who fought the Taliban, told me: 'The Taliban were appreciated for their swiftness; cases were quickly resolved. The use of the law of an eye for an eye made it possible to obtain judgments which, without it, would never have happened.'[24] The application of particularly harsh sentences in certain cases of theft or murder effectively underpinned the reputation of the Taliban justice system. The summary nature of the court procedures also responded to the movement's limited resources and the precarious conditions under which the judges held court.[25]

Still, some cases could take months or even years to resolve: 'Usually Taliban courts decide a case in a short period of time. However, some cases take more than a month. Such complicated cases are sent to the Military Commission, which passes it on to the Council of Ten in Quetta [the Leadership Council]. The Council's decision is sent to the judge through the Military Commission. This process takes time.'[26] Unlike expedited resolutions, these cases were subject to painstaking investigation or in-depth study by the judge. An appeals court judge in Alishang district recounted one such case:

[20] I-2, Taliban appeals court judge, Karagai district (Laghman), 2011.
[21] E-30, Taliban court judge, Mohamad Agha district (Logar), May 2013.
[22] I-35, a woman living in Charkh district (Logar), 2013.
[23] I-40, a resident of Arghandab district (Kandahar), 2011.
[24] E-68, a notable of Alingar district (Laghman), April 2011.
[25] E-57, veterinarian in Laghman province, April 2011.
[26] I-26, Taliban appeals court judge, Alishang district (Laghman), 2011.

> I have decided quite a few cases but the most emotional case for me was that of X's three sons. This was a conflict over inheritance. The man had three sons. Two of them were living with him while one was living apart. The father had disowned his third son for his alleged disobedience and did not give him his share in property. This made him angry and he shot his father dead. Then, the third son claimed again his share of the inheritance. But the two other sons refused to give him his share. As a result, the eldest son killed the third son. It was a complicated case, and it took me three months, the longest time for a case in my entire judicial career. I was particularly moved when I saw the mother torn apart. But by the grace of Allah, I handled this matter very successfully.[27]

Another judge recalled a case that was investigated for two months before he reached a verdict:

> A person had married off his daughter to a man for 400,000 rupees [$3,500]. The man fathered three children but he had not paid the amount [of the bride price]. The father-in-law filed a petition against his son-in-law. He also made his own daughter a co-accused in the case as she was also siding with her husband. That was a complicated case and it took me more than nine weeks to decide.[28]

Judges generally explained that the distinction between a simple case and a complicated one related to the seriousness of the offence:

> There are different cases that take a lot of time, for example the land disputes take a long time, but thefts, murders and disputes between two people are resolved very quickly. For example, if someone has killed another person, we give a gun to his brother to execute the killer of his brother in public; if someone steals something, we cut his hand off in front of people. So, such cases are concluded very rapidly, but disputes between communities take time to resolve.[29]

In practice, protracted trials seemed to be related less to the seriousness of the crime than to the politically sensitive nature of the dispute. The above two

[27] Ibid.
[28] I-1, Taliban appeals court judge, Nahrin district (Baghlan), 2011.
[29] I-7, Taliban court judge, Logar province, 2013.

cases cited by the judges concerned inheritance and marriage matters that had implications for the social status of the families involved. Moreover, a conflict that mobilized families or groups on a tribal or ethnic basis added a political dimension, especially in the context of war, and obliged the judge to decide it carefully or even refer it to his hierarchical superiors. Thus, in the case of conflict between two villages in Khogiani district (Nangarhar, see Chapters 5 and 6), the Peshawar branch of the Supreme Court cautiously declined to weigh in, postponing any decision until the end of the war.[30]

Once the preliminary inquiry was completed, the judge would summon the parties to an adversarial, public hearing:

> After receiving a complaint from a petitioner, he asks him to come on a specific date and bring all relevant documents and witnesses so that his case can be decided. The petitioner comes on the given date and defends his case in person. He enters as an ordinary citizen and is free to offer whatever he wants in his defense.[31]

While the judge and the clerics assisting him might have conducted an inquiry ahead of time, the hearing was a public moment during which each party gave their version, presented additional documents, and called witnesses. The hearing proceeded in a mostly informal manner: neither the plaintiff nor the defendant could have counsel at the hearing. The judges interviewed often stressed the Islamic, even authentically Afghan, nature of this way of doing things, as opposed to the importation of Western judicial practices, which they blamed for the dysfunction of the regime's courts:

> The Taliban courts decide cases according to Islamic laws instead of Western Law, which has been imposed on the country. So, there are no lawyers with neckties in Taliban courts. No Taliban judges wear colorful suits. Taliban judges are simple religious scholars, who follow guidance of Islam. They meet the criteria required by Islam for judging. The same goes for the people who appear before them. They come as ordinary men, no matter who they are; regardless of their importance, they must justify themselves before the court. If they can, they are honorably acquitted. If convicted, they must face the punishment accordingly.[32]

[30] E-8, resident of one of the two villages involved, Shirzad district (Nangarhar), August 2015.
[31] I-22, Taliban appeals court judge, Ghormach district (Badghis), 2011.
[32] I-12, Taliban trial court judge, Nahrin district (Baghlan), 2011.

Nevertheless, the proceedings appeared to follow a standard pattern. During the hearing, the judge and his assistants sat cross-legged on a mat or on a cushion. People who came to plead their case usually sat across from them and waited their turn, as in the reception rooms of the notables:

> The Taliban judge sits on a prayer mat. The local mullahs, who assist the judge in deciding cases, also sit beside him. People come and hand over their petitions to the judge. Taliban judges receive complaints in their own hands and tell the petitioners to come on the following date so that their cases can be decided. […] We follow our own path and cases are decided in the light of sharia laws, not according to the English laws.[33]

The judges' verdicts were usually written down in the format of the former Islamic Emirate of Afghanistan's official documents, with a header, a stamp, and a judge's signature. Several photocopies would be made for the parties and for the archive:

> Taliban judges hand over copies of their verdicts to both parties and also forward the original to the Military Commission. The paper, on which a verdict is written, bears the logo of the Islamic Emirate of Afghanistan, the stamp, and the judge's signature so that no one can challenge its authenticity. […] A copy of the verdict is given to both the petitioner and the defendant. […] Anyone filing an appeal will have to produce a copy of the verdict for the new judge.[34]

Again, there were exceptions to the rule: to cite an example, a judge in Ghazni said he only wrote down his verdicts in the most important cases:

> We do provide certificates for both sides of the dispute, if they ask for it and if the case is important, not for all cases. We always look at the importance of a case in determining whether a certificate is really required to prove that a verdict has been reached, and we give it to them. As many people witness our judgment and trial, even if we do not give them a certificate or keep any record, neither of the parties can challenge it in the future. However for small cases, we only announce our decision and that's it for both sides, and we do not give them any type of official document.[35]

[33] I-23, Taliban trial court judge, Dahan-i Ghuri district (Baghlan), 2011.
[34] I-5, Taliban trial court judge, Karagai district (Laghman), 2011.
[35] I-20, Taliban appeals court judge, Qarabagh district (Ghazni), 2011.

Documenting verdicts was fundamental to their durability and value outside the Taliban courts. In effect, they served as property titles in areas controlled by the insurgency and were often also recognized by the regime's courts.

In principle, the law allowed the dismissed plaintiff or the convicted defendant to appeal the verdict in cases where the investigation was conducted in a cursory manner. As one appeals court judge explained: 'The plaintiffs inform us of their objections and we review the verdict of the lower court, and then we either tell them that the verdict is correct or we give them a new verdict.'[36] The cases in appeal courts proceeded in a manner similar to the trial courts:

> Look, I am a judge of the Qala-i-Naw superior court. I sit in the court and people come to me to submit their requests. These people, who want to challenge the verdicts of the lower court, come to the high court. [. . .] After deliberations and collection of information based on evidences and witnesses produced before the court, the case is sent to the Military Commission and then, as soon as possible, a verdict is rendered. We try to decide cases as quickly as possible.[37]

If the appeals court's judgment does not satisfy them, the parties can bring a challenge before the Military Commission or they may even appeal to the Supreme Court based in Nawzad, northern Helmand province:

> One can file an appeal against the verdict with the superior court. He will have to submit the verdict of the lower court with his appeal. [. . .] The appeal is usually disposed of by the superior court judge. But he sends it to the Military Commission if he cannot come to a decision. The Military Commission decides on such appeal with the approval of the Council of Ten [the Leadership Council in Quetta]. The petitioner can file an appeal with the Supreme Court against the decision of the Military Commission if he has any objection to it. But this happens very rarely.[38]

Appealing a decision of the Military Commission was a delicate matter, as it was the supreme Taliban authority in a province and appeals were regarded as a challenge to the senior cadres. For example, a Baghlan judge warned that this was a dangerous move if it did not convince the highest Taliban

[36] I-26, Taliban appeals court judge Alishang district (Laghman), 2011.
[37] I-15, Taliban appeals court judge, Qala-i Naw district (Badghis), 2011.
[38] I-18, Taliban appeals court judge, Alingar district (Laghman), 2011.

authorities: 'An appeal against a superior court verdict can be submitted to the Military Commission. If the person has objection to the verdict of the Military Commission, then he should be careful, because the verdicts of all these tiers of the Taliban judicial system cannot be incorrect. The Military Commission can punish him for rejecting its verdict.'[39] In practice, only people with connections within the Taliban, or who had a relative in the movement, or notables could get away with filing an appeal:

> In general, most locals cannot complain against the Taliban judges, because people are afraid that the Taliban will kill them. But there are some people in the villages, who were previously with the Taliban movement and now they are just normal notables or some people who have very good contact with the Taliban, these people can appeal or complain about the Taliban judges and their judgment. They complain to the Military Commission or the governor of Qarabagh district.[40]

Furthermore, the losing party could question the integrity of the judge before the Military Commission:

> Anyone in any district can come to the weekly meeting of Taliban judges if he has a complaint against a judge. Such meetings are held between members of the Military Commission and the judges in each district in turn. A person having a complaint against a judge may lodge it with the members of the Military Commission during such meetings. The members of the Military Commission will discuss his problem in that meeting. The judge will be punished if he is found guilty, otherwise his verdict will be implemented and the complaint will be dismissed.[41]

At the meeting, the complainant had to face the judge, in principle a respected official of the movement. The judges mentioned this procedure and were unanimous in saying that a judge convicted of nepotism or corruption would be punished:

> If someone has a valid objection against a judge, he can lodge his complaints with the Military Commission. The commission intervenes in response to the

[39] I-12, Taliban trial court judge, Nahrin district (Baghlan), 2011.
[40] I-31, a resident of Qarabagh district (Ghazni), 2011.
[41] I-21, Taliban trial court judge, Ghormach district (Badghis), 2011.

> requests from common people. It checks the verdict concerned. The judge is allowed to carry on his duty if the objection is baseless. If the objection is valid, then the judge is duly punished and dismissed.[42]

In Andar (Ghazni) district, a fired judge was sent back to Quetta and punished. However, regardless of the merits of the charge, only those who know Taliban militants or have significant support would risk denouncing a judge.

Carrying out the verdicts

The Taliban had no police force separate from their fighting arm. A Kunar resident told me: 'In every district, the Taliban have a security commander (*qomandan-i amniat*) who sees to it that people obey the judges and the governor's orders.'[43] A Taliban court user living in Qarabagh district (Ghazni) detailed that official's prerogatives: 'This commander has his fighters in most villages of Qarabagh district and these fighters are responsible for arresting the criminals and bringing them to the security commander. These fighters in the villages have contact among the people and gather information from the villagers. They are not the police, but they do the job of the police.'[44] In Asmar, Kunar, the security commander sat in on court hearings and regularly patrolled the market unbothered by soldiers from the nearby government post.[45] The Taliban also relied on networks of informants and sympathizers: 'Taliban commanders have secretly recruited people in every village, and their job is to keep an eye on everyone, and if someone works with the Afghan government, then they report it to the Taliban commanders. Those people are the Taliban's police.'[46] Whatever the true effectiveness of Taliban informant networks, they were perceived as all-knowing and all-seeing by many of my respondents, for example this resident of Sayid Abad district:

> Every commander, in every village, has some people secretly working for him among the villagers. If a villager does something wrong or gets in contact with government people or tries to turn the villagers to the government side, these secret people quickly inform on them. These secret people are watching that

[42] I-1, Taliban appeals court judge, Nahrin district (Baghlan), 2011.
[43] E-20, a trader, resident of Kunar province, July 2011.
[44] I-31, a resident of Qarabagh district (Ghazni), 2011.
[45] E-31, a notable of Kunar province, July 2011.
[46] I-20, Taliban appeals court judge, Qarabagh district (Ghazni), 2011.

the local villagers are not doing something wrong or against the Taliban. No one knows who these people are. But they know that there are some villagers who work for the Taliban and will inform the Taliban if villagers do something wrong.[47]

The punishments mix literal application of Islamic law and negotiations with the inhabitants. The most severe punishments (*hudud*) prescribed by the Koran are meted out by the Taliban. These include stoning fornicators to death, usually by a mob, or amputating a limb for theft. On being questioned about this by a journalist, a judge in Ghazni estimated that the two butchers he employed as executioners had severed some forty limbs over a period of eighteen months.[48] Yet these punishments rarely came up during my interviews. When asked about the last amputation or stoning they had ordered or witnessed, judges generally responded evasively. While this silence could be construed as wishing to conceal or refusing to answer the question, the cases reported to me were generally the same as those that made the pages of the newspapers, which suggests that these draconian punishments were fairly rare. In addition, Taliban judges punished homicide, bodily harm, and destruction of property by ordering beatings (*tazir*), administering a penalty equivalent to the damage inflicted, or requiring compensation (*diya*). Corporal punishment could also be imposed in cases of gambling or fraud. Espionage and collaboration with the regime were crimes for which the judge had latitude in deciding the sentence (*tazir*); more often than not, it would mean execution. For 2012, the United Nations Assistance Mission in Afghanistan (UNAMA) counted thirty-three executions and, in an interview with Antonio Giustozzi, a cadre on the Peshawar Judicial Committee estimated that the Taliban courts ordered several hundred that same year.[49] Mostly, executions were reserved for cases of espionage, collaboration with the regime or with Western troops, and rarely for private conflicts. In 2008, an order signed by Mullah Omar was circulated to commanders to stop beheadings. A Taliban commander in Helmand stated that 'the orders are driven by growing public aversion to beheadings. From now on, we will be executing the secret agents by shooting instead of slaughtering

[47] I-33, a resident Sayid Abad district (Wardak), 2011.

[48] Miles Amoore, 'Afghans Flock to Judge Dread and his Butcher Boys', *The Sunday Times*, 23 January 2011.

[49] For a tally of executions compiled by the United Nations Office for Human Rights in Kabul, see *Afghanistan Annual Report 2012: Protection of Civilians in Armed Conflict*, Kabul, UNAMA, 2012, p. 24. For an estimate by an executive of the Peshawar Judicial Committee, see Antonio Giustozzi and Adam Baczko, 'The Politics of the Taliban's Shadow Judiciary, 2003–2013', *Central Asian Affairs*, 2014, vol. 1, nº 2, p. 221.

them.'[50] Finally, given the dearth of prisons, imprisonment happened infrequently, but the Taliban often detained suspects while an investigation was underway. Prisons existed in some areas; in others, people were sequestered in insurgency hideouts.[51]

While the most severe sentences prescribed by the Quran were carried out, several judges told of how they avoided imposing them. While they may have tempered their remarks in an interview to avoid being seen as cruel, how they described certain negotiations and their underlying issues did in fact point to conciliation playing a role in judgments. Judges pushed for agreements between the parties, such as a marriage to avoid a conviction for fornication. Thus, a judge recounted how he avoided passing the death sentence on a couple by mandating an arrangement:

> Before Eid al-Azha, a girl named H. fled with a Laghman resident named I. The father of the girl was determined to kill them both. I made them appear before the court where the girl said that she would only marry I. and no one else. I solemnized their marriage and told all that the girl's father would be responsible if the couple was harmed. I also solemnized the marriage of I.'s sister with the brother of H. So the issue was resolved. And I take pride in this case where, I believe, I saved the couple from the girl's angry father who was out to kill the couple in the name of honor.[52]

In this situation, by marrying the young man's sister to the girl's brother, the judge in effect ordered an exchange of women that solved the bride price dilemma to the benefit of both families. Another judge recounted how he engineered an arrangement in a case that he could not resolve satisfactorily in his own mind by relying on Islamic law:

> I have decided many cases in my career. One of the cases was about a couple. The husband was a cruel man and he would torture his wife. The woman was seeking a divorce but he was not ready to divorce her. According to Sharia, a woman can't divorce her husband. I convinced the man to divorce his wife. It was a case of Laghman province.[53]

[50] Janullah Hashimzada and Akram Noorzai, 'Omar to Taliban: Stop Beheadings', *Pajhwok*, 3 February 2008.

[51] E-74, a notable of Maywand district (Kandahar), who was jailed for several days, August 2010. See also the account by a journalist who was kept in a Taliban prison, Ghaith Abdul-Ahad, 'Five Days inside a Taliban Jail', *The Guardian*, 25 November 2010.

[52] I-5, Taliban trial court judge, Karagai district (Laghman), 2011.

[53] I-18, Taliban appeals court judge, Alingar district (Laghman), 2011.

This turns out to have been a fairly standard practice in rural areas during the Islamic Emirate of Afghanistan. In a case of fornication dating to 1996, which I learned about from an eyewitness, a judge holding court in Mihtarlam, the capital of Laghman, would have liked to have prevented the stoning that he ultimately ordered. A few months after the woman's execution, the judge held the victim responsible for the outcome, claiming he had offered her a way out. When he interrogated her explicitly if she had sex with the man who kidnapped her, she reportedly nodded. However, the judge said that he had implicitly been offering to exonerate her: all she needed to do was deny the accusation for him to dismiss her case, since there were no eyewitnesses willing to testify to the sexual act.[54]

Other judges, however, applied the sentences prescribed in the reference texts, in spite of social pressure and even their personal feelings. A judge told of a case that left a deep impression on him:

> A man had pronounced his wife divorced three times on a single occasion, which is enough to prove that the divorce had happened, but then he wanted to patch up with her. According to Islamic laws when you say the word 'divorce' three times, divorce happens. But he did not want to leave her anyway. The case was brought before me. I told him: 'According to Sharia, if someone divorces his wife and then wants to keep her again as his wife, the woman will have to marry another man and then get a divorce from him before living as a wife with the first husband.' I handed over a divorce letter to them and both the man and his wife left the court. Though according to the rules and Sharia laws I had done the right thing, as a human being this really left me shocked but I had to abide by Sharia laws.[55]

Another judge recalled an execution he ordered:

> I have decided lots of cases. But the most shocking case for me was the case of G. which I can't forget. G., an accused in a double murder case started weeping in front of me when I announced the death sentence for him. I really got emotional when I saw him weeping and begging for his life, but I had to kill the emotions of the man and maintain the decision of the judge. I still remember that hair-raising moment.[56]

[54] Interview with Alain de Bures, humanitarian zootechnician working in Afghanistan since the 1980s, April 2011. For a press article reporting this stoning, see 'Afghan Woman Stoned to Death for Adultery', *RAWA News*, 30 March 1997.

[55] I-4, Taliban appeals court judge, Dahan-i Ghuri district (Baghlan), 2011.

[56] I-18, Taliban appeals court judge, Alingar district (Laghman), 2011.

A third judge claimed to have ordered a stoning despite the pressure on him:

> One of the sensitive cases brought before my court involved a man who had illicit relations with his wife's sister. His sister-in-law had become pregnant as a result of these illicit relations. The case was brought before me. It took me a lot of time to reach a verdict, because it was socially complicated and there was an enormous pressure from the notables, but I had to abide by the Islamic laws and I issued a sentence of death by stoning. Although this led to a hostile reaction from society, later people were convinced that the principle of punishment was to make them better Muslims and that it was only to deter crimes.[57]

In some cases, Taliban judges may even have scotched an informal agreement between the parties. This was specifically the situation in the highly publicized agony of Siddiqa and Khayyam in Kunduz in 2010. While an agreement had been reached between the two families, the Taliban judge sentenced the young couple to be stoned and told the crowd:

> When a married woman commits adultery, she will be struck by stones—this is called *sangsar* in Arabic. The woman you see here today committed adultery with this man. She has admitted this herself not once, but many times. [...] Islamic law will be enforced here in Kunduz, by the grace of God. They will both be punished, these two people.[58]

As Torunn Wimpelmann showed, the girl's family played an ambiguous role. The couple had fled to Kunar province but were convinced by members of the young man's family that an agreement could be reached, and the regime's district governor had even offered to shelter the lovers until an arrangement that suited both families could be sealed. But the girl's father demanded that the lovers be kept at the home of a mullah close to the Taliban who then asked the judge to intervene. The girl's father reportedly said: 'I shall hand over my daughter to the Taliban and will ask them to do what religion orders.'[59] When questioned following the execution of a pregnant woman convicted of fornication (*zina*), a Taliban spokesman justified the violence of the sentences as a deterrent: 'We gave this decision so that in future no one should have these

[57] I-8, Taliban trial court judge, Dushi district (Baghlan), 2011.

[58] Torunn Wimpelmann, *The Pitfalls of Protection: Gender, Violence, and Power in Afghanistan*, Berkeley, University of California Press, 2017, pp. 141–2.

[59] Ibid., p. 145.

illegal affairs. We whipped her in front of all the local people, to show them an example. Then we shot her.'[60]

In any event, the Taliban and users of its courts agreed that people who failed to abide by the verdicts should be severely punished:

> We will be informed very quickly if someone who has lost the trial refuses the verdicts of the Taleban judge or court. It didn't happen yet, but if we hear about something like this in the future, then we will administer a very harsh punishment, because they did not accept the holy Quran decision, since I am judging according to the holy Quran.[61]

The Taliban reserved special punishment for those who turned to government courts or to an alternative form of settling disputes following one of their verdicts. Cases of resistance to Taliban decisions appear to have been rare and punishments particularly brutal. As one notable from Faryab province explained, 'People here are afraid of the Taliban. I know many people who lost Taliban trials and are not happy with this court. But they are afraid of the Taliban and can't do anything against Taliban trials or courts.'[62] Moreover, the Taliban can mobilize their resources to arrest fugitives:

> Once, I was presented a case that someone had kidnapped a young boy. The kidnapper had fled the area. He had kidnapped the 11-year-old boy at gunpoint for ransom. Kidnapping a boy is a serious crime. I informed the Taliban militants and passed on the name and identity of the kidnapper to them. The two kidnappers were produced before me. That day I felt satisfied when I handed over the boy to his father and sent the culprits to jail where they are still languishing.[63]

Ultimately, recruiting and inserting judges into a bureaucratic system and establishing due process contributed to the objectivization of the Taliban justice system. In this respect, sticking to the procedures played a key role in the recognition of the system by its users and by the population at large. Those present at the trial, which was public, could observe the judges' going by the book, so to speak. It was on this condition that the force of the law operated and that a conflict before a Taliban court could be reduced to a legal case involving only the

[60] 'Taliban Judges Kill Pregnant Woman', *Asian News International*, 10 August 2010.
[61] I-9, Taliban court judge, Dawlat Abad district (Faryab), 2011.
[62] I-28, a notable from Dawlat Abad district (Faryab), 2011.
[63] I-8, Taliban trial court judge, Dushi district (Baghlan), 2011.

parties recognized by the judge. In a war where private disputes were exploited and involved broader social issues, compliance with procedures allowed conflicts to be individualized and reduced to the legally recognized object of litigation: a parcel of land, a marriage. Moreover, the emphasis on adhering to even rudimentary procedures, more than on formal attributes, offered the Taliban a way of distinguishing themselves from the regime's justice system.

PART III

PRODUCING A SOCIAL ORDER THROUGH THE LAW

8

Judges as an instrument of centralization

Introduction

The Taliban's judicial system was part of a shadow administration organized according to the formal principles of state functioning. The monopoly of violence and its bureaucratic supervision were key aims of the movement as a senior Taliban official claimed in 2015 on the official website (www.alamarah.com—now no longer functioning):

> [The Taliban] did not let the war conditions morph into anarchy and mayhem. […] The Taliban did not allow anyone amongst the populace to form unauthorised groups or raise weapons that took advantage of the turmoil, but disciplined all civil and military conditions under a framework of methodical management while spreading the struggle countrywide. They assigned provincial and district governors, judicial authorities, military commanders, group leaders, and at the top assigned commissions for overseeing under the direct command of the leadership. In doing so, they not only kept the fight orderly, but also kept in check disorder, injustices and unauthorised groups and gunmen from prevailing among the populace.[1]

Under Mullah Omar and his Leadership Council (Rahbari Shura), specialized committees (military affairs, judicial affairs, culture and information, foreign affairs, education, finance, health) acted like ministries responsible for coordinating the movement's activities in each of these sectors. This functional division was replicated at the provincial administration level, headed up by officials appointed under the Taliban governor.

In the late 2000s, Taliban leaders instructed judges to uphold the chain of command. The independence of the courts from the military hierarchy allowed the movement to use these magistrates for disciplining combatants.

[1] Reproduced in Mawlawi Abdul Hadi, 'Hallmarks of the Islamic Emirate's Jihadi Management' in Alex Strick van Linschoten and Felix Kuehn (eds), *The Taliban Reader: War, Islam and Politics*, London, Hurst, 2018, pp. 489–94.

The Taliban Courts in Afghanistan. Adam Baczko, Oxford University Press. © Adam Baczko 2023.
DOI: 10.1093/oso/9780198896777.003.0009

Deploying the judges in this way was based on their privileged relationship with the senior officials, sharing as they did their bureaucratic *habitus* and worldview, shaped by each of them having attained a higher level of religious education than the commanders. However, in practice, judges depended on the respect paid to their office by the commanders to be able to exercise their judicial functions. Moreover, the war fostered the independence of the most powerful military leaders vis-à-vis the movement's top leaders sequestered in their Pakistan refuge.[2] These commanders were therefore able to shake off the judges' influence, especially when it came to meting out political justice. The Taliban exemplified the problems posed by the differentiation of civilian and military functions in war. The relative autonomy of the judicial system was part of a cross-legitimization between fields. In return for recognizing the judge, which would reinforce the magistrate's credibility, the commander would obtain a legal grounding for his action. In practice, however, wartime conditions placed constraints on the autonomy of judges and their ability to legitimize the commanders.

Judicial control of combatants

Once the Taliban judicial system was well established, the leadership used judges to help centralize the movement. In 2006, a Code of Conduct was circulated to combatants entitled *Instructions* (layeha) *to the Mujahideen of the Islamic Emirate of Afghanistan*. Modified and expanded versions were distributed in 2009 and 2010, and while the first version drew relatively little media coverage, the updates aroused considerable interest:[3] US officers pored over the text to see how they could use it against the movement,[4] a professor

[2] These tensions between the leadership and the commanders only superficially resembled the situation of the 1980s. Unlike the exiled parties of the 1980s in Pakistan, the Taliban now were a unified organization. Regarding relations between parties and commanders in the 1980s–90s, see Gilles Dorronsoro, *Revolution Unending: Afghanistan, 1979 to the Present*, New York, Columbia University Press, 2005; Barnett R. Rubin, *The Fragmentation of Afghanistan: State Formation and Collapse in the International System*, New Haven, Yale University Press, 2002.

[3] Several translations in English have been published, including by the Afghan Analysts Network, the ICRC, and the journal *Studies in Conflict & Terrorism*. Kate Clark, *The Layha: Calling the Taleban to Account*, Kabul, Afghanistan Analysts Network, 2011; Muhammad Munir, 'The Layha for the Mujahideen: An Analysis of the Code of Conduct for the Taliban Fighters under Islamic Law', *International Review of the Red Cross*, 2011, vol. 93, n° 881, pp. 81–102; Niaz A. Shah, 'The Islamic Emirate of Afghanistan: A Layeha [Rules and Regulations] for Mujahidin', *Studies in Conflict & Terrorism*, 2012, vol. 35, n° 6, pp. 456–70. Here I rely on the version from the Afghan Analysts Network, which is the most complete.

[4] They suggested using the Code of Conduct to identify the weaknesses of the insurgency and propagandize its recurring failures. See Greg Kleponis, 'Throwing the Book at the Taliban: Undermining Taliban Legitimacy by Highlighting their Own Hypocrisy, *Small Wars Journal*, 1 September 2010;

of Islamic law discussed its conformity with Islamic law,[5] other law professors analysed it for compliance with international humanitarian law,[6] and the British researcher Kate Clark called on the Taliban to uphold the standards they set.[7] While there is no doubt that the document was ordered by the movement's leadership, precisely who authored it is difficult to establish. According to Kate Clark, the initiative came from the movement's number two man, Mullah Abdul Ghani Baradar. More is known about the sequels, said to have been drafted by Amir Khan Muttaqi, the Information and Culture Committee chairman, who had also headed the ministry of the same name in the Islamic Emirate (1996–2001). Various versions would have been reviewed and amended by the Council of Ulama and the Leadership Council.[8] Written in Pashto, the text was intended for internal consumption, primarily as guidelines for the movement's militants. The 2006 version appears to have had a modest circulation in contrast to the 2009 and 2010 editions.[9] In 2011, its distribution seemed to have been more systematic in the southern and central regions, but the document circulated in other regions as well, as reported by an Afghan researcher who watched it being printed in Kabul for dissemination in the northern provinces.[10] Copies recovered in the South from the bodies of Taliban fighters killed by Western troops indicated that these documents made it to their intended audience.[11]

The Code of Conduct was also used in Taliban courts as a legal document. All versions uniformly referred to sharia law and borrowed its vocabulary. Mullah Omar was called 'Imam' in all versions of the Code, a religious name associated with the title 'Commander of the Faithful'. The 2010 version referred

Thomas Johnson and Matthew DuPee, 'Analysing the New Taliban Code of Conduct (Layeha): An Assessment of Changing Perspectives and Strategies of the Afghan Taliban', *Central Asian Survey*, 2012, vol. 31, n° 1, pp. 77–91.

[5] Muhammad Munir, 'The Layha for the Mujahideen: An Analysis of the Code of Conduct for the Taliban Fighters under Islamic Law', *International Review of the Red Cross*, 2011, vol. 93, n° 881, pp. 81–102.

[6] Dapo Akande, *The Taliban's New 'Code of Conduct', Compliance with the Laws of War and POW Status*, 31 August 2009, www.ejiltalk.org/the-talibans-new-code-of-conduct-compliance-with-the-laws-of-war-and-pow-status/; Niaz A. Shah, 'The Taliban Layeha for Mujahidin and the Law of Armed Conflict', *Journal of International Humanitarian Legal Studies*, 2012, vol. 3, n° 1, pp. 192–229.

[7] Kate Clark, *The Layha: Calling the Taleban to Account*, Kabul, Afghanistan Analysts Network, 2011.

[8] Ibid., pp. 3, 6.

[9] Yoshinobu Nagamine, *The Legitimization Strategy of the Taliban's Code of Conduct*, New York, Palgrave Macmillan, 2015, pp. 31–3.

[10] Kate Clark, *The Layha: Calling the Taleban to Account*, Kabul, Afghanistan Analysts Network, 2011, p. 6.

[11] Thomas Johnson and Matthew DuPee, 'Analysing the New Taliban Code of Conduct (Layeha): An Assessment of Changing Perspectives and Strategies of the Afghan Taliban', *Central Asian Survey*, 2012, vol. 31, n° 1, p. 88.

to three works of classical Deobandi jurisprudence, *Al Hidaya*, *Fath ul-Qadir*, and *Alamgiriya* (Article 3) and the words of the prophet's companion Abu Huraira, an essential hadith reference in Sunnism (Article 79). Judges cited the *Instructions to the Mujahideen* in several decisions convicting a fighter or commander. Beyond the booklet's legal character, it pointed to the movement's growing institutionalization and the place of judges in this evolution. Indeed, by placing the inviolability of the chain of command at the centre of the *Instructions to the Mujahideen* and revising each edition to address problems identified by the cadres, the movement's leadership affirmed the disciplinary role of judges and their monopoly on handling disputes between fighters and non-combatants.

Most articles in all three versions dealt with respect for the hierarchy and discipline. In the 2006 version, specific articles aimed to hedge in the prerogatives of commanders, for instance by prohibiting them from collecting money for the release of a prisoner (Article 7) or signing agreements with NGOs (Article 8). The 2009 and 2010 versions went into lengthy detail on the chain of command and the obligations of combatants to obey it. Nearly half of the eighty-five articles in the 2010 version dealt with discipline, starting with the following:

> The mujahideen must obey their group leader; group leaders must obey their district leaders; district leaders must obey the senior provincial officials; senior provincial officials must obey their head of the zone; heads of the zones must obey the Imam [Mullah Omar] and his deputy [nayeb]. This is a duty [*wajeb*, a quranic term] if [the order] is in accordance with sharia.

The booklet also took the planning and conduct of military operations out of the individual commander's hands by making them the prerogative of the Military Commissions (Article 42, 2010). With specified exceptions, the text prohibited the forming of groups and subgroups of combatants unless authorized by the provincial and national hierarchy (Article 36, 2010). The same article ordered governors to integrate 'unofficial' and 'unregistered' groups into 'larger' and 'official' units and to disarm any that refused. Along these lines, Article 37 (2010) prohibited cadres from communicating with the media, something only the movement's spokespersons were authorized to do. Other articles banned extorting money, confiscating private property, and selling looted property, if any. In several of his speeches, Mullah Omar stressed the need for fighters to follow the booklet's directives: 'Observe obedience to your Amir and ensure the implementation of the codes of conduct of Mujahideen which have been delivered to you. The Jihadic chiefs nominated by us in all parts of the country are your Sharia-based leaders. You should obey them.'[12]

The Code of Conduct's evolution could be gauged from the different successive versions. The most significant changes came with the 2009 revision; the 2010 edition on the other hand only supplemented it. The first edition of 2006 was a relatively skimpy text of thirty articles, with a hardline tone, ordering the burning of schools and dispensaries and the killing of anyone working for the regime. In contrast, the 2009 version had sixty-seven articles organized into thirteen sections and the 2010 version had eighty-five articles arranged in fourteen sections. In addition, both of these versions contained a procedure for recourse to higher levels when it came to resolving any ambiguities in the text. While the majority of articles still focused on purely military matters, especially the centralization of operations, the text seems also to be designed to help garner popular support:

> Provincial, district and group officials and all mujahedin with all their power must be careful with regard to the lives of the common people and their property, such as cars. Those who do not pay care with the lives and belongings of the common people shall be held responsible and, taking into account their prestige [rank], will be punished accordingly. (Article 46, 2009)

> Mujahideen are obliged to adopt Islamic behaviour and good conduct with the people and try to win over the hearts of the common Muslims and as mujahideen be such representatives of the Islamic Emirate that all compatriots shall welcome and give the hand of cooperation and help. (Article 59, 2009)

The latter provision reflects the Taliban's reappropriation of standards and practices imported with the Western intervention. In addition to referencing the classic maxim of counterinsurgency 'winning hearts and minds' regularly espoused by the American military,[13] the movement's texts and speeches echoed the language of international institutions with phrases like 'civilian victims' and 'human rights'. Similarly, from 2009 onwards, many articles mandated respect for schools, humanitarian organizations, or clinics against the

[12] Mullah Omar's Eid al-Fitr Address for 2011.

[13] This maxim comes from a 1952 declaration by the commander-in-chief of British forces in Malaysia, General Sir Harold Templer, who declared that against the communist insurgency, 'the answer lies not in pouring more troops into the jungle, but in the hearts and minds of the Malayan people'. The term came into considerable vogue with European and American military personnel who theorized the doctrine of counterinsurgency, especially in the context of the Vietnam War (1964–75), followed by those in Afghanistan since 2001 and in Iraq since 2003. In 1968, faced with its success—and the euphemizing of the violence it induces—its inventor wryly called it 'this nauseating phrase that I think I invented'.

background of increased exchanges with the International Committee of the Red Cross (ICRC) and the United Nations.[14] More generally, both texts corresponded to two very different moments in time for the Taliban. In 2006, the movement reconstituted itself and sought to mobilize fighters, whereas it was just getting started with reconstructing institutions. Three years later, however, the Taliban already controlled many rural districts and had established an administration whose size and responsibilities burgeoned year by year. Hence, the problem for the movement was getting some of the veteran commanders to obey the hierarchy.

The 2009 and 2010 versions assigned the supervision of combatants to judges, with the authority over the judges vested in the Military Commissions. Where the 2006 version of the *Instructions to the Mujahideen* made no mention of judges, later versions ordered the establishment of courts composed of a judge and two religious scholars in all provinces where the movement had a presence (Article 20, 2009). Notably, the power to adjudicate complaints against combatants was delegated to the judges, as Mullah Omar confirmed in a 2011 speech:

> If civilian casualties are caused in IED strikes, martyrdom attacks and other operations but the Mujahideen of the area repudiate these allegations while all testimonials and evidence point otherwise then all the suspects should be forwarded to the legal offices. If it is irrefutably proven that the blood of innocent Muslims is spilled by the negligence of Mujahideen then a penalty should be implemented in accordance with sharia after extensive investigation and all steps should be taken to seek the pardon and pleasure of the inheritors and affectees. If the same officials persist in their neglectfulness in relation to civilian casualties then more Islamic penalties should be handed out in addition to his termination from post.[15]

[14] Beginning in the late 2000s, committees to deal with education and health issues were established in Quetta and officials were appointed in each province to coordinate the insurgency's activities in these areas. Where they were in control, the Taliban allowed schools to remain open provided they changed their programmes. A notable from Mohmand Dara district (Nangarhar province) explained: 'The Taliban send their curriculum to schools; they select teachers in agreement with the local administration. They have banned computers, but allow English.' E-75, head of a madrasa and Taliban vice-chief of education in Ghazni province, May 2013; E-12, a notable from Mohmand Dara district (Nangarhar), August 2015. Negotiations were regularly conducted between Ministry of Education officials and the Taliban. As some international funding was conditional on the number of schools in operation, the Kabul regime had an interest in keeping schools in Taliban-controlled areas open and therefore it continued to pay teachers' salaries. E-77, an Afghan analyst with UNAMA specializing in Khost province, September 2014. For an overview of the insurgency's education policy, see Antonio Giustozzi and Claudio Franco, *The Battle for the Schools*, Kabul, Afghanistan Analysts Network, 2012; Antonio Giustozzi and Claudio Franco, *The Ongoing Battle for the Schools: Uprisings, Negotiations and Taleban Tactics*, Kabul, Afghanistan Analysts Network, 2013.

[15] Mullah Omar's Eid al-Adha Address for 2011.

Two years later, he again mentioned the military oversight function of the courts, suggesting the difficulty judges were still having in imposing their authority: 'Occasionally, when a Mujahid is found being careless as regards the prevention of the civilian casualties, he must be referred to the leadership after identification for handing over to the judicial courts.'[16]

Finally, the latest (2010) version of the Code of Conduct explicitly gave judges—as well as Mullah Omar and his deputy—the monopoly on applying the law within the movement. Two articles formally prohibited commanders from interfering in judicial matters:

> If local residents with legal or other disputes come to the mujahideen and hand in petitions, group commanders do not have the right to intervene in the people's issues. Only provincial officials, district governors and their deputies can consider petitions concerning a dispute and must then seek the help of relevant bodies and a legitimate jirga to resolve the dispute in a way that is not in conflict with holy sharia. If the peace *jirga* can not solve the dispute, then it should be referred to a court, if it exists. If there is no court, the decision should be made according to the views of prominent ulema. (Article 62, 2010)

> Mujahideen commanders and individuals are not allowed to intervene in public disputes. They are not allowed to recommend anyone to a judge, or go to court with them. They cannot take sides in any dispute. (Article 64, 2010)

Thus, commanders were banned from deciding disputes or intervening in a judicial process. In the interviews, Taliban judges asserted they were independent from military leaders and administrators: 'The Taliban governor has nothing to do with courts and judges. Taliban judges have been directed to decide all cases in the light of sharia without caring about anybody, including governors, commanders and district administrators.'[17] Several judges pointed to the instructions from the movement's leadership. 'Taliban judges have been directed by the Commander of the Faithful [Mullah Omar] to obey no one except the members of the Military Commission.'[18] This independence allowed them to pass judgment on certain Taliban cadres. 'No Taliban leaders can interfere in the affairs of the courts and judges. However, Taliban judges can interfere in

[16] Mullah Omar's Eid al-Fitr Address for 2013.
[17] I-1, a Taliban appeals court judge, Nahrin district (Baghlan), 2011.
[18] I-23, a Taliban trial court judge, Dahan-i Ghuri district (Baghlan), 2011.

the affairs of all officials including provincial governors, district administrators and military commanders.'[19]

The local autonomy of commanders

While successive versions of *Instructions to the Mujahideen* showed the increased reliance that Taliban leaders placed on judges in enforcing obedience to the chain of command, the constant need to reiterate these orders implies that they met with resistance. The authority of the judges over the combatants was in fact limited by the local autonomy of the most powerful commanders.

In the early years of the uprising, judges rarely enjoyed enough authority and independence to arrest fighters and commanders. However, as the judicial system matured, the power and legitimacy of the courts within the movement grew. The arrest of a commander in Kandahar in 2006 suggested that judges were by then able to confront military leaders. In this incident, the Quetta Leadership Council conspicuously supported the judge and disarmed the intransigent commander.[20] In Kunduz, a northern province where the insurgency took hold later, the first arrest of a commander was reported around the end of 2009.[21] The provincial commissions and governors directly appointed by the movement's leadership gave judges backing in confronting the military. For example, in 2012, in Kajaki district, Helmand province, following a complaint filed with the district commission, the Taliban judge ordered the arrest of a commander who publicly beat a farmer. When the commander refused to surrender, the commander of another group was authorized to arrest him. The judge, citing the *Instructions to the Mujahideen*, suspended the commander from his post for forty-five days and let him off with a warning.[22]

Beginning in the late 2000s, arrests or cashiering of commanders by judges or Military Commissions increased in frequency. In 2007, the Zabul Provincial Commission forced one of the commanders to return a truck that he had unjustifiably confiscated from a villager. The following year, the Commission ordered the release of three Afghan ICRC staffers kidnapped by a commander.[23]

[19] I-25, a Taliban appeals court judge, Bala Mughab district (Badghis), 2011.
[20] E-22, a Taliban fighter, Kandahar province, July 2011.
[21] Antonio Giustozzi and Christoph Reuter, *The Insurgents of the Afghan North*, Kabul, Afghanistan Analysts Network, 2011, p. 19.
[22] E-11, a resident of Kajaki district (Helmand), September 2012.
[23] Abdul Awwal Zabulwal, 'Taliban in Zabul: a Witness' Account' in Antonio Giustozzi (ed.), *Decoding the New Taliban: Insights from the Afghan Field*, New York, Columbia University Press, 2009, pp. 179–90.

In 2008, the fighters under one of the most feared commanders in Andar district (Ghazni) were disarmed and dispersed.[24] In late 2010–early 2011, in Qasin district (Ghazni), a commander was flogged and imprisoned for beating residents who had refused to heat their mosque to keep militants from quartering themselves in it.[25]

However, the authority conferred on judges by the leadership was diluted by their lack of a police force, which left judges reliant on Taliban commanders and fighters in their jurisdictions to enforce their decisions. One judge hinted at the problem: 'You know, it is not an easy exercise. To have your own courts and then get your decisions implemented you need to have strong backing in the region where you are exercising justice.'[26] Relying on local commanders to carry out verdicts became highly problematic in cases where the accused was a Taliban fighter, much less a military leader. In a land dispute involving a personage close to the Taliban, the judge's ruling against him was simply ignored.[27] On the other hand, with the coalition and the regime treating judges as combatants, they needed the commanders' protection. Beginning in the late 2000s, the US military became aware of the role of judges in the insurgency and from then on tracked them down. The influx in 2010 of 30,000 US military personnel in Kandahar and Helmand provinces, where the Taliban justice system was most developed, further increased judges' dependence on combatants. The authority of judges thus rested on the respect of the commanders for the chain of command. That made the independence of the judges a function of the relationship between the commanders and the movement's leadership in Pakistan.

Furthermore, the insurgency's mobilization of what were initially local groups, together with the fog of war, limited the power of judges in other ways. In the early years, the insurgency grew by integrating various local networks. A charismatic military leader like Mullah Dadullah enjoyed significant autonomy in the South. Famous for having led the offensive against the Hizb-i Wahdat in Bamiyan in 1999–2000 and Yakawland in 2001, he was accused of carrying out several massacres of Hazaras. In 2003, he was among the first to publicly call for taking up arms to wage jihad against Western troops in Afghanistan before taking his seat on the ten-member Leadership Council. He recruited his own commanders, was filmed at public beheadings, and gave

[24] Christoph Reuter and Borhan Yunus, 'The Return of the Taliban in Andar District' in Antonio Giustozzi (ed.), *Decoding the New Taliban: Insights From the Afghan Field*, New York, Columbia University Press, 2009, p. 116.

[25] Miles Amoore, 'Afghans Flock to Judge Dread and his Butcher Boys', *The Sunday Times*, 23 January 2011.

[26] I-10, a Taliban trial court judge, Tala wa Barfak district (Baghlan), 2011.

[27] E-36, user of a Taliban court in Andar district (Ghazni), September 2014.

interviews to Al Jazeera.[28] Although he was the most notorious figure among the commanders, he was no exception: other groups emerged that maintained a certain autonomy of action vis-à-vis the leadership in Quetta. The movement was plagued by internal dissent, for example, over the use of suicide bombings which, since 2003, had proved their effectiveness in Iraq but which, according to some, violated the religious prohibition against suicide.[29] In addition, conflicts regularly broke out between cadres dispatched from Quetta and local commanders: for example, in 2006 in Badghis, between Mawlawi Dastargir and Abdul Rahman Haqqani—the latter dispatched by Quetta to take command of all groups in the province.[30]

Over time, three other factors increased the independence of local commanders: the creation of their own economic networks, the presence of foreign fighters, and operations by the Western armed forces. First, the movement was short of resources, so it fell to the commanders to find ways of financing the armed struggle. Many groups armed themselves by taxing traders and poppy growers. Others demanded a percentage of private company and NGO project budgets. Some commanders made money by kidnapping foreigners, civil servants, and employees of foreign organizations.[31] Others set up roadblocks to extort money from vehicular traffic. Although the commanders were expected to pass a share of these proceeds upstream to the leadership, some did so little or not at all. Personal enrichment and extortion by commanders were recurring complaints among rural residents. 'People see Taliban commanders getting richer and richer, acquiring new clothes, a new woman, a new motorcycle. This creates a suspicion about the Taliban's judicial system, that judges are influenced, not necessarily by money, but by relationships (*wasta*).'[32] More generally, conflicts over controlling resources set Taliban commanders against one another and threatened the movement's cohesion in several regions.[33]

[28] Alex Strick van Linschoten and Felix Kuehn, *An Enemy we Created: The Myth of the Taliban-al Qaeda Merger in Afghanistan*, Oxford, Oxford University Press, 2012, pp. 275–8.

[29] Anand Gopal, 'The Taliban in Kandahar' in Peter Bergen and Katherine Tiedemann (eds), *Talibanistan: Negotiating the Borders between Terror, Politics, and Religion*, Oxford, Oxford University Press, 2013, pp. 54–5.

[30] Matthew DuPee, 'Badghis Province: Examining the Taliban's Northwestern Campaign', *The Culture and Conflict Review*, 2008, vol. 2, nº 4.

[31] For example, in the Andar district of Ghazni province. See Christoph Reuter and Borhan Yunus, 'The Return of the Taliban in Andar District' in Antonio Giustozzi (ed.), *Decoding the New Taliban: Insights From the Afghan Field*, New York, Columbia University Press, 2009, pp. 113–14.

[32] E-79, resident of Ghazni province, September 2014.

[33] For a case in Zabul, see Abdul Awwal Zabulwal, 'Taliban in Zabul: a Witness' Account' in Antonio Giustozzi (ed.), *Decoding the New Taliban: Insights from the Afghan Field*, New York, Columbia University Press, 2009, pp. 187–8.

Secondly, some commanders leveraged privileged ties with groups of foreign fighters attached to them into greater autonomy.[34] The best known of these was Jalaludin Haqqani, who had maintained close ties with foreign fighters, including members of Al Qaeda, since the war against the Soviet occupation. After the US intervention, other Taliban commanders forged relationships with foreign fighters pouring into Afghanistan. Thus, in the late 2000s, a commander close to Al Qaeda and internationalist jihadist networks, Qari Zia ul-Rahman, established himself as the most important commander in Kunar province.[35] Educated in one of the Kunar Salafi madrasas and linked to the Arab networks in the region, he did not fit the classical profile of Taliban cadres. He achieved his place in the insurgency through spectacular operations against American troops in the eastern provinces. Tied in with the complex web of Pakistani and international groups present in the region, Qari Zia ul-Rahman sheltered them whenever the Pakistani army launched operations across the border. Groups like his fought alongside the Taliban against the US military, but they guarded their autonomy.

Thirdly, targeted killings thinned out the Taliban chain of command and led to a turnover in the composition of the movement. In the 2000s, many fighters were uneducated or had merely attended a village madrasa. They differed therefore from the seasoned cadres in the movement who were usually ulama. While in the early years the presence of veteran militants provided a link to the new generation, many of the experienced cadres were killed in the 2000s, only to be replaced in the ensuing years by fighters between the ages of fifteen and twenty-five. The new commanders were not much older, rarely past their thirties, and only the most senior cadres survived by sheltering in their Pakistani sanctuary. This rejuvenation fanned considerable tensions: the new generation was less accommodating towards the population and disposed to a more aggressive strategy.[36]

Some commanders could thus sustain themselves on a territorial base enough to allow them to stand up to the movement hierarchy. To curtail the autonomy of these commanders, Taliban leaders initiated a regular rotation of military units, but succeeded in imposing it only in areas where the latter's local

[34] Men from Pakistan in particular, but also from Central Asia and the Middle East fought alongside the Taliban. Specifically, militants of Al Qaeda, the Islamic Movement of Uzbekistan, and the Pakistani Tehrik-i Taliban-i Pakistan, Lashkar-i Jhangvi, and Lashkar-i Taiba regularly took part in operations against Western troops and regime security forces.

[35] For a biography, see Syed Saleem Shahzad, *Inside Al-Qaeda and the Taliban: Beyond Bin Laden and 9/11*, London, Pluto Press, 2011, pp. 111–15.

[36] Alex Strick van Linschoten and Felix Kuehn, *An Enemy we Created: The Myth of the Taliban-al Qaeda Merger in Afghanistan*, Oxford, Oxford University Press, 2012.

grounding was shallow. For instance, in Ghazni province, commanders were usually locals, while in the adjacent Wardak province, they were rotated in and out. Indeed, while the movement's leadership asserted direct control over the combatants quite early in Wardak, in Ghazni it was another story. Here one of the top commanders, *Mawlawi* Ismael, managed to place his men in the provincial administration, starting in the first years of the war. Subsequently, working his way up the hierarchy, he was first appointed governor of Zabul, then chairman of the Military Council, the movement's highest military authority—while still keeping his men in Ghazni. Ironically, one of the cases of resistance to the movement's leadership occurred in Farah in 2012, when the province's top commander, Mullah Baz Mohamad, detained the same Mawlawi Ismael, then head of the Military Council, who had been sent by Quetta to force the mullah to disgorge to it some of the revenue that his commanders had been collecting.[37]

In the end, the judges only managed to exert control over the second-tier commanders. The frequent interventions in these types of conflicts by the provincial commission, or even by the Taliban leadership, revealed how precarious the power of judges really was. Between 2009 and 2012, facing resistance from commanders and complaints from the population, the Taliban leaders established regional judicial commissions covering several provinces. Antonio Giustozzi reported the account given by the head of one of the commissions:

> As you know, most of the Taliban commanders and fighters are not educated and I am sure that there are lots of problems in their behaviour with the local villagers and if we don't try them and don't impose rules on them, it's very difficult to bring changes in their behaviour. Every month our team receives three or four cases mostly about Taliban commanders, who misused their positions and disturbed or beat a villager, we also hear cases regarding Taliban commanders taking money by force from a villager and other problems; then according to their crimes we try them and punish them. [. . .] Just around 10 days ago we had a case where a Taliban commander took money from a villager to interfere in a land dispute case and tried to threaten the other side to take his complaint back and not to tell anyone about the threats;

[37] Ron Moreau, 'Taliban Feud: Tribal Rivalries, Limited Resources Splinter Commanders', *The Daily Beast*, 17 August 2011; Anand Gopal, 'Serious Leadership Rifts Emerge in Afghan Taliban', *CTC Sentinel*, 2012, vol. 5, n° 11, pp. 9–11. For two additional cases where appointees sent by the Quetta Leadership Council were weaker than local commanders, see Martina Van Biljert, 'The Taliban in Zabul and Uruzgan' in Peter Bergen and Katherine Tiedemann (eds), *Talibanistan: Negotiating the Borders between Terror, Politics, and Religion*, Oxford, Oxford University Press, 2013, pp. 111–12.

> otherwise he would kill him. The other side was a very brave man, he told the district judge about the threat by this Taliban commander and the judge informed us, then immediately we took action and brought the commander to court and as a punishment we demoted him to simple fighter.[38]

These jurisdictions moved commanders out of the territories in which they enjoyed support within the movement and among the population. To arrest a military leader, judges often had to call in fighters from other districts or even provinces.

Unable to bring its most powerful commanders to heel, the leadership in Quetta preserved the movement's unity by integrating them into its supreme bodies. Mullahs Dadullah and Jalaludin Haqqani were appointed to the Leadership Council in 2003; Mawlawi Ismael was appointed to the Military Council and then took over as its head; Qari Zia ul-Rahman was made Quetta's representative in Kunar and Nuristan. Even Mullah Abdul Rauf Khadem, whose open preaching of Salafism put him at odds with the movement's ideology, was appointed Mullah Omar's deputy in 2010. In several cases involving particularly difficult commanders, it appears the movement resorted to letting the Western coalition crush them. The capture by the International Security Assistance Force of Mawlawi Dastargir, a military leader in Badghis who refused to submit to Quetta's representative Abdul Rahman Haqqani, was reportedly facilitated through information provided by his relatives.[39] Similarly, Mullah Dadullah, the influential and increasingly rebellious commander, was killed in a Special Forces raid. Two weeks after swearing allegiance to the Islamic State, Abdul Rauf Khadem was eliminated by a drone strike. It is, of course, impossible to confirm the rumours that the Taliban were behind the information that led to these killings. However, in each of these cases, coalition forces relieved the insurgency of maverick commanders who were thorns in the leadership's side. In retrospect, the fact that the movement was able to hold together throughout the period—including after the announcement in 2015 of Mullah Omar's death two years earlier and the elimination of his successor, Mullah Akhtar Mansour, by a drone strike in 2016—demonstrated the success of this combination of judicial and political actions.

[38] Antonio Giustozzi, 'The Taliban's "Military Courts"', *Small Wars & Insurgencies*, 2014, vol. 25, n° 2, pp. 292–3.

[39] Matthew Dupee, 'Badghis Province: Examining the Taliban's Northwestern Campaign', *The Culture and Conflict Review*, 2008, vol. 2, n° 4.

The treatment of enemy agents

Executing those accused of spying or collaboration with the regime or Western troops constituted an essential element of Taliban control in the rural areas. In the early years of the war, insurgents executed people working for the government, especially mullahs who refused to side with them, but also notables, teachers, policemen, judges, and administrators. The insurgency usually followed the same procedure: 'night letters' (*shabnamah*) would be posted on the walls of mosques, official buildings, and even on the doors of residences. Some were simply lists warning those whose names appeared on them to quit their jobs; others threatened anyone working with the regime and coalition forces, calling them 'infidels' or 'unbelievers'.[40] These threats were taken extremely seriously, and many rural residents chose to quit their jobs and take refuge in the nearest city, Kabul, or even outside the country.[41] If individuals ignored the warning, the Taliban would summon them or abduct them. In 2010, a notable siding with the government in Maywand district (Kandahar) told me how he was taken to a Taliban-held village. He was detained overnight and again told to either stop his activities or get out, causing him to flee to Kandahar city.[42] Taliban leaders openly acknowledged the practice, for example, when one of their spokesmen said: 'Assassinations of government officials is part of the military strategy of the Taliban. Our fight was with the foreigners, but unfortunately there are lots of government officials who are willing to be used by the foreigners so we have increased our assassinations of them.'[43] In discussions with United Nations Assistance Mission in Afghanistan (UNAMA)'s Human Rights Department, they defended the legitimacy of their campaign to eliminate people working with the government, denying their civilian status.[44]

As Special Forces raids and targeted strikes increased, the losses among the Taliban cadres created a state of paranoia. Fighters responded by summarily executing suspects. In the mid-2000s, Mullah Dadullah, as a warning to informers, filmed the beheading of people accused of spying on behalf of the United States. The story told by a Kunar resident speaks of the fear of being held responsible for the death of a Taliban member:

[40] For examples of night letters, see Thomas Johnson, 'The Taliban Insurgency and an Analysis of Shabnamah (Night Letters)', *Small Wars & Insurgencies*, 2007, vol. 18, n° 3, pp. 317–44.

[41] Aryn Baker, 'Deadly Notes in The Night', *Time*, 7 May 2006; Christoph Reuter and Borhan Yunus, 'The Return of the Taliban in Andar District' in Antonio Giustozzi (ed.), *Decoding the New Taliban: Insights From the Afghan Field*, New York, Columbia University Press, 2009, pp. 108–9.

[42] E-74, a notable of Maywand district (Kandahar), August 2010.

[43] Solomon Moore, 'Taliban Assassination Campaign Impedes Governance', *Washington Post*, 22 March 2011.

[44] E-5, head of UNAMA's Human Rights Department, September 2012.

> Last winter I was in Jalalabad, I went to the Torkham market [under government control] and I bumped into someone who was an important person in the Taliban. [Out of fear of being denounced,] he turned pale when he saw me and I was very scared thinking that if he was killed by a drone, I would be blamed for it.[45]

Summary executions quickly became a problem for the insurgency as false denunciations became prevalent, similar to the challenges faced by Western troops (see Chapter 4). In 2011, Mullah Omar obliquely acknowledged the syndrome by calling on the movement's leaders to fight it: 'All the provincial governors should hone in on civilian casualties and make a point of stopping the name of Taliban from being falsely utilized against victims in warning letters and phone calls.'[46] For example, one of my interlocutors recounted how his brother was killed by a neighbour, a young man about fifteen years old, who justified his act to the Taliban by explaining that his victim worked for the Americans. To prevent reprisals from my interlocutor's family, the Taliban gave the assassin a letter declaring that he was now under their protection because he had eliminated a spy.[47] Summary executions caused discontent, and complaints about them regularly surfaced during my interviews. In many cases, villagers mobilized and sometimes even took up arms against the Taliban. In October 2008, for example, the massacre of twenty-six passengers on a bus led to protests; the commander behind it, Mullah Adam, was quietly summoned to Quetta and disarmed.[48] In August 2011, in Helmand, villagers killed a Taliban commander and his bodyguard after he summarily executed an elderly man.[49]

Beginning in the late 2000s, the leadership tried to manage this problem by giving judges the sole authority to try those accused of espionage or collaboration with the government. The 2009 and 2010 versions of the *Instructions to the Mujahideen* dedicated an entire section to the topic and stipulated an appearance before a judge before any execution could be ordered: 'The authority to execute a spy lies with the Imam [Mullah Omar], his deputy or the provincial judge, or if no judge has been appointed, it lies with the authority of the provincial governor. No one else has the authority to order an execution' (Article 17,

[45] E-56, a resident of Kunar province, September 2014.
[46] Mullah Omar's Eid al-Adha Address for 2011.
[47] Subsequently, the Taliban would try to check what happened, E-40, a resident of Kunar province, August 2015.
[48] Anand Gopal, 'The Taliban in Kandahar' in Peter Bergen and Katherine Tiedemann (eds), *Talibanistan: Negotiating the Borders between Terror, Politics, and Religion*, Oxford, Oxford University Press, 2013, p. 40.
[49] Ray Rivera and Taimoor Shah, 'Afghan Villagers Stone a Taliban Commander to Death', *New York Times*, 22 August 2011.

2010 version). The code of conduct specified the need for an unforced confession, direct witnesses, or physical evidence.

Subsequently, I was told several times of death sentences handed down by judges. In 2010, the foreign manager of an irrigation program in Baghlan recalled how a seventeen-year-old was hanged in execution of a verdict.[50] The same year, the press reported on the case of a Taliban commander in Paktya, sentenced to death as an informant for American troops.[51] In 2012, following a Special Forces raid in Kunar that killed more than a dozen Taliban fighters, two people who regularly commuted to Asadabad, the provincial capital, were executed after a trial.[52] The following year, in the same province, a man was sentenced to death by a judge after chips used to tag targets for airstrikes were found on him.[53] A reporter from an Afghan television station, accused of working for an Indian construction company,[54] was released after his appearance before a Taliban judge in the Logar. Interviewed by telephone by a Western journalist, the judge said that the arrest of the Afghan journalist had been based on false information.[55]

People living in areas under the influence of the insurgency noticed this judicialized treatment of persons accused of collaboration or espionage. In 2014, a Kunar resident told me that 'before, the Taliban were particularly zealous in their treatment of regime officials. They could be punished arbitrarily. Today, officials go on trial before Taliban judges who demand witnesses or a confession.'[56] Similarly, in answer to questions from a *New York Times* reporter in 2010, a notable from Kandahar contrasted the movement's contemporaneous practices with those of previous years:

> There is a tremendous change in the Taliban's behavior. They don't behead people or detain those they suspect of spying without an investigation. But sometimes they still make mistakes, people still fear them, but now generally they behave well with people. They had to change because the leadership of the Taliban did not want to lose their grass roots support.[57]

[50] E-66, head of a programme by the Aga Khan Foundation in Baghlan province, August 2010.
[51] Miles Amoore, 'Afghans Flock to Judge Dread and his Butcher Boys', *The Sunday Times*, 23 January 2011.
[52] E-59, a resident of Nari district (Kunar), April 2013.
[53] E-53, a resident of Ghaziabad district (Kunar), April 2013.
[54] In conflict with Pakistan, which supported the Taliban, India backed the Kabul regime, so that the insurgency regularly took aim at Indian interests.
[55] Soraya Nelson, 'Rural Afghans Resistant to Official Judicial System', *NPR*, 17 December 2008.
[56] E-47, a resident of Kunar province, September 2014.
[57] Alissa Rubin, 'Taliban Overhaul Image to Win Allies', *New York Times*, 10 January 2010.

To avoid misunderstandings, Taliban judges issued certificates to those found innocent or who had quit their jobs in response to the insurgency's warnings. However, these documents also led to their being suspected of collaborating with the Taliban in the eyes of coalition or government forces.[58] Moreover, around 2014, in Helmand, the Taliban realized that most of the strikes did not involve denunciations:

> The Taliban have stopped beheading people they suspect of espionage because they understand that Americans do not use spies to finger people, but that they use them only to obtain general information. The drones followed them from place to place, even when no one was around. They understood that it was not because of local spies. So they adapted their ways of moving around; more by motorcycle and every time they moved, three or four people left at the same time, each in a different direction to fool the drone.[59]

However, while having the accused appear before a judge may have stopped some of the worst abuses, it did not necessarily cut down on executions. Judges were instructed to severely punish those who worked for the government. A judge of the court of appeals for Karagai District (Laghman) explained: 'Taliban judges have repeatedly told people to pull out their sons and nephews from government departments, otherwise killing them is allowed. The Military Commission has told Taliban judges that the killing of government officials is allowed to set an example for others.'[60] Contrary to provisions in the *Instructions to the Mujahideen*, extracting a confession by force was a widespread practice. On the other hand, judicialization sometimes prevented the making of arrangements that could have avoided the death sentence. 'In the past, those who worked for the government would often go free by promising to help the insurgency', said a resident of Kunar province.[61] All the ambiguity of Taliban policy on this issue surfaced in judicial practice. Those accused of espionage and collaboration were seen both as criminals and as enemies. For example, the judge of the Karagai Court of Appeals told of a case where he disagreed with the Military Commission:

> Recently the Taliban captured a soldier of the National Army of Afghanistan. He was released after assuring the Taleban that he would quit the army. But

[58] E-59, a resident of Nari district (Kunar), September 2012.
[59] E-51, analyst for an Afghan think tank, September 2014.
[60] I-2, a Taliban appeals court judge, Karagai district (Laghman), 2011.
[61] E-37, a resident of Kunar province, September 2014.

> he rejoined the army. He was arrested again in Laghman and presented before the court. I said that it was someone else and, therefore, he should be again released on bail. But the Military Commission sentenced him to death. He is still in the custody of the Taliban.[62]

Above all, an appearance before a judge never became automatic. Many commanders continued to summarily execute people accused of working for the government or coalition forces without trying them first. Qari Zia ul-Rahman, the most powerful commander of Kunar province, massacred a whole family, accusing the father of giving information to the Special Forces. The man had travelled with his sick pregnant wife to an American base for treatment at a Western military hospital (a common practice).[63] That same year, the same commander levied fines on about twenty notables in the Marawara district for collaborating with the regime.[64] There were times, however, when commanders were punished after ordering executions:

> There was a 65 years old man who was called X, he was working for the National ID department of the Afghan government and everyone knew that he was not a spy of the government. But a Taliban commander killed him without bringing him to justice or a court. After a lot of pressure from the notables on the Taliban commanders in Sayid Abad district, the Taliban high-ranking officials took action and disarmed the Taliban commander, who had killed the 65 years old man without informing the Taliban leadership.[65]

However, these remained exceptional cases, and judges never dictated the treatment of accused collaborators or spies.

The way in which people accused of collaborating with the enemy were dealt with is a paradigmatic illustration of the limits to the movement's judicialization. By decreeing that a spy or government employee had to appear before a judge before being executed, the leadership relied on their jurisdiction to reclaim a prerogative that the commanders had arrogated to themselves. However, the Taliban leaders never managed to impose the procedure, thus revealing the limited success of their efforts to centralize the movement.

62 I-2, a Taliban appeals court judge, Karagai district (Laghman), 2011.
63 E-44, a resident of Kunar province, September 2014.
64 E-59, a resident of Nari district (Kunar), April 2013. For other cases, see Antonio Giustozzi, 'The Taliban's "Military Courts"', *Small Wars & Insurgencies*, 2014, vol. 25, n° 2, p. 290.
65 Ibid., p. 289.

9
Legitimation through law

Introduction

> The Taliban court is for all people of Afghanistan but the government's court is only for rich people.
>
> Wardak province resident[1]

> We are popular among the people because with the government everything is about money. If you have money, you get to choose who is right and who is wrong. You are the law.
>
> A Taliban judge in Ghazni province[2]

The insurgency set up its courts in a society pervaded by drastic legal uncertainty that was worsened by the nepotistic justice of the Kabul regime and by Western troops trampling on the law. Against this backdrop, resolving conflicts opened the door for the Taliban to establish their authority and have it recognized.

In the interviews, the judges claimed both strategic and political value for their judicial activity. Asked about the place of the courts in the insurgency, this judge replied:

> This is most important to us, the Taliban. I'll give you an example. I admit there was nothing in Afghanistan when the Taliban were in power, but one thing was there for sure, that was peace. Now, I am asking you, how did we manage that in a country where there was no food for the people to eat, no business opportunities and no economic activity? It was thanks to this justice system that we brought back those who had strayed from the right path. Had we not hanged Dr. Najibullah and his brother Ahmadzai,[3] you would

[1] I-33, a resident of Sayid Abad district (Wardak), 2011.

[2] Miles Amoore, 'Afghans Flock to Judge Dread and his Butcher Boys', *The Sunday Times*, 23 January 2011.

[3] Najibullah headed the intelligence services (KHAD) of the People's Republic of Afghanistan and was placed at the head of the country by the USSR in 1986. As Kabul fell in 1992, he and his brother

The Taliban Courts in Afghanistan. Adam Baczko, Oxford University Press. © Adam Baczko 2023.
DOI: 10.1093/oso/9780198896777.003.0010

> not have seen this exemplary peace in this war-ridden country. Besides, the Taliban gained the support of the common people by establishing these courts. You see, none of the government courts decide as many cases as the Taleban courts do.[4]

The presence of their courts demonstrated daily how shaky the Kabul regime's grip was and strengthened the Taliban's hold. 'Our primary focus is on these courts and giving people access to justice. The Karzai government and its masters should be ashamed that students of seminaries come to an area and set up their courts there. The Taliban should be proud that their courts are working and becoming more active.'[5] Other judges pointed out that the effectiveness of their judicial system boosted the movement's popularity: 'Making their courts work is very beneficial for the Taliban, as these courts help them increase their number and gain the sympathy and support of the common people. People realize that the Taliban are making sacrifices for them and setting up courts to help them.'[6] Most users of the Taliban courts interviewed echoed this conception of them as gaining an edge in the political contest. 'This is also very important for the Taliban, because having an impartial court is the only way for the Taliban to reach the heart of Afghans.'[7]

In practice, assessing the strategic impact of the Taliban courts presents difficulties. While the justice system generally contributed to the movement's implantation, establishing the causal link at the micro-sociological level is tricky and the mechanisms that allowed the insurgents to grow their social base still need to be clarified. Many Afghans turned to Taliban judges while remaining opposed to the movement returning to power. Nevertheless, at a macrosocial level, the cumulative political effects of the law's penetration notably eased the movement's making inroads in regions that were formerly hostile to them.

More than a political adherence per se, resorting to the Taliban courts was part of a calculation by Afghans that compared this judicial system to the regime courts.[8] These evaluations fit into a juridical field characterized by an unrelenting struggle between judicial systems. Thus, the greater efficacy of

found refuge in the United Nations building. When the Taliban seized Kabul four years later, fighters entered the building, ignoring its diplomatic status, and executed him before hanging his body in the street.

[4] I-15, a Taliban appeals court judge, Qala-i Naw district (Badghis), 2011.
[5] I-25, a Taliban appeals court judge, Bala Mughab district (Badghis), 2011.
[6] I-10, a Taliban trial court judge, Tala wa Barfak district (Baghlan), 2011.
[7] I-33, a resident of Sayid Abad district (Wardak), 2011.
[8] It is important to repeat that I was only able to interview men and could only do a few interviews with women. As we will see in Chapter 10, women have much less access to Taliban courts.

Taliban judgments, the fact that they earned more respect than those of the government—making them a source of predictability in daily life—consecrated the legality of their verdicts and therefore their legitimacy. However, the international and social recognition lavished on the Kabul regime gave its courts an official, and therefore more sustainable, imprimatur—something that the Taliban judicial system lacked and which rendered its authority more fragile.

The difficult conversion to political gain

How the Taliban's use of the judicial system translated into political gain is difficult to demonstrate. The logics of adherence to the Taliban movement were multiple and complex: a mix of ideology, moral shock, local rivalries, and family dynamics.[9] There is some evidence to suggest that Taliban judgments sometimes produced changes in loyalty. In disputes over land especially, satisfaction with verdicts created material incentives for wanting the Taliban to remain in power—their departure would have led to the reopening of many disputes. As one Wardak resident put it, having seen someone else's claim to his land rejected in the Taliban court: 'The Taliban judge announced the result of the court in my favour and he told X not to disturb me, otherwise he would punish him severely. I know that as long as the Taliban are active in this district, X can't do anything, but if the Taliban leave this place, he will cause me problems.'[10] In some cases, valuing the Taliban justice system justified broader support for the insurgency. For example, in Kunar province in 2013–14, members of two quarrelling families addressed their complaints and denunciations to the regime's justice system, to the US military, and to the Taliban. They experienced first-hand the contrast between the inaction of the former two and the ability of the insurgency to investigate—and even countermand—a decision of their judicial system when additional evidence revealed that it had erred. A family member involved in the conflict, previously opposed to the insurgency, told me how this changed his position: 'If you are on the side of the

[9] One of the few insights into the motivations of the fighters comes from the forty-two interviews with Taliban fighters led by Canadian journalist Graeme Smith. When asked about the reasons for their involvement, the militants justified it not only by a nationalist and religious discourse of fighting foreign invaders and infidels, but also by the death of their relatives, civilians or combatants in the bombings or ground operations of the American and Canadian military. Graeme Smith, 'What Kandahar's Taliban Say' in Antonio Giustozzi (ed.), *Decoding the New Taliban: Insights from the Afghan Field*, New York, Columbia University Press, 2009, pp. 191–210. The taped interviews are accessible on the *Globe and Mail* website: http://v1.theglobeandmail.com/talkingtothetaliban/.

[10] I-32, a resident of Sayid Abad district (Wardak), 2011.

Taliban, they support you, they pay attention to you. The Americans and the government, they don't do that.'[11]

In other cases, while satisfaction with the judicial treatment may not have garnered support for the movement itself, nevertheless it did lead some opponents to recognize its authority. They praised the functioning of the Taliban courts in absolute terms and—most importantly in the context of war—relative to that of the government. Even if these people did not adhere to the Taliban's political agenda, they wanted a government that treated their most pressing concerns fairly. Thus, in 2010, a notable linked to President Karzai's family networks, who had taken refuge in Kandahar city after being threatened by the Taliban, praised their system of justice after volubly criticizing the movement itself. His neighbour, with connections in the insurgency, had taken advantage of his absence and opposition to the Taliban to claim ownership of his land but his claim had been rejected by the Taliban court.[12] Similarly, during an interview in Asadabad in 2010, someone close to the former governor of Kunar, *sayid* Faizal Akbar (2002–5), while voicing strong anti-Taliban sentiments, told me about filing a complaint over cattle rustling with the Taliban judge in his district. He described the regime's judges as 'corrupt', always 'on the side of the strongest', highlighting that the Taliban judges were 'not corrupt'. He also explained to me that the cost of a complaint to the police and the regime's justice system would have far exceeded the value of the stolen cattle. Living in a remote village in Kunar province but travelling regularly to Kabul and back, he contrasted the rural people who appreciated Taliban judges because they guaranteed ownership and respected local customs with the city dwellers who feared and rejected them and their justice system.[13]

The political implications of effectively functioning Taliban courts are reflected in statements by some opponents of the insurgency. As the head of the Kunar Provincial Council in 2011 explained to me:

> The Taliban are popular for two reasons. First, because of the weakness of the government. Its relationship with the population is bad, its agents keep harassing people. Then, there are the Taliban who are among the people; they have more influence, they are able to enforce their decisions. They have the Pakistani resources to establish their order. They have their own government,

[11] E-40, a resident of Kunar province, August 2015.
[12] E-74, a notable in Maywand district (Kandahar), August 2010.
[13] E-6, a resident of Ghaziabad district (Kunar), July 2010.

> with district governors, judges. People can turn to them by filing formal complaints, they have written procedures.[14]

Similarly, a member of parliament from Helmand told a British journalist in 2008: 'Security is 100 per cent under Taliban, there are no robber in the whole district. Justice is very effective.'[15] A civilian adviser to the US Army, deployed between 2009 and 2011 in Helmand province, conceded the impartiality of Taliban judges, as exemplified by one of the judges in Garmsir district: 'The people were obliged to accept his judgment. If they did not, he could call in fighters to enforce his decision. That said I never heard any complaints about Mawlawi Mohammedullah's judgments. I suspect people heeded his decisions because they were fair rather than because they feared him.'[16] Beginning in the early 2010s, the political effectiveness of Taliban judges started to register with the coalition. One of General Petraeus's closest advisers, David Kilcullen, wrote: 'We can beat the Taliban in any military engagement, but we're losing in Afghanistan not because we're being outfought but because the Afghan government is being outgoverned.'[17] In a backhanded compliment to the effectiveness of Taliban courts, the American Special Forces and intelligence agencies made the judges priority targets for elimination.[18]

These elements taken together provide a number of clues to the strategic and political effects of Taliban justice. These remain eminently contextual: the advances made by the Taliban since 2002 rode on the back of popular discontent with the predations of the regime's administrators and the practices of Western troops. Many areas whose populations had been hostile to the Taliban in the 1990s thus turned into insurgency strongholds in the 2000s. For example, the predominantly Uzbek district of Qaysar (Faryab) had suffered greatly from the Taliban presence in the late 1990s, because the Taliban favoured the province's Pashtun commanders over its Uzbek commanders. The ethnicization of local political divides translated into many abuses against civilians. However, in the 2000s, with the nepotism of local regime representatives on full display, with Uzbek ulama having assumed leadership roles in the insurgency, and with the effectiveness of its own administration, the Taliban moved on from ethnic

[14] E-41, head of the Kunar Provincial Council, July 2011.

[15] Tom Coghlan, 'The Taliban in Helmand: An Oral History' in Antonio Giustozzi (ed.), *Decoding the New Taliban: Insights from the Afghan Field*, New York, Columbia University Press, 2009, p. 140.

[16] Carter Malkasian, *War Comes to Garmser: Thirty Years of Conflict on the Afghan Frontier*, Oxford, Oxford University Press, 2013, p. 113.

[17] David Kilcullen here paraphrases the journalist Bernard Fall who predicted, starting in the late 1950s, that the American intervention in Vietnam was destined to fail. David Kilcullen, *Counterinsurgency*, Oxford, Oxford University Press, 2010, p. 158.

[18] Communication with US Army officers, 2010 and 2011.

divisions and turned Qaysar into one of its strongholds.[19] Similarly, in Kunar, Ghazni, Kandahar, or Kunduz, many of my interlocutors told me of their disdain for the Islamic Emirate's policies before 2001. However, a few years later, the economic takeover by regime-linked potentates, the practices of Western troops, and the establishment of a Taliban judicial system in villages also turned regions such as the Korengal Valley (Kunar), Arghandab (Kandahar), and Andar (Ghazni) into insurgency strongholds.[20] More recently, in 2013, Pashtun nomads facilitated the Taliban's inroads into Deh Sabz, on the outskirts of Kabul, to defend their land against the 'New Kabul City' development project. With the private developers and the Japan International Cooperation Agency, the project funders and coordinator respectively, ignoring their land rights, the Taliban appeared as the last line of defence for their ownership.[21]

More accessible but less official courts

My interlocutors repeatedly described Taliban courts as *more* accessible, *more* familiar, *more* affordable, *more* reliable, but *less* official and therefore *less* durable. These comparative assessments were a crucial dimension of the judgements made by the users, revealing that their views of the Taliban judicial system was underpinned by a more or less explicit critique of the government's courts and of the Western intervention.

The first determining factor was the accessibility of the courts. Taliban courts sitting in the villages spared their users having to take the risk of travel during wartime. With the regime's judges confined to the cities (see Chapter 3), the insurgency's judicial system was often the only option for residents of rural districts. Indeed, in contrast to the dozen regime judges confined to Kandahar City in 2010, the Taliban fielded several dozen magistrates who covered the

[19] Obaid Ali, *Moving East in the North: Transitioned Faryab and the Taleban*, 17 May 2013, www.afghanistan-analysts.org/en/reports/war-and-peace/moving-east-in-the-north-transitioned-faryab-and-the-taleban/.

[20] For more on the shift of the Korengal Valley from *a priori* favourable to the American intervention to a stronghold of the Taliban insurgency, see Adam Baczko, 'Les revers de l'armée américaine dans la Guerre d'Afghanistan: Le cas de la Kounar', *Politique américaine*, 2012, vol. 19, n° 1, pp. 11–26.

[21] Hervé Nicolle, 'Qu'elle était verte ma vallée: L'avenir sans terre des populations Kuchi dans le district de Deh Sabz', *Revue des mondes musulmans et de la Méditerranée*, 2013, n° 133, pp. 227–38; Fabrizio Foschini, *Land Grabs in Afghanistan (2): Deh Sabz, the New and the Old*, 15th August 2013, www.afghanistan-analysts.org/en/reports/rights-freedom/land-grabs-2-deh-sabz-the-new-and-the-old/. The expansion of the city of Kabul to areas where nomads had customary rights caused many land conflicts. Nick Miszak and Alessandro Monsutti, 'Landscapes of Power: Local Struggles and National Stakes at the Rural-Urban Fringe of Kabul, Afghanistan', *The Journal of Peasant Studies*, 2014, vol. 41, n° 2, pp. 183–98.

entire province. Concurrently, the situation was similar in the provinces of Helmand, Zabul, Nuristan, or Kunar. In the ensuing years, as the security forces unravelled and Western troops withdrew, similar conditions prevailed in most provinces, for example in Uruzgan, Ghazni, Wardak, Kunduz, and Faryab. A resident of Qarabagh district explained:

> Qarabagh district is one of the remote districts of Ghazni province. Most villages in Qarabagh district are under Taliban control; of course there are Afghan army and ISAF troops, but they are in the district center and make not much of an impact in the villages. [. . .] There is no government court and the villagers can't come to the district center to solve their problems. That's why all the villagers, whether or not they like the Taliban courts, are forced to use them.[22]

As its grip tightened, the insurgency shifted from a conception of its courts as complementary to those of the regime, to seeing them as a means for monopolizing the law. Initially, the use of Taliban courts was optional for the population, the Taliban allowing the parties to a case to choose which judicial system they preferred. The Taliban only banned resorting to the regime's courts after their own judges had delivered verdicts. Yet, beginning in the late 2000s, the movement banned government judges from the areas under its control and set ambushes for them. Moreover, the Taliban would now punish residents who turned to government courts, as one notable from Andar district pointed out: 'Only those who live in the vicinity of the city of Ghazni can go to the regime court, that is, those who live outside the Taliban's control. People who live under Taliban control would be punished if they went there.'[23] A resident of Sayid Abad district (Wardak) feared appealing to the regime's courts against the wishes of a movement seen as omniscient:

> It's very difficult for people to come and solve their problem with the Afghan government because if the Taliban learn that someone used the government court, then he will soon be killed by the Taliban. That's why people are afraid and don't go to the Afghan government court, and I can say without hesitation that most people use the Taliban court.[24]

22 I-36, a resident of Qarabagh district (Ghazni), 2011.
23 E-13, a notable of Andar district (Ghazni), September 2012.
24 I-32, a resident of Sayid Abad district (Wardak), 2011.

Without a bona fide reason for going to the district or provincial capital (for medical care, education, or employment), the mere fact of doing so was suspect. Moreover, while in the past Taliban judges had agreed to try a case already decided by the regime's judges only if the complainant could show he had been treated unjustly, they now changed their policy: 'What is new is that Taliban judges now agree to try all those who turn to them after having been before a government court. Before, they took a case only if someone complained of having been unfairly judged.'[25]

Secondly, Afghans living in rural areas were more familiar with the law and procedures followed in Taliban courts than those used in the regime courts. The Taliban courts promoted public ownership of the judicial system through abiding by the interactional mechanisms of rural sociability (the seating of persons in the room according to status, sitting on cushions, centrality and modalities of speech, absence of legal representation). Moreover, in the villages, the majority of people with even a basic education had received it in a madrasa and therefore had some notions of Islamic law.

Though regime judges also based rulings on Islamic law, appealing regularly to Hanafi jurisprudence under Article 130 of the Constitution,[26] the intricacies of state law seemed alien to a population two-thirds of whose members were illiterate. This familiarity gave Islamic law a consensual character and reinforced the legitimacy of trials. The reference to sharia law redounded to the credit of Taliban courts, even with people who opposed the movement, such as this resident of Zhari district (Kandahar):

> If I do not respect the decision of Taliban, it means that I do not respect the Sharia law, it means that I do not respect the Holy Quran. I am against the Taliban system in general and do not want them, but when we talk about their judgement, they are really judging according to sharia law and I really respect their judgement, not their activities in Afghanistan, nor their fighting or their killing.[27]

The appreciation of a verdict's Islamic character in particular conditioned its acceptance, regardless of the result: 'I personally used the Taliban court in our village around one month ago. Unfortunately, I lost the trial, but I am not angry on the Taliban judges, because they judged according to the sharia law

[25] E-37, a resident of Kunar province, September 2014.

[26] Lutforahman Saeed, *Islam, Custom and Human Rights: A Legal and Empirical Study of Criminal Cases in Afghanistan After the 2004 Constitution*, New York, Springer, 2021.

[27] I-29, a resident of Zhari district (Kandahar), 2011.

and I can't stand against the sharia law.'[28] This elementary knowledge of codes and standards allowed court users to assess the consistency and impartiality of the decision. As long as the trial was conducted according to the rules, which those present at the hearing could see with their own eyes, the decisions of the Taliban judges were difficult to argue with.

Thirdly, Taliban courts were low-cost venues. My interlocutors regularly contrasted the regime's judges and police officers, notorious for holding their hands out for bribes, with the Taliban judges, whom they generally described as having integrity. However, the absence of lawyers, which essentially denied the right to legal defence in criminal investigations and political charges, resulted in a considerable saving in land or family disputes (the majority of cases handled by the courts). Without fees and with few if any court costs, people with modest incomes were more inclined to initiate legal proceedings:

> For poor villagers, who don't have enough money to pay for government court, the Taleban's sharia court is very good. [. . .] they want it because, first, they don't have money to pay the bribes in the Afghan court and, second, they don't have enough energy or time to follow the Afghan court rules which take years and years.[29]

This contrast came up time and again in interviews: 'If I were rich, I would appeal to the judges of the government, just pay and you win. But when you're poor, the Taliban are the only solution.'[30] The problem of cost often went hand in hand with the issue of proceedings dragging on: in the regime's courts, prolonging the trial was one of the stratagems public servants and judges used to extract money from the opposing parties. Thus, a shopkeeper in Kandahar province involved in an accident, after recounting how he had to pay off police officers even though the alleged victim hadn't filed a complaint, concluded:

> As everyone knows, the Afghan government officials are not honest and they are corrupted, and they know many ways to get money from people. That is why they always delay the cases of the people. [. . .] From the first days of the accident till the time I was released from jail, I handed over 140,000 Afs ($3,000) in different places.[31]

[28] I-44, a resident of Panjway district (Kandahar), 2011.
[29] I-32, a resident of Sayid Abad district (Wardak), 2011.
[30] E-72, a user of the Taliban court in Mohamad Agha district (Logar), May 2013.
[31] I-41, a resident of Argandhab district (Kandahar), 2011.

The speed with which the Taliban courts worked therefore formed part of their image of integrity. The head of a construction company in Kandahar explained: 'I don't like our current government at all, and I don't really like the Taliban, either. But I can either spend months in the government court and pay bribes, or I can go to the Taliban and have the matter settled in one day. It's an easy choice to make.'[32] However, in criminal or political cases, this promptness became a source of criticism. For example, a man whose brother was executed following the verdict of a Taliban judge told an Afghan journalist: 'The desert courts[33] are organized at very short notice, they accuse and then punish defendants without any evidence or witnesses. And because they have neither the time nor the resources to do a proper investigation, they end up doing injustice to people.'[34]

Finally, users of the Taliban courts made explicit mention of their ability to enforce rulings as a key characteristic of the movement's justice system. They contrasted it with the inability of the regime's courts to make their verdicts stick, compounded by their absence from many parts of the country. One of my interlocutors, politically opposed to the Taliban, recounted a dispute between two families over the ownership of a forest that paralysed the entire village of Marid (Kunar). The dispute involving a Gujar family and a Nuristani family had taken on an ethnic dimension. The hostility between the two families, and more broadly between the two communities, had men carrying weapons when they went out. The parties filed a complaint with the court in Asadabad, the provincial capital, but the losing parties rejected the verdict, which the police were unable to enforce because they were confined to the city. The losers also called on Malik Zarin, one of the top strongmen associated with American troops in Kunar province, but to no avail. In 2011, as a last resort, they turned to the Taliban, who held an early morning hearing in the village with dozens of fighters in a show of force. The judge threatened that he would burn down the house of the party that did not abide by his verdict. My contact, a staunch opponent of the Taliban, told me how satisfied the people of Marid were to see a cycle of revenge interrupted. He then went on to tell me that he had himself just filed a complaint with the Taliban following a cattle theft. He concluded: 'The difference between the government and the Taliban is that when the Taliban

[32] Dan Murphy, 'Dent in Afghanistan War Strategy: Why Kandahar Locals Turn to Taliban', *Christian Science Monitor*, 6 July 2010.

[33] None of my interlocutors ever used this expression, which appears here with an orientalist tinge shared by many city dwellers towards a justice whose summary character is implicitly explained by the movement's rural nature.

[34] Rahmat Alizada, 'Reign of the Desert Court', *Afghanistan Today*, 11 August 2011.

pronounce a verdict, they implement their decision. When they say something, they do it.'[35] A Logar notable similarly told me: 'It's a good system and the Taliban judgment is comparatively better than the government's, because people can't reject the Taliban's decision.'[36] One of the few press articles based on interviews with both a Taliban judge and users of his court reported on a similar case in Ghazni province, where the judge threatened the parties with flogging if they refused the verdict, much to the contentment of the sanctioned person:

> Two weeks ago, [Taliban judge] Qasim ruled on the case of Naqibullah Noori, who shot and killed two men with an assault rifle after his cousins stormed his land with 15 accomplices and beat him and his brother with shovels. The cousins said the land was theirs. Noori spent a month in jail before tribal elders secured his release by vouching for him. However, after four years of weekly trips to a local government judge and $5,000 in bribes, his case had still not been heard. 'Friends of mine told me I should go to the Taliban court', said the 32-year-old Noori. 'In four years, the government hadn't even bothered to send a delegation to look into our case. They never once asked for the deeds to the land.' Within two weeks, the Taliban judge had made a decision. Noori was ordered to pay $37,000 compensation to his cousins. The land was divided between the two families and they were warned that if the dispute arose again, the Taliban would beat them. 'I was incredibly happy with the decision', Noori said. 'The Taliban's justice system is far more efficient. They don't care about money and they decide quickly and they always look at the truth. It is a fair system.' Noori said that many people in his village had begun to feed the Taliban fighters who pass through their area out of gratitude to them for solving disputes.[37]

In each of these examples, impartiality smoothed the way for acquiescence to the enforcement measures. The threats by Taliban judges (burning down the house of one resister or administering a beating to another) met with approval because they helped enforce an impartial verdict: 'They don't care about money and they decide quickly and they always look at the truth. It is a fair system', to quote Naqibullah Noori again. As revealed in my other interviews with Taliban users, the impartiality resided less in the respect for procedures—the topic

[35] E-6, a resident of Ghaziabad district (Kunar), July 2010.
[36] E-14, a notable of Logar province, May 2013.
[37] Miles Amoore, 'Afghans Flock to Judge Dread and his Butcher Boys', *The Sunday Times*, 23 January 2011.

rarely came up—than in the fact that the judge had links with neither party to the case. Moreover, this valuing of force was part of the context of legal uncertainty on which my interviewees dwelt at length. They were sometimes less interested in winning at trial than in putting an end to a dispute without losing face with a judgment that would stand—in short, that the verdict decided the matter (*res iudicata*). My interlocutors emphasized the prevalence of land and family conflicts and the related violence to explain their satisfaction with a system that effectively and fairly resolved disputes. The words of a Kandahar landowner interviewed by an American journalist furnish a particularly telling example of this. The operator of a minibus service between the town and the adjoining villages, he said that he accepted a Taliban verdict awarding half of his land to his opponent because '[t]he key thing was that the dispute was ended. I have to live and work here. I choose what works.'[38] He also pointed out that fear of the Taliban could be beneficial in other respects, for example in obtaining certain documents without having to bribe the regime's administrators: 'I walked in [the office] and they asked me why—I told them I was taking a dispute to the Taliban. They were scared, and they gave me the documents without any hassles.'[39]

However, the insurgency winning was the *sine qua non* for the sustainability of judgments. 'Some people are not happy with the Taliban's judgments, because they think that the Taliban's judgments don't have a high authority, because they are not an official government. If tomorrow they leave the district, all their judgments and courts become nothing, because all these decisions and judgments depend on their power and their position.'[40] Many Afghans interviewed stressed that the value of the decisions issued by the movement's judges depended on the fortunes of war. 'The problem with the Taliban is that they may leave from one day to the next.'[41] In 2010–11, the move to mobile courts in many districts was sometimes seen as a sign of the Taliban's weakening and with it a lessening of the value of their decisions. If the Taliban lost the war, the verdicts they handed down might be questioned by those on the losing end of a case. 'The problem is that their judgment and their court are unofficial and whenever the Taliban leave this district, all their courts and judgments will no longer be acceptable by those people who lost their case. [. . .] People consider that the Taliban courts are temporary and once the Taliban will leave

[38] Dan Murphy, 'Dent in Afghanistan War Strategy: Why Kandahar Locals Turn to Taliban', *Christian Science Monitor*, 6 July 2010.

[39] Ibid.

[40] I-31, a resident of Qarabagh district (Ghazni), 2011.

[41] E-6, a resident of Ghaziabad district (Kunar), April 2013.

the district, no one will recognize their [previous] judgments anymore.'[42] The issue of officialdom, regularly raised in interviews, was more than a nuance of the overall positive reception of the Taliban judicial system. Instead, it reintroduces the considerations on accessibility, familiarity, cost, fairness, and reliability into a broader context in which this court system was not the recognized official system. This reflection even surfaced in some interviews with Taliban judges, for example the one quoted in the lead-in to this chapter, who underlined the irony of it all: 'The Karzai government and its masters should be ashamed that students of seminaries come to an area and set up their courts there.' Recalling the modest origin of the judges, he skewered the regime in place, conceding with these same words that the task of exercising justice was first and foremost up to 'the Karzai government and its masters'. The official nature of the regime's courts was the basis on which my interlocutors compared the two systems, highlighting both the flaws in the Kabul regime's judicial system and what motivated people to turn to the Taliban courts.

[42] I-36, a resident of Qarabagh district (Ghazni), 2011.

10
The society project

Introduction

The Taliban judicial system participated in the production of an alternative to the regime's social order, one characterized by social conservatism and moral rigour. This social project was especially apparent in the areas most affected by legal uncertainty, namely the identity regime, property, and gender relations, which the judges most often had to deal with.

Taliban judges imposed an identity regime with their rulings that resembled one in existence before the war, during the 1970s, which favoured the Pashtuns by denying the ethnic question and relegated the Shiites to a subordinate position. In adjudicating land disputes, while they guaranteed private property, combating the forcible hoarding by the commanders of the 1990s and the regime's potentates, they also ensured the reproduction of economic inequalities centred on land. Finally, with respect to gender relations, the Taliban's apparent flexibility regarding certain behaviours went out of the window. The judges ruled with particular severity in these cases, which had the effect of shoring up a system of patriarchal domination based on repressing deviance in the public sphere and delegating violence in the domestic space to the heads of families.

This attention paid to the public good by judges concealed their work of universalizing the particular interests of the clerics. By reshaping the state and society through the application of Islamic law, judges promoted an order in which religious capital determined access to positions of power. The Taliban judicial system then established the rise of the clerics who, in areas held by the insurgency, sought to eclipse the non-religious elites.

'The interest in disinterestedness' of the clerics

The Taliban judicial system participated in the production of a social order in which the ulama claimed to represent the public good, the definition of which,

The Taliban Courts in Afghanistan. Adam Baczko, Oxford University Press. © Adam Baczko 2023.
DOI: 10.1093/oso/9780198896777.003.0011

however, was itself a contentious issue in the war. The religious thus universalized their own interests through the courts and worked to impose themselves in the villages at the expense of other social elites.

The movement's judicial system enshrined the rise of religious elites, which had already made itself felt early on in the civil war. In the 1980s and 1990s, the Islamist insurgency, the fall of the Communist regime, and the rise of the Islamic Emirate (1996–2001) offered the mullahs and ulama a historic opportunity for social climbing (see Chapter 1). In the 1990s, the Taliban leadership governed by relying on their peers, who were integrated into the public service and headed up the various administrative bodies.[1] Whereas in the 1970s the state relied on delegating certain aspects of local governance to the notables, the Taliban called on the mullahs who then displaced the tribal elites from their intermediary positions. In continuity with the 1980s insurrection, the Taliban transformed the social hierarchy by allowing the mullahs to no longer rely on the *khan* or *bay* to insert themselves among the village elites.[2] Sunni clerics, because of their large number and dispersion across all regions and ethnic groups (except in the Shia areas), operated as a particularly effective administrative lever.[3] Thanks to their madrasa networks, the mullahs were much better connected to the political elites of the Islamic Emirate than the notables had been to the monarchy of Zaher Shah or to Daoud Khan's republic. In the 2000s, the insurgency reproduced this model and, with the extension of its administrative and judicial system, again concentrated military, political, and judicial functions in clerical hands.

The Taliban judicial system advantaged people with a religious education who had mastered the language and essential concepts of Islamic law. By having attended madrasas, members of the movement often knew each other, providing channels for recourse and appeals against adverse decisions. In addition, ulama often assisted the Taliban judges and, in general, acted as privileged witnesses during trials. Inasmuch as they were sympathizers of

[1] 'Les oulémas afghans au XXe siècle: Bureaucratisation, contestation et genèse d'un État clérical', *Archives de sciences sociales des religions*, 2001, n° 115, pp. 63–79.

[2] For the case of Helmand, see Carter Malkasian, *War Comes to Garmser: Thirty Years of Conflict on the Afghan Frontier*, Oxford, Oxford University Press, 2013; Mike Martin, *An Intimate War: An Oral History of the Helmand Conflict, 1978–2012*, Oxford, Oxford University Press, 2014.

[3] In the 1970s, Soviet researchers estimated the proportion of clerics in Afghan society at 10 per cent of adult men. This estimate is unverifiable, especially since it depends on the criteria for defining this group: educated in a madrasa, exercising a sacerdotal activity, possessing a socially recognized religious competence? Whatever this figure may have been, it increased sharply in the following two decades during which madrasas were the only educational offer for most refugees and residents in mujahideen-controlled areas. Antonio Giustozzi, 'Local Politics and the Taliban' in Conrad Schetter (ed.), *Local Politics in Afghanistan: A Century of Intervention in the Social Order*, Oxford, Oxford University Press, 2013, p. 78.

the movement, their opinions tended to carry greater weight in the scales of justice. Here we see one of the typical effects of a juridical field that produces social hierarchies as a function of the degree of familiarity with the system and its actors. As is relatively traditional for the legal profession, the ulama had 'an interest in disinterestedness',[4] which partly explains their personal investment in the objectivization of the Taliban judicial system: as soon as sharia became state law, Islamic jurisconsults had a vested interest in the state. In effect, by defending the application of a law and of judicial procedures regardless of the specific issues in a court case, the clerics universalized their own interest, that of a social group holding no economic capital and with low pre-war social status. Through their moral discourse and judicial practice, they promoted a society in which the religious form of cultural capital held the key to power and decision-making.

In areas under their control, the Taliban imposed a clerical monopoly on the definition and representation of the common interest to the detriment of two other social elites with claims to acting for the public good: the Afghan executives of humanitarian or development organizations and the landowners (*khan, bay*) who historically had acted as intermediaries between the people and the state. First, the Taliban excluded or marginalized people who worked for the international intervention. To carry out development projects, foreign organizations employed Afghans who had educational capital, spoke English or French, and had mastered Western social norms—especially anyone who had lived for several years in Europe, North America, or Australia. In the early years of the intervention, these actors mattered in the countryside because of their access to international resources. Thus, they championed a project of social and economic modernization that universalized their particular interests. As the insurgency spread, they were forced out of their areas—many left the country—or had to abort their activities with a consequent loss of social status. Secondly, the Taliban's attitude towards the rural notables was more ambivalent. The latter's pretensions of representing the common good stemmed from their position as intermediaries with the state, a position that regime changes largely invalidated.[5] Still, while the inroads made by the insurgency on the whole weakened the influence of these rural elites relative to that of the mullahs

[4] Pierre Bourdieu, *On the State: Lectures at Collège de France, 1989–1992*, Stanford, Stanford University Press, 2014, pp. 342–4.

[5] The situation varied greatly from region to region and within some areas. Especially in the South, on the eve of the war large landowners had already lost much of their influence. Jon Anderson, 'There Are no Khans Anymore: Economic Development and Social Change in Tribal Afghanistan', *Middle East Journal*, 1978, vol. 32, n° 2, pp. 167–83.

and ulama, the Taliban judges also helped cement their—subordinate—social status in two ways: on the one hand, the conservative Taliban judicial system preserved private property, and thus the economic resources that buttressed their position as notables. On the other hand, the Taliban granted them some status as intermediaries—albeit at a lower level than the religious—in their administration of the population.

The identity regime

The Taliban's justice system contributed to the imposition of an identity regime that largely reproduced pre-war ethnic and denominational hierarchies. These linked the predominance of the Pashtuns within the movement to a discourse negating the question of ethnicity, while relegating the Shiites to an inferior position. This identity regime did not hinder the movement, since the multi-ethnic recruitment of judges, the non-ethnic nature of the madrasa networks, and the reputation of impartiality of its courts attracted people who did not identify as Pashtuns.

While their numbers are impossible to estimate, the insurgency fielded many Uzbek, Tajik, and Turkmen judges, especially in the northern provinces.[6] Judges also relied on mullahs from different ethnic groups to set up and operate their courts:

> All religious leaders of Baghlan, including Pashtuns, Uzbeks and Tajiks, are always in contact with the Taliban Military Commission. They extend all kinds of help to the Taliban. These religious leaders have played a key role in the establishment of the Taliban courts. They would visit the houses of tribal leaders at night to persuade them to provide land for Taliban facilities.[7]

[6] Instances of Uzbek, Tajik, and Turkmen judges recur often in reports and press articles dealing with the northern provinces. See Antonio Giustozzi and Christoph Reuter, *The Northern Front: The Afghan Insurgency Spreading beyond the Pashtuns*, Kabul, Afghanistan Analysts Network, 2010; Antonio Giustozzi and Christoph Reuter, *The Insurgents of the Afghan North*, Kabul, Afghanistan Analysts Network, 2011; Obaid Ali, *The Non-Pashtun Taleban of the North: A Case Study from Badakhshan*, 3 January 2017, www.afghanistan-analysts.org/en/reports/war-and-peace/the-non-pashtun-taleban-of-the-north-a-case-study-from-badakhshan/; Obaid Ali, *Non-Pashtun Taleban of the North (2): Case Studies of Uzbek Taleban in Faryab and Sar-e Pul*, 17 March 2017, www.afghanistan-analysts.org/en/reports/war-and-peace/non-pashtun-taleban-of-the-north-2-case-studies-of-uzbek-taleban-in-faryab-and-sar-e-pul/; Obaid Ali, *The Non-Pashtun Taleban of the North (3): The Takhar Case Study*, 29 July 2017, www.afghanistan-analysts.org/en/reports/war-and-peace/the-non-pashtun-taleban-of-the-north-the-takhar-case-study/; Obaid Ali, *Non-Pashtun Taleban of the North (4): A Case Study from Jawzjan*, 18 September 2017, www.afghanistan-analysts.org/en/reports/war-and-peace/non-pashtun-taleban-of-the-north-4-a-case-study-from-jawzjan/.

[7] I-4, Taliban appeals court judge, Dahan-i Ghuri district (Baghlan), 2011.

Minorities were not recruited only for the judicial system—the provinces of Ghazni, Badakhshan, Takhar, Sar-i Pul, Jawzjan, and Faryab had ethnic minority governors and commanders.[8] In 2016, the Taliban had a Tajik, an Uzbek, and a Turkman on its twelve-member Leadership Council, giving its supreme ruling body a multi-ethnic make-up while still remaining tilted toward the Pashtuns (who held 75 per cent of positions although they made up only around 40 per cent of the population).[9]

In part, this recruitment was motivated by strategic considerations—the movement had to give pledges to the non-Pashtuns so that it could implant itself in the North. But it also fitted in primarily with the Taliban movement's historical structuring around Pakistan's Deobandi madrasas. Already in the 1990s, among the non-Pashtun students and ulama who joined the Taliban were hundreds of Tajiks, mostly from Badakhshan province.[10] In 1995, the Afghan Students' Association (Jamiat-i Tulaba-yi Afghanistan), composed mainly of Uzbek students from Pakistan-based madrasas, pledged allegiance to Mullah Omar. Several hundred of its members fought for the movement, and its leader Mawlawi Abdul Raqib, an Uzbek from Takhar province, was appointed a commander and then rose to Minister for Refugees and Repatriation.[11] These religious served as go-betweens that the movement mobilized after 2001 in non-Pashtun areas. Many members of minority groups continued to study in Pakistan's Deobandi madrasas, and by 2010 two-thirds of the mullahs in the northern provinces—mostly inhabited by non-Pashtuns—had received their religious education in Pakistan. Graduates of these schools also opened their own madrasas in the northern provinces. From 2006 onwards, the Taliban exploited this clerical network, which shared their ideology, to establish themselves in the North.[12]

On a parallel track, judges also regularly rendered verdicts favourable to non-Pashtuns. The Taliban leadership had issued orders that the movement should be blind to affiliations. Thus, the 2010 version of the *Instructions to the Mujahideen* advised that:

[8] For example, between 2008 and 2011, the Taliban governor of Ghazni, Mullah Najib, was a Tajik.

[9] Tahir Khan, 'Afghan Taliban Expel Two Dissenting Leaders', *The Express Tribune*, 7 January 2016.

[10] Antonio Giustozzi, 'Local Politics and the Taliban' in Conrad Schetter (ed.), *Local Politics in Afghanistan: A Century of Intervention in the Social Order*, Oxford, Oxford University Press, 2013, p. 80; Obaid Ali, *The Non-Pashtun Taleban of the North: A Case Study from Badakhshan*, 3 January 2017, www.afghanistan-analysts.org/en/reports/war-and-peace/the-non-pashtun-taleban-of-the-north-a-case-study-from-badakhshan/.

[11] Obaid Ali, *Non-Pashtun Taleban of the North (2): Case Studies of Uzbek Taleban in Faryab and Sar-e Pul*, 17 March 2017, www.afghanistan-analysts.org/en/reports/war-and-peace/non-pashtun-taleban-of-the-north-2-case-studies-of-uzbek-taleban-in-faryab-and-sar-e-pul/.

[12] Antonio Giustozzi and Christoph Reuter, *The Northern Front: The Afghan Insurgency Spreading beyond the Pashtuns*, Kabul, Afghanistan Analysts Network, 2010.

> Mujahedin shall protect themselves completely from any tribal, linguistic, and regional prejudice. It has been narrated by Hazrat Abu Hurairah that: if someone fights under an unknown flag […] or has become angry for tribal reasons or encourages tribalism or helps someone for tribal reasons, if he dies, he will be dead in ignorance (*jahil*), as if he had not been a Muslim. (Article 79)

The movement leadership here relied on words of the Prophet transmitted by Abu Huraira, the most important rapporteur of hadiths, to threaten excommunication for anyone found to be favouring members of specific tribes or the Pashtuns in general (see also Chapter 6). The Taliban judges stressed the diversity of the public in their courts: 'All of them, including Pashtuns, Tajiks and Uzbeks, support the Taliban courts and have cordial relations with Taliban judges. And you can easily deduce it by their crowding into these courts.'[13] The judges claimed that the universality of Islamic law enabled their rulings to surmount ethnic and social barriers:

> Taliban courts don't distinguish between rich and poor. Similarly, masters and slaves, blacks and whites, all are treated the same when it comes to justice in the Taliban's court of law. This is also the case with cultural values that must be eclipsed when we administer justice. We decide all cases within the framework of sharia law. There is no mention of Pashtun in the Taliban constitution.[14]

In settling land disputes, the movement could also demonstrate the impartiality of its judges in deciding cases regardless of the litigants' ethnicity or tribal affiliations. Thus, in an ownership dispute over a forest in Marid, Kunar (see Chapter 9), the Taliban judge was able to impose his decision not only with a big show of force but also by negating the ethnic framing of the contesting families. In doing so, he reduced the case to a private ownership litigation between two parties.[15] Here we encounter the mechanism of individuating disputes through law raised by Pierre Bourdieu in his article on the juridical field: 'Recourse to the law in many cases implies recognition of a definition of the forms of grievance or of struggle which gives primacy to individual (and legal) conflicts over other forms of struggle.'[16] In the Afghan context,

[13] I-1, a Taliban appeals court judge, Nahrin district (Baghlan), 2011.
[14] I-2, a Taliban appeals court judge, Karagai district (Laghman), 2011.
[15] E-6, a resident of Ghaziabad district (Kunar), July 2010.
[16] Pierre Bourdieu, 'The Force of Law: Toward a Sociology of the Juridical Field', *Hastings Law Journal*, 1986, vol. 38, n° 5, p. 830, fn 41.

individuating and judicializing conflicts in this manner was all the more effective when contrasted with, for one thing, the strong bias Western troops exhibited by taking sides in local conflicts, and, for another, the functioning or lack thereof of the regime's local administration. The latter relied on former commanders, who built their authority precisely by exploiting private conflicts in an ethnic logic. While the Western military fielded militias that operated outside any legal framework and were mobilized on an ethnic basis, Taliban judges provided welcome relief from the identity logics which echoed the hated period of the 1990s. The institutionalization of their court system and the reliance on sharia served to counterbalance the communal framing of some disputes, effectively diminishing their communitarian dimensions and refocusing them on interpersonal issues. However, the Hanafite jurisprudence applied by the Taliban relegated Shiite populations to a lower status. While Islamic law practised by the Taliban facilitated the circumvention of ethnic barriers, it widened the sectarian divide. Where possible, Shiites therefore went before regime courts or settled their conflicts in other ways, for example by turning to a Shiite mullah. A Shiite Hazara journalist from Ghazni explained this dynamic:

> I do not know of any example of Hazaras who went to the Taliban to resolve their differences. One time, one of my acquaintances thought about going to the Taliban, because the regime's courts leaned in favor of the culprit. This was a case caused by a marriage, where on the first night it turned out that the girl was not a virgin. The groom's family wanted to get back the money they had paid, but the other family refused. The groom's father took it as an insult. A doctor confirmed that the girl was not a virgin, but the court still leaned in favor of the woman's family, as had the local mullahs. Eventually he did not go to see the Taliban but got satisfaction by turning to Ayatollah Mosseini who proved him in the right. The bride's family gave her money back and made a public apology.[17]

However, other interviewees in the same province reported that some Shiite Hazaras did use Taliban judges to settle disputes. Shah Jahan Noori, a member of parliament in Ghazni province, explained that 'Hazaras living near Taliban areas prefer to go to the Taliban judge and they do not suffer discrimination'.[18]

[17] E-29, a journalist in Ghazni province, September 2014.

[18] Interview with Shah Jahan Noori, MP for Ghazni province, September 2012. Similar cases were reported in other provinces, including Wardak and Uruzgan. In a 2011 countrywide survey, 2 per cent of Hazaras responded that they had used a Taliban court. Antonio Giustozzi, *Justice and State-Building in Afghanistan: State vs. Society vs. Taliban. Reflections on a Survey of the Afghan People, Part 4 of 4*, San Francisco, Asia Foundation, 2012, p. 7.

Although few in number, these cases provide evidence of the insurgency's effort to provide local security to Shiite Hazaras. This effort was particularly visible in the conflict between Pashtun nomads and Hazara farmers over land in the country's middle region, in which the Pashtun nomads relied on local Taliban networks. While Taliban commanders routinely sided with the nomads, the judges conspicuously stayed above the conflict.[19] Similarly, in a conflict in Khas Uruzgan district caused by the elopement of a Shiite Hazara man and a Sunni Pashtun woman, the judge referred the two sides to his hierarchy, which directed them to the Taliban authorities in Quetta. In the end, the Taliban chose not to issue a ruling. Indeed, the case turned the ethnic-confessional hierarchy on its head (Pashtun men could marry Hazara women but not the reverse). A ruling either way would have risked displeasing not only the insurgency's Pashtun base but also the Hazara communities living in a particularly strategic valley that permitted passage between Uruzgan and Ghazni provinces.[20]

Securing (male) property

For many of the Taliban judges I interviewed, land disputes accounted for most of the cases that came before them. In a situation where land rights were particularly shaky and vulnerable, the Taliban judicial system contributed to securing property. The literal interpretations in Islamic law—particularly detailed on property issues—eased the deliberations of the judges and the social recognition of the verdict. In one case, the brothers of a child born several months after their father's death exploited the suspicion that weighed on the newborn's paternity to seize its inheritance. The Taliban judge's decision strictly applied Islamic law:

> A woman gave birth to a child after the death of her husband. Her other sons were not willing to give her husband's share of his property to their newborn brother. I asked her how long time had passed after her husband's death when the child was born. I was told the time, which was less than nine months. So, I ordered her sons to restore his rights to their newborn brother.[21]

[19] Liz Alden Wily, 'The Battle over Pastures: The Hidden War in Afghanistan', *Revue des mondes musulmans et de la Méditerranée*, 2013, n° 133, pp. 95–113; Hervé Nicolle, 'Qu'elle était verte ma vallée: L'avenir sans terre des populations Kuchi dans le district de Deh Sabz', *Revue des mondes musulmans et de la Méditerranée*, 2013, n° 133, pp. 227–38.

[20] E-9, a resident of Khas Uruzgan district (Uruzgan), April 2011.

[21] I-12, a Taliban trial court judge, Nahrin district (Baghlan), 2011.

Absent formal evidence of adultery, Islamic law pragmatically deduces paternity from the number of months elapsed between the husband's death and a child's birth. In like fashion, many inheritance rules prescribed by Islamic law are applied according to the letter of the law. For example, one interviewee recounted how the Taliban resolved a dispute with his uncle, who took advantage of the fall of the Islamic Emirate of Afghanistan to grab my respondent's inheritance when he was fourteen years old:

> When my father died in 2001, we were living together with my uncle. When I wanted to stop living with my uncle, he would not give me my right and inheritance, which was due to me. He told me: 'you are one, the property belongs to more people.' I told him that I was my father's only son, that I had no brother. My uncle had five sons, he wanted to divide the property into six parts, but I told him: 'You have to divide it into two portions, one is your part and the other is that of my father, which is my inheritance. Then you can divide your own part into five for each of your sons, not my inheritance.' He warned me that I was alone and that if I wanted to go in that direction, he would kill me.
>
> After this, I called on the village notables, we organized a *jirga* on it and […] The notables ruled, 'we will give four portions to your uncle and two portions to you', but I refused. […] Then I went to the district governor and brought a complaint against him. The case dragged on for six months without progress. I paid 200,000 afghanis [$4,000] to the governor, but they take their time in the district office. After that, the governor said to me, 'if you want to share the property with me, I will confiscate the property from your uncle, otherwise I can't do anything.'
>
> I had no other solutions, so there was an elderly person, he took me to the Taliban, to whom I told my problems. They said, 'Why didn't you bring your case to us first instead of going to the government? You made a mistake, for that we will fine you 20,000 Pakistani rupees [$200].' They gave me a piece of paper and told me to give this to my uncle and after that, it would be their business. They took the address of the village and house of my uncle and told me they would come.
>
> The next night, the Taliban came to our village and rounded up all the notables of the village and my uncle. First, they beat the notables with a stick and told them, 'Why did you make a bad judgment?' After that, they took from my uncle the money that I had spent in six months, half the property […] and told him that if he argued with me in the future, they would kill him in front of the villagers. The Taliban also asked the villagers whether or not

> I was my uncle's nephew. The villagers answered yes, so the Taliban gave me the plot, wrote a letter of this judgment, gave me one copy and took one with themselves. I am really happy with their judgment because they solved my problems in two days, but before that, I had spent two years between the government and the judgment of the local people without solving my problems.[22]

As in other cases of land disputes interviewees shared with me, the aggrieved party turned to Taliban judges following several abortive appeals to other dispute resolution bodies, which the Taliban judge in this case penalized. His verdict was a strict application of Islamic law: one share for each son—the interviewee's father and uncle—with the deceased father's share going entirely to his son. Also exemplary are the prompt—even summary—nature of the judgments and the centrality of coercion in making the verdict stick by threatening the uncle should he flout their ruling. Another account of land conflict, involving a woman stripped of her share of inheritance by her brothers-in-law, brought together most of the recurring elements of how Taliban judges handled property disputes:

> My husband was in the National Army and he was killed in Helmand province in 2008. After my husband died, my brother-in-law asked me to marry him to recover all of my husband's inheritance, but I refused. So he warned me: 'If you do not marry me, I will not give you your rights to the land and other things.' I warned my brothers that this problem had occurred. They came here and my brothers fought with him and were beaten. […] I went to the notables, they did not reach any decision. In addition, I spent a lot of money on these notables, 10,000 afghanis [$200] for their food expenses for every month and this problem took three months without being solved. Nothing happened, then I went to the government court and there the judge demanded 600,000 afghanis [$12,000], but I didn't have that kind of money. […]
>
> Therefore, the last solution for me was to go to the Taliban and ask them for help. One of the village notables advised me [to go see the Taliban] and he went with me. He told me that you cannot trust the notables and the government court. We started walking in the morning and reached there in the evening and [the Taliban judge] was in Kharwar district. There were 20 people with him […] they all came with the judge and us to my brother-in-law's house. They obeyed him. When they arrived at my brother-in-law's

[22] I-30, a resident of Azra district (Logar), 2013.

> house, [. . .] they called three or four notables and asked them: 'Does this land belong to this woman?' The notables answered, 'Yes.' Then, the Taliban beat my brother-in-law badly and said, 'If you do not give her the land or money, we will kill you next time' and the Taliban had a letter written [certifying the woman's rights]. I came to see him the next day, he gave me the money. I spent two years on this case with both the government's and the notables' court systems, but my problems did not end. But the Taliban settled them in two days.[23]

As we will see, decisions affirming women's ownership interests proved to be particularly problematic. In this case, the Taliban judge enforced Islamic law, which assigns a half-share of inheritance to the widow of the deceased. We see again the role of coercion which, combined with the Islamic legitimacy of judgments and the impartiality of judges, made Taliban judges' verdicts difficult to dispute.[24] Finally, in the most ambiguous cases, judges sometimes made pragmatic decisions. Thus, in a particularly intractable land dispute case, the judge, unable to determine the rightful owner of a plot from the documentary and testimonial evidence before him, referred it to the Military Commission. In the absence of conclusive evidence, it rendered a Solomonic solution by dividing the land into two equal parts.[25]

This assertion of property rights implies that judges and the Taliban movement had to confront the practical fallout from juridical uncertainty, including the shaky validity of titles. Many titles were issued under irregular circumstances or were falsified. Conversely, many genuine deeds were lost during decades of war (see Chapter 2). Faced with this uncertainty, Taliban judges treated the titles with suspicion, calling for witnesses or ascertaining the validity of the certificates with others in the village. A resident of Kandahar province recounted how he prevailed against his neighbour, despite the fact that the latter was able to produce a title:

> I used the Taliban court around 5 months ago. At that time Taliban did not have any specific place for their court, they asked me to come two days later with my rival and five notables from our area in the village of X for trial. My

[23] I-35, a woman resident of Charkh district (Logar), 2013.

[24] In another context, Nick Miszak shows the role that threats play in negotiating an agreement between parties to a land dispute. Nick Miszak, 'Land-based Conflict in Afghanistan: On the Right of Preemption (*shuf'a*) as "Back-Channel" Diplomacy and a Show of Indignation' in Martin Sökefeld (ed.), *Spaces of Conflict in Everyday Life*, Bielefeld, Transcript Verlag, 2015, pp. 117–35.

[25] I-27, a Taliban court judge in Arghandab district (Kandahar), 2011.

> case was a land dispute with a man called H. He claimed that one jerib [2,000 m^2] of my land in reality belonged to him and he produced a fake title for that land. For almost 6 months we were fighting each other and always H. with his sons attacked me [. . .]. Then I went to see the Taliban commander and complained about H. The Taliban commander came to H. to ask about the issue, H. showed the fake title and, because the Taliban commander was not educated, he sent us to the Taliban judges.
>
> When we went to the Taliban judges, they heard the case and asked for witnesses, but as we did not bring any witnesses, the Taliban postponed the court for two days. They told us to bring two witnesses, our papers and to try to bring one or two notables. [After this audience] the Taliban judges told us to come back after three days to the same place and that they would announce their decision. During the three days, the Taliban came to our village. They questioned many people and found out that H. had in fact made a fake title. After three days H. and I went to the same place and the judges announced that the land belonged to me. He said that H. had lied to the Taliban and produced a fake title. The judges gave him 20 lashes and warned him that he would be punished again if in the future he dared bothering me.[26]

In this case, the judge checked with neighbours for past use and inferred the falsity of the title produced by the rival party. As in the previous cases, the Taliban judge had the person he found guilty flogged for the falsification or for using violence. The testimony and the Taliban judges being outsiders were decisive in deciding these disputes. After decades of questioning property rights, distrust of recent deeds was widespread. As a cleric from Logar province explained, 'the ownership certificates are not trustworthy for us because if someone gives $2,000 or $3,000, the government makes the documents for him or her.'[27] Similarly, one notable observed that the fragility of property deeds made it necessary to verify their validity with other villagers: 'The state-issued land ownership certificates are no good because some people give money to the government to make such certificates. But when the claim on land is clearly known by all the villagers, then [the deed] is good.'[28] Moreover, regardless of their uncertain value, some deeds were refused for contradicting the Taliban's interpretation of Islamic law:

[26] I-42, a resident of Zhari district (Kandahar), 2011.
[27] I-34, a cleric of Baraki Barak district (Logar), 2013.
[28] I-16, a notable of Mohamad Agha district (Logar), 2013.

> Those people who have land, they have ownership certificates, but there will still be problematic cases. For example, a father may put the land certificate in the name of only one of his sons and that son may refuse to give the rights that are due to his brothers. So, in this case we do not bother with the ownership certificates. We apply sharia law and ask their relatives if the other brothers have not sold their share to him, and if not, we take the rights of other brothers from that one who has the land certificate.[29]

While such questioning of rights did not happen without provoking tensions, the movement's coercive powers and the Islamic legitimacy of decisions made them difficult to contradict.

By resolving conflicts, the Taliban assumed the role of the guaranteeing authority for the definition and allocation of property. As Christian Lund has shown, control over land issues is an essential component of effective sovereignty, in the sense that it allows a political actor, be it a state or not, to apply its vision of social order.[30] The regulation of land conflicts allowed the Taliban to impose a conservative view of social relations. In the wake of the Islamist insurrection against the Communist regime of the 1980s, the Taliban had categorically rejected using land as an instrument of social reform. In some cases, the verdicts favoured people who were robbed and powerless in the post-2001 political configuration, such as the widow of the Afghan army soldier or the orphaned teenager in the earlier examples. But in many cases, verdicts benefited the most well-heeled party, the landowner. The movement advocated neither land reform nor redistribution of resources. Its discourse on inequality limited itself to criticizing the regime's nepotism and the resulting land grabs, a critique that targeted the enrichment less than its illegality. Their attachment to legal sources and their strict application was part of a focus on stabilizing social relations, which in practice meant reproducing them.

This social conservatism was evident from the exceptions that Taliban judges made to their own rules when they did not apply their interpretation of Islamic law. As Jean Carbonnier, Pierre Bourdieu, and Michel Foucault have shown, 'illegalisms' and 'free passes' are not anomalies of the law, but rather the other facet of the same phenomenon. As Pierre Bourdieu

[29] I-11, a Taliban court judge, Logar province, 2013.

[30] Christian Lund, 'Fragmented Sovereignty: Land Reform and Dispossession in Laos', *The Journal of Peasant Studies*, 2011, vol. 38, nº 4, pp. 885–905; Christian Lund, 'Rule and Rupture: State Formation through the Production of Property and Citizenship', *Development and Change*, 2016, vol. 47, nº 6, pp. 1199–228.

explains: 'The law does not operate without the special treatment, the derogation, the exemption, the waiver, that is, without all the kinds of special authorizations to violate the regulation which, paradoxically, can only be granted by the authority responsible for enforcing it.'[31] The tensions recurred in conflicts involving the granting of the half-share of inheritance that Islamic law grants to single women or widows. In the Pashtun regions of the South and East, this legal status tended to be more favourable to women than the custom that deprived them of any right of inheritance.[32] As one notable explained:

> Of course, she can [own land] from an Islamic point of view, but in our culture, we do not give land to women. From the Islamic point of view, two sisters have an inheritance right equal to a brother. But if the father gives her the inheritance, then her brother refuses it. Here, in our area, a father gave land to his daughter and her brother denied it and killed her husband. So, people do not give up the rights, there are maybe two percent of people who give their share [to women]. This is the case even when the deceased does not have a son.[33]

While the Taliban were generally adamant in their application of Islamic law, they displayed a willingness to compromise on this issue. If in the previously mentioned case a Taliban judge enforced the allocation of the half-share, another judge in Kunar province admitted that in fact the families often refused to give it up and that he did not object.[34] In Ghazni province, another judge explained to me the controversy surrounding the allocation of the half-share to women and that he took the time to persuade the men to grant it.[35] On this issue, the judges showed a surprising pliancy for a movement that on other occasions brutally imposed its own interpretation of the law. The social logic behind these decisions is obvious: in line with past use and judicial practices in rural areas, Taliban judges reproduced the exclusion of women from property rights.

[31] Pierre Bourdieu, 'Droit et passe-droit [Le champ des pouvoirs territoriaux et la mise en oeuvre des règlements]', *Actes de la recherche en sciences sociales*, 1990, vol. 81, n° 1, p. 91.

[32] Nancy Tapper, 'Causes and Consequences of the Abolition of Brideprice in Afghanistan' in M. Nazif Shahrani and Robert Canfield (eds), *Revolutions and Rebellions in Afghanistan*, Berkeley, University of California Press, 1984, p. 303.

[33] I-43, a notable of Baraki Barak district (Logar), 2013.

[34] E-7, a Taliban court judge, Kunar province, April 2013.

[35] E-55, a Taliban trial court judge, Ghazni province, May 2013.

Moral order and patriarchal domination

Just as in the 1990s, the judges' verdicts overlaid a moral conception on regulating social relations, with individual deviancies from it blamed for perpetuating the war. In his 2008 Eid al-Fitr message, Mullah Omar outlined this interpretation of the war, which underpinned judgments by the Taliban courts:

> Our poor country is just like a lawless jungle due to the illegitimate attacks. Forces of many countries and thousands of internal forces in the name of police and national army march in the country but still the casualties, looting and plundering of the people has turned this country into a wild jungle that neither life, nor property are safe, nor dignity and honour. [...] How can one imagine and expect peace and harmony where national and international thieves are in power? If police and security forces of a state consist of such people who are characterless, unbelieving, addicted to drugs, and strayed from houses, how can they safeguard the lives and property of the people?[36]

The use of characterizations targeting deviant behaviours and personal failings featured repeatedly in Mullah Omar's discourses. He explained the war and the disorder suffered by Afghans as being caused by the presence of international forces eager to exploit the country's resources, but he also blamed the moral weakness of some Afghans. In another of his speeches, he touched on the situation of women but only to underline this state of moral decay: 'It is a matter of sorrow to say that the common people, particularly women, are grappling with various hardships following the invasion of the invaders. Even many women have immolated themselves or have been martyred miserably or their honor has been violated. Still this brutal trend continues.'[37] From this perspective, judges took on the role of combating the deviance and uncertainty he blamed for being root causes of the perpetuation of the civil war. A judge gave this interpretation of why people resorted to the Taliban courts: 'This provides them with a protected life. Otherwise there is a chaos, disruption and disorder and might is right becomes the order of the day. So they have to go for a kind of system where they feel secure.'[38]

However, while 1990s edicts about beard length, turban wearing, make-up, high heels, music, or images remained in force, they were only observed in the breach. In 2015, a student who passed a daily Taliban checkpoint from

[36] Mullah Omar's Eid al-Fitr Address for 2008.
[37] Mullah Omar's Eid al-Fitr Address for 2012.
[38] I-6, a Taliban trial court judge, Qala-i Naw district (Badghis), 2011.

his village to Jalalabad University wore a short beard and had music on his phone. However, the Taliban who regularly checked the same phone did not bother him.[39] Many such testimonies echoed each other in the different provinces where the Taliban had a presence: a beard that was too short, flying a kite, and not wearing a turban were no longer punished by flogging. The British journalist Tom Coghlan, who penned an oral history of the war in Helmand province, dates the change of attitude of the movement from 2007. It was then that the Taliban took over many villages and pragmatically avoided punishing minor transgressions. As a resident of the province put it: 'They are not like the old Taliban who destroyed your cassettes, shouted at you and beat you.'[40] In an interview, a judge corroborated this change of policy:

> We have committed blunders in the past. I would say blunders because that was the need of the day, but we were blamed for that. Anyways, there is a growing realization that things are different now with the changes on the international environment and that we must also bring changes in our society if we want to go with the international community. So, a little bit of changes are definitely there, but that doesn't mean that we changes in the sharia law.[41]

However, there was one area where the Taliban remained as strict as they had been during the Islamic Emirate: gender relations. Death by stoning was the most striking practice of a broader system that guaranteed radical patriarchal domination. Gender issues effectively allowed the Taliban to advance an essential point of their ideology since their formation in the 1990s, namely drawing a distinction between the public and private spheres. In the public space, judges played a direct role in regulating behaviour, especially that of women; but they avoided intervening in the domestic domain. The 2010 version of the *Instructions to the Mujahideen* reserved an entire article for this question and set very strict conditions for fighters entering houses: 'Mujahedin shall not search people's houses and if the need to search a house is urgent, they shall obtain the permission of the district official and take the Imam of the mosque and two elders of the area with them' (Article 72).[42]

[39] E-45, a student at Jalalabad University, residing in Shirzad district (Nangarhar), August 2015.

[40] Tom Coghlan, 'The Taliban in Helmand: An Oral History' in Antonio Giustozzi (ed.), *Decoding the New Taliban: Insights from the Afghan Field*, New York, Columbia University Press, 2009, p. 140.

[41] I-6, a Taliban trial court judge, Qala-i Naw district (Badghis), 2011.

[42] This insistence on respect for the private space echoes some of the stories I heard from my male interlocutors. When I asked a resident of Ghaziabad (Kunar) about his worst experience with American troops, far from telling me about drone strikes or civilians killed or tortured in detention centres, he recalled how angry he felt when American troops broke down his door to search his house. An American

The private space that the Taliban set up corresponds to Christine Delphy's definition of a 'state of exception' and 'derogation from the common law' but whose contours are defined by law. The Afghan situation of course differs from that analysed by Delphy, as the gender domination relationships are dramatically more blatant and violent. However, her conceptualization of the private space shines a light on how an authority redefines the domestic sphere through a law essentially applied in the public space.[43] As long as the deviations and their effects remained behind the walls of the houses, the Taliban judges did not intervene. As soon as they spilled over into the village, into the streets, they became the responsibility of a judicial system that was stacked in favour of men. Thus, far from the convenient but false image of a totalitarian movement, the Taliban avoided penetrating domestic spaces and interfering with cases relegated to the private sphere. This respect for homes, which they derived from their patriarchal vision of society, made them the guarantors of husbands, fathers, and brothers dominating wives, daughters, and sisters. In other words, they were rebuilding, by strictly regulating behaviour in the public space, a private sphere whose essential trait was the delegation of the legitimate use of violence to heads of families. This distinction between the private and public spheres was part of a broader project to rebuild society based on the family unit.

While the few cases I collected of women using Taliban courts suggested that they could win their cases, women generally did not have access to judges. Two women already mentioned won when the Taliban court awarded the first her share of the inheritance following her husband's death and granted the daughter of the second a divorce from a husband who abused her.[44] However, these cases remained rare, and the Taliban maintained an ambivalent relationship with women as court users. They had the right to file a suit, but only if they were accompanied by a relative (*mahram*, literally someone whom she cannot marry). As one judge in Ghazni province explained:

soldier came into the kitchen where his wife, whose face was not covered, tried to hide herself by turning toward the wall and pulling up her scarf. A young soldier stood leaning against the wall, looking at her with an amused and curious look. My interlocutor told me that he had never felt so humiliated. E-6, a resident of Ghaziabad district (Kunar), July 2010.

[43] Christine Delphy, 'L'état d'exception: la dérogation au droit commun comme fondement de la sphère privée', *Nouvelles Questions Féministes*, 1995, vol. 16, nº 4, pp. 73–114. For a similar perspective in the American context, see Elizabeth Schneider, 'The Violence of Privacy', *Connecticut Law Review*, 1991, vol. 23, pp. 973–99.

[44] I-35, a resident of Charkh district (Logar), 2013; I-38, a resident of Mohamad Agha district (Logar), 2013.

> Women can come with a parent (*mahram*) or choose someone they trust as a representative (*wakil*). Most of the time, they do not dare to come to us, but in serious cases, sometimes they do. The main problem is culture, they face particularly strong barriers. Traditionally, people send a representative of the woman. They think it's not correct that they come themselves.[45]

Blaming the inaccessibility of the courts to women on the culture was a recurrent theme among the judges. Another judge in Kunar province told me of the shame that Pashtun women 'who behave well' would feel before him, suggesting that women complainants, by the simple act of appealing to him, would not be so well behaved.[46] A third judge, who asserted that he had received two to three complaints from women a month, justified the de facto exclusion of women by the physical distance and insecurity that would keep women from going to the judges: 'Women face many barriers, for example our courts are so far away from cities and villages, they are in the mountains, so it is hard for women to come there and, on the way, they may also face other problems.'[47] By remaining out of reach for women, and thus unresponsive to their demands, the Taliban judicial system guaranteed the patriarchal structure of Afghan society. Once the complaint was filed, women sometimes had a chance, if only because the objectivization mechanisms also worked for their benefit, but the judicial system remained fundamentally tilted against them.

On the other hand, when dealing with these issues, the Taliban courts judged with particular strictness any deviance detrimental to the gender and power relationship within the family. Generally, Taliban judges avoided involvement until a case had a public dimension. A Kunar resident explained: 'The Taliban avoid intervening when a woman is abused by her husband, she is unhappy, she wants a divorce, but which he refuses. They wouldn't take the risk of provoking the people.'[48] Cases where they did intervene were rare and most of the time signified the existence of male support in the woman's family who brought matters out into the open. A Taliban judge said: 'There was a woman who was always beaten by her husband, and then her father came to us to get a divorce for his daughter, but her husband refused to grant her a divorce. We went to see her husband and forced him to grant the divorce.'[49] Here, the fact that the

[45] E-63, a Taliban court judge, Ghazni province, May 2013.
[46] E-7, a Taliban court judge, Kunar province, April 2013.
[47] I-11, a Taliban court judge, Logar province, 2013.
[48] E-37, a resident of Kunar province, September 2012.
[49] I-11, a Taliban court judge, Logar province, 2013.

young woman's father decided to bring the case made appealing to the Taliban judge possible.

Conversely, whenever a case broke out into the public space, either because of an irremediable act (runaway lovers, homicides) or because of a complaint, Taliban judges often delivered the harshest verdicts. As we have seen, sexual relations outside marriage were particularly repressed and judges emphasized the deterrent aspect of public stoning as a punishment (see Chapter 7). In this respect, one of the reasons for the movement's rigour here was the popular acceptance of—and sometimes joining in—severe punishment for any deviant practice in marital and family relations. The case of Siddiqa and Khayyam in Kunduz, in which the girl's father allegedly made it possible for the Taliban to take up the case, which ended with the couple's stoning, illustrates the congruence of interests between maintaining a patriarchal authority within the family and the insurgency's assertion of sovereignty.[50] While the ban on music or the prescribed beard length caused discontent, the violent punishments of women manifestly were not protested by men—and women living in rural areas only had few means of challenging the social order. In a context where disputes, especially those involving the family's reputation, could escalate into violent conflicts, a collective punishment turned victims of stoning into convenient scapegoats.[51]

The violence of the sentences passed by the Taliban courts was part of a broader discourse drawing on a fantasized pre-war Afghanistan where such conflicts would not have occurred. A number of my male interlocutors—including those opposed to the Taliban—shared this idealized vision of a society in which family relations had been destabilized by the social and economic transformations linked to war and moral corruption imported from the West.[52] In talking with a notable in Andar province about the handling of cases of fornication by the Taliban court, he explained to me:

> Young people tend to form relationships by escaping the supervision of their parents, by calling each other on the phone. Running away is often a way for the boy and girl to force their family members, who are then stuck, to

[50] Torunn Wimpelmann, *The Pitfalls of Protection: Gender, Violence, and Power in Afghanistan*, Berkeley, University of California Press, 2017, pp. 141–51.

[51] Torunn Wimpelmann notes that while the stoning in Kunduz led to moral outrage from the regime's officials, they did not target the principle of stoning itself, but the summary nature of the investigation, the large size of the stones, and the fact that the Taliban were not a legitimate legal authority. Ibid., 147.

[52] In this connection, see Julie Billaud, *Kabul Carnival: Gender Politics in Postwar Afghanistan*, Philadelphia, University of Pennsylvania Press, 2015, pp. 111–46.

> accept their marriage and find a compromise. Families lose control of their children.[53]

The proliferation of mobile phones had provided a whole generation of young women and men with the chance to communicate out of earshot and unsupervised by other family members.[54] The expansion of education during the Western intervention also fed into such narratives of parents losing control of children.

Finally, the war and the tide of cash that it brought also led to rampant inflation in the bride price, making marriage out of reach financially for a large part of society. While discourses on the problematic nature of the bride price were highly consensual, unanimity on the subject had not ended this practice and the considerable increase in the sums that had to be raised. The same notable from Andar explained:

> The bride price doubled in five years. Before people paid between $4,000 and $8,000, now you have to raise between $8,000 and $16,000, buy gold, other things in the city to give to the girl, which is new and not traditional. Before the war, with 1,000 dollars, it was possible to find a woman. Some women reach the age of thirty without getting married. The common solution is to exchange girls, but when you don't have a daughter to marry off, you have to find another solution. [. . .] A father I knew had to pay $18,000 to get a wife for his son. He had to mortgage all his land and what's on it.[55]

The Taliban thus made themselves popular by capping the bride price, for example at $3,800 in 2010 in Kapisa province, where it sometimes might reach $20,000.[56] As for Andar, the same notable concluded:

> The Taliban limited the bride price in the province to $6,000, in accord with the local religious scholars and elders. But the same mullahs are demanding more money for their own daughters and the Taliban have not punished these people. Some Taliban even participated in this violation of their own rules.[57]

[53] E-61, a notable of Andar district (Ghazni), September 2014.
[54] For cases, see Torunn Wimpelmann, *The Pitfalls of Protection: Gender, Violence, and Power in Afghanistan*, Berkeley, University of California Press, 2017, p. 133.
[55] E-61, a notable in Andar district (Ghazni), September 2014.
[56] 'Taleban Try Hearts-and-Minds Tactics', *Institute for War and Peace Reporting*, 8 September 2010.
[57] E-61, a notable of Andar district (Ghazni), September 2014.

Thus, even if the insurgency's ability to transform society through the application of Islamic law was limited, its vision of society emerged from the sum of its judgments. It was a vision characterized by moral rigorism and social conservatism linked to the movement's genesis and the social norms prevailing in the South. In keeping with their practices of the 1990s, these decisions were intended to preserve—that is, to reproduce—property rights and the patriarchal structure of the family. They also legitimized the rise of the religious, who universalized their particular interests by presenting themselves as the guarantors of social peace. The resumption of the historical elements of their political agenda was accompanied by the easing of the moral order—except when it came to gender relations. This formed part of the—limited—deference to international standards and widespread social demands for education, health, and development.

Conclusion

The internationalization of law in civil war

The role of the courts in the 2021 Taliban victory attest to the force of law in civil wars. Even more than in peaceful contexts, the objectivization of social relations in juridical institutions is essential to having judges recognized as such. Through recruiting, erecting an institutional architecture, instituting procedures, and employing coercion, the Taliban insurgency established mechanisms for maintaining the impartiality of its judges and conditioning the acceptance of their verdicts.

Two distinctive features that set the Taliban apart from other insurgent movements are the priority given to delivering justice and the recruitment of its judges from among the graduates of the Deobandi madrasas in the Afghan-Pakistan border region. This recruitment strategy provided the Taliban with personnel who possessed pre-established legal competence was widely recognized in the countryside. Thanks to the dual membership of Taliban judges in the religious and the juridical fields, the insurgency was able to legitimize verdicts that might have been disputed, considering they had been issued by members of an armed movement. By relying on an independent educational authority like the Deobandi madrasas, the Taliban partially alleviated the difficulties of recognizing legal competence in a war context. They could counter the suspicion that political affiliations would determine legal acts with personnel certified as qualified in Islamic law by outside institutions recognized in the religious field and, more generally, in Afghan society.

Next, this study refutes the dominant perception of the Taliban in the literature as fragmented, as an aggregate of local and tribal interests, failing to account for the integration of the courts into a hierarchy of institutions. Mechanisms for rotating judges, monitoring their practices, and appealing their judgments ensured that they would remain outsiders with respect to the social issues within their jurisdiction. However, the centralization of the Taliban judicial system depended in the first place on the degree of control they exerted over a territory and therefore this court system remained vulnerable to

The Taliban Courts in Afghanistan. Adam Baczko, Oxford University Press. © Adam Baczko 2023.
DOI: 10.1093/oso/9780198896777.003.0012

military setbacks. In addition, the stakes of the war limited the independence of judges. Repeated interference by the movement's executive bodies was a reminder that political objectives took priority in a context of constant tension between immediate necessities and the advantage of fielding a legitimate judicial system.

Finally, rudimentary but predictable procedures framed the practices of Taliban judges from the moment they received a complaint to the point at which they handed down a verdict. The methods of securing access to judges were largely constrained by the clandestinity necessitated by the operations of Western Special Forces. Nevertheless, the movement's extensive network in rural areas ensures the accessibility of the judges. The adherence to established procedures also played a pivotal role in securing recognition for the justice system among its users and the wider public. It was on this foundation that the force of law operated and that a conflict brought before a Taliban court could be distilled into a case involving only the parties recognized and sanctioned by the judge. In a war where private disputes were easily instrumentalized and overlapped with broader social issues, due process reduced conflicts to the legally recognized object of the litigation.

The ideological consistency of the Taliban was evident in their verdicts, which underpinned a vision of society that they promoted even before they took power. Their enforcement enabled Taliban judges to influence day-to-day practices and thus participate in the production of an alternative social order. In the regions under their jurisdiction, they guaranteed property, favoured the rise of the religious, implemented an identity regime akin to that of the pre-war period, and reinforced the power of the male in the domestic sphere. Thus, under the guise of deciding private conflicts, the formalization of the judicial system permitted the installation of a social order that diverged from that of the official authorities in Kabul.

The Taliban case shows how the articulation between law and violence naturalizes domination. Users of Taliban courts valued coercion when the judgment to be enforced was regarded as fair. Here we encounter a classic idea from the philosophy of law developed by Pascal, Rousseau, or Kant. 'Justice without force is powerless; force without justice is tyrannical' writes Pascal. The articulation between law and violence relates to the underpinnings of domination, to the necessity of legitimizing the use of coercion to ensure the sustainability of social order. The Taliban thus packaged their authority as an expression of the public good more than as rule by ulama. Even as civil war leads to a radical questioning of its legitimacy, the law becomes, more than ever, a necessary resource for dominance.

The efficacy of the Taliban courts was inseparable from the legal uncertainty caused by decades of armed conflict and Western intervention. Indeed, Afghans rated the Taliban courts by comparing them to the practices of the regime and international operators. In a zero-sum game, the recognition of the authority of Taliban judges was inversely related to that of the regime's magistrates. The value placed on insurgent judges by the rural population carried an implicit critique of the government's judicial system and the effects of the international intervention. People described the Taliban courts as more accessible and predictable, but also feared that their verdicts were not durable. Judgments therefore created an interest—even for the losing parties—in having the Taliban continue in power. However, the existence of an internationally recognized state in Kabul limited the insurgency's ability to sustain its judicial decisions, and the implementation of its verdicts ultimately depended on maintaining its territorial grip, a preoccupation that was ended by the takeover of the country in 2021.

Contemporary civil wars such as the war in Afghanistan are a laboratory for law and politics: a space and a time when norms are tested and reinvented. In this *sui generis* environment, legal categories and institutions are born of interactions between governments, the armed movements that challenge them, transnational operators, international institutions, and customary bodies. While social scientists have long established that the state is not the only producer of law, it remains widely regarded as an essential intermediary for implementing international norms and the source of national laws. Civil wars, which are radical challenges to the central authority, allow us to question the production of law in renewed ways.

The Taliban courts show that civil wars are not internal conflicts, but international phenomena. Far from the common intuition of a pre-eminence of local modes of regulation in civil wars, the Afghan case suggests that, on the contrary, they are characterized by an increased influence of the international system on the modes of organization and exercise of the law by the warring parties. Legal practices appear to be dependent on the international system both directly thanks to the involvement of foreign countries or transnational institutions (International Criminal Court, United Nations, World Bank, International Monetary Fund, International Committee of the Red Cross), but also indirectly due to the constraints imposed by international law. Paradoxically, while prosecutions by international courts, starting with the ICC, have met with mixed results, their actions, together with those by the United Nations and Western powers, strongly influenced the combatants' practices.[1] The sharp reaction of the United States to the opening of an investigation

[1] In the case of Sierra Leone and Liberia in the 1990s, Mariane Ferme and Danny Hoffman show the adaptation of fighting practices to international interventions. See Mariane Ferme and Daniel

into war crimes in Afghanistan that would include crimes committed by US military officials confirms that its effects are not merely anecdotal.

Contrary to the idea that international norms do not apply in civil wars, they in fact constrain the action of the warring parties. The Taliban, a movement ostracized by the international system for hosting Al Qaeda, adapted their practices to international law and engaged with organizations that implement it (ICRC, UN). Although it did not formally recognize international humanitarian law or the Universal Declaration of Human Rights, the movement regularly adopted their vocabulary and principles by justifying them in the light of Islamic law. It also cooperated with the United Nations in counting civilian casualties and in the investigations aimed at attributing responsibility for this violence. This taking into account of international norms is recurrent among armed movements, such as the PYD (Democratic Union Party), which affirms its respect for the rights of women and minorities in all its official documents, a reiteration of the human rights agenda in a campaign to obtain recognition of its de facto legal authority in northeast Syria.

Vice versa, strategies for violating international humanitarian law implicitly reveal the effectiveness of these standards. Perpetrating abuses is a strategy that paid off for armed groups in the Congo or Mali when their brutalizing of civilians garnered them invitations to the negotiating table.[2] Even one of the few movements that totally rejected the international system, the Islamic State, confirmed the prominence of these norms through the offences that its militants publicized to *mark* their breaking with them (cutting the throats of prisoners of war, enslaving civilians, committing sexual abuse). Also evidencing the importance of international norms is the Israeli army's initiative of setting up a legal department to mitigate the legal consequences of violations of international law by its soldiers. These jurists, who cynically call themselves 'anarchists against the law',[3] were inspired by the critical approaches to law developed in the United States in the 1970s to devise legal countermeasures and eventually transform jurisprudence.[4]

Hoffman, 'Hunter Militias and the International Human Rights Discourse in Sierra Leone and Beyond', *Africa Today*, vol. 50, n° 4, pp. 72–95; Danny Hoffman, 'The Civilian Target in Sierra Leone and Liberia: Political Power, Military Strategy, and Humanitarian Intervention', *African Affairs*, 2004, vol. 103, n° 411, pp. 211–26.

[2] Séverine Autesserre, 'Dangerous Tales: Dominant Narratives on the Congo and their Unintended Consequences', *African Affairs*, 2012, vol. 111, n° 443, p. 217; Denia Chebli, 'Cette paix qui divise: Une analyse de la médiation au Mali par ses effets', *Critique internationale*, 2020, n° 88, pp. 9–30.

[3] The phrase 'anarchists against the law' hijacks the 'anarchists against the wall' name of an activist group opposed to the construction of the separation wall in Israel.

[4] Eyal Weizman, *The Least of All Possible Evils: Humanitarian Violence from Arendt to Gaza*, New York, Verso Books, 2011. In 2005, Lisa Hajjar had already shown that '[t]he *[Israeli]* military court system also

Civil wars thus appear as a privileged space for reconfigurations of the law led by the major powers and international organizations since the end of the Cold War, but also for local actors reclaiming these norms. Civil wars are the theatre of a radical form of internationalizing the law, for the disordered entanglement of norms and jurisdictions due to armed competition between different belligerents claiming a legal monopoly.[5] Involvement in the law by transnational actors, extreme in Afghanistan, could also be observed in Somalia following the intervention under a United Nations mandate of 1992, in the Democratic Republic of the Congo with the involvement of multiple foreign countries since 1996, in Côte d'Ivoire after 2002, in Iraq after the 2003 invasion, or in Mali since the 2013 French intervention.[6] These external interventions, whether under United Nations mandate or not, were supported and led by a complex web of transnational organizations and operators specializing in 'legal reform', 'legal training', and 'legal capacity building'. The same actors involved in Afghanistan are found in other civil wars, interacting with the regime or insurgency as the case may be. Private companies like Checchi and Company Consulting, Adam Smith International, and Chemonics, among others, which were engaged in the juridical field in Afghanistan, are also on the ground in Mali, Ukraine, Syria, and Libya. The International Development Law Organization, the subcontractor of the Italian legal assistance mission, conducts programmes in Mali, Libya, Somalia, and Yemen.

The involvement of the same actors in various civil wars fosters the flow of people and ideas.[7] The reinvention of custom is a paradigmatic case because of the paradox that underlies it: transnational organizations promoting the establishment of traditional bodies claim to take local norms into consideration while applying Western legal concepts and practices. For example, in 2009, the United States Institute for Peace, the US State Department agency that

has been a setting for the deployment of legal strategies and the cultivation of legal discourses to contend with the conflict'. Lisa Hajjar, *Courting Conflict: The Israeli Military Court System in the West Bank and Gaza*, Berkeley, University of California Press, 2005, pp. 2–3.

5 Mireille Delmas-Marty, *Ordering Pluralism. A Conceptual Framework for Understanding the Transnational Legal World*, London, Hart Publishing, 2009.

6 Roland Marchal and Christine Messiant underlined the entanglement between interstate, national, and local conflicts through the concept of 'system of wars'. Roland Marchal and Christine Messiant, 'Une lecture symptomale de quelques théorisations récentes des guerres civiles', *Lusotopie*, 2006, vol. XIII, n° 2, pp. 45–46. For an analysis of how these different scales were entangled in the Ivorian civil war, see Richard Banégas and Ruth Marshall-Fratani (eds), 'La Côte d'Ivoire en guerre: Dynamiques du dedans et du dehors', *Politique africaine*, 2003, n° 89, pp. 5–11.

7 Sandrine Lefranc, 'Du droit à la paix: La circulation des techniques internationales de pacification par le bas', *Actes de la recherche en sciences sociales*, 2008, n° 174, pp. 4–13; Sara Dezalay, 'Des droits de l'homme au marché du développement: Note de recherche sur le champ faible de la gestion de conflits armés', *Actes de la recherche en sciences sociales*, 2008, n° 174, pp. 68–79.

promoted neotraditional councils in Afghanistan, organized a conference in Washington headlined as *Customary Justice and Legal Pluralism in War-Torn Societies*. In the book that it spawned, researchers and development experts uniformly affirmed the need to refrain from imposing a model of formal justice specific to the West, but to rely instead on the customary norms more familiar to people.[8] In fact, in Afghanistan as elsewhere, the promotion of customary justice justified the importation of mediation mechanisms and bodies in use in North America and Europe since the 1980s, fuelling the 'globalization of informal law' that anthropologist Laura Nader noted in the late 1990s.[9]

This internationalization of law is obvious when considering the central issues in the struggle between juridical systems within each civil war, particularly the recurrent focus on Islamism following the attacks of 9/11.[10] Negotiations that began in 2018 under US auspices exposed the scant ideological differences between the Afghan belligerents as to the foundation of the legal system or women's rights. Between 2001 and 2014, Western intervention, justified by the fight against Islamic terrorism and for women's emancipation, exerted significant pressure. This pressure prompted the former mujahideen on the regime side to soften their positions, while the Taliban—who were not always recognized as a political movement—were relegated to religious fundamentalism. In practice, with the prospect of the complete withdrawal of American troops, the introduction of sharia law appeared to meet with a consensus among the conflicting parties. In the last years prior to the country's fall to the Taliban in August 2021, the regime's leaders engaged in a race to demonstrate religious rigor, although this had little impact on preventing the eventual takeover.

Similarly, in the Syrian civil war, competition between legal actors revolved around the application of Islamic law and its modalities. The Syrian regime, which referred to the war as a fight against Islamist terrorism, emphasized the secular nature of its juridical system (although in reality Islamic law applies to issues of personal status). Similarly, the PYD, seeking support in Europe and North America, showcased the secular nature of its law and earned support in the name of the fight against Al Qaeda and the Islamic State. The Syrian insurgency, hoping for help from both the West and the Gulf countries, highlighted

[8] Deborah Isser, *Customary Justice and the Rule of Law in War-torn Societies*, Washington, US Institute of Peace Press, 2011.

[9] Laura Nader, 'The Globalization of Law: ADR as "Soft" Technology', *Proceedings of the Annual Meeting (American Society of International Law)*, 1999, vol. 93, pp. 304–11.

[10] More broadly, this dynamic is a resource for some countries, which therefore frame their suppression of dissent as a fight against a terrorist movement, for example Russia or Pakistan in the 2000s. Kim Lane Scheppele, 'Le droit de la sécurité internationale: Le terrorisme et l'empire sécuritaire de l'après-11 Septembre 2001', *Actes de la recherche en sciences sociales*, 2008, n° 173, pp. 28–43.

its codification work, while affirming the Islamic inspiration of its law. In contrast, the Islamic State, at odds with all the world and regional powers, claimed the purity of its Islamic law as opposed to the falsity of the modes of application of other movements and regimes claiming to be Islamic. Similarly, in Mali, the application of Islamic law and the characterization of 'Islamist' constituted one of the barriers to bringing certain armed groups into the negotiation process sponsored by France and the United Nations. As in Afghanistan, the action of international powers in Syria and Mali fuelled the struggle over the law and thus, in times of war, its strategic character.

Afghanistan, where modern forms of Western humanitarianism and political Islam developed in the 1980s and 1990s, occupies a defining place in the tangled history of these antagonistic transnationalisms.[11] By reviving an armed conflict that ended up lasting more than four decades, the 2001 military intervention accelerated the revolutionary dynamic that has made that country a stage for contemporary reconfigurations of law. Although the Taliban took over the country and the war is now over, Afghanistan shows itself to be a young society (half the population is under the age of eighteen) that is more globalized than ever and open to cultural forms and ideological currents from the Indian subcontinent, the West, and the Middle East. The emergence of a local branch of the Islamic State in 2014 suggests that the succession of revolutions experienced by the Afghan people is far from over. For the thirty million Afghans, these upheavals have placed them in a no-win situation: struggling to survive in a country devastated by violence or suffering the agonies of exile in a world that has become inhospitable to them.

[11] For an argument along these lines concerning Bosnia-Herzegovina, see Darryl Li, *The Universal Enemy: Jihad, Empire, and the Challenge of Solidarity*, Stanford, Stanford University Press, 2019.

APPENDICES

Methodology

This research follows a qualitative methodology (formal interviews, informal discussions, and direct observations) adapted to the constraints posed by the armed conflict.[1] Every year, between 2010 and 2016, I sojourned in Afghanistan for one to three months of fieldwork, conducting interviews in Kunar, Nangarhar, Laghman, Paktya, Kandahar, Ghazni, and Kunduz provinces in the East, South, and North. The journeys and stays, even when short, raised logistical and security concerns. Thus, my navigating from one network of sociability to another could not be left to chance encounters in the face of the suspicion, mistrust, and legitimate fears of the people I met with. Several key interlocutors opened their networks to me and reassured my respondents that I had no political axe to grind.[2] All presented the same profile of straddlers: respectively from Kabul, Kunar, Kandahar, and Ghazni provinces, they were enrolled in kinship and proximity networks relating them to the Taliban movement. However, their individual paths were disrupted by the 2001 intervention, which also put them into contact with its various operators (humanitarians, journalists, military, development agencies). Thus, I could navigate from one region to the next with the necessary precautions, trying to escape notice (clothing, beard, modes of travel, choice of houses in which I stayed) when travelling in the areas held by the insurgency. My repeated stays then allowed me to establish relationships of trust and to compensate for some of the prejudicial effects related to being coopted in one network due to the constraints on movement.[3] Moreover, these long-term relationships compensated

[1] For similar methodologies, see Jeffrey Sluka, 'Participant Observation in Violent Social Contexts', *Human Organization*, 1990, vol. 49, n° 2, pp. 114–26; Koen Vlassenroot, 'War and Social Research: The Limits of Empirical Methodologies in War-Torn Environments', *Civilisations*, 2006, n° 54, pp. 191–8.

[2] While research assistance or collaboration is a recurring feature of many long-term research projects, it is rarely addressed in scientific works. For an exception, see Townsend Middleton and Jason Cons (eds), 'Special issue on Fieldwork(ers): Research Assistants, Researchers, and the Production of Ethnographic Knowledge', *Ethnography*, 2014, vol. 15, n° 3.

[3] Jean-Pierre Olivier de Sardan, *Epistemology, Fieldwork, and Anthropology*, New York, Palgrave Macmillan, 2015.

for the gaps in my language proficiency. Despite my efforts to learn Persian, the frequent use of Pashto in the South and East, as well as surveys in other countries, gave me limited working proficiency that sufficed strictly for casual use. While I was able to check the translations during the interviews, conducting them was beyond me. In this respect, the chance of being able to benefit from interpreting by people I worked with from year to year was decisive.

In addition to the informal discussions that made possible the deeper insights essential to contextualize discourses and observations, I recorded in notebooks many interviews that I conducted; 137 of these I quote in the book. I use them to provide elements of information (description of an institution, personal career paths) and to convey points of view (ideological commitment, subjective perception of a situation). They comprise an empirical body of material simultaneously providing conflict cases, a general panorama of the functioning of the Taliban courts, as well as of how people perceived them. In particular, I conducted many long, detailed interviews with Taliban court users and the population of the areas administered by the insurgency. Interviews with members of the Taliban, including judges, required particularly complicated logistics and flexibility in the questions posed to my often suspicious contacts. To ease the discussions, the interviews with judges focused on courtroom techniques, Islamic jurisprudence, and the description of cases dealt with: in other words, subjects perceived as non-political.

My participation in two studies on Taliban justice allowed me to enrich my data and verify variations in my results by province. As the Taliban juridical system became of interest to intervention actors (see Chapter 3), Antonio Guistozzi invited me to collaborate with him on two studies sponsored by Integrity Watch Afghanistan and Samuel Hall.[4] I helped design the semi-structured questionnaires that were then used by Afghan investigators to interview the Taliban judges, Taliban commanders, notables, and court users throughout the country. This corpus, which gave me access to the discourse of a much greater number of people, also had a limitation stemming from the need to delegate these interviews: the questions were fixed, preventing me from revisiting or deepening a particular point. I also lacked the insights gained from

[4] Antonio Giustozzi, Claudio Franco, and Adam Baczko, *Shadow Justice*, Kabul, Integrity Watch Afghanistan, 2012; Antonio Giustozzi and Adam Baczko, 'The Politics of the Taliban's Shadow Judiciary, 2003–2013', *Central Asian Affairs*, 2014, vol. 1, n° 2, pp. 199–224; *Gender & Justice Study: Obstacles to Justice*, Kabul, World Bank/Samuel Hall, 2014. This last report was never disseminated—in the run-up to the 2014 presidential elections and the withdrawal of Western troops, the World Bank considered the report's findings too sensitive.

observation before, during, and after an interview, which can be crucial for placing discourses within their proper context. Nevertheless, interviews with respondents who had also been interviewed for the other two studies allowed me to cross-check their validity; and, more generally, I saw my information on the functioning of the Taliban courts confirmed, albeit with some regional variations. Thus, *integrated into* my fieldwork and *triangulated* by my own interviews, the corpus of outsourced interviews (coded differently because of how they were realized—see the Table of interviews) allowed me to verify how systematically court procedures were applied in other areas controlled by the Taliban.

The fieldwork led to some frustrations and disappointments. Chief among these was not having the chance to sit in on a Taliban court hearing and of observing the judges in their daily lives. On two occasions, my presence at a trial was approved and then cancelled at the last minute due to military operations in the area. The facts concerning practices during hearings therefore were gleaned from interviews, confirmed by the rare pictures available. This limitation leads to my smoothing the hesitations and contradictions that are a feature in all trials. It also prevents me from anchoring the Taliban's judicial process in the course of a single conflict and in the social relations that it brings into play more broadly. Furthermore, I was unable to conduct interviews with women living in rural areas; the few interviews I cite were conducted by Afghan investigators.[5] I have tried to take this important bias of my corpus into account in analysing my data, focusing more on highlighting the position of women as a stake, as revealed in male discourse, their experiences remaining inaccessible to me.

Despite these difficulties and setbacks, the fieldwork proved vital. Due to access difficulties, it is now increasingly common to approach armed conflicts from a distance, either from the outside or by focusing on past violence.[6] However, beyond the collection of data, the fieldwork was essential for discovering the importance of the Taliban court and formulating the sociological problem they posed. It was also a most fertile time for theoretical work, during which I formulated the main hypotheses that underlie my argument, hypotheses that I was able to refine and confront with various local

[5] The impossibility of a man interviewing women in rural areas was already a given before the war. Surveys of Afghan women have always been conducted by female researchers. See the literature review on the issue by Robert Canfield, 'Reviews', *Iranian Studies*, 2004, vol. 37, n° 2, pp. 323–33.

[6] For such approaches, see Antonius Robben (ed.), *Iraq at a Distance: What Anthropologists Can Teach Us about the War*, Philadelphia, University of Pennsylvania Press, 2011; Chowra Makaremi, 'États d'urgence ethnographiques: Approches empiriques de la violence politique', *Cultures & Conflits*, 2016, vol. 103–4, pp. 15–34.

configurations.[7] Even the vagaries, constraints, and limitations we have discussed turned into events the analysis of which shed additional light on the subject.[8] Thus, while my key interlocutors were constantly assessing their ability to guarantee my safety during travel and stays, I could observe between 2010 and 2016 the evolution of what they considered feasible or not. The drastic reduction of possibilities from 2014 onwards (when even simple trips or short stays entailed great difficulties) constituted the best barometer of the war's intensification, making the fall of Kabul a predictable result even while the dwindling media coverage suggested otherwise.

[7] Daniel Bizeul, 'Que faire des expériences d'enquête? Apports et fragilité de l'observation directe', *Revue française de science politique*, 2007, vol. 57, n° 1, pp. 69–89; Lisa Wedeen, 'Reflections on Ethnographic Work in Political Science', *Annual Review of Political Science*, 2010, vol. 13, n° 1, pp. 255–72; Jean Copans, 'L'appel de la théorie: Le terrain le plus difficile', *Civilisations*, 2015, vol. 64, n° 1, pp. 165–75; Adam Baczko, Gilles Dorronsoro, and Arthur Quesnay, 'The Epistemological Privilege of Fieldwork: A Collective Investigation in War-Torn Syria', *Bulletin of Sociological Methodology*, vol. 151, n° 1, 2021, pp. 96–116.

[8] Olivier Grojean, 'Les aléas d'un terrain comme révélateurs de sa structuration: Gestion et objectivation d'une relation d'enquête sur une mouvance radicale et transnationale', *Revue internationale de politique comparée*, 2010, vol. 17, n° 4, pp. 63–76; Adèle Blazquez, 'Ethnographie d'un contexte violent (Sinaloa, Mexique): L'immanence de l'enquête', *Monde commun*, 2018, n° 1, pp. 188–205.

Table of interviews

The interviews are listed according to two different codings: 'E' refers to interviews conducted as part of my field investigations; 'I' to semi-structured interviews conducted through Afghan interviewers. For security reasons, I anonymize my interlocutors, and those I name are public figures whose words reported in the book concern the 1980s and 1990s and do not put them in harm's way.[1]

Code	Interview Date	Interview Location	Position
E-1	August 2010	Kandahar	Militia commander in Dand district, Kandahar
E-2	April 2013	Kabul	Senior leader of the Taliban movement
E-3	July 2011	Kunar	Former US Army supplier
E-4	July 2010	Kabul	Employee of a private company conducting the civil-military component of the American counterinsurgency in the East
E-5	September 2012	Kabul	Director of UNAMA's Human Rights Department
E-6	July 2010 April 2013	Kunar	Resident of Ghaziabad district, Taliban court user
E-7	April 2013	Kunar	Judge of a Taliban court in Kunar
E-8	August 2015	Nangarhar	Resident of Shirzad district (Nangarhar)
E-9	April 2011	Kabul	Resident of Khas Uruzgan district (Uruzgan)

[1] Research in an area of armed conflict calls for particular attention to its ethical implications, from fieldwork to publication. Jonathan Goodhand, 'Research in Conflict Zones: Ethics and Accountability', *Forced Migration Review*, 2000, vol. 8, pp. 12–15; Elisabeth Wood, 'The Ethical Challenges of Field Research in Conflict Zones', *Qualitative Sociology*, 2006, vol. 29, nº 3, pp. 373–86.

Code	Interview Date	Interview Location	Position
E-10	April 2011	Laghman	Resident of Alishang district (Laghman)
E-11	September 2012	Kabul	Resident of Kajaki district (Helmand)
E-12	August 2015	Nangarhar	Notable, Mohamad Dara district (Nangarhar)
E-13	September 2012	Ghazni	Notable, Andar district (Ghazni)
E-14	May 2013	Kabul	Elder, Baraki Barak district, Logar province
E-15	July 2010	Kabul	Professor of Constitutional Law, consultant for Checchi and Company Consulting
E-16	April 2013	Kunar	Resident of Kunar province
E-17	August 2010	Kandahar	Former NDS agent, executive of a private Afghan security company
E-18	July 2011	Kunar	Elected official from Kunar province
E-19	July 2011	Kandahar	Notable of Arghandab district (Kandahar)
E-20	July 2011	Kunar	Kunar resident, trader
E-21	July 2011	Kabul	Analyst of an Afghan think tank
E-22	July 2011	Kandahar	Taliban fighter
E-23	May 2013	Kabul	UNAMA political officer in charge of electoral issues
E-24	September 2014	Kabul	Senior official of the Afghan mission of Doctors Without Borders
E-25	September 2014	Kabul	Director of an Afghan NGO
E-26	May 2013	Kabul	Cleric regularly sitting in *jirgas* (Logar)
E-27	July 2010	Kabul	Afghan translator for US Special Forces between 2003 and 2007
E-28	September 2014	Kabul	Expert from an Afghan anti-corruption NGO
E-29	September 2014	Ghazni	Journalist in the city of Ghazni

Code	Interview Date	Interview Location	Position
E-30	May 2013	Kabul	Taliban judge in Mohamad Agha district (Logar)
E-31	July 2010 July 2011 September 2012	Kunar	Notable in Kunar province
E-32	July 2010	Kunar	US Officer, Rural Development Program Manager for the Provincial Reconstruction Team in Asadabad, Kunar
E-33	September 2014	Ghazni	Assitant to the governor of Ghazni province
E-34	September 2012	Kunduz	Landowner in Kunduz province
E-35	August 2015	Nangarhar	Notable in Achin district (Nangarhar)
E-36	September 2014	Ghazni	Taliban court user in Andar district (Ghazni)
E-37	July 2010 July 2011 September 2012 September 2014	Kunar	Resident of Kunar province
E-38	September 2014	Kunduz	Employee of a private company conducting the US counterinsurgency in the North
E-39	July 2010	Kabul	UNAMA's head in the Southeast
E-40	August 2015	Kunar	Resident of Kunar province
E-41	July 2011	Kunar	Head of the Kunar Provincial Council
E-42	September 2014	Paktya	UNAMA Afghan analyst specializing in Paktika province
E-43	May 2013	Kabul	Cleric residing in Logar province
E-44	September 2014	Kunar	Resident of Kunar province
E-45	August 2015	Nangarhar	Jalalabad University student, resident in Shirzad district (Nangarhar)

Code	Interview Date	Interview Location	Position
E-46	September 2014	Paktya	Head of UNAMA's human rights department in the Southeast
E-47	September 2012	Kunar	Resident of Kunar province
E-48	July 2011	Kabul	European officer attached to ISAF command
E-49	September 2012	Kabul	Consultant for Adam Smith International at the Afghan Ministry of Justice
E-50	September 2014	Ghazni	President of the Ghazni Provincial Council
E-51	August 2010	Kandahar	Analyst of an Afghan think tank
E-52	September 2012	Kabul	US Special Forces officer
E-53	April 2013	Kunar	Resident of Ghaziabad district (Kunar)
E-54	July 2011	Kandahar	Senior local government official in Kandahar province
E-55	May 2013	Ghazni	Judge of a Taliban Trial Court, Ghazni province
E-56	September 2014	Kunar	Resident of Kunar province
E-57	April 2011	Laghman	Veterinarian in Laghman province
E-58	September 2014	Kabul	United Nations political officer working with ISAF
E-59	September 2012 April 2013	Kunar	Resident of Nari district (Kunar)
E-60	April 2013	Kandahar	Taliban commander in Kandahar province
E-61	September 2014	Ghazni	Notable in Andar district (Ghazni)
E-62	July 2011	Kandahar	Senior Kandahar Provincial Administration official
E-63	May 2013	Ghazni	Judge of a Taliban court, Ghazni province
E-64	September 2014	Paktya	UNAMA Afghan analyst specializing in Paktya province
E-65	August 2010	Kandahar	Afghan translator for the US Army between 2002 and 2006

Code	Interview Date	Interview Location	Position
E-66	August 2010	Kabul	Head of programme for the Aga Khan Foundation
E-67	September 2014	Ghazni	Notable in Ghazni province
E-68	April 2011	Laghman	Notable in Alingar district (Laghman)
E-69	April 2013	Kabul	Taliban cadre, inspector of courts for Command Council
E-70	April 2013	Kabul	UNAMA political officer
E-71	September 2012	Kabul	Abdul Wahid Baghran's political representative in Kabul
E-72	May 2013	Kabul	Taliban court user in Mohamad Agha district (Logar)
E-73	August 2015	Kunar	mullah residing in Kunar province
E-74	August 2010	Kandahar	Notable in Maywand district (Kandahar)
E-75	May 2013	Ghazni	Vice-head of education for the Taliban in Ghazni province, director of madrasa
E-76	September 2014	Ghazni	Second-in-command of the Afghan Local Police in Andar district (Ghazni), Hizb-i Islami activist
E-77	September 2014	Paktya	UNAMA Afghan analyst specializing in Khost province
E-78	September 2014	Ghazni	Taliban court user in Andar district (Ghazni)
E-79	September 2012 April 2013 September 2014	Kabul Ghazni	Resident of Ghazni province
E-80	September 2012	Kabul	Senior official of Madera
E-81	August 2015	Nangarhar	Notable resident in Achin district (Nangarhar)
Alain de Bures	April 2011	Nangarhar	Humanitarian zootechnician working in Afghanistan since the 1980s

Code	Interview Date	Interview Location	Position
Mawlawi Mohamad Qalamuddin	July 2011	Kabul	Minister of the Promotion of Virtue and the Prevention of Vice during the Islamic Emirate of Afghanistan
Hyder Akbar	July 2010	Kunar	Son of the governor of Kunar province *sayid* Faizal Akbar
Khial Mohamad	September 2012	Ghazni	Deputy to Qari baba, governor of Ghazni under the Taliban
Shah Jahan Noori	September 2012	Kabul	Commander allied with Qari Baba during the 1980s, MP
Mohammed Osman Tariq	September 2012	Kabul	Cleric, a Foreign Ministry official during the Islamic Emirate of Afghanistan
Abdul Malik	September 2012	Ghazni	Son of Qari Baba
Mullah Wazir	September 2012	Ghazni	Commander for Qari Baba
Ali Amiri	September 2012	Ghazni	Political secretary of the Mohaqiq branch of Hizb-i Wahdat
Mualim Aziz	September 2012	Ghazni	School principal in Kabul, intellectual
I-1	2011	N/A	Judge of a Taliban Appeals Court, Nahrin district (Baghlan)
I-2	2011	N/A	Judge of a Taliban Appeals Court, Karagai district (Laghman)
I-3	2011	N/A	Judge of a Taliban Trial Court, Ab Kamari district (Badghis)
I-4	2011	N/A	Judge of a Taliban Appeals Court, Dahan-i Ghuri district (Baghlan)
I-5	2011	N/A	Judge of a Taliban TrialCourt, Karagai district (Laghman)
I-6	2011	N/A	Judge of a Taliban Trial Court, Qala-i Naw district (Badghis)
I-7	2013	N/A	Judge of a Taliban court, Logar province
I-8	2011	N/A	Judge of a Taliban TrialCourt, Dushi district (Baghlan)

Code	Interview Date	Interview Location	Position
I-9	2011	N/A	Judge of a Taliban court, Dawlat Abad district (Faryab)
I-10	2011	N/A	Judge of a Taliban Trial Court, Tala wa Barfak district (Baghlan)
I-11	2013	N/A	Judge of a Taliban court, Logar province
I-12	2011	N/A	Judge of a Taliban Trial Court, Nahrin district (Baghlan)
I-13	2011	N/A	Head of the Military Commission, Laghman province
I-14	2011	N/A	Judge of a Taliban Trial Court, Alingar district (Laghman)
I-15	2011	N/A	Judge of a Taliban Appeals Court, Qala-i Naw district (Badghis)
I-16	2013	N/A	Notable, Mohamad Agha District (Logar)
I-17	2011	N/A	Judge of a Taliban Appeals Court, Dushi district (Baghlan)
I-18	2011	N/A	Judge of a Taliban Appeals Court, Alingar district (Laghman)
I-19	2011	N/A	Judge of a Taliban TrialCourt, Alishang district (Laghman)
I-20	2011	N/A	Judge of a Taliban court, Qarabagh district (Ghazni)
I-21	2011	N/A	Judge of a Taliban Trial Court, Ghormach district (Badghis)
I-22	2011	N/A	Judge of a Taliban Appeals Court, Ghormach district (Badghis)
I-23	2011	N/A	Judge of a Taliban Trial, Dahan-i Ghuri district (Baghlan)
I-24	2013	N/A	Judge of a Taliban court, Logar province
I-25	2011	N/A	Judge of a Taliban Appeals Court, Bala Mughab district (Badghis)
I-26	2011	N/A	Judge of a Taliban Appeals Court, Alishang district (Laghman)

Code	Interview Date	Interview Location	Position
I-27	2011	N/A	Judge of a Taliban court in Arghandab district (Kandahar)
I-28	2011	N/A	Notable of Dawlat Abad district (Faryab)
I-29	2011	N/A	Resident of Zhari district (Kandahar)
I-30	2013	N/A	Resident of Azra district (Logar)
I-31	2011	N/A	Resident of Qarabagh district (Ghazni)
I-32	2011	N/A	Resident of Sayid Abad district (Wardak)
I-33	2011	N/A	Resident of Sayid Abad district (Wardak)
I-34	2013	N/A	Cleric of Baraki Barak district (Logar)
I-35	2013	N/A	Woman Resident of Charkh district (Logar)
I-36	2011	N/A	Resident of Qarabagh district (Ghazni)
I-37	2013	N/A	Resident of Baraki Barak district (Logar)
I-38	2013	N/A	Resident of Mohamad Agha district (Logar)
I-39	2011	N/A	Resident of Arghandab district (Kandahar)
I-40	2011	N/A	Resident of Arghandab district (Kandahar)
I-41	2011	N/A	Shopkeeper, resident of Arghandab district (Kandahar)
I-42	2011	N/A	Resident of Zhari district (Kandahar)
I-43	2013	N/A	Notable of Baraki Barak district (Logar)
I-44	2011	N/A	Resident of Panjwai district (Kandahar)

Chronology

April 1978	coup d'état of the PDPA
December 1979	Soviet intervention in Afghanistan
August 1980	a million Afghan refugees in Pakistan
May 1981	millions of Afghan refugees in Pakistan
February 1989	last Soviet troops withdraw from Afghanistan
April 1992	capture of Kabul by the mujahideen
August 1994	emergence of the Taliban in Kandahar province
November 1994	Taliban capture of Kandahar
September 1995	Taliban takeover of Herat
April 1996	Mullah Omar proclaimed Commander of the Faithful by an assembly of ulama
September 1996	Taliban capture of Kabul, proclamation of the Islamic Emirate
August 1998	Taliban capture of Mazar-i Sharif
November 1999	United Nations sanction against the Taliban regime
July 2000	Taliban ban on poppy cultivation
March 2001	destruction of Bamyan Buddhas by the Taliban
9 September 2001	assassination of Ahmad Shah Massoud
11 September 2001	attacks on the World Trade Center towers and the Pentagon
October 2001	launch of Operation Enduring Freedom, US military intervention
November 2001	capture of Mazar-i Sharif, Bamiyan, Kabul, Kunduz, and Jalalabad by the Northern Alliance
December 2001	Bonn agreement, Hamid Karzai appointed interim leader
	surrender of Taliban fighters entrenched in Kandahar
	Resolution 1386, the creation of ISAF, deployed in and around Kabul

June 2002	Loya jirga appoints Hamid Karzai as interim administration president
2002–3	emergence of Taliban-aligned insurgent groups in the south and east
March 2003	US invasion of Iraq
June 2003	establishment of the Leadership Council (Rahbari Shura) by the Taliban
January 2004	adoption of a new constitution
October 2004	presidential election, election of Hamid Karzai
2005	131 Western military killed in Afghanistan, increased Taliban attacks in the south and east
September 2005	parliamentary election
July 2006	Battle of Panjwai
May 2007	death of Mullah Dadullah
November 2007	ISAF and Operation Enduring Freedom have 55,000 troops
September 2008	Bush announces the deployment of an additional 31,000 troops
August 2009	presidential election, massive fraud, Karzai's reelection
December 2009	Obama announces the deployment of 30,000 additional troops (*the Surge*) and the start of withdrawal in eighteen months
2010	711 Western military killed in Afghanistan
September 2010	parliamentary election
May 2011	Abbotabad raid, special forces soldiers execute Osama bin Laden
April–June 2014	disputed presidential election
September 2014	agreement under US leadership, Ashraf Ghani is appointed President and Abdullah Chief Executive Officer
December 2014	withdrawal of most US troops
January 2015	Islamic State's proclamation of a Khorasan governorate, covering Afghanistan and Pakistan
September 2015	temporary conquest of Kunduz city by the Taliban
May 2018	temporary conquest of the city of Farah by the Taliban
August 2018	temporary conquest of the city of Ghazni by the Taliban
July 2021	Completion of the withdrawal of Western troops
August 2021	Fall of Kabul, Taliban Takeover

Glossary

adat	custom
afghani	Afghan currency
akhound	theologian
amir al-mouminin	Commander of the Faithful
aqida	faith
arbab	village headman, equivalent to *khan* in Hazarajat
arbaki	militiamen, tribal levy
baad	women offered as compensation in a conflict
bay	large landowner, equivalent to *khan* in the north
biswa	surface measurement, approx. 100 m^2
shabnamah	night letters, usually a flyer posted in a village warning a person or group of persons
chadri	veil worn by women
diya	financial compensation; blood price, Quranic term
fatwa	nonbinding legal opinion by an alim
fazilat	graduate diploma in theology or Islamic law
firman	order or decree by the emir
fiqh	Islamic jurisprudence
hadith	precept attributed to the prophet Muhammad, source of Islamic law
had, hudud	punishment fixed by the Quran
imam	leader of an Islamic community, from the umma to a prayer group
jarib	surface measurement (about 0.2 hectares)
jihad	holy war
jirga	assembly, tribal council

khan	great property owner, notable
lashkar	army, troop
madrasa	religious school
mahram	parent
malik	village chief, historically designated by the state
mawlana, mawlawi	spiritual master, alim (term of address)
millat	nation
mirab	responsible for the distribution of water
mollah	member of the clergy
mujahid, mujahideen	fighter in holy war
nawruz	Persian New Year
umma	community of believers
pashtunwali	Pashtun customary code
qanoun-i wizarat	inheritance law
qari	one who recites the Qur'an following the rules of recitation (*tajwid*)
qawm	solidarity group (lineage, tribe, ethnic or professional group)
rais	political leader
sayid, sadat	descendant of the prophet Muhammad
saranwali	Attorney General
sharia	Islamic law, literally 'the path'
shura	assembly, Islamic council, Quranic term
sunna	reported deeds and words of the prophet Muhammad, literally 'tradition', source of Islamic law
taliban	seminarians, students of a madrasa
tazir	sentence set by the judge or legislator, a term of Islamic law
ushr	Islamic tax on crops
wasta	influence
wakil	representative
waqf, awqaf	pious foundation
zina	fornication, Quranic term

Bibliography

ABEL Richard, 'Delegalization: A Critical Review of its Ideology, Manifestations, and Social Consequences' in Erhard Blankenburg, Ekkehard Klausa, and Hubert Rottleuthner (eds), *Alternative Rechtsformen und Alternativen zum Recht*, Opladen, West-deutscher Verlag, 1980, pp. 27–47.

ADELKHAH Fariba, 'Religious Dependency in Afghanistan: Shia Madrasas as a Religious Mode of Social Assertion?' in Keiko Sakurai and Fariba Adelkhah (eds), *The Moral Economy of the Madrasa: Islam and Education Today*, London, Taylor & Francis, 2011, pp. 103–29.

ADELKHAH Fariba, 'Afghanistan: La guerre des *qumandan* pour le contrôle des terres', *Moyen-Orient*, 2012, vol. 14, pp. 72–7.

ADELKHAH Fariba (ed.), 'Guerre et terre en Afghanistan', *Revue des mondes musulmans et de la Méditerranée*, 2013, n° 133.

ADELKHAH Fariba, 'War and State (Re)Construction in Afghanistan: Conflicts of Tradition or Conflicts of Development?', *International Development Policy*, 2017, vol. 8.

AGIER Michel, 'Le camp des vulnérables: Les réfugiés face à leur citoyenneté niée', *Les Temps Modernes*, 2004, n° 627, pp. 120–37.

AHMAD Aisha, *Jihad & Co: Black Markets and Islamist Power*, New York, Oxford University Press, 2017.

AHMED Akbar, *Millennium and Charisma among Pathans: A Critical Essay in Social Anthropology*, London, Routledge, 2012.

AHMED Faiz, 'Judicial Reform in Afghanistan: A Case Study in the New Criminal Procedure Code', *Hastings International and Comparative Law Review*, 2005, vol. 29, pp. 93–134.

AHMED Faiz, *Afghanistan Rising: Islamic Law and Statecraft Between the Ottoman and British Empires*, Cambridge, Harvard University Press, 2017.

ALEF-SHAH zadran, *Socio-Economic and Legal-Political Processes in a Pashtun Village, Southeastern Afghanistan*, New York, State University of New York, 1977.

ANDERSON Jon W., 'There Are no Khans Anymore: Economic Development and Social Change in Tribal Afghanistan', *Middle East Journal*, 1978, vol. 32, n° 2, pp. 167–83.

ARENDT Hannah, *On Revolution*, New York, Viking, 1963.

ARJONA Ana, *Rebelocracy: Social Order in the Colombian Civil War*, Cambridge, Cambridge University Press, 2016.

ARJONA Ana, KASFIR Nelson, and MAMPILLY Zachariah (eds), *Rebel Governance in Civil War*, Cambridge, Cambridge University Press, 2015.

ARMYTAGE Livingston, 'Justice in Afghanistan: Rebuilding Judicial Competence after the Generation of War', *Heidelberg Journal of International Law*, 2007, vol. 67, pp. 185–210.

ASSIER-ANDRIEU Louis, *Le droit dans les sociétés humaines*, Paris, Nathan, 1996.

AUDOIN-ROUZEAU Stéphane, *Combattre: une anthropologie historique de la guerre moderne, XIXe-XXIe siècle*, Paris, Seuil, 2008.

AUDREN Frédéric and LINHARDT Dominique, 'Un procès hors du commun?', *Annales. Histoire, Sciences Sociales*, 2008, vol. 63, n° 5, pp. 1003–34.

AUGUSTIN, *The City of God Against the Pagans*, Cambridge, Cambridge University Press, 1998.

AUSTIN John, *How to Do Things with Words*, Oxford, Clarendon Press, 1962.

AUTESSERRE Séverine, 'Dangerous Tales: Dominant Narratives on the Congo and their Unintended Consequences', *African Affairs*, 2012, vol. 111, n° 443, pp. 202–22.

AUTESSERRE Séverine, *Peaceland: Conflict Resolution and the Everyday Politics of International Intervention*, Cambridge, Cambridge University Press, 2014.

AZERBAIJANI-MOGHADDAM Sippi, 'Afghan Women on the Margins of the Twenty-First Century' in Antonio Donini, Norah Niland, and Karin Wermester (eds), *Nation-building Unraveled? Aid, Peace and Justice in Afghanistan*, Bloomfield, Kumarian Press, 2004, pp. 95–116.

AZOY G. Whitney, *Buzkashi, Game and Power in Afghanistan*, Philadelphia, University of Pennsylvania Press, 1982,

BACON Francis, *The Essays*, London, Penguin Books, 1985.

BACZKO Adam, 'Les revers de l'armée américaine dans la Guerre d'Afghanistan: le cas de la Kounar', *Politique américaine*, 2012, vol. 19, n° 1, pp. 11–26.

BACZKO Adam, 'Legal Rule and Tribal Politics: The US Army and the Taliban in Afghanistan (2001–13)', *Development and Change*, 2016, vol. 47, n° 6, pp. 1412–33.

BACZKO Adam and DORRONSORO Gilles, 'For a Sociological Approach to Civil Wars', *Revue française de science politique*, 2017, vol. 67, n° 2, pp. 309–27.

BACZKO Adam, DORRONSORO Gilles, and QUESNAY Arthur, *Civil War in Syria: Mobilization and Competing Social Orders*, Cambridge, Cambridge University Press, 2017.

BACZKO Adam and DORRONSORO Gilles, and QUENAY Arthur, 'The Epistemological Privilege of Fieldwork: A Colloective Investigation in War-Torn Syria', *Bulletin of Sociological Methodology*, vol. 151, n° 1, 2021, pp. 96–116.

BAILY John, 'Music and Censorship in Afghanistan, 1973–2003' in Laudan Nooshin (ed.), *Music and the Play of Power in the Middle East, North Africa and Central Asia*, London, Ashgate, 2009, pp. 143–63.

BANÉGAS Richard and MARSHALL-FRATANI Ruth (eds), 'La Côte d'Ivoire en guerre: dynamiques du dedans et du dehors', *Politique africaine*, 2003, n° 89, pp. 5–11.

BANO Masooda, *The Rational Believer: Choices and Decisions in the Madrasas of Pakistan*, Ithaca, Cornell University Press, 2012.

BARFIELD Thomas, *Afghanistan: A Cultural and Political History*, Princeton, Princeton University Press, 2010.

BARFIELD Thomas and NOJUMI Neamatollah, 'Bringing More Effective Governance to Afghanistan: 10 Pathways to Stability', *Middle East Policy*, 2010, vol. 17, n° 4, pp. 40–52.

BARNES Cedric and HASSAN Harun, 'The Rise and Fall of Mogadishu's Islamic Courts', *Journal of Eastern African Studies*, 2007, vol. 1, n° 2, pp. 151–60.

BARRY Mike, 'Afghanistan: Les séminaristes de la guerre', *Politique internationale*, 1997, n° 74, pp. 60–96.

BARTH Fredrik, *Political Leadership among Swat Pathans*, London, Athlone Press, 1959.

BAYART Jean-François, *The State in Africa: The Politics of the Belly*, London, Longman, 1993.

BAYART Jean-François, ELLIS Stephen, and HIBOU Béatrice, *Criminalization of the State in Africa*, Bloomington, Indiana University Press, 2009.

BAYART Jean-François, MBEMBE Achille, and TOULABOR Comi, *Le politique par le bas en Afrique noire*, Paris, Karthala, 2008.

BENDA-BECKMANN Keebet VON, 'Forum Shopping and Shopping Forums: Dispute Processing in a Minangkabau Village in West Sumatra', *The Journal of Legal Pluralism and Unofficial Law*, 1981, vol. 13, n° 19, pp. 117–59.

BERRY Sara, *No Condition is Permanent: The Social Dynamics of Agrarian Change in Sub-Saharan Africa*, Madison, University of Wisconsin Press, 1993.

BILLAUD Julie, *Kabul Carnival: Gender Politics in Postwar Afghanistan*, Philadelphia, University of Pennsylvania Press, 2015.

BIZEUL Daniel, 'Faire avec les déconvenus: Une enquête en milieu nomade', *Sociétés Contemporaines*, 1999, vol. 33, n° 1, pp. 111–37.

BIZEUL Daniel, 'Que faire des expériences d'enquête? Apports and fragilité de l'observation directe', *Revue française de science politique*, 2007, vol. 57, n° 1, pp. 69–89.

BLANCHARD Emmanuel, 'Recours à la force and demandes de justice en situation (post-coloniale)', *Crime, Histoire & Sociétés*, vol. 21, n° 2, pp. 87–102.

BLAZQUEZ Adèle, 'Ethnographie d'un contexte violent (Sinaloa, Mexique): L'immanence de l'enquête', *Monde commun*, 2018, n° 1, pp. 188–205.

BOESEN Inger, 'Women, Honour and Love: some Aspects of the Pashtun Woman's Life in Eastern Afghanistan', *Afghanistan Journal*, 1980, vol. 7, n° 2, pp. 50–9.

BOESEN Inger, 'Conflicts of Solidarity in Pakhtun Women's Lives' in Bo Utas (ed.), *Women in Islamic Societies: Social Attitudes and Historical Perspectives*, London, Curzon Press, 1983, pp. 104–23.

BOESEN Inger, 'What Happens to Honour in Exile? Continuity and Change among Afghan Refugees' in Bo Huldt and Erland Jansson (eds), *The Tragedy of Afghanistan: The Social, Cultural and Political Impact of the Soviet Invasion*, London, Croom Helm, 1988, pp. 219–39.

BOHANNAN Paul, *Justice and Judgment among the Tiv*, Oxford, Oxford University Press, 1957.

BONY Jérome and PONFILLY Christophe de, 'A Valley Against an Empire', *Central Asian Survey*, 1983, vol. 1, n° 4, pp. 133–48.

BOURDIEU Pierre, 'Les modes de domination', *Actes de la Recherche en Sciences Sociales*, 1976, vol. 2, n° 2, pp. 122–32.

BOURDIEU Pierre, 'The Force of Law: Toward a Sociology of the Juridical Field', *Hastings Law Journal*, 1986, vol. 38, n° 5, pp. 814–53.

BOURDIEU Pierre, 'Droit et passe-droit [Le champ des pouvoirs territoriaux et la mise en oeuvre des règlements]', *Actes de la Recherche en Sciences Sociales*, 1990, vol. 81, n° 1, pp. 86–96.

BOURDIEU Pierre, 'Genesis and Structure of the Religious Field', *Comparative Social Research*, 1991, vol. 13, pp. 1–44.

BOURDIEU Pierre, *Pascalian Meditations*, Stanford, Stanford University Press, 2000.

BOURDIEU Pierre, *On the State: Lectures at the Collège de France, 1989–1992*, Stanford, Stanford University Press, 2014.

BRAITHWAITE John and WARDAK Ali, 'Crime and War in Afghanistan Part I: The Hobbesian Solution', *British Journal of Criminology*, 2013, vol. 53, n° 2, pp. 179–96.

BRUBAKER Rogers and COOPER Frederick, 'Beyond "Identity"', *Theory and Society*, 2000, vol. 29, n° 1, pp. 1–47.

BUTLER Judith, *Precarious Life: The Powers of Mourning and Violence*, New York, Verso, 2004.

BUUR Lars, 'The Sovereign Outsourced: Local Justice and Violence in Port Elizabeth' in Thomas Blom Hansen and Finn Stepputat (eds), *Sovereign Bodies: Citizens, Migrants, and States in the Postcolonial World*, Princeton, Princeton University Press, 2005, pp. 192–217.

CANFIELD Robert, 'The Ecology of Rural Ethnic Groups and the Spatial Dimensions of Power', *American Anthropologist*, 1973, vol. 75, n° 5, pp. 1511–28.

CANFIELD Robert, 'New Trends among the Hazaras: From "The Amity of Wolves" to "The Practice of Brotherhood"', *Iranian Studies*, 2004, vol. 37, n° 2, pp. 241–62.

CANFIELD Robert, 'Reviews', *Iranian Studies*, 2004, vol. 37, n° 2, pp. 323–33.

CENTLIVRES Pierre, *Un bazar d'Asie centrale: Forme et organisation du bazar de Tashqurghan (Afghanistan)*, Wiesbaden, Dr Ludwig Reichert Verlag, 1972.

CENTLIVRES Pierre, 'Identité et image de l'autre dans l'anthropologie populaire en afghanistan', *Revue européenne des sciences sociales*, 1980, vol. 18, n° 53, pp. 29–41.

CENTLIVRES Pierre, *Paysannerie et pouvoir en Afghanistan: De la fin de la monarchie à l'intervention soviétique*, Geneva, Institut universitaire de hautes études internationales, 1985.

CENTLIVRES Pierre, 'Exil, relations interethniques et identité dans la crise afghane', *Revue du monde musulman et de la Méditerranée*, 1991, vol. 59, n° 1, pp. 70–82.

CENTLIVRES Pierre, 'Tribus, ethnies et nations en Afghanistan' in Hosham Dawod (ed.), *Tribus et pouvoirs en terre d'Islam*, Paris, Armand Colin, 2004, pp. 115–43.

CENTLIVRES Pierre and CENTLIVRES-DEMONT Micheline, 'The Afghan Refugee in Pakistan: An Ambiguous Identity', *Journal of Refugee Studies*, 1988, vol. 1, pp. 141–52.

CENTLIVRES Pierre and CENTLIVRES-DEMONT Micheline, *Et si on parlait de l'Afghanistan? Terrains et textes, 1964–1980*, Paris, Les Éditions de la MSH, 1988.

CENTLIVRES Pierre and CENTLIVRES-DEMONT Micheline, 'Les réformes agraires en Afghanistan, de la fin de la monarchie à la chute des talibans', *Revue des mondes musulmans and de la Méditerranée*, 2013, n° 133, pp. 45–61.

CHABAL Patrick and DALOZ Jean-Pascal, *Africa Works: Disorder as Political Instrument*, Oxford, James Currey, 1999.

CHAMAYOU Grégoire, *A Theory of the Drone*, New York, The New Press, 2015.

CHAYES Sarah, *The Punishment of Virtue: Inside Afghanistan after the Taliban*, New York, Penguin Press, 2006.

CHEBLI Denia, 'Cette paix qui divise: Une analyse de la médiation au Mali par ses effets', *Critique internationale*, 2020, n° 88, p. 9–30.

CLUNAN Anne and TRINKUNAS Harold, *Ungoverned Spaces: Alternatives to State Authority in an Era of Softened Sovereignty*, Stanford, Stanford University Press, 2010.

COBURN Noah and DEMPSEY John, *Informal Dispute Resolution in Afghanistan*, Washington, United States Institute for Peace, 2010.

COGHLAN Tom, 'The Taliban in Helmand: An Oral History' in Antonio Giustozzi (ed.), *Decoding the New Taliban: Insights from the Afghan Field*, New York, Columbia University Press, 2009, pp. 119–53.

COLE Juan, 'The Taliban, Women, and the Hegelian Private Sphere' in Robert D. Crews and Amin Tarzi (eds), *The Taliban and the Crisis of Afghanistan*, Cambridge, Harvard University Press, 2009, pp. 118–54.

COLIN Jean-Philippe, LE MEUR Pierre-Yves, and LÉONARD Éric, 'Identifier les droits et dicter le droit: La politique des programmes de formalisation des droits fonciers' in Jean-Philippe Colin, Pierre-Yves Le Meur, and Éric Léonard (eds), *Les politiques d'enregistrement des droits fonciers: Du cadre légal aux pratiques locales*, Paris, Karthala, 2010, pp. 5–67.

COLLIER Paul and HOEFFLER Anke, 'On Economic Causes of Civil War', *Oxford Economic Papers*, 1998, vol. 50, n° 4, pp. 563–73.

COLLIER Paul and HOEFFLER Anke, *Justice-Seeking and Loot-Seeking in Civil War*, Washington, World Bank 1999.

COLLIER Paul, ELLIOTT V. L., HEGRE Håvard, HOEFFLER Anke, REYNAL-QUEROL Marta, and SAMBANIS Nicholas, *Breaking the Conflict Trap: Civil War and Development Policy*, Washington, World Bank, 2003.

COMAROFF Jean and COMAROFF John, 'Law and Disorder in the Post-Colony: An Introduction' in Jean Comaroff and John Comaroff (eds), *Law and Disorder in the Postcolony*, Chicago, University of Chicago Press, 2006, pp. 1–56.

COMMAILLE Jacques and DUMOULIN Laurence, 'Heurs et malheurs de la légalité dans les sociétés contemporaines. Une sociologie politique de la "judiciarisation"', *L'Année sociologique*, 2009, vol. 59, n° 1, pp. 63–107.

COPANS Jean, 'L'apple de la théorie: Le terrain le plus difficile', *Civilisations*, 2015, vol. 64, n° 1, pp. 165–75.
COULSON Noel, 'Muslim Custom and Case-Law', *Die Welt des Islams*, 1959, vol. 6, n° 1-2, pp. 13–24.
CRAMER Christopher, 'Homo Economicus Goes to War: Methodological Individualism, Rational Choice and the Political Economy of War', *World Development*, 2002, vol. 30, n° 11, pp. 1845–64.
CREVELD Martin Van, *Transformation of War*, New York, Free Press, 1991.
DAS Veena and POOLE Deborah (eds), *Anthropology in the Margins of the State*, Oxford, Oxford University Press, 2004.
DAULATZAI Anila, 'The Discursive Occupation of Afghanistan', *British Journal of Middle Eastern Studies*, 2008, vol. 35, n° 3, pp. 419–35.
DAVIS Anthony, 'How the Taliban Became a Military Force' in William Maley (ed.), *Fundamentalism Reborn? Afghanistan and the Taliban*, London, Hurst, 1998, pp. 43–71.
DE LAURI Antonio, 'Access to Justice and Human Rights in Afghanistan', *Crime, Law and Social Change*, 2013, vol. 60, n° 3, pp. 261–85.
DE LAURI Antonio, 'Corruption, Legal Modernisation and Judicial Practice in Afghanistan', *Asian Studies Review*, 2013, vol. 37, n° 4, pp. 527–45.
DE LAURI Antonio, 'Between Law and Customs: Normative Interconnections in Kabul's Tribunals', *Diogenes*, 2015, vol. 60, n° 3–4, pp. 45–57.
DELMAS-MARTY Mireille, *Ordering Pluralism. A Conceptual Framework for Understanding the Transnational Legal World*, London, Hart Publishing, 2009.
DELPHY Christine, 'L'état d'exception: La dérogation au droit commun comme fondement de la sphère privée', *Nouvelles Questions Féministes*, 1995, vol. 16, n° 4, pp. 73–114.
DELPHY Christine, 'Une guerre pour les femmes afghanes?', *Nouvelles Questions Féministes*, 2002, vol. 21, n° 1, pp. 98–109.
DEZALAY Sara, 'Des droits de l'homme au marché du développement: Note de recherche sur le champ faible de la gestion de conflits armés', *Actes de la recherche en sciences sociales*, 2008, n° 174, pp. 68–79.
DOBBINS James, *America's Role in Nation-Building from Germany to Iraq*, Santa Monica, Random House, 2003.
DORRONSORO Gilles, *La ville d'Hérat dans la guerre*, DEA d'histoire, EHESS, Paris, 1987.
DORRONSORO Gilles, 'Politique et ethnicité en Afghanistan: Le cas tadjik', *Cahiers d'Études sur la Méditerranée Orientale et le monde Turco-Iranien*, 1994, n° 18, pp. 131–47.
DORRONSORO Gilles, 'Désordre et légitimité du politique en Afghanistan', *Cultures & Conflits*, 1997, n° 24–25, pp. 135–57.
DORRONSORO Gilles, 'Les oulémas afghans au XXe siècle: Bureaucratisation, contestation et genèse d'un État clérical', *Archives de sciences sociales des religions*, 2001, n° 115, pp. 63–79.
DORRONSORO Gilles, *Revolution Unending: Afghanistan, 1979 to the Present*, New York, Columbia University Press, 2005.
DORRONSORO Gilles, 'Dynamiques entre champs religieux et politique. Le cas de l'Afghanistan', *Purusartha*, 2012, n° 30, pp. 363–76.
DORRONSORO Gilles, 'Le déclin de l'institution tribale en Afghanistan' in Hosham Dawod, *La constante 'tribu', variations arabo-musulmanes*, Paris, Démopolis, 2014, pp. 93–117.
DORRONSORO Gilles, *Le gouvernement transnational en Afghanistan. Une si prévisible défaite*, Paris, Karthala, 2021.
DORRONSORO Gilles and GROJEAN Olivier (eds), *Identity, Conflict and Politics in Turkey, Iran and Pakistan*, New York, Oxford University Press, 2018.
DORRONSORO Gilles and LOBATO Chantal, 'The Militia in Afghanistan', *Central Asian Survey*, 1989, vol. 8, n° 4, pp. 95–108.

DUBOS Nicolas, *Mal extrême: La guerre civile vue par les philosophes des origines à nos jours*, Paris, CNRS Éditions, 2010.

DUFFIELD Mark R., *Global Governance and the New Wars: The Merging of Development and Security*, London, Zed Books, 2001.

DUPEE Matthew, 'Badghis Province: Examining the Taliban's Northwestern Campaign', *The Culture and Conflict Review*, 2008, vol. 2, n° 4.

DUPREE Louis, 'The Changing Character of South-Central Afghanistan Villages', *Human Organization*, 1955, vol. 14, n° 4, pp. 26–9.

DUPREE Louis, *Afghanistan*, Princeton, Princeton University Press, 1973.

DUPREE Louis, 'Afghanistan under the Khalq', *Problems of Communism*, 1979, vol. 28, n° 4, pp. 34–50.

DUPREE Louis, 'Tribal Warfare in Afghanistan and Pakistan: A Reflexion of the Segmentary Lineage System' in Akbar S. Ahmed (ed.), *Islam in Tribal Societies: From the Atlas to the Indus*, London, Routledge, 1984, pp. 266–86.

DUPREE Nancy, 'Behind the Veil in Afghanistan', *Asia*, August 1978.

DUPREE Nancy, 'Revolutionary Rhetoric and Afghan Women' in Robert L. Canfield and M. Nazif Shahrani (eds), *Revolutions & Rebellions in Afghanistan: Anthropological Perspectives*, Berkeley, University of California Press, 1984, pp. 306–40.

DUPREE Nancy, 'Afghan Women under the Taliban' in William Maley (ed.), *Fundamentalism Reborn? Afghanistan and the Taliban*, London, Hurst, 1998, pp. 145–66.

DUPREE Nancy, 'The Family During Crisis in Afghanistan', *Journal of Comparative Family Studies*, 2004, vol. 35, n° 2, pp. 311–31.

DUPREE Nancy Hatch, 'The Demography of Afghan Refugees in Pakistan' in Hafeez Malik (ed.), *Soviet-American Relations with Pakistan, Iran and Afghanistan*, Basingstoke, Palgrave Macmillan, 1987, pp. 366–94.

DUPRET Baudoin, *Droit et sciences sociales*, Paris, Armand Colin, 2006.

EDGAR Iain, *The Dream in Islam: From Qur'anic Tradition to Jihadist Inspiration*, New York, Berghahn, 2011.

EDWARDS David, 'Mad *mullahs* and Englishmen: Discourse in the Colonial Encounter', *Comparative Studies in Society and History*, 1989, vol. 31, n° 4, pp. 649–70.

EDWARDS David, *Heroes of the Age: Moral Fault Lines on the Afghan Frontier*, Berkeley, University of California Press, 1996.

EDWARDS David, 'Learning from the Swat Pathans: Political Leadership in Afghanistan, 1978–97', *American Ethnologist*, 1998, vol. 25, n° 4, pp. 712–28.

EDWARDS David, *Before Taliban Genealogies of the Afghan Jihad*, Berkeley, University of California Press, 2002.

EDWARDS David, *Caravan of Martyrs: Sacrifice and Suicide Bombing in Afghanistan*, Berkeley, University of California Press, 2017.

EISENSTADT Shmuel, *Traditional Patrimonialism and Modern Neopatrimonialism*, Thousand Oaks, Sage Publishing, 1973.

EISENSTEIN Zillah, 'Feminisms in the Aftermath of September 11', *Social Text*, 2002, vol. 20, n° 3, pp. 79–99.

EMADI Hafizullah, 'The Hazaras and their Role in the Process of Political Transformation in Afghanistan', *Central Asian Survey*, 1997, vol. 16, n° 3, pp. 363–87.

ETIENNE Gilbert, *L'Afghanistan ou les aléas de la coopération*, Paris, Presses universitaires de France, 1972.

FARRELL Theo and GIUSTOZZI Antonio, 'The Taliban at War: Inside the Helmand Insurgency, 2004–2012', *International Affairs*, 2013, vol. 89, n° 4, pp. 845–71.

FERME Mariane and HOFFMAN Daniel, 'Hunter Militias and the International Human Rights Discourse in Sierra Leone and Beyond', *Africa Today*, 2004, vol. 50, n° 4, pp. 72–95.

FRANKS Tommy, *American Soldier*, New York, Harper Collins, 2009.

FUKUYAMA Francis, *Nation-Building: Beyond Afghanistan and Iraq*, Baltimore, Johns Hopkins University Press, 2008.

GANT Jim, *One Tribe at a Time: A Strategy for Success in Afghanistan*, Los Angeles, Nine Sisters Imports, 2009.

GEFFRAY Christian, 'État, richesse et criminels' in Yann Guillaud and Frédéric Létang (eds), *Du social hors la loi: L'anthropologie analytique de Christian Geffray*, Marseille, IRD Éditions, 2009, pp. 243–70.

GHANI Ashraf, 'Disputes in a Court of Sharia, Kunar Valley, Afghanistan, 1885–1890', *International Journal of Middle East Studies*, 1983, vol. 15, n° 03, pp. 353–67.

GHANI Ashraf and LOCKHART Clare, *Fixing Failed States: A Framework for Rebuilding a Fractured World*, Oxford, Oxford University Press, 2009.

GIUSTOZZI Antonio, *Koran, Kalashnikov, and Laptop: The Neo-Taliban Insurgency in Afghanistan*, New York, Columbia University Press, 2008.

GIUSTOZZI Antonio, *Empires of Mud: War and Warlords of Afghanistan*, London, Hurst, 2009.

GIUSTOZZI Antonio, 'Hearts, Minds, and the Barrel of a Gun: The Taliban's Shadow Government', *Prism*, 2012, vol. 3, n° 2, pp. 71–80.

GIUSTOZZI Antonio, 'Local Politics and the Taliban' in Conrad Schetter (ed.), *Local Politics in Afghanistan: A Century of Intervention in the Social Order*, Oxford, Oxford University Press, 2013, pp. 77–94.

GIUSTOZZI Antonio, 'The Taliban's "Military Courts"', *Small Wars & Insurgencies*, 2014, vol. 25, n° 2, pp. 284–96.

GIUSTOZZI Antonio and BACZKO Adam, 'The Politics of the Taliban's Shadow Judiciary, 2003–2013', *Central Asian Affairs*, 2014, vol. 1, n° 2, pp. 199–224.

GLATZER Bernt, 'Is Afghanistan on the Brink of Ethnic and Tribal Disintegration?' in William Maley (ed.), *Fundamentalisme Reborn? Afghanistan and the Taliban*, New York, New York University Press, 1998, pp. 167–81.

GLUCKMAN Max, 'Analysis of a Social Situation in Modern Zululand. A. The Social Organization of Modern Zululand', *Bantu Studies*, 1940, vol. 14, pp. 1–30.

GLUCKMAN Max, *The Judicial Process among the Barotse of Northern Rhodesia*, Manchester, Manchester University Press, 1955.

GLUCKMAN Max, *Politics, Law and Ritual in Tribal Society*, Oxford, Blackwell, 1955.

GONZÁLEZ Roberto, 'Towards Mercenary Anthropology? The New US Army Counterinsurgency Manual FM 3-24 and the Military-Anthropology Complex', *Anthropology Today*, 2007, vol. 23, n° 3, pp. 14–19.

GONZÁLEZ Roberto, *Militarizing Culture: Essays on the Warfare State*, Walnut Creek, Left Coast Press, 2010.

GOODHAND Jonathan, 'Research in Conflict Zones: Ethics and Accountability', *Forced Migration Review*, 2000, vol. 8, pp. 12–15.

GOODHAND Jonathan, 'Corrupting or Consolidating the Peace? The Drugs Economy and Post-conflict Peacebuilding in Afghanistan', *International Peacekeeping*, 2008, vol. 15, n° 3, pp. 405–23.

GOODWIN Jan, *Price of Honor: Muslim Women Lift the Veil of Silence on the Islamic World*, London, Penguin, 2002.

GOPAL Anand, 'The Taliban in Kandahar' in Peter Bergen and Katherine Tiedemann (eds), *Talibanistan: Negotiating the Borders between Terror, Politics, and Religion*, Oxford, Oxford University Press, 2013, pp. 1–69.

GOPAL Anand, *No Good Men among the Living: America, the Taliban, and the War through Afghan Eyes*, New York, Metropolitan Books, 2014.

GREVEMEYER Jan-Heeren, 'Ethnicity and National Liberation: The Afghan Hazara between Resistance and Civil War' in Jean-Pierre Digard (ed.), *Le fait ethnique en Iran et en Afghanistan*, Paris, Éditions du CNRS, 1988, pp. 211–18.

GRIFFITHS John, 'What is Legal Pluralism?', *The Journal of Legal Pluralism and Unofficial Law*, 1986, vol. 18, n° 24, pp. 1–55.

GRIMM Sonja, Nicolas LEMAY-HÉBERT, and Olivier NAY (eds), 'Fragile States: A Political Concept', *Third World Quarterly*, 2014, vol. 35, n° 2, pp. 197–209.

GROJEAN Olivier, 'Les aléas d'un terrain comme révélateurs de sa structuration: Gestion et objectivation d'une relation d'enquête sur une mouvance radicale et transnationale', *Revue internationale de politique comparée*, 2010, vol. 17, n° 4, pp. 63–76.

GROTE Rainer, 'Separation of Powers in the New Afghan Constitution', *Zeitschrift für ausländisches öffentliches Recht und Völkerrecht*, 2004, vol. 64, pp. 897–915.

HABERMAS Jürgen, *The Structural Transformation of the Public Sphere: An Inquiry into a Category of Bourgeois Society*, Cambridge, Polity, 1989.

HAGMANN Tobias and PÉCLARD Didier (eds), *Negotiating Statehood: Dynamics of Power and Domination in Africa*, Oxford, Wiley-Blackwell, 2011.

HAJJAR Lisa, *Courting Conflict: The Israeli Military Court System in the West Bank and Gaza*, Berkeley, University of California Press, 2005.

HAKIMI Aziz, 'Getting Savages to Fight Barbarians: Counterinsurgency and the Remaking of Afghanistan', *Central Asian Survey*, 2013, vol. 32, n° 3, pp. 388–405.

HALLAQ Wael, 'Was the Gate of Ijtihad Closed?', *International Journal of Middle East Studies*, 1984, vol. 16, n° 1, pp. 3–41.

HALLAQ Wael, *Authority, Continuity and Change in Islamic Law*, Cambridge, Cambridge University Press, 2001.

HALLAQ Wael, *Shari'a: Theory, Practice, Transformations*, Cambridge, Cambridge University Press, 2009.

HAMRE John and SULLIVAN Gordon, 'Toward Postconflict Reconstruction', *The Washington Quarterly*, 2002, vol. 25, n° 4, pp. 83–96.

HANIFI M. Jamil, 'Editing the Past: Colonial Production of Hegemony through the "Loya Jerga" in Afghanistan', *Iranian Studies*, 2004, vol. 37, n° 2, pp. 295–322.

HANIFI Shah, *Connecting Histories in Afghanistan: Market Relations and State Formation on a Colonial Frontier*, Stanford, Stanford University Press, 2011.

HAROON Sana, *Frontier of Faith: Islam in the Indo-Afghan Borderland*, London, Hurst, 2011.

HARPVIKEN Kristian Berg, *Political Mobilization among the Hazara of Afghanistan: 1978–1992*, Oslo, Department of Sociology, University of Oslo, 1996.

HARTMANN Michael and KLONOWIECKA-MILART Agnieszka, 'Lost in Translation: Legal Transplants without Consensus-based Adaptation' in Whit Mason (ed.), *The Rule of Law in Afghanistan: Missing in Inaction*, Cambridge, Cambridge University Press, 2011, pp. 266–98.

HAUNER Milan, 'One Man against the Empire: The Faqir of Ipi and the British in Central Asia on the Eve of and during the Second World War', *Journal of Contemporary History*, 1981, vol. 16, n° 1, pp. 183–212.

HEDGES Chris, *War Is a Force that Gives Us Meaning*, New York, PublicAffairs, 2002.

HIBOU Béatrice, 'Retrait ou redéploiement de l'Etat?', *Critique internationale*, 1998, n° 1, pp. 151–68.

HIRSCHKIND Charles and MAHMOOD Saba, 'Feminism, the Taliban, and Politics of Counter-Insurgency', *Anthropological Quarterly*, 2002, vol. 75, n° 2, pp. 339–54.

HOBBES Thomas, *On the Citizen*, Cambridge, Cambridge University Press, 1998.

HOBSBAWM Eric and RANGER Terence (eds), *The Invention of Tradition*, Cambridge, Cambridge University Press, 1983.

HOFFMAN Danny, 'The Civilian Target in Sierra Leone and Liberia: Political Power, Military Strategy, and Humanitarian Intervention', *African Affairs*, 2004, vol. 103, n° 411, pp. 211–26.

HOFFMAN Danny, *The War Machines: Young Men and Violence in Sierra Leone and Liberia*, Durham, Duke University Press, 2011.

HOFFMANN Kasper and KIRK Tom, *Public Authority and the Provision of Public Goods in Conflict-Affected and Transitioning Regions*, London, London School of Economics, 2013.

HOPKINS Benjamin, *The Makings of Modern Afghanistan*, Basingstoke, Palgrave Macmillan, 2008.

HOPKINS Benjamin, 'The Problem with "Hearts and Minds" in Afghanistan', *Middle East Report*, 2010, n° 255, pp. 24–9.

HOPKINS Benjamin, 'The Frontier Crimes Regulation and Frontier Governmentality', *The Journal of Asian Studies*, 2015, vol. 74, n° 2, pp. 369–89.

HOWARD-MERRIAM Kathleen, 'Afghan Refugee Women and their Struggle for Survival' in Grant Farr and John Merriam (eds), *Afghan Resistance: The Politics of Survival*, London, Westview Press, 1987, pp. 103–25.

IACOPINO Vincent, RASEKH Zohra, YAMIN Alicia Ely, FREEDMAN Lynn, BURKHALTER Holly, and HEISLER Michele, *The Taliban's War on Women: a Health and Human Rights Crisis in Afghanistan*, Boston, Physicians for Human Rights, 1998.

IGNATIEFF Michael, *Empire Lite: Nation Building in Bosnia, Kosovo, Afghanistan*, London, Vintage Books, 2004.

ISRAËL Liora, *Robes noires, années sombres. Avocats et magistrats en résistance pendant la Seconde guerre mondiale*, Paris, Fayard, 2005.

ISRAËL Liora, *L'arme du droit*, Paris, Presses de Sciences Po, 2009.

ISSER Deborah, *Customary Justice and the Rule of Law in War-torn Societies*, Washington, US Institute of Peace Press, 2011.

JACKSON Ashley, *Negotiating Survival: Civilian-Insurgent Relations in Afghanistan*, London, Hurst, 2021.

JACOB Jean-Pierre and LE MEUR Pierre-Yves (eds), *Politique de la terre et de l'appartenance: Droits fonciers et citoyenneté locale dans les sociétés du sud*, Paris, Karthala, 2010, pp. 5–57.

JASPER James, *The Art of Moral Protest: Culture, Biography, and Creativity in Social Movements*, Chicago, University of Chicago Press, 1997.

JOAS Hans, *War and Modernity*, Cambridge, Polity Press, 2003.

JOAS Hans and KNÖBL Wolfgang, *War in Social Thought: Hobbes to the Present*, Princeton, Princeton University Press, 2012.

JOHNSON Thomas, 'The Taliban Insurgency and an Analysis of Shabnamah (Night Letters)', *Small Wars & Insurgencies*, 2007, vol. 18, n° 3, pp. 317–44.

JOHNSON Thomas and DUPEE Matthew, 'Analysing the New Taliban Code of Conduct (Layeha): An Assessment of Changing Perspectives and Strategies of the Afghan Taliban', *Central Asian Survey*, 2012, vol. 31, n° 1, pp. 77–91.

JONES Seth, *In the Graveyard of Empires: America's War in Afghanistan*, New York, W. W. Norton & Company, 2010.

KAKAR Hasan, 'The Fall of the Afghan Monarchy in 1973', *International Journal of Middle East Studies*, 1978, vol. 9, n° 2, pp. 195–214.

KALDOR Mary, *New and Old Wars: Organized Violence in a Global Era*, London, Polity Press, 1999.

KALDOR Mary, *New and Old Wars: Organized Violence in a Global Era*, 3rd edn, London, Polity Press, 2012.

KALYVAS Stathis, '"New" and "Old" Civil Wars: A Valid Distinction?', *World Politics*, 2001, vol. 54, n° 01, pp. 99–118.

KALYVAS Stathis, *The Logic of Violence in Civil War*, Cambridge, Cambridge University Press, 2006.

KAMALI Mohammad Hashim, *Law in Afghanistan: A Study of the Constitutions, Matrimonial Law and the Judiciary*, Leiden, Brill, 1985.

KANDIYOTI Deniz (ed.), *Women, Islam and the State*, London, Macmillan, 1991.

KANDIYOTI Deniz, 'Old Dilemmas or New Challenges? The Politics of Gender and Reconstruction in Afghanistan', *Development and Change*, 2007, vol. 38, n° 2, pp. 169–99.

KANT Immanuel, *Idea for a Universal History with a Cosmopolitan*, Cambridge, Cambridge University Press, 2009.

KEANE Conor, *US Nation-Building in Afghanistan*, London, Routledge, 2016.

KILCULLEN David, *The Accidental Guerrilla: Fighting Small Wars in the Midst of a Big One*, Oxford, Oxford University Press, 2009.

KILCULLEN David, *Counterinsurgency*, Oxford, Oxford University Press, 2010.

KLEPONIS Greg, 'Throwing the Book at the Taliban: Undermining Taliban Legitimacy by Highlighting their Own Hypocrisy', *Small Wars Journal*, 2010, vol. 6, n° 10, pp. 1–16.

LACROIX Stéphane, *Les islamistes saoudiens: Une insurrection manquée*, Paris, Presses universitaires de France, 2015.

LAGROYE Jacques, *La vérité dans l'Église catholique: Contestations et restauration d'un régime d'autorité*, Paris, Belin, 2006.

LAHIRE Bernard, *Monde pluriel: Penser l'unité des sciences sociales*, Paris, Le Seuil, 2012.

LAU Martin, *Afghanistan's Legal System and its Compatibility with International Human Rights Standards*, Geneva, International Commission of Jurists, 2002.

LAZAREV Egor, *State-Building as Lawfare: Custom, Sharia, and State Law in Postwar Chechnya*, Cambridge, Cambridge University Press, 2023.

LEDWIDGE Frank, 'Justice and Counter-Insurgency in Afghanistan: A Missing Link', *The RUSI Journal*, 2009, vol. 154, n° 1, pp. 6–9.

LEDWIDGE Frank, 'Justice in Helmand: The Challenge of Law Reform in a Society at War', *Asian Affairs*, 2009, vol. 40, n° 1, pp. 77–89.

LEDWIDGE Frank, *Rebel Law: Insurgents, Courts and Justice in Modern Conflict*, Oxford, Oxford University Press, 2017.

LEFRANC Sandrine, 'Du droit à la paix: La circulation des techniques internationales de pacification par le bas', *Actes de la recherche en sciences sociales*, 2008, n° 174, pp. 4–13.

LI Darryl, *The Universal Enemy: Jihad, Empire, and the Challenge of Solidarity*, Stanford, Stanford University Press, 2019.

LINDHOLM Charles, 'The Structure of Violence among the Swat Pukhtun', *Ethnology*, 1981, vol. 20, n° 2, pp. 147–56.

LINHARDT Dominique, 'Un monopole sous tension: La double nature de la violence d'État', *Politika*, 2019.

LOBATO Chantal, *Un islam conservateur au service du communisme: Kaboul 1980–1985*, DEA d'histoire, EHESS, 1986.

LUND Christian, 'Fragmented Sovereignty: Land Reform and Dispossession in Laos', *The Journal of Peasant Studies*, 2011, vol. 38, n° 4, pp. 885–905.

LUND Christian, 'Of What is This a Case? Analytical Movements in Qualitative Social Science Research', *Human Organization*, 2014, vol. 73, n° 3, pp. 224–34.

LUND Christian, 'Rule and Rupture: State Formation through the Production of Property and Citizenship', *Development and Change*, 2016, vol. 47, n° 6, pp. 1199–228.
MACEK Ivana, *Sarajevo Under Siege: Anthropology in Wartime*, Philadelphia, University of Pennsylvania Press, 2009.
MAJROOH Parwin Ali, 'Afghan Women between Marxism and Islamic Fundamentalism', *Central Asian Survey*, 1989, vol. 8, n° 3, pp. 87–98.
Makaremi Chowra, '"États d'urgence ethnographiques": Approches empiriques de la violence politique', *Cultures & Conflits*, 2016, vol. 103-4, pp.15–34.
MALIK Jamal, *Colonialization of Islam: Dissolution of Traditional Institutions in Pakistan*, New Delhi, Manohar, 1996.
MALIKYAR Helena, 'Development of Family Law in Afghanistan: The Roles of the Hanafi *Madhhab*, Customary Practices and Power Politics', *Central Asian Survey*, 1997, vol. 16, n° 3, pp. 389–99.
MALINOWSKI Bronislaw, 'Introduction' in Ian Hogbin, *Law and Order in Polynesia: A Study of Primitive Legal Institutions*, London, Christophers, 1934, pp. xvii–lxii.
MALKASIAN Carter, *War Comes to Garmser: Thirty Years of Conflict on the Afghan Frontier*, Oxford, Oxford University Press, 2013.
MAMDANI Mahmood, *Citizen and Subject: Contemporary Africa and the Legacy of Late Colonialism*, Princeton, Princeton University Press, 1996.
MAMPILLY Zachariah Cherian, *Rebel Rulers: Insurgent Governance and Civilian Life During War*, Ithaca, Cornell University Press, 2011.
MANSFIELD David, *A State Built on Sand: How Opium Undermined Afghanistan*, Oxford, Oxford University Press, 2016.
MARCHAL Roland and MESSIANT Christine, 'De l'avidité des rebelles: L'analyse économique de la guerre civile selon Paul Collier', *Critique internationale*, 2002, vol. 16, n° 3, pp. 58–69.
MARCHAL Roland and MESSIANT Christine, 'Les guerres civiles à l'ère de la globalisation: Nouvelles réalités et nouveaux paradigmes', *Critique internationale*, 2003, vol. 18, n° 1, pp. 91–112.
MARCHAL Roland and MESSIANT Christine, 'Une lecture symptomale de quelques théorisations récentes des guerres civiles', *Lusotopie*, 2006, vol. XIII, n° 2, pp. 3–46.
MARKS Zoe, 'Sexual Violence in Sierra Leone's Civil War: "Virgination", Rape, and Marriage', *African Affairs*, 2014, vol. 113, n° 450, pp. 67–87.
MARTIN Mike, *An Intimate War: An Oral History of the Helmand Conflict, 1978–2012*, Oxford, Oxford University Press, 2014.
MASON Whit, 'Introduction' in Whit Mason (ed.), *The Rule of Law in Afghanistan: Missing in Inaction*, Cambridge, Cambridge University Press, 2011, pp. 1–12.
MASSOUD Mark Fathi, *Law's Fragile State: Colonial, Authoritarian, and Humanitarian Legacies in Sudan*, Cambridge, Cambridge University Press, 2013.
MASSOUD Mark Fathi, *Shari'a, Inshallah: Finding God in Somali Legal Politics*, Cambridge, Cambridge University Press, 2021.
MÉDARD Jean-François, 'L'État néo-patimonial en Afrique noire' in Jean-François Médard (ed.), *États d'Afrique noire: Formations, mécanismes et crises*, Paris, Karthala, 1991, pp. 323–53.
MÉDARD Jean-François, 'Le "big man" en Afrique: Esquisse d'analyse du politicien entrepreneur', *L'Année sociologique*, 1992, vol. 42, pp. 167–92.
MENKHAUS Ken, 'Governance without Government in Somalia: Spoilers, State Building, and the Politics of Coping', *International Security*, 2007, vol. 31, n° 3, pp. 74–106.
MERRY Sally Engle, 'Legal Pluralism', *Law & Society Review*, 1988, vol. 22, n° 5, pp. 869–96.

MERRY Sally Engle, *Human Rights and Gender Violence: Translating International Law into Local Justice*, Chicago, University of Chicago Press, 2006.

METCALF Barbara, *'Traditionalist' Islamic Activism: Deoband, Tablighis, and Talibs*, Leiden, ISIM, 2002.

METCALF Barbara, *Islamic Revival in British India: Deoband, 1860–1900*, Princeton, Princeton University Press, 2014.

MIDDLETON Townsend and CONS Jason (eds), 'Special Issue on Fieldwork(ers): Research Assistants, Researchers, and the Production of Ethnographic Knowledge', *Ethnography*, 2014, vol. 15, n° 3.

MIGDAL Joel, *Strong Societies and Weak States: State-Society Relations and State Capabilities in the Third World*, Princeton, Princeton University Press, 1988.

MISZAK Nick, 'Land-based Conflict in Afghanistan: On the Right of Pre-emption (*shuf'a*) as "Back-Channel" Diplomacy and a Show of Indignation' in Martin Sökefeld (ed.), *Spaces of Conflict in Everyday Life*, Bielefeld, Transcript Publication, 2015, pp. 117–35.

MISZAK Nick and MONSUTTI Alessandro, 'Landscapes of Power: Local Struggles and National Stakes at the Rural-Urban Fringe of Kabul, Afghanistan', *The Journal of Peasant Studies*, 2014, vol. 41, n° 2, pp. 183–98.

MOGHADAM Valentine, 'Patriarchy, the Taleban, and Politics of Public Space in Afghanistan', *Women's Studies International Forum*, 2002, vol. 25, n° 1, pp. 19–31.

MOGHADAM Valentine, 'A Tale of Two Countries: State, Society, and Gender Politics in Iran and Afghanistan', *The Muslim World*, 2004, vol. 94, n° 4, pp. 449–67.

MONSUTTI Alessandro, *War and Migration: Social Networks and Economic Strategies of the Hazaras of Afghanistan*, London, Routledge, 2005.

MONSUTTI Alessandro, 'Fuzzy Sovereignty: Rural Reconstruction in Afghanistan, between Democracy Promotion and Power Games', *Comparative Studies in Society and History*, 2012, vol. 54, n° 3, pp. 563–91.

MONSUTTI Alessandro, 'Anthropologizing Afghanistan: Colonial and Postcolonial Encounters', *Annual Review of Anthropology*, 2013, vol. 42, n° 1, pp. 269–85.

MONTAIGNE Michel, *Les essais*, Paris, Hachette, 1972.

MOORE Sally Falk, 'Certainties Undone: Fifty Turbulent Years of Legal Anthropology, 1949–1999', *The Journal of the Royal Anthropological Institute*, 2001, vol. 7, n° 1, pp. 95–116.

MOUSAVI Sayed Askar, *The Hazaras of Afghanistan: An Historical, Cultural, Economic and Political Study*, Basingstoke, Palgrave Macmillan, 1998.

MUKHOPADHYAY Dipali, *Warlords, Strongman Governors, and the State in Afghanistan*, Cambridge, Cambridge University Press, 2014.

MUNIR Muhammad, 'The Layha for the Mujahideen: An Analysis of the Code of Conduct for the Taliban Fighters under Islamic Law', *International Review of the Red Cross*, 2011, vol. 93, n° 881, pp. 81–102.

MURTAZASHVILI Jennifer Brick, *Informal Order and the State in Afghanistan*, Cambridge, Cambridge University Press, 2016.

NADER Laura, 'The Anthropological Study of Law', *American Anthropologist, New Series*, 1965, vol. 67, n° 6, pp. 3–32.

NADER Laura (ed.), *Law in Culture and Society*, Berkeley, University of California Press, 1997.

NADER Laura, 'The Globalization of Law: ADR as "Soft" Technology', *Proceedings of the Annual Meeting (American Society of International Law)*, 1999, vol. 93, pp. 304–11.

NADER Laura, *The Life of the Law: Anthropological Projects*, Berkeley, University of California Press, 2002.

NAGAMINE Yoshinobu, *The Legitimization Strategy of the Taliban's Code of Conduct*, New York, Palgrave Macmillan, 2015.

NAGARAJ Vijay Kumar, '"Beltway Bandits" and "Poverty Barons": For-Profit International Development Contracting and the Military-Development Assemblage', *Development and Change*, 2015, vol. 46, n° 4, pp. 585–617.

NAHOUM-GRAPPE Véronique, 'La purification ethnique et les viols systématiques. Ex-Yougoslavie 1991–1995', *Clio. Femmes, Genre, Histoire*, 1997, n° 5, pp. 163–75.

NEUMANN Ronald E., *The Other War: Winning and Losing in Afghanistan*, Lincoln, Potomac Books, 2011.

NGUYEN Vinh-Kim, *The Republic of Therapy: Triage and Sovereignty in West Africa's Time of AIDS*, Durham, Duke University Press, 2010.

NICOLLE Hervé, 'Qu'elle était verte ma vallée: L'avenir sans terre des populations Kuchi dans le district de Deh Sabz', *Revue des mondes musulmans et de la Méditerranée*, 2013, n° 133, pp. 227–38.

OLESEN Asta, *Islam and Politics in Afghanistan*, London, Routledge, 1995.

OLIVIER DE SARDAN Jean-Pierre, *Epistemology, Fieldwork, and Anthropology*, New York, Palgrave Macmillan, 2015.

OLSEN Mary Kay Gilliland, 'Bridge on the Sava. Ethnicity in Eastern Croatia, 1981–1991', *Anthropology of Eastern Europe Review*, 1993, vol. 11, n° 1 & 2, pp. 54–62.

PAIN Adam, 'Land, Power and Conflict in Afghanistan: Seeking to Understand Complexity', *Revue des mondes musulmans et de la Méditerranée*, 2013, n° 133, pp. 63–81.

PANDOLFI Mariella, 'Une souveraineté mouvante et supracoloniale', *Multitudes*, 2000, vol. 3, n° 3, pp. 97–105.

PÉLISSE Jérôme, 'Judiciarisation ou juridicisation? Usages et réappropriations du droit dans les conflits du travail', *Politix*, 2009, n° 86, pp. 73–96.

POLANYI Karl, *The Great Transformation: The Political and Economic Origins of Our Time*, New York, Farrar & Rinehart, 1944.

POULLADA Leon B., *Reform and Rebellion in Afghanistan, 1919–1929: King Amanullah's Failure to Modernize a Tribal Society*, Ithaca, Cornell University Press, 1973.

PROVOST René, *Rebel Courts: The Administration of Justice by Armed Insurgents*, New York, Oxford University Press, 2021.

RABASA Angel, BORAZ steven, CHALK peter, CRAGIN kim, KARASIK theodore, MORONEY jennifer, O'BRIEN kevin, and PETERS john E. (eds), *Ungoverned Territories: Understanding and Reducing Terrorism Risks*, Santa Monica, RAND, 2007.

RAEYMAEKERS Timothy, *Violent Capitalism and Hybrid Identity in the Eastern Congo*, Cambridge, Cambridge University Press, 2014.

RANDERIA Shalini, 'Cunning States and Unaccountable International Institutions: Legal Plurality, Social Movements and Rights of Local Communities to Common Property Resources', *European Journal of Sociology*, 2003, vol. 44, n° 1, pp. 27–60.

RANDERIA Shalini, 'Glocalization of Law: Environmental Justice, World Bank, NGOs and the Cunning State in India', *Current Sociology*, 2003, vol. 51, n° 3-4, pp. 305–28.

RANDERIA Shalini, 'The State of Globalization: Legal Plurality, Overlapping Sovereignties and Ambiguous Alliances between Civil Society and the Cunning State in India', *Theory, Culture & Society*, 2007, vol. 24, n° 1, pp. 1–33.

RASEKH Zohra, BAUER Heidi, MANOS Michele, and IACOPINO Vincent, 'Women's Health and Human Rights in Afghanistan', *JAMA: Journal of the American Medical Association*, 1998, vol. 280, n° 5, pp. 449–55.

RASHID Ahmed, *Taliban: Militant Islam, Oil and Fundamentalism in Central Asia*, New Haven, Yale University Press, 2000.

RASHID Ahmed, *Descent into Chaos: How the War Against Islamic Extremism is Being Lost in Pakistan, Afghanistan and Central Asia*, London, Penguin, 2008.

REETZ Dietrich, 'The Deoband Universe: What Makes a Transcultural and Transnational Educational Movement of Islam?', *Comparative Studies of South Asia, Africa and the Middle East*, 2007, vol. 27, n° 1, pp. 139–59.

RENO William, *Warlord Politics and African States*, Boulder, Lynne Rienner Publishers, 1998.

REUTER Christoph and YUNUS Borhan, 'The Return of The Taliban in Andar District' in Antonio Giustozzi (ed.), *Decoding the New Taliban: Insights From the Afghan Field*, New York, Columbia University Press, 2009, pp. 101–18.

RIBOT Jesse and PELUSO Nancy Lee, 'A Theory of Access', *Rural Sociology*, 2009, vol. 68, n° 2, pp. 153–81.

ROBBEN Antonius (ed.), *Iraq at a Distance: What Anthropologists Can Teach Us about the War*, Philadelphia, University of Pennsylvania Press, 2011.

ROY Olivier, 'État et société en Afghanistan', *Revue française de science politique*, 1985, vol. 35, n° 3, pp. 402–23.

ROY Olivier, 'Afghanistan: Modèles anthropologiques et pacification', *Cahiers du monde russe et soviétique*, 1990, vol. 31, n° 2, pp. 405–11.

ROY Olivier, *Islam and Resistance in Afghanistan*, Cambridge, Cambridge University Press, 1990.

ROY Olivier, 'Ethnic Identity and Political Expression in Northern Afghanistan' in Jo-Ann Gross (ed.), *Muslims in Central Asia: Expressions of Identity and Change*, Durham, Duke University Press, 1992, pp. 73–87.

RUBIN Barnett R., *The Fragmentation of Afghanistan: State Formation and Collapse in the International System*, New Haven, Yale University Press, 2002.

RUBIN Barnett R., 'Crafting a Constitution for Afghanistan', *Journal of Democracy*, 2004, vol. 15, n° 3, pp. 5–19.

RUTTIG Thomas, 'The Haqqani Network as an Autonomous Entity' in Antonio Giustozzi (ed.), *Decoding the New Taliban: Insights from the Afghan Field*, New York, Columbia University Press, 2009, pp. 57–88.

SAEED Lutforahman, *Islam, Custom and Human Rights: A Legal and Empirical Study of Criminal Cases in Afghanistan After the 2004 Constitution*, New York, Springer, 2021.

SAHLINS Marshall, 'Poor Man, Rich Man, Big-Man, Chief: Political Types in Melanesia and Polynesia', *Comparative Studies in Society and History*, 1963, vol. 5, n° 3, pp. 285–303.

SCHACHT Joseph, *An Introduction to Islamic law*, Oxford, Clarendon Press, 1964.

SCHEPPELE Kim Lane, 'Le droit de la sécurité internationale: Le terrorisme et l'empire sécuritaire de l'après-11 septembre 2001', *Actes de la recherche en sciences sociales*, 2008, n° 173, pp. 28–43.

SCHETTER Conrad, 'Introduction' in Conrad Schetter (ed.), *Local Politics in Afghanistan: A Century of Intervention in the Social Order*, Oxford, Oxford University Press, 2013, pp. 1–20.

SCHMEIDL Susanne, 'Engaging Traditional Justice Mechanisms in Afghanistan: State-Building Opportunity or Dangerous Liaison?' in Whit Mason (ed.), *The Rule of Law in Afghanistan: Missing in Inaction*, Cambridge, Cambridge University Press, 2011, pp. 149–71.

SCHNEIDER Elizabeth, 'The Violence of Privacy', *Connecticut Law Review*, 1991, vol. 23, pp. 973–99.

SEDRA Mark, 'Security Sector Reform and State Building in Afghanistan' in Geoffrey Hayes and Mark Sedra (eds), *Afghanistan: Transition under Threat*, Waterloo, Wilfrid Laurier University Press, 2008, pp. 193–218.

SHAH Niaz, 'The Islamic Emirate of Afghanistan: A Layeha [Rules and Regulations] for Mujahidin', *Studies in Conflict & Terrorism*, 2012, vol. 35, n° 6, pp. 456–70.

SHAH Niaz, 'The Taliban Layeha for Mujahidin and the Law of Armed Conflict', *Journal of International Humanitarian Legal Studies*, 2012, vol. 3, n° 1, pp. 192–229.

SHAHRANI Nazif M., 'War, Factionalism, and the State in Afghanistan', *American Anthropologist*, 2002, vol. 104, n° 3, pp. 715–22.

SHAHZAD Syed Saleem, *Inside Al-Qaeda and the Taliban: Beyond Bin Laden and 9/11*, London, Pluto Press, 2011.

SHALINSKY Audrey C., 'Women's Roles in the Afghanistan Jihad', *International Journal of Middle East Studies*, 1993, vol. 25, n° 4, pp. 661–75.

SIKOR Thomas and LUND Christian, 'Access and Property: A Question of Power and Authority', *Development and Change*, 2009, vol. 40, n° 1, pp. 1–22.

SINGH Amrit, *Globalizing Torture: CIA Secret Detention and Extraordinary Rendition*, New York, Open Society, 2013.

SIRAT A. S., 'The Modern Legal System of Afghanistan', *The American Journal of Comparative Law*, 1968, vol. 16, n° 4, pp. 563–69.

SIVAKUMARAN Sandesh, 'Courts of Armed Opposition Groups: Fair Trials or Summary Justice?', *Journal of International Criminal Justice*, 2009, vol. 7, n° 3, pp. 489–513.

SLUKA Jeffrey, 'Participant Observation in Violent Social Contexts', *Human Organization*, 1990, vol. 49, n° 2, pp. 114–26.

SMITH Graeme, 'What Kandahar's Taliban Say' in Antonio Giustozzi (ed.), *Decoding the New Taliban: Insights from the Afghan Field*, New York, Columbia University Press, 2009, pp. 191–210.

SOMER Jonathan, 'Jungle Justice: Passing Sentence on the Equality of Belligerents in Non-International Armed Conflict', *International Review of the Red Cross*, 2007, vol. 89, n° 867, pp. 655–90.

SOUSA SANTOS Boaventura DE, *Toward a New Common Sense: Law, Science and Politics in the Paradigmatic Transition*, London, Routledge, 1995.

STANILAND Paul, 'States, Insurgents, and Wartime Political Orders', *Perspectives on Politics*, 2012, vol. 10, n° 2, pp. 243–64.

STRICK VAN LINSCHOTEN Alex and KUEHN Felix (eds), *The Taliban Reader: War, Islam and Politics*, London, Hurst, 2018.

STRICK VAN LINSCHOTEN Alex and KUEHN Felix, *An Enemy We Created: The Myth of the Taliban-al Qaeda Merger in Afghanistan*, Oxford, Oxford University Press, 2012.

STRICK VAN LINSCHOTEN Alex, *Mullah Wars: The Afghan Taliban between Village and State, 1979–2001*, Ph.D., King's College London, 2016.

STRICK VAN LINSCHOTEN Alex and KUEHN Felix, *Poetry of the Taliban*, New York, Columbia University Press, 2012.

SUHRKE Astri, 'Democratizing a Dependent State: The Case of Afghanistan', *Democratization*, 2008, vol. 15, n° 3, pp. 630–48.

SUHRKE Astri, *When More is Less: The International Project in Afghanistan*, London, Hurst, 2011.

TAMANAHA Brian, SAGE Caroline, and WOOLCOCK Michael (eds), *Legal Pluralism and Development: Scholars and Practitioners in Dialogue*, Cambridge, Cambridge University Press, 2012.

TAPPER Nancy, 'Causes and Consequences of the Abolition of Brideprice in Afghanistan' in M. Nazif Shahrani and Robert Canfield (eds), *Revolutions and Rebellions in Afghanistan*, Berkeley, University of California Press, 1984, pp. 291–305.

TAPPER Nancy, *Bartered Brides: Politics, Gender and Marriage in an Afghan Tribal Society*, Cambridge, Cambridge University Press, 1991.

TAPPER Richard, 'Who Are the Kuchi? Nomad Self-Identities in Afghanistan', *The Journal of the Royal Anthropological Institute*, 2008, vol. 14, n° 1, pp. 97–116.

TARIQ Mohammed Osman, *Tribal Security System (Arbakai) in Southeast Afghanistan*, London, Crisis States Research Centre, 2008.

TARZI Amin, 'Islam, Shari'a, and State Building under 'Abd al-Rahman Khan' in Nile Green (ed.), *Afghanistan's Islam: From Conversion to the Taliban*, Berkeley, University of California Press, 2016, pp. 129–44.

TARZI Shah, 'Afghanistan in 1992: A Hobbesian State of Nature', *Asian Survey*, 1993, vol. 33, n° 2, pp. 165–74.

TERRAY Emmanuel, 'Le climatiseur et la véranda' in Pierre Bonnafé (ed.), *Afrique plurielle, Afrique actuelle: Hommage à Georges Balandier*, Paris, Karthala, 1986, pp. 37–59.

THE UNITED STATES ARMY AND MARINE CORPS, *The U.S. Army/Marine Corps Counterinsurgency Field Manual*, Chicago, University of Chicago Press, 2007.

THOMPSON Edward, *Whigs and Hunters: The Origin of the Black ACT*, New York, Pantheon Books, 1975.

TILLY Charles, *From Mobilization to Revolution*, New York, McGraw-Hill, 1978.

TILLY Charles, 'War Making and State Making as Organized Crime' in Dietrich Rueschemeyer, Peter B. Evans, and Theda Skocpol (eds), *Bringing the State Back In*, Cambridge, Cambridge University Press, 1985, pp. 169–91.

TOMSEN Peter, *The Wars of Afghanistan: Messianic Terrorism, Tribal Conflicts, and the Failures of Great Powers*, New York, Public Affairs, 2013.

TONDINI Matteo, *Statebuilding and Justice Reform: Post-Conflict Reconstruction in Afghanistan*, London, Routledge, 2010.

TROTSKY Leon, *History of the Russian Revolution*, Chicago, Haymarket Books, 2008.

TURNER Simon, 'New Opportunities: Angry Young Men in a Tanzanian Refugee Camp' in Philomena Essed, Georg Frerks, and Joke Schrijvers (eds), *Refugees and the Transformation of Societies: Agency, Policies, Ethics, and Politics*, New York, Berghahn Books, 2004, pp. 94–105.

UTAS Mats, *Sweet Battlefields: Youth and the Liberian Civil War*, Uppsala, Uppsala University, 2003.

UTAS Mats, *African Conflicts and Informal Power: Big Men and Networks*, London, Zed Books, 2012.

VALLÉE Olivier, *La police morale de l'anticorruption: Cameroun, Nigeria*, Paris, Karthala, 2010.

VAN BILJERT Martina, 'Unruly Commanders and Violent Power Struggles: Taliban Networks in Uruzgan' in Antonio Giustozzi (ed.), *Decoding the New Taliban: Insights from the Afghan Field*, New York, Columbia University Press, 2009, pp. 155–78.

VAN BILJERT Martina, 'The Taliban in Zabul and Uruzgan' in Peter Bergen and Katherine Tiedemann (eds), *Talibanistan: Negotiating the Borders between Terror, Politics, and Religion*, Oxford, Oxford University Press, 2013, pp. 94–127.

VENDRELL Francesc, 'The International Community's Failures in Afghanistan' in Whit Mason (ed.), *The Rule of Law in Afghanistan: Missing in Inaction*, Cambridge, Cambridge University Press, 2011, pp. 53–60.

VERGÈS Jacques, *De la stratégie judiciaire*, Paris, Éditions de Minuit, 1981.

VIGH Henrik, *Navigating Terrains of War: Youth and Soldiering in Guinea-Bissau*, New York, Berghahn Books, 2006.

VLASSENROOT Koen, 'War and Social Research: The Limits of Empirical Methodologies in War-Torn Environments', *Civilisations*, 2006, n° 54, pp. 191–8.

WARDAK Ali, 'Jirga: A Traditional Mechanism of Conflict Resolution in Afghanistan' in John Strawson (ed.), *Law after Ground Zero*, London, Cavendish, 2002, pp. 187–203.

WARDAK Ali, 'Building a Post-War Justice System in Afghanistan', *Crime, Law and Social Change*, 2004, vol. 41, n° 4, pp. 319–41.

WATSON Alan, *Legal Transplants: An Approach to Comparative Law*, Athens, University of Georgia Press, 1974.

WEBER Max, *Economy and Society*, Berkeley, University of California Press, 1978.

WEDEEN Lisa, 'Reflections on Ethnographic Work in Political Science', *Annual Review of Political Science*, 2010, vol. 13, n° 1, pp. 255–72.

WEINBAUM Marvin, 'Legal Elites in Afghan Society', *International Journal of Middle East Studies*, 1980, vol. 12, n° 1, pp. 39–57.

WEINER Tim, *Legacy of Ashes: The History of the CIA*, New York, Knopf Doubleday, 2007.

WEIZMAN Eyal, *The Least of All Possible Evils: Humanitarian Violence from Arendt to Gaza*, New York, Verso Books, 2011.

WHITMAN James, 'At the Origins of Law and the State: Supervision of Violence, Mutilation of Bodies, or Setting of Prices', *Chicago-Kent Law Review*, 1995, vol. 71, pp. 41–84.

WILLARD Marcel, *La défense accuse*, Paris, Éditions sociales, 1955.

WIMPELMANN Torunn, 'The Informal Justice Paradigm and the Appropriation of Local Reality', *Northern Ireland Legal Quarterly*, 2013, vol. 64, n° 3, pp. 397–411.

WIMPELMANN Torunn, 'Nexuses of Knowledge and Power in Afghanistan: The Rise and Fall of the Informal Justice Assemblage', *Central Asian Survey*, 2013, vol. 32, n° 3, pp. 406–22.

WIMPELMANN Torunn, *The Pitfalls of Protection: Gender, Violence, and Power in Afghanistan*, Berkeley, University of California Press, 2017.

WOOD Elisabeth, 'The Ethical Challenges of Field Research in Conflict Zones', *Qualitative Sociology*, 2006, vol. 29, n° 3, pp. 373–86.

WOODWARD Bob, *Obama's Wars*, New York, Simon and Schuster, 2010.

ZABULWAL Abdul Awwal, 'Taliban in Zabul: A Witness' Account' in Antonio Giustozzi (ed.), *Decoding the New Taliban: Insights from the Afghan Field*, New York, Columbia University Press, 2009, pp. 179–90.

ZAEEF Abdul Salam, *My Life with the Taliban*, New York, Columbia University Press, 2010.

ZAMAN Muhammad Qasim, *The Ulama in Contemporary Islam: Custodians of Change*, Princeton, Princeton University Press, 2002.

ZAMAN Muhammad Qasim, 'Tradition and Authority in Deobandi Madrasas of South Asia' in Robert W. Hefner and Muhammad Qasim Zaman (eds), *Schooling Islam: The Culture and Politics of Modern Muslim Education*, Princeton, Princeton University Press, 2007, pp. 61–86.

ZARTMAN I. William, *Collapsed States: The Disintegration and Restoration of Legitimate Authority*, Boulder, Lynne Rienner Publishers, 1995.

Index

For the benefit of digital users, indexed terms that span two pages (e.g., 52–53) may, on occasion, appear on only one of those pages.